Machine Learning Advances and Applications on Natural Language Processing (NLP)

Machine Learning Advances and Applications on Natural Language Processing (NLP)

Guest Editors

Leonidas Akritidis
Panayiotis Bozanis

MDPI

Basel • Beijing • Wuhan • Barcelona • Belgrade • Novi Sad • Cluj • Manchester

Guest Editors
Leonidas Akritidis
Department of Science and Technology
International Hellenic University
Thessaloniki
Greece

Panayiotis Bozanis
Department of Science and Technology
International Hellenic University
Thessaloniki
Greece

Editorial Office
MDPI AG
Grosspeteranlage 5
4052 Basel, Switzerland

This is a reprint of the Special Issue, published open access by the journal *Electronics* (ISSN 2079-9292), freely accessible at: https://www.mdpi.com/journal/electronics/special_issues/CR7ISFW633.

For citation purposes, cite each article independently as indicated on the article page online and as indicated below:

Lastname, A.A.; Lastname, B.B. Article Title. *Journal Name* **Year**, *Volume Number*, Page Range.

ISBN 978-3-7258-5177-5 (Hbk)
ISBN 978-3-7258-5178-2 (PDF)
https://doi.org/10.3390/books978-3-7258-5178-2

Contents

About the Editors

Leonidas Akritidis

Leonidas Akritidis is a post-doctoral research fellow in the Department of Science and Technology of the International Hellenic University. He is also a contracted lecturer in the same department. His overall teaching experience exceeds 10 years in this and other departments. He holds a diploma in Electrical and Computer Engineering (Aristotle University of Thessaloniki, 2003) and a PhD in Electrical and Computer Engineering (University of Thessaly, 2013). His research activity is focused on the fields of machine learning (especially in natural language processing and deep generative models), data mining, information retrieval, parallel algorithms, data structures, and high-performance storage devices. In this context, he has published numerous novel research articles in leading international journals and scientific conferences. Moreover, he has designed and developed a broad collection of scientific systems and commercial applications. He has contributed to the successful preparation and completion of various research projects with national and international funding.

Panayiotis Bozanis

Panayiotis Bozanis has been a full Professor at the School of Science and Technology, International Hellenic University, Greece since September 2019. Currently, he serves as the Deputy Dean of the School and Director of five postgraduate programs of study (an MSc in Cybersecurity, MSc in Data Science, MSc in e-Business and Digital Marketing, MSc in Mobile and Web Computing: Internet of Things Applications, and MSc in Information & Communication Technology Systems). He holds a diploma and a PhD degree in computer engineering and informatics, both from University of Patras, Greece. Previously, he served as full Professor, Head of Department, Deputy Dean, Director of the MSc Programme "Applied Informatics", and Director of the DaSELab at the ECE Dept., University of Thessaly, Greece. His publications comprise several journal/conference papers, book chapters, eight books (in Greek) about data structures, algorithms and an introduction to computer science, and he has been involved in editing seven books. His research interests include data structures, algorithms, information retrieval, databases, cloud computing, big data, machine learning, and smart grids, among others. He has taught/teaches several courses: Data structures, algorithms, discrete mathematics, computer graphics (undergraduate), algorithm engineering, ICT Essentials, statistical methods for data science, machine learning principles and concepts, big data and cloud computing, information retrieval (postgraduate).

Preface

In recent years, the utilization of machine learning (ML) techniques in the area of natural language processing (NLP) has witnessed tremendous growth. Innovative studies in the field have revolutionized numerous applications, including human–computer interaction, information retrieval, and language understanding. This rapid evolution is mainly driven by advances in ML techniques, particularly deep learning, transformer architectures, and unsupervised learning methods. These innovations have significantly enhanced the ability of machines to comprehend human language and respond with a remarkable naturalness.

This Reprint contains 10 research studies that explore novel solutions with cutting-edge machine learning models and their impact on diverse NLP tasks. Sentiment analysis, linguistic improvement and text classification are among the most significant problems to which the contributions of machine learning are central. The introduction of large-scale pre-trained language models such as BERT, GPT, and their successors demonstrates how data-driven learning, combined with scalable computational resources, has enabled breakthroughs previously thought unachievable.

The goal of this Reprint is twofold: first, we aim to offer the scientific community a rich collection of state-of-the-art studies in the area on NLP; second, we wish to provide a comprehensive overview of the most significant ML advancements that have contributed to the progress of NLP. Emphasis is placed not only on technical achievements but also on the broader implications, including ethical considerations and bias in language models.

This Reprint serves as a valuable resource for researchers, practitioners, and students seeking to understand the state of the art in ML-driven NLP. As the field continues to evolve at a rapid rate, we hope this work provides a foundation for deeper exploration and inspires further innovation.

Leonidas Akritidis and Panayiotis Bozanis
Guest Editors

electronics

Editorial

Machine Learning Advances and Applications on Natural Language Processing (NLP)

Leonidas Akritidis * and Panayiotis Bozanis *

Department of Science and Technology, International Hellenic University, 57001 Thessaloniki, Greece
* Correspondence: lakritidis@ihu.gr (L.A.); pbozanis@ihu.gr (P.B.)

The recent technological advances in the research field of machine learning have played a crucial role in the improvement of Natural Language Processing (NLP). Today, state-of-the-art models and algorithms are allowing machines to understand, interpret, and generate human language of unprecedented quality. These advances allowed researchers to introduce effective tools and solutions for a wide variety of applications, including sentiment analysis, machine translation, conversational AI, question answering, named entity recognition, and others.

Deep learning stands at the heart of most modern NLP applications. Initially, the introduction of Recurrent Neural Networks (RNNs) [1] and their improved variants (i.e., Long-Short Term Memory–LSTM [2], Gated Recurrent Units–GRUs [3], etc.) allowed the effective processing of sequential data and the capture of contexts in text. Despite their inherent problems (i.e., unstable training due to the phenomenon of the vanishing and exploding gradients), these models have largely managed to overcome the severe limitations of the traditional NLP approaches.

Another milestone in the development of NLP was the introduction of word embeddings. Algorithms such as Word2Vec [4], GloVe [5], and FastText [6] have been designed to transform each word into a vector representation in a continuous space, while capturing the semantic relationships among words. These embeddings significantly improved the performance of the aforementioned NLP models across various tasks, replacing the sparse, non-informational TF-IDF vector representations [7].

The introduction of the Transformer architecture by Vaswani et al. in 2017 marked the beginning of the revolution era of NLP [8]. Unlike Convolutional Neural Networks (CNNs) [9] and RNNs, Transformers are not based on convolution or recurrence operations. Instead, they rely entirely on an innovative attention mechanism that enables the modeling of long-range dependencies in text. More specifically, the mechanism weighs the importance of different tokens in a sequence relative to a specific token. This is achieved by computing three vectors for each token: Query, Key, and Value. Each vector is obtained by multiplying the input embeddings with learned weight matrices.

Through its attention mechanism, the Transformer model became the building block of powerful pre-trained language models that revolutionized the area of NLP. In particular, BERT (Bidirectional Encoder Representations from Transformers) introduced a Transformer-based architecture that processes the entire sequence of words simultaneously, considering the context from both directions (namely, left-to-right and right-to-left) [10]. This bidirectional nature allows BERT to capture deeper semantic relationships in text.

After the introduction of BERT, numerous variants have been developed to enhance its performance and adapt it to different use cases. RoBERTa (Robustly optimized BERT approach) improves BERT by using a larger training corpus, eliminating the next-sentence prediction task, and training for longer periods [11]. On the other hand, DistilBERT is a smaller and faster variant of BERT that is considered to be more suitable when the underlying computational resources are limited [12].

In contrast, GPT (Generative Pre-trained Transformer) adopts a different approach compared to BERT. More specifically, GPT is a unidirectional language model trained to predict the next word in a sentence, generating text based on the left-to-right context. While BERT excels in tasks requiring deep understanding of bidirectional context, GPT is designed for tasks such as text generation, language modeling, and conversational AI [13,14].

This Special Issue explores the most recent machine learning advancements in the research field of NLP. It includes ten original articles that systematically study popular NLP problems and introduce novel technologies, models, and algorithms to address them.

Sentiment analysis is a traditional NLP problem that focuses on the identification of the emotional tone behind a body of text. It is frequently treated as a typical classification problem that classifies the content of a text as positive, negative, or neutral. The relevant techniques can be applied to various data sources, including product reviews, social media posts, user comments, and customer feedback. These elements render them particularly important, since they provide the businesses and organizations with tools that allow them to gain insight into public opinion, customer satisfaction, and brand perception.

Motivated by the significance of the sentiment analysis techniques, the present Special Issue published five articles on the topic. More specifically, Y. Fu et al. (Contributor 5) introduced Self-HCL, a new method for multimodal sentiment analysis. Self-HCL first enhances the unimodal features using a unimodal feature enhancement module, and then, it jointly trains both multimodal and unimodal tasks. The proposed framework integrates a hybrid contrastive learning strategy with the aim of improving multimodal fusion and performance, even when unimodal annotations are lacking.

On the other hand, Faria et al. (Contributor 8) studied the emerging problem of sentiment analysis for memes in under-resourced languages. In this context, they developed three deep learning-based approaches: (i) a text-based model that uses Transformer architectures; (ii) an image-based model leveraging visual data for sentiment classification; and (iii) SentimentFormer, a hybrid model that integrates both text and image modalities. The authors evaluated the three models with the MemoSen dataset and concluded that the hybrid SentimentFormer model was the most effective. Moreover, Papageorgiou et al. (Contributor 1) investigated stock market prediction using reinforcement learning (specifically, a double deep Q-network), combined with technical indicators and sentiment analysis. The proposed model predicts short-term stock movements of NVIDIA, using data from Yahoo Finance and StockTwits. The results indicate that the inclusion of sentiment analysis elements in the prediction improves profitability and decision making.

Apart from the articles that introduce original models and techniques, this Special Issue also contains survey and investigation papers on sentiment analysis. More specifically, Kampatzis et al. (Contributor 2) conducted a survey that examined sentiment classification techniques in texts containing scientific citations. The authors explored various methods (from lexicon-based to machine and deep learning approaches) and highlighted the importance of interpreting both the emotional tone and intent behind citations. In another study, Kang et al. (Contributor 9) explored the use of GPT and FinBERT for sentiment analysis in the finance sector. The investigation focuses on the impact of news and investor sentiment on market behavior, and compares the performance of GPT and FinBERT, using a refined prompt design approach to optimize GPT-4o.

Text classification is not just limited to sentiment analysis applications. It is extended to cover other downstream tasks, such as named entity classification (e.g., news, products, articles, etc.), document categorization, acceptability of linguistic quality, and others. This Special Issue includes two studies related to the generic field of text classification. The first one is the work of Kalogeropoulos et al. (Contributor 3), which enhances the Graphical Set-based model by integrating node and word embeddings in its edges. In particular, the proposed technique employs the well-established Word2Vec, GloVe, and Node2Vec algorithms with the aim of generating vector representations of the text. Subsequently, it utilizes these representations to augment the edges of the model in order to improve its classification accuracy. The second study was authored by Guarasci et al. (Contributor 4) and introduced a new methodology for automatically evaluating linguistic acceptability judgements using the Italian Corpus of Linguistic Acceptability. By leveraging the ELECTRA language model, the proposed approach outperformed the existing baselines and exhibited a capability in addressing language-specific challenges.

Named Entity Recognition (NER) constitutes another fundamental NLP task. Given a corpus of text, the goal of NER is to automatically identify and classify named entities into predefined categories. In other words, NER facilitates the recognition of key pieces of information within unstructured text. This is often proved to be crucial for tasks, such as information retrieval, question answering, and text summarization. In this spirit, Gao et al. (Contributor 6) presented a NER framework for extracting entities from Chinese equipment fault diagnosis texts. The framework integrates the following three models: RoBERTa-wwm-ext for extracting context-sensitive embeddings, a Bidirectional LSTM for capturing context features, and CRF for improving the accuracy of sequence labeling.

Finally, two research groups presented original studies on other interesting topics. More specifically, the work of Hirota et al. (Contributor 7) explored the use of descriptive text as an alternative to visual features in Visual Question Answering (VQA) tasks. Instead of relying on visual features, the proposed approach employs a language-only Transformer model to process description–question pairs. The authors also investigate strategies for data augmentation, with the aim of improving the diversity of the training set and reducing statistical bias.

Furthermore, Fernandes et al. (Contributor 10) evaluated the performance of 16 LLMs in automating engineering tasks related to Low-Power Wide-Area Networks. The main focus is whether lightweight, locally executed LLMs can generate correct Python code for these tasks. The models were compared with state-of-the-art models, such as GPT-4 and DeepSeek-V3. The evaluation revealed that while GPT-4 and DeepSeek-V3 consistently provided correct solutions, smaller models like Phi-4 and LLaMA-3.3 also performed well.

The diversity of the studies of this Special Issue indicates that NLP-related research constantly improves and evolves toward the introduction of models that truly understand the meaning of text. However, there are still many challenges on the way, including ambiguity and context understanding, performance improvement for low-resource languages, model explainability, and multimodal integration. Addressing these challenges is crucial for building more accurate and generalizable NLP systems.

Conflicts of Interest: The authors declare no conflicts of interest.

List of Contributions:

1. Papageorgiou, G.; Gkaimanis, D.; Tjortjis, C. Enhancing Stock Market Forecasts with Double Deep Q-Network in Volatile Stock Market Environments. *Electronics* **2024**, *13*, 1629. https://doi.org/10.3390/electronics13091629.

2. Kampatzis, A.; Sidiropoulos, A.; Diamantaras, K.; Ougiaroglou, S. Sentiment Dimensions and Intentions in Scientific Analysis: Multilevel Classification in Text and Citations. *Electronics* **2024**, *13*, 1753. https://doi.org/10.3390/electronics13091753.
3. Kalogeropoulos, N.-R.; Ioannou, D.; Stathopoulos, D.; Makris, C. On Embedding Implementations in Text Ranking and Classification Employing Graphs. *Electronics* **2024**, *13*, 1897. https://doi.org/10.3390/electronics13101897.
4. Guarasci, R.; Minutolo, A.; Buonaiuto, G.; De Pietro, G.; Esposito, M. Raising the Bar on Acceptability Judgments Classification: An Experiment on ItaCoLA Using ELECTRA. *Electronics* **2024**, *13*, 2500. https://doi.org/10.3390/electronics13132500
5. Fu, Y.; Fu, J.; Xue, H.; Xu, Z. Self-HCL: Self-Supervised Multitask Learning with Hybrid Contrastive Learning Strategy for Multimodal Sentiment Analysis. *Electronics* **2024**, *13*, 2835. https://doi.org/10.3390/electronics13142835.
6. Gao, F.; Zhang, L.; Wang, W.; Zhang, B.; Liu, W.; Zhang, J.; Xie, L. Named Entity Recognition for Equipment Fault Diagnosis Based on RoBERTa-wwm-ext and Deep Learning Integration. *Electronics* **2024**, *13*, 3935. https://doi.org/10.3390/electronics13193935.
7. Hirota, Y.; Garcia, N.; Otani, M.; Chu, C.; Nakashima, Y. A Picture May Be Worth a Hundred Words for Visual Question Answering. *Electronics* **2024**, *13*, 4290. https://doi.org/10.3390/electronics13214290.
8. Faria, F.T.J.; Baniata, L.H.; Baniata, M.H.; Khair, M.A.; Bani Ata, A.I.; Bunterngchit, C.; Kang, S. SentimentFormer: A Transformer-Based Multimodal Fusion Framework for Enhanced Sentiment Analysis of Memes in Under-Resourced Bangla Language. *Electronics* **2025**, *14*, 799. https://doi.org/10.3390/electronics14040799.
9. Kang, J.-W.; Choi, S.-Y. Comparative Investigation of GPT and FinBERT's Sentiment Analysis Performance in News Across Different Sectors. *Electronics* **2025**, *14*, 1090. https://doi.org/10.3390/electronics14061090.
10. Fernandes, D.; Matos-Carvalho, J.P.; Fernandes, C.M.; Fachada, N. DeepSeek-V3, GPT-4, Phi-4, and LLaMA-3.3 Generate Correct Code for LoRaWAN-Related Engineering Tasks. *Electronics* **2025**, *14*, 1428. https://doi.org/10.3390/electronics14071428.

References

1. Schuster, M.; Paliwal, K.K. Bidirectional Recurrent Neural Networks. *IEEE Trans. Signal Process.* **1997**, *45*, 2673–2681. [CrossRef]
2. Hochreiter, S.; Schmidhuber, J. Long Short-Term Memory. *Neural Comput.* **1997**, *9*, 1735–1780. [CrossRef] [PubMed]
3. Cho, K.; Van Merriënboer, B.; Bahdanau, D.; Bengio, Y. On the Properties of Neural Machine Translation: Encoder-Decoder Approaches. *arXiv* **2014**, arXiv:1409.1259. [CrossRef]
4. Mikolov, T.; Chen, K.; Corrado, G.; Dean, J. Efficient Estimation of Word Representations in Vector Space. *arXiv* **2013**, arXiv:1301.3781. [CrossRef]
5. Pennington, J.; Socher, R.; Manning, C.D. Glove: Global Vectors for Word Representation. In Proceedings of the 2014 Conference on Empirical Methods in Natural Language Processing (EMNLP), Doha, Qatar, 25–29 October 2014; pp. 1532–1543.
6. Bojanowski, P.; Grave, E.; Joulin, A.; Mikolov, T. Enriching Word Vectors with Subword Information. *Trans. Assoc. Comput. Linguist.* **2017**, *5*, 135–146. [CrossRef]
7. Akritidis, L.; Bozanis, P. How Dimensionality Reduction Affects Sentiment Analysis NLP Tasks: An Experimental Study. In Proceedings of the IFIP International Conference on Artificial Intelligence Applications and Innovations, Hersonissos, Greece, 17–20 June 2022; Springer: Berlin/Heidelberg, Germany, 2022; pp. 301–312.
8. Vaswani, A.; Shazeer, N.; Parmar, N.; Uszkoreit, J.; Jones, L.; Gomez, A.N.; Kaiser, Ł.; Polosukhin, I. Attention is All you Need. *Adv. Neural Inf. Process. Syst.* **2017**, *30*. Available online: https://papers.nips.cc/paper_files/paper/2017/hash/3f5ee243547dee91fbd053c1c4a845aa-Abstract.html (accessed on 1 July 2025).
9. LeCun, Y.; Bengio, Y.; Hinton, G. Deep Learning. *Nature* **2015**, *521*, 436–444. [CrossRef] [PubMed]
10. Devlin, J.; Chang, M.W.; Lee, K.; Toutanova, K. BERT: Pre-training of Deep Bidirectional Transformers for Language Understanding. In Proceedings of the 2019 Conference of the North American Chapter of the Association for Computational Linguistics: Human Language Technologies, Minneapolis, MN, USA, 2–7 June 2019; Volume 1 (Long and Short Papers), pp. 4171–4186.
11. Liu, Y.; Ott, M.; Goyal, N.; Du, J.; Joshi, M.; Chen, D.; Levy, O.; Lewis, M.; Zettlemoyer, L.; Stoyanov, V. RoBERTa: A Robustly Optimized BERT Pretraining Approach. *arXiv* **2019**, arXiv:1907.11692.

12. Sanh, V.; Debut, L.; Chaumond, J.; Wolf, T. DistilBERT, a distilled version of BERT: Smaller, faster, cheaper and lighter. *arXiv* **2019**, arXiv:1910.01108.
13. Radford, A.; Wu, J.; Child, R.; Luan, D.; Amodei, D.; Sutskever, I. Language models are unsupervised multitask learners. *OpenAI Blog* **2019**, *1*, 9.
14. Brown, T.; Mann, B.; Ryder, N.; Subbiah, M.; Kaplan, J.D.; Dhariwal, P.; Neelakantan, A.; Shyam, P.; Sastry, G.; Askell, A.; et al. Language Models are Few-Shot Learners. *Adv. Neural Inf. Process. Syst.* **2020**, *33*, 1877–1901.

electronics

MDPI

Article

Enhancing Stock Market Forecasts with Double Deep Q-Network in Volatile Stock Market Environments

George Papageorgiou, Dimitrios Gkaimanis and Christos Tjortjis *

School of Science and Technology, International Hellenic University, 57001 Thessaloniki, Greece; gpapageorgiou2@ihu.edu.gr (G.P.); dgkaimanis@ihu.edu.gr (D.G.)

* Correspondence: c.tjortjis@ihu.edu.gr

Abstract: Stock market prediction is a subject of great interest within the finance industry and beyond. In this context, our research investigates the use of reinforcement learning through implementing the double deep Q-network (DDQN) alongside technical indicators and sentiment analysis, utilizing data from Yahoo Finance and StockTwits to forecast NVIDIA's short-term stock movements over the dynamic and volatile period from 2 January 2020, to 21 September 2023. By incorporating financial data, the model's effectiveness is assessed in three stages: initial reliance on closing prices, the introduction of technical indicators, and the integration of sentiment analysis. Early findings showed a dominant buy tendency (63.8%) in a basic model. Subsequent phases used technical indicators for balanced decisions and sentiment analysis to refine strategies and moderate rewards. Comparative analysis underscores a progressive increase in profitability, with average profits ranging from 57.41 to 119.98 with full data integration and greater outcome variability. These results reveal the significant impact of combining diverse data sources on the model's predictive accuracy and profitability, suggesting that integrating sentiment analysis alongside traditional financial metrics can significantly enhance the sophistication and effectiveness of algorithmic trading strategies in fluctuating market environments.

Keywords: data mining; machine learning (ML); double deep Q-network (DDQN); reinforcement learning; sentiment analysis; stock forecasting

1. Introduction

The field of stock market forecasting has always been a subject of great interest within the finance industry. It has been the focus of extensive research and innovative practices, with various traditional methods utilized to predict market trends. These methods include technical analysis, which examines historical market data such as price and volume, and fundamental analysis, which assesses a stock's intrinsic value. Additional techniques involve quantitative and econometric models, applying mathematical, statistical, and economic analyses to forecast market directions [1].

However, these traditional approaches face challenges in managing the vast and intricate datasets prevalent in today's financial markets. Machine learning (ML) has led to the introduction of revolutionary methodologies in stock market prediction, leveraging advanced algorithms to analyze vast quantities of data beyond human capacity. These models identify intricate patterns and relationships by training on extensive historical datasets, mirroring the learning process of human traders but with superior processing power [2]. Notably, ML has been employed in the field of finance for algorithmic trading. This strategy employs computer algorithms to execute trades at optimal speeds and volumes based on predefined criteria derived from various data sources, including market indicators and news events. Algorithmic trading enhances trade execution, minimizes costs, and improves risk management, with algorithms capable of evolving in response to market dynamics, thereby continuously optimizing trading strategies [3].

In addition to conventional data sources, social media platforms have become a great source of insightful information for analyzing the stock market. Popular platforms such as Twitter, StockTwits, and Reddit offer forums for users to share their views, expectations, and analyses of stock and market trends, making user-generated content a powerful source of sentiment data. These data reflect the collective mood and outlook of individuals concerning specific stocks or the market at large. The integration of social media sentiment analysis into stock market prediction models is an expanding field of interest. Sentiment analysis applies natural language processing (NLP), text analysis, and computational linguistics to identify, quantify, and examine emotional states and subjective insights from text [4,5].

By evaluating sentiments from social media content, researchers and analysts can assess public sentiment toward certain stocks or the overall market. This approach is invaluable for predicting short-term market movements influenced by public sentiment. Merging traditional market data with social media sentiment analysis offers a comprehensive approach to stock market forecasting [6]. ML models that assimilate and scrutinize both types of data can achieve more precise and holistic market predictions, capturing not only historical market trends but also market participants' prevailing sentiments and expectations [7].

The potential of ML to enhance stock market predictions is significant. These models can analyze vast amounts of data and technical indicators beyond human capabilities and excel at detecting intricate patterns that may elude human analysts. This proficiency promises to refine trading strategies and improve returns. However, it is crucial to acknowledge the inherent challenges and limitations given the susceptibility of the stock market to unpredictable factors [8]. With ongoing technological advancements and the increasing availability of data, the landscape of stock market prediction is poised for further innovation. The dynamic interplay between technology and finance is exemplified by the merger of ML and social media sentiment analysis, which offers advanced and effective trading strategies. As exploration and refinement of these methods continue, the future of stock market forecasting appears vibrant and promising [9,10].

This study aims to explore the potential of using reinforcement learning, specifically through the double deep Q-network (DDQN) [11], to predict stock market trends. The research focuses on NVIDIA, a company with a reputation for volatility and significant market presence. The main goal and contribution of this research is the methodological application of the DDQN to predict short-term stock movements into three sequential phases, focusing on the NVIDIA stock and providing valuable insight into the ML model's efficiency, integrating diverse data sources, including traditional financial indicators and sentiment analysis, to enhance predictive accuracy and profitability. The study comprehensively analyzes how combining these data sources refines trading strategies and increases profitability, demonstrating a clear progression as model complexity increases. Furthermore, it focuses on the impact of sentiment analysis, using NLP to integrate market sentiments from social media. Ultimately, this study aims to lay the groundwork for a more nuanced understanding of how data integration impacts algorithmic trading efficacy in the dynamic stock market environment by demonstrating that layered data integration can optimize algorithmic trading strategies in dynamic market environments.

2. Related Work

Stock market forecasting has evolved significantly, moving from traditional theories to leveraging cutting-edge technologies and incorporating psychological insights. Foundational theories such as the efficient market hypothesis (EMH) [12] and random walk theory [13] initially framed the understanding of market dynamics, suggesting that stock prices fully reflect all available information and follow unpredictable paths. These concepts have been instrumental in shaping investment strategies and financial analyses. However, criticisms from the realm of behavioral finance have exposed gaps in these theories, emphasizing the need to consider the psychological aspects that influence market movements and investor decisions. This has paved the way for a more nuanced understanding of market behaviors that incorporate both rational and irrational factors [14].

The field has since witnessed a shift toward integrating diverse forecasting methodologies, including fundamental and technical analysis, alongside advanced statistical and computational models [1]. The application of ML techniques, such as support vector machines (SVMs) [15], long short-term memory (LSTM) networks [16,17], and deep reinforcement learning (DRL) [18,19], represents a significant step toward enhancing predictive accuracy and processing complex datasets. These technological advancements have led to the development of sophisticated algorithmic trading strategies that can more effectively navigate the complexities of financial markets. Additionally, sentiment analysis, fueled by the wide spread of social media, has introduced a novel dimension to forecasting by capturing the collective mood and opinions of market participants. This convergence of quantitative analysis and qualitative insights underscores the multifaceted nature of stock market forecasting, reflecting an ongoing journey of adaptation and innovation in the face of financial market intricacies [20].

2.1. Core Theories of Stock Market Forecasting

The EMH, in [21], states that stock prices reflect all available information, making modern investment strategies possible. It is categorized into three forms: the weak form, which negates the predictive value of historical prices; the semi-strong form, which states that all public information is already priced; and the strong form, which suggests that no investor can consistently outperform the market due to the immediate incorporation of all information into stock prices [22,23]. Despite its widespread influence on passive investment strategies, EMH is assessed by behavioral finance to overlook human biases that may delay information assimilation [24].

Random walk theory, developed in [25] and later promoted in [26], declares that stock prices follow an unpredictable path, indicating that traditional forecasting methods are ineffective. This theory argues that stock movements are independent and random, challenging the ability of actively managed funds to surpass passive index funds in performance. However, this theory was reinforced in [24] by illustrating the futility of attempting to outguess market trends. Moreover, the analysis in [27] for random walk theory underscores the importance of developing economic models that account for observable patterns in asset pricing without necessarily disputing market efficiency.

Compared to related work and studies focused on the evolution of stock market forecasting from foundational theories to incorporating diverse statistical and machine learning methodologies, our study centers on the practical application of the DDQN and its benefits. We investigate integrating a multi-layered data strategy, including technical indicators, financial data, and sentiment analysis, highlighting not only the enhancement of the predictive accuracy of our DDQN model for NVIDIA's short-term stock movements, but also presenting the methodology which advances those results and significantly improves algorithmic trading strategies in a volatile market. Unlike broad theoretical explorations, our research provides a detailed analysis of how layering distinct data types incrementally benefits the predictive capabilities of DDQN, demonstrating its practical implications.

2.2. Stock Market Prediction Methodologies

Stock market forecasting combines fundamental and technical analysis, time series, and momentum investing strategies to predict market movements. Fundamental analysis evaluates a stock's value through economic indicators, company performance, and market demand [23,28,29]. Influential research has highlighted the importance of using financial ratios and accounting data for valuation, advocating for sector-specific studies [30–33].

Technical analysis utilizes historical price data and indicators such as the simple moving average (SMA), exponential moving average (EMA), moving average convergence divergence (MACD), relative strength index (RSI), and on-balance volume (OBV) to forecast trends [34–37]. In [38], it was emphasized that market prices reflect all available information, trends can be identified and exploited, and historical patterns often repeat. Moreover, time series analysis predicts stock prices by analyzing past trends and employing models such as ARIMA to account for seasonality and trends [39]. Additionally, the EMH challenges the premise of prediction based on historical data by stating that prices already reflect all known information [21]. Additionally, momentum investing is based on the observation that stocks with strong past performance tend to continue outperforming stocks with weak past performance in the short term. Studies [40–42] support this trend but also note concerns regarding transaction costs and the sustainability of momentum strategies. Behavioral finance studies, such as [43], show the complex influence of market trends on investor behavior.

2.3. Advances in Stock Market Forecasting through Machine Learning

A study in [44] aimed at predicting daily fluctuations in the Korea Composite Stock Price Index (KOSPI) utilized technical indicators as predictive variables. The goal was to forecast daily index movements, categorizing outcomes into two types: a decrease ("0") or an increase ("1") relative to the current day's index value. The study analyzed data from 2928 trading sessions between January 1989 and December 1998, with 20% reserved for testing and the rest reserved for model training. Data normalization ensured consistent scaling within $[-1.0, 1.0]$ to balance the influence of different variables and improve prediction accuracy. The research evaluated support vector machines (SVMs) using polynomial and Gaussian radial basis kernels against back propagation neural networks (BPNs) and case-based reasoning (CBR), and revealed that the performance of SVMs is superior due to their reliance on the structural risk minimization principle, suggesting that SVMs are effective at predicting financial time series and stock indices. These findings underscore the potential of SVM in enhancing stock market forecasting methods, offering significant implications for academic and practical applications in finance.

Researchers [45] studied the effectiveness of ML techniques, specifically the back propagation technique (BPN) and support vector machine (SVM) technique, in forecasting futures prices in the Indian stock market. Using real index futures data from the National Stock Exchange of India, this study compared these methods using statistical metrics such as the normalized mean squared error (NMSE), mean absolute error (MAE), and directional symmetry (DS) to evaluate the prediction accuracy. The results indicated SVM's superior performance over BPN in forecasting accuracy for futures prices, highlighting SVM's potential in financial forecasting within the Indian market context.

Furthermore, the application of long short-term memory (LSTM) models for stock market trend prediction has gained prominence due to their ability to capture complex temporal patterns in financial data. A study in [46] developed a classification model using LSTM networks aimed at predicting short-term price movements of Brazilian stocks, showcasing its efficacy in real-time trading with the model being retrained daily. This model, which integrates past pricing data and technical indicators, demonstrated significant predictive accuracy over baseline methods, underscoring the utility of LSTM in enhancing stock market prediction strategies. In another study [17], LSTM networks were applied to predict stock returns in the Chinese market, demonstrating a significant improvement in prediction accuracy from 14.3% to 27.2% over random predictions. The research utilized 900,000 training sequences of 30-day spans with 10 learning features and 3-day return rate labels and tested them on an additional 311,361 sequences, highlighting the potential of LSTM for financial forecasting within the volatile Chinese stock market.

The emergence of deep reinforcement learning (DRL), particularly deep Q-networks (DQNs), has influenced stock market prediction. DQN integrates reinforcement learning with deep neural networks to navigate the financial market's inherent uncertainty and volatility, making informed sequential decisions based on historical data [47]. Previous research [48] introduced a DQN-based algorithmic trading (AT) system designed for single-stock trading with daily actions—"hold", "long", or "short"—and a reward system encouraging trend-compliant actions. By incorporating trading charges, the model outperformed the decision tree and buy-and-hold strategies across various metrics, including the accumulated return and Sharpe ratio, indicating that the DQN is effective at enhancing trading strategies and reducing portfolio volatility. This work presented the potential of the DQN in algorithmic trading, particularly in handling single-stock investments for improved financial performance. In managing the complexities of financial markets, the robustness and stability provided by methods used in fractional-order uncertain BAM neural networks [49] prove beneficial for ensuring reliable predictive performance under volatile conditions. Similarly, applying deep neural networks for probabilistic state estimation demonstrates their ability to surpass traditional methods, enabling real-time, uncertainty-aware decision making in dynamic environments [50].

2.4. The Role of Sentiment Analysis in Stock Market Forecasting

Researchers in [51] highlight the innovative use of time-specific data divisions to analyze investor sentiment through tweets and news articles, focusing on the more predictive value of sentiments expressed during stock market hours than natural day cycles, applying their methodology to companies' stocks like Amazon, Netflix, Apple, and Microsoft, and showcasing that sentiment analysis during opening hours can better forecast next-day stock trends. Another study in [52] expands this concept by developing a user-facing application that dynamically assembles stock-related news to predict stock prices in real time using deep learning models. Additionally, in [53], a more general exploration of sentiment analysis on Twitter showcases its potential to estimate public sentiment towards specific stocks or sectors. They conclude that the effectiveness of such tools depends mainly on data quality and the precision of sentiment analysis algorithms.

Researchers in [54] present a sophisticated approach using neutrosophic logic to refine sentiment analysis processes by effectively handling uncertain and indeterminate data within social media content. Their methodology is based on feeding into a long short-term memory network, which uses the results from the sentiment analysis combined with historical stock data to predict market movements more accurately than previously compared models. Moreover, in [55], researchers integrated sentiment analysis with graph neural networks for stock predictions, highlighting the synergy between graph neural networks' structural data representation capabilities and sentiment interpretation. They explored various graph structures, like stock and investor networks, and how those can incorporate sentiment data extracted from news articles, social media feeds, and financial reports.

The rise of social media has transformed societal interaction, enabling a digital landscape where "online individualism" continues to increase, enhancing dialog and collective action. This digital era emphasizes the importance of sentiment analysis, which aims to automate the extraction of subjective information—opinions, feelings, and attitudes—from natural language texts [56–59]. In financial contexts, sentiment reflects market participants' collective optimism or pessimism, significantly influencing asset prices. Discrepancies between trading prices and inherent values often highlight the impact of sentiment, incorporating emotional responses and other exogenous factors into pricing mechanisms. This is central to behavioral finance, which investigates the effect of biases on financial decisions, and technical analysis, where price movements are seen as combinations of factual and emotional responses. Analysts and researchers have focused on identifying price levels that indicate emotional extremes, predicting potential corrections and market backsliding to mean values [60]. This approach underscores the critical role of sentiment in financial markets, offering insights into price deviations and correction predictions.

A study in [61] analyzed the impact of Twitter sentiment on stock market trends, specifically examining Microsoft ($MSFT). They collected 2.5 million tweets over a year, filtering them with Microsoft-related keywords. Preprocessing procedures, which included tokenization, stop word removal, and special character elimination, were used to prepare the tweets for analysis. Tweets were annotated for sentiment, and ML models classified the emotions of the remaining dataset. The logistic regression and LibSVM models achieved accuracies of 69.01% and 71.82%, respectively, demonstrating a significant correlation between Twitter sentiment and stock market movements, with model performance improving as the data volume increased. Researchers in [62] further investigated Twitter's influence on stock markets during the COVID-19 pandemic, comparing its effect to that during the H1N1 pandemic. Their findings indicated that a lexicon-based method combined with correlation analysis could uncover subtle relationships between Twitter sentiment and financial indices, with the SenticNet lexicon proving particularly effective. This study confirmed social media's increasingly pivotal role in forecasting stock market trends.

3. Data

This research's methodology is based on the systematic collection of necessary data from three distinct sources chosen for their unique contributions to the research. This section details the selection criteria for these datasets and the preparation steps for analytical readiness, aiming for transparency in the data acquisition and modeling process.

3.1. Data Collection

This research specifically focuses on NVIDIA stocks, spanning from 2 January 2020 to 21 September 2023, a period denoted by significant volatility and changes in NVIDIA's market valuation, thus making it an ideal period for investigating the dynamics of stock behavior and the efficacy of the DDQN integrating diverse data sources. The data were sourced from StockTwits, Yahoo Finance, and the yfinance Python library, with each source's contribution detailed in subsequent sections.

3.1.1. StockTwits

The StockTwits platform [5,7], which is consistent with the platform's user engagement patterns, was utilized for the sentiment analysis component of the study. Posts related to NVIDIA tagged as $NVDA were collected. StockTwits is a unique social media platform designed specifically for investors and traders. It was launched in 2008 and has grown into a vibrant community where participants share insights, strategies, and real-time market trends. Unlike traditional social media platforms, StockTwits is focused on the financial market, offering an environment for discussing stocks, bonds, cryptocurrencies, and other investment vehicles. The study gathered a range of attributes for each post on the StockTwits platform to ensure a comprehensive analysis. These attributes include:

- ID: A unique identifier for each post.
- Body: The main content or message of the post.
- Created_at: The original timestamp at which the post was created.
- User.home_country: The user's home country.
- User.followers: The number of followers the user has on StockTwits.
- Likes.total: The total number of likes the post received.
- Entities.sentiment.basic: A basic sentiment analysis of the post, if available, categorizing it as bullish or bearish.

3.1.2. Technical Indicator Overview

Technical indicators are crucial for traders worldwide, assisting in making informed decisions. This study focuses on five widely recognized and effective indicators sourced from the yfinance Python library, chosen for their analytical relevance:

- SMA Fast;
- RSI;
- SStoch RSI;
- MACD;
- Volume weighted average price (VWAP).

SMA Fast is utilized for its responsiveness to recent price movements and for identifying short-term trends [63]. RSI, a momentum oscillator [64] ranging from 0 to 100, is employed for spot overbought or oversold conditions, with values above 70 indicating overbought situations and values below 30 indicating oversold situations. Stoch RSI offers a more sensitive measure for detecting these conditions [65]. MACD, a trend-following momentum indicator, identifies buy or sell signals through the relationship between two moving averages of stock prices [66]. Finally, VWAP [67] provides a day-trading benchmark, reflecting the average price a security trades at, weighted by volume, which is useful for institutional investors managing large trades.

3.1.3. Historical and Financial Data

Yahoo Finance [68], a well-known financial news and data platform, offers extensive financial resources such as real-time stock quotes, market data, portfolio management tools, and comprehensive news coverage. Its design facilitates easy monitoring of personal investments and market analysis, supplemented by interactive charts, historical stock data, and live earnings call webcasts.

For this study, historical data on NVIDIA stocks were retrieved from Yahoo Finance. The data encompasses key metrics such as closing, opening, high, and low prices, trading volume, and adjusted prices for the study period, with a focus on trading days only. Particular attention was given to analyzing the closing prices of NVIDIA stocks.

3.2. Data Wrangling

In our study, we used data wrangling techniques to enhance ML and sentiment analysis efficacy, utilizing the advanced RoBERTa model [69] for analyzing social media sentiments on StockTwits. This progression from conventional models to RoBERTa, notable for its adeptness with informal social media language, enables more accurate sentiment analysis, revealing a generally positive sentiment toward NVIDIA stocks. This finding is consistent with user engagement trends on the platform and NVIDIA's market performance, illustrating the tendency of users to actively participate in discussions when they presented positive sentiments toward a stock.

Furthermore, our analysis incorporates essential technical indicators such as SMA, RSI, Stoch RSI, MACD, and VWAP, which were chosen for their ability to provide a detailed understanding of market behavior and assist in trading decisions. Coupled with Yahoo Finance data, which focus on active trading days and omit nontrading days for dataset consistency, our approach provides a robust foundation for reinforcement learning model development. This compact, focused strategy for data preparation and analysis sets the groundwork for leveraging reinforcement learning and sentiment analysis in financial market predictions, ensuring relevance and coherence with real-world trading activities.

3.2.1. Sentiment Analysis Methodology

In sentiment analysis, various models, such as VADER [70] and TextBlob [71], assess text sentiment polarity, categorizing it as positive, negative, or neutral. This study, however, utilizes the more recent and advanced RoBERTa model, an evolution of the BERT architecture, marking significant progress in the field. RoBERTa, which was introduced in "RoBERTa: A Robustly Optimized BERT Pretraining Approach" [69], is the basis for numerous specialized models for distinct text analysis tasks.

The chosen model for this analysis is the "Twitter-roBERTa-base for Sentiment Analysis", detailed in "TWEETEVAL: Unified Benchmark and Comparative Evaluation for Tweet Classification" [72]. This model, fine-tuned on approximately 58 million tweets via the TweetEval benchmark, is especially effective for sentiment analysis of concise, often informal social media texts, like those found on StockTwits. Its selection was strategic, considering the dataset's resemblance to Twitter's content, enabling precise sentiment analysis of StockTwits posts.

Figure 1 indicates a generally positive sentiment toward NVIDIA stocks, demonstrated by a sentiment scale ranging from -1 (negative) to +1 (positive), with a median sentiment value of 0.10, indicating a modestly positive average sentiment. The lower quartile (Q1) shows that 25% of sentiments are neutral or less, while the upper quartile (Q3) at 0.21 confirms a positive sentiment trend. The absence of negative outliers and a cluster of positive outliers highlight days with notably positive sentiment. This trend aligns with NVIDIA's significant stock price growth in recent years, capturing user interest.

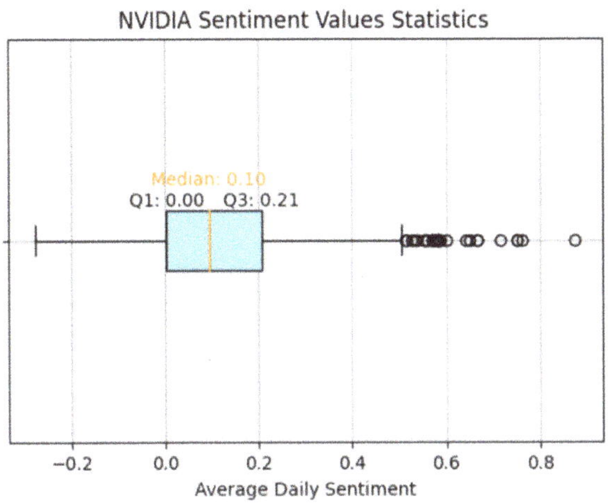

Figure 1. NVIDIA sentiment value statistics.

In summary, the analysis shows that the NVIDIA stock has a mildly positive sentiment on StockTwits. Users expressing positive sentiment toward a stock tend to be more active, leading to an increased presence of positive sentiment in posts. This reflects the natural tendency of optimists to share their views and follow related stock pages, suggesting that sentiment analysis on such platforms tends to lean positive, fueled by the enthusiasm of supportive users.

3.2.2. Technical Indicators

This study incorporates key technical indicators calculated using specified parameters, focusing on SMA, RSI, Stoch RSI, moving MACD, and VWAP.

SMA [63] is calculated over a 14-day period using closing stock prices, a method chosen for balancing recent price trends and volatility smoothing. The closing price, the last trade price during regular trading hours, offers a reliable market sentiment indicator.

RSI [64], a momentum oscillator, assesses the speed and change of stock price movements within a 14-day window to identify overbought or oversold conditions, with values over 70 indicating potential pullbacks and values below 30 indicating price rebounds. It underscores market strengths or weaknesses.

Stoch RSI [65], which enhances RSI's sensitivity, applies stochastic calculations to RSI values to detect earlier market sentiment changes. Values above 0.8 suggest overbought conditions, and values below 0.2 indicate oversold states, aiding in identifying market trends.

MACD [66], a trend-following momentum indicator, illustrates the relationship between two EMAs, specifically the 12-period and 26-period EMAs. The MACD line is derived by subtracting the 26-period EMA from the 12-period EMA, with a nine-day EMA of MACD serving as a signal line for buying or selling cues.

VWAP [67] provides the average price a security has traded throughout the day, combining price and volume data. It offers a benchmark for evaluating trade efficiency, with purchases below VWAP and sales above it considered favorable.

Each indicator offers unique insights into market behavior, contributing to the development of a comprehensive technical analysis framework for informed trading decisions.

3.2.3. Yahoo Finance

The Yahoo Finance dataset captures daily trading activities, excluding weekends and holidays, to focus exclusively on active market days. This study primarily analyzes closing prices, confronting challenges associated with missing data on nontrading days.

Two prevalent methods address this issue: linear interpolation and the complete omission of nontrading days. This research removed nontrading data from the analysis to ensure a consistent and uninterrupted dataset for modeling, as further explored in a subsequent section on reinforcement model structuring. Similarly, this exclusion principle applies to sentiment analysis of StockTwits posts, where nontrading days are ignored to prevent their influence on sentiment metrics. This strategy maintains the relevance and consistency of the sentiment analysis with actual trading periods.

4. Modeling

In the Modeling section of our study, we focus on developing and implementing an advanced stock market trading agent, leveraging the DDQN methodology to address and mitigate the overestimation biases commonly found in DQN models. This refinement allows for a more precise assessment of action values by separating the processes of action selection and evaluation. The agent is programmed with the capability to perform "BUY" and "SELL" actions based on predictive analyses of daily market changes, supported by a meticulously designed reward system that aligns with the fundamental trading principle of buying low and selling high. By integrating a policy network for decision making and a target network to enhance training stability, along with employing experience replay for a varied and efficient learning experience, our model simulates a realistic trading environment requiring nuanced daily market evaluations.

This section further explores the created reinforcement learning environment that frames the agent's operational context, detailing the structure of the action space and the formulation of the reward function to encapsulate a realistic trading scenario. By creating multiple DDQN environments, each incorporating varying levels of market data complexity, our study aims to assess the impact of different data types—ranging from closing prices and technical indicators to market sentiment—on the agent's ability to forecast short-term stock movements. This comprehensive approach highlights the versatility of DDQN in adapting to complex market conditions and emphasizes the potential of reinforcement learning to transform financial market strategies, demonstrating the way for future advancements in algorithmic trading.

4.1. Agent

This study introduces a stock market trading agent for daily operations. It utilizes the DDQN technique to overcome the overestimation bias prevalent in DQN models. By decoupling action selection from evaluation, DDQN ensures more accurate value assessments [73].

The agent employs "BUY" and "SELL" actions in response to daily market dynamics. BUY actions are predicated on expected stock value increases, while SELL actions anticipate decreases, aiming to capitalize on or mitigate market fluctuations. The reward system is drafted to promote sound trading decisions, with "BUY" rewards based on subsequent price increases and "SELL" rewards based on decreases, signifying the principle of buying low and selling high. Figure 2 presents the schema of the Q-network process.

DDQN's framework includes a policy network for decision making and a target network for stability during training, with the latter's parameters periodically refreshed to minimize volatility. A key learning mechanism is experience replay, which stores and randomly samples experiences to enhance training inputs and improve learning efficiency. The emphasis on daily trading aligns the agent's operation with real-world trading environments, requiring daily market assessments to inform actions [74]. This DDQN-based approach aims to simulate effective trading strategies, highlighting the potential of advanced reinforcement learning in stock trading applications.

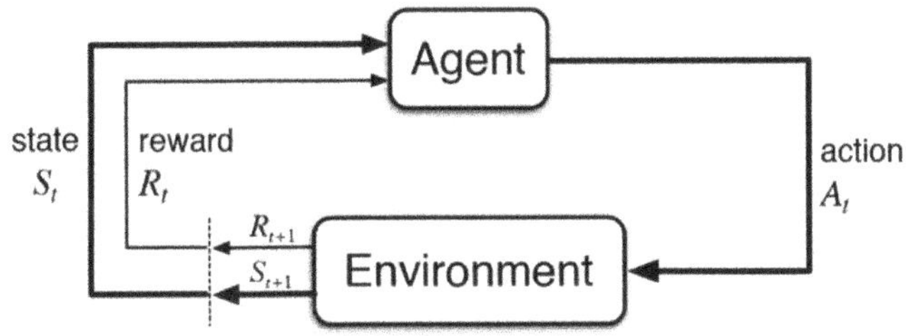

Figure 2. Schematic representation of the Q-network process.

4.2. Environment in Reinforcement Learning

In reinforcement learning (RL), the environment is a crucial element that outlines the context for agent operations, defining external conditions and parameters for decision making. Specifically, within the DDQN, the environment is instrumental in directing the agent's learning and decision-making processes. It encompasses the state space, action space, and reward system, presenting the agent with states and evaluating its actions through rewards or penalties, consequently facilitating learning and adaptation to environmental dynamics.

This study explores three DDQN environments, each adding complexity through additional market data:

1. Closing Price Environment: This environment focuses on daily stock closing prices, serving as a foundational framework for understanding basic market fluctuations.
2. Technical Indicators with Closing Price Environment: Enhances the closing price data with technical indicators (SMA, MACD, RSI, Stoch RSI, VWAP), offering a multi-faceted market perspective that includes trend, momentum, and volume analysis.
3. Technical Indicators, Sentiment, and Closing Price Environment: Integrates closing price, technical indicators, and market sentiment (from StockTwits) for comprehensive stock market analysis, encouraging the agent to consider quantitative and qualitative data in decision making.

Normalization across these environments utilizes RobustScaler [75], which is notably suitable for financial data prone to volatility and outliers. This scaler ensures data integrity and consistent model training, and its stability to outliers and trend accommodation maintains data point relevance during normalization.

This environmental setup presents agents with escalating market complexities, from basic price trends to combined technical and sentiment analysis. Employing RobustScaler ensures uniform input scaling, promoting unbiased learning. This progressive environmental design prepares the DDQN agent for diverse trading scenarios, reflecting the complexity of real-world stock trading.

4.3. Action Space

In this reinforcement learning experiment, the action space [76] is critically designed to enable the agent's decision making with two fundamental actions: "BUY" (0) and "SELL" (1). This binary structure serves the experiment's goal of evaluating the agent's ability to predict daily stock price movements, either upward or downward, thereby assessing its capability for making profitable trading decisions.

4.4. Reward Function

The reward function [77] in our study is designed to be direct and impactful, focusing on the financial consequences of the agent's actions using real financial figures without normalization. This approach ensures that the rewards genuinely reflect the outcomes of trading decisions, thereby motivating the agent to develop effective trading strategies. The reward mechanism operates as follows:

- SELL action: The reward is calculated based on the difference between the selling day's closing price and the following day's closing price. A positive reward indicates a profitable sell (price dropped the next day), and a negative reward suggests a loss (price increased the next day).

- BUY action: The reward is the difference between the next day's closing price and the current day's closing price, with a positive reward indicating a gain (price increased the next day) and a negative reward indicating a loss (price decreased the next day).

This method of calculating rewards based on actual price movements provides a realistic measure of trading success and offers the agent clear feedback on its decisions.

This study focuses on analyzing the impact of different data types on agents' predictive abilities rather than simulating a comprehensive trading scenario. By simplifying the reward structure and limiting the action space to buying and selling, this study aims to directly evaluate how closing prices, technical indicators, and sentiment analysis influence short-term stock predictions.

This simplified approach examines the contribution of each data layer to the agent's decision-making process, avoiding the complexity of more intricate trading simulations that could weaken the clarity of these insights. This methodology underlines the potential of reinforcement learning in financial market applications, demonstrating its capacity for profit generation, and deepening our understanding of market dynamics.

4.5. *Advanced Techniques in DDQN Model Optimization*

This section presents the intricate mechanisms and strategic methodologies underpinning our DDQN model, aimed at refining the decision-making processes in stock market trading. Central to our model's learning and adaptation capabilities is the experience replay memory technique, a cornerstone in DRL that significantly enhances algorithmic performance by mitigating the correlation among sequential learning samples. This technique, supplemented by a capacity of 100,000 steps, ensures a rich repository of experiences for the agent, facilitating a sophisticated learning process across varied market scenarios.

Additionally, we implement a step-decaying learning rate and a decaying epsilon-greedy strategy, which are crucial for balancing the exploration of new strategies against exploiting known profitable actions. The step-decaying learning rate methodically reduces the learning rate to fine-tune the model's adjustments for precision. At the same time, the decaying epsilon-greedy strategy systematically lowers epsilon and shifts focus from exploration to exploitation as the agent acquires additional information. These methodologies optimize the training process and ensure a well-rounded and adaptive learning experience, highlighting the sophisticated design and execution of our DDQN model.

4.5.1. Experience Replay Memory in Deep Q-Networks

Experience replay memory is a key strategy in DQNs and is essential for enhancing learning stability and efficiency in DRL. Researchers in [78] used this method, involving the storage and reutilization of past transitions (state, action, reward, next state) for learning. This approach mitigates the correlation among sequential learning samples, which is a challenge in deep RL, particularly with high-dimensional inputs such as Atari game frames.

The utility of experience replay stems from its capacity to ensure a diversified and uncorrelated selection of experiences for training batches, thereby improving algorithmic performance and learning robustness. It randomizes the learning updates by drawing samples from a replay buffer, granting even rare but crucial experiences repeated opportunities to impact the learning outcome and aid in retaining knowledge over time [79].

For our study, experience replay memory was essential, given the limited size of the dataset. With a capacity of 100,000 steps, it provided a comprehensive repository of encountered experiences, enabling the agent to leverage and learn from various situations. This extensive memory allowed for the revisiting of past transitions, contributing to a well-informed and refined learning process by utilizing every piece of data within the dataset for informed decision making.

4.5.2. Step-Decaying Learning Rate

In the DDQN framework, the implementation of a step-decaying learning rate [80] serves to strategically refine the learning process. This technique, in contrast to a static learning rate, systematically lowers the learning rate at predetermined periods, facilitating several advantages:

- Efficient convergence: Starting with a higher learning rate to achieve quick convergence to a viable solution, the rate to fine-tune the adjustments gradually decreases, culminating in a more refined and precise model.
- Adaptability: Adjusts the learning pace according to the agent's progression, employing larger steps for swift initial learning and smaller steps for meticulous model refinement in later stages.
- Prevention of oscillations: A reduced learning rate in advanced training phases shortens fluctuations near the optimal solution, enhancing the model's precision and stability.

This approach effectively balances exploration and exploitation by modulating the learning velocity in sync with the agent's incremental task comprehension.

The step-decay procedure is illustrated in Figure 3 for a model starting with an initial learning rate of 0.0045. A decay factor of 0.8, applied at fixed intervals—every 20 epochs—characterizes this method. The learning rate is kept constant within each interval before being reduced multiplicatively by the decay factor. This creates a staircase effect on the learning rate across 300 epochs, optimizing the training process and allowing the model to adjust smoothly to the evolving learning rate for an efficient and effective learning experience. Additionally, this controlled approach assists in reducing the risk of exceeding the minimum of the loss function, which can be particularly useful in the later stages of training when finer adjustments are essential for stabilizing the model.

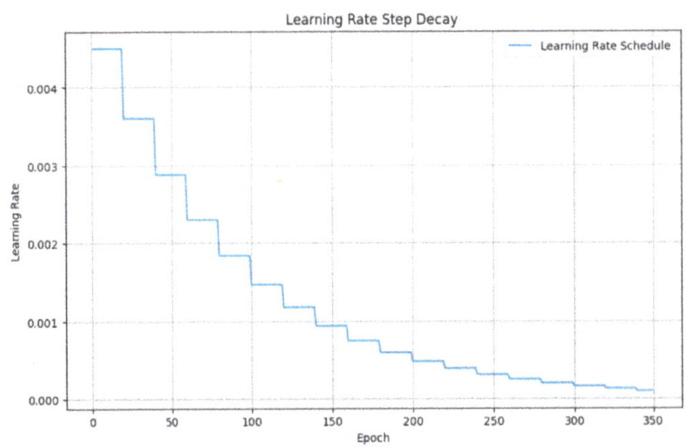

Figure 3. Learning rate step decay.

4.5.3. Decaying the Epsilon-Greedy Strategy

The epsilon-greedy strategy, which is pivotal in the realm of DQNs for reinforcement learning, is formulated to strike an optimal balance between the exploration of new actions and the exploitation of familiar ones [81]. It operates on a mechanism where the agent, based on a predefined probability epsilon (ε), either randomly selects an action or commits to the most advantageous known action with a probability of $1 - \varepsilon$. Starting with a higher ε promotes exploration, facilitating the acquisition of varied environmental insights. Over time, ε decreases to enhance the focus on exploiting accumulated knowledge for optimal decision making. This methodology enables the agent's learning by ensuring a balanced approach to discovering new strategies and applying learned experiences.

In our DDQN model, the decaying epsilon-greedy approach is essential for modulating the exploration–exploitation trade-off. Initially, set high, epsilon propels the agent toward exploration, enabling a broad sampling of actions for environmental learning. As the agent becomes more knowledgeable, epsilon decays, gradually orienting the strategy toward exploiting learned behaviors.

The key advantages of this strategy include the following:

- Balanced exploration and exploitation: This prevents the agent from being overly cautious or excessively daring, ensuring a well-rounded learning experience by integrating discoveries with existing knowledge.
- Adaptive learning: The strategy's decaying nature allows the agent's exploration-exploitation balance to adjust over time, which is tailored to the pace of learning, ensuring a smooth transition from exploration to exploitation.
- Enhanced decision making: With the reduction in epsilon, the agent increasingly relies on its learned Q-values for making decisions, resulting in more accurate and optimal choices reflecting its cumulative experiences.

Therefore, the decaying epsilon-greedy strategy is fundamental to the DDQN model, facilitating effective navigation between exploring novel strategies and leveraging known rewards, which significantly contributes to a sophisticated and efficient learning process.

Our research examined the epsilon decay strategy across 350 epochs, which is integral to balancing exploration and exploitation in reinforcement learning. Initially, at 1.0, epsilon indicates the likelihood of the model taking a random action to promote exploration. Throughout the training, we applied a decay rate of 0.991 per epoch, reducing epsilon to a floor of 0.05. This methodical reduction in epsilon facilitates a smooth transition from an exploration-dominant approach to one that favors exploitation, progressively favoring informed decisions over random actions. The observed epsilon trend depicted a consistent exponential decrease, illustrating the effectiveness of this strategy in adjusting the model's learning focus over time.

5. Results

This section evaluates the performance of a DDQN agent within the stock market prediction context by examining its behavior through diverse training stages and environmental conditions. We focus on the agent's performance during the training and testing phases across three distinct and complex environmental settings.

The initial environment is based on the stock's closing price, providing a basic understanding of market trends. The second setting incorporates technical indicators to enrich the model's inputs, which is crucial for analyzing market patterns and predicting future price shifts. These indicators offer insights into market momentum, trends, and volatility, providing the agent with a more detailed awareness of market dynamics. The last set includes sentiment analysis, introducing a component that captures the sentiment and subjective dimensions of the market. This addition aims to mirror the impact of public sentiment, as reflected on social media, on stock prices.

Throughout the training phase, the agent's goal is to refine its strategy for optimal performance based on the state representations of each environment. This phase is essential for the agent to enhance its prediction and market strategy skills. Performance is measured by the total profits achieved by the agent in each episode.

During the DDQN model training phase, 890 active trading days were utilized, excluding weekends, public holidays, and market closure days, starting on 2 January 2020, with an opening stock price of USD 59.97, and ending on 17 July 2023, with a closing price of USD 464.60. This period encompasses various market conditions, from volatility triggered by global events in 2020 to recovery and growth in the following years, providing a rich dataset that likely improved the training robustness and enabled the DDQN model to adjust to different trading environments.

5.1. Experiment Setup

In this research, we conducted a series of experiments to evaluate the efficacy of DDQN within three uniquely defined environmental states. Each state was subjected to three distinct tests, employing predetermined random seeds to ensure consistency and reproducibility of the results. The strategic application of these seeds across all tests was critical for maintaining the integrity and comparability of our findings.

In ML and, more specifically, reinforcement learning, random seeds serve as the foundation for generating reproducible sequences of random numbers. These sequences are essential to numerous aspects of the learning process, including but not limited to the initial setting of network weights, the selection of actions, and the sampling from experience replay buffers. The value of a random seed lies in its ability to generate a consistent sequence of "random" numbers across different runs, provided that the seed value is unchanged.

A uniform set of random seeds across various experiments guarantees that each trial is conducted under the same initial conditions and random processes. This uniformity was crucial for accurately comparing the performance of the DDQN agent across different environmental states, as it minimizes the impact of random variations in the learning process.

Furthermore, the fixed random seed methodology directly links the observed performance differences to the modifications in environmental states, eliminating random variability as a confounding factor. This practice significantly strengthens the trustworthiness of our experimental conclusions.

Reinforcement learning frameworks, such as the DDQN, are prone to overfitting, particularly in intricate scenarios such as predicting stock market movements. Overfitting describes a scenario where a model excessively learns from the training data to the detriment of its performance on unseen data by capturing noise and anomalies as if they were significant patterns. This issue is a prominent concern in reinforcement learning due to the critical balance required between the exploration of new strategies and the exploitation of known rewards.

To reduce the risk of overfitting in our study, we meticulously calibrated the number of training episodes. This planning aimed to provide the agent with satisfactory learning opportunities while safeguarding against the potential for overfitting to the training data patterns. By adopting this approach, we aimed to cultivate a strategy within the agent that is both generalizable and resilient rather than overly tailored to the specific instances presented during training.

5.2. Training Phase

During the training phase of this study, the DDQN model was evaluated across three sequential experiments, each designed to progressively integrate layers of information and assess their impact on the model's ability to predict stock market movements. Starting with a basic environment that utilized only NVIDIA's closing stock prices, this phase set a foundational benchmark for the model's performance, highlighting the limitations of relying on a singular data point for decision making. As the study advanced, the environment was enriched first with technical indicators, offering a broader perspective on market dynamics, and then with sentiment analysis from the StockTwits platform, incorporating qualitative insights into market sentiment. This enhancement allowed for a detailed examination of how varying types and complexities of data influence the model's trading strategies and effectiveness.

The findings of these experiments revealed a clear trajectory toward improved profitability and strategic sophistication within the DDQN model's operations. Experiment 1 demonstrated the inherent limitations of a closing price-based model, prompting a move toward a more nuanced approach in Experiment 2 with the introduction of technical indicators. This shift yielded a more balanced distribution of buy and sell actions, paving the way for Experiment 3's integration of sentiment analysis, which further refined the trading strategies by incorporating public opinion and market sentiment. Through this phased approach, the research showcased the progressive enhancement of the model's predictive accuracy and profitability and underscored the necessity of embracing a multifaceted data integration strategy. The insights gleaned from this training phase, which will be presented in the following subsections, emphasize the significance of combining diverse data sources, including both quantitative and qualitative information, to bolster the sophistication and effectiveness of algorithmic trading strategies in navigating the complexities of the stock market.

5.2.1. Closing Price Environment (Experiment 1)

The initial experiment within our investigation sets the stage with the most basic configuration, focusing exclusively on the stock's closing price. This environment, the simplest of the three evaluated, bases its entire premise on this singular data point, offering a foundational yet narrow perspective for the trading agent's decision-making process.

This simplified approach has several limitations. While the closing price reflects the stock's final trading position each day, it does not provide a comprehensive view of the market's broader movements. Consequently, the agent is bereft of critical information that could facilitate a more rounded understanding of market behaviors and trends.

Figure 4 illustrates the agent's buy and sell actions in the final episode. A dominance of buy actions is noted, indicating an expectation of higher returns from buying rather than selling. The absence of deeper market insights, such as those from technical indicators on market momentum or comprehensive trends, significantly restricts the agent's ability to distinguish and respond to market developments. Given the agent's limited operational scope, any perceived short-term trends based solely on closing prices are vulnerable to sudden and inexplicable changes.

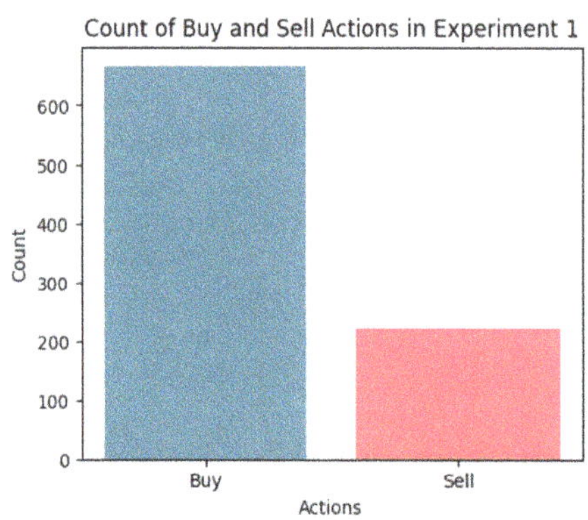

Figure 4. Experiment 1—buy/sell actions.

Figure 5 reveals the variability in total profits across episodes, highlighting the agent's struggle to stabilize its trading strategy. This fluctuation suggests that without a broader array of market data, the agent struggles to form a consistent approach to trading, hindered by the sparse information available in this elementary environment.

Thus, while this initial setting provides an introductory platform for the agent's engagement with the stock market, its basic nature significantly constrains the agent's capacity to develop a sophisticated market analysis. The findings underscore the need for a more enriched environmental setup, incorporating a wider spectrum of market data, to empower the agent with the knowledge necessary for executing informed and strategic trading decisions.

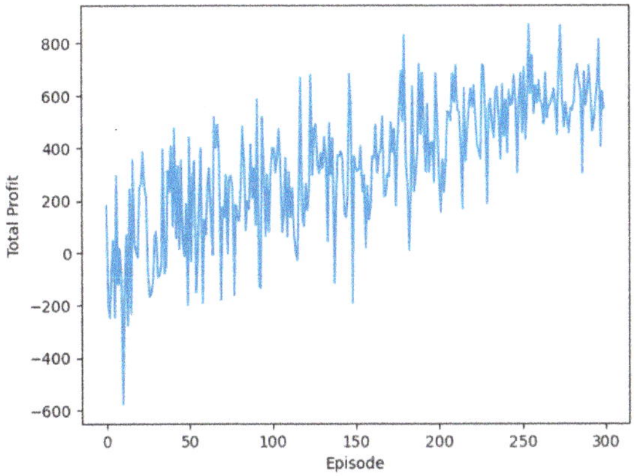

Figure 5. Experiment 1—evolution of total profits per episode.

5.2.2. Enhanced Environment with Technical Indicators (Experiment 2)

In this phase of our study, the environment for the DDQN model incorporates technical indicators, providing a richer dataset for the agent's decision-making processes. This augmentation significantly influences the agent's trading behavior, as evidenced in Figure 6, where the agent executed a balanced mix of 483 buy and 406 sell actions. This contrasts with the previous experiment's dominance of buy actions, illustrating how technical indicators have equipped the agent with a deeper understanding of market dynamics, facilitating a finer strategy in trading decisions. This development underscores the pivotal role of comprehensive data in refining trading strategies and enhancing market analysis.

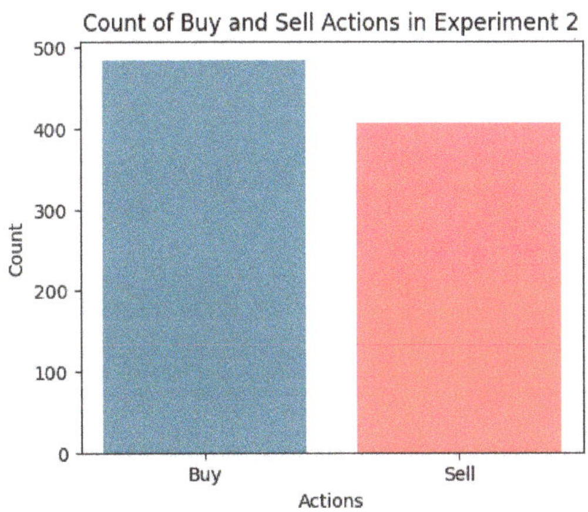

Figure 6. Experiment 2—buy/sell actions.

The training progress in this enriched environment shows less volatility across episodes than that observed in the initial experiment, suggesting a more stable and comprehensible environment for the agent. This stability indicates that the introduction of technical indicators provides sufficient information for the agent to discern optimal actions early in the training process, indicating the effectiveness of these indicators in improving performance.

In Figure 7, the trajectory of total profits during training episodes demonstrates a marked improvement in the agent's ability to identify optimal trading actions, with profits peaking at approximately USD 3500 before reaching a plateau. This enhanced performance relative to the initial experiment highlights the value of integrating technical indicators into the trading environment, enabling the agent to achieve better-informed trading decisions and, consequently, more consistent profits.

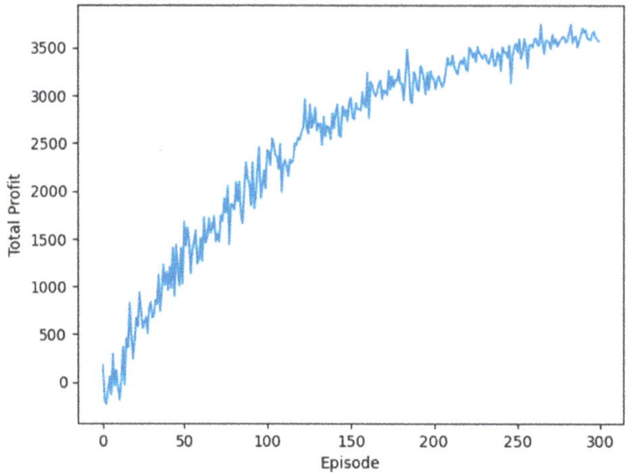

Figure 7. Experiment 2—evolution of total profits per episode.

5.2.3. Comprehensive Environment with Closing Prices, Technical Indicators, and Sentiment Analysis (Experiment 3)

In this concluding experiment of the training phase, the environment encompasses closing prices, technical indicators, and market sentiment analysis, providing a comprehensive market overview. This multifaceted approach merges quantitative data (such as closing prices and technical indicators) with qualitative insights (derived from sentiment analysis), challenging the agent to navigate through empirical evidence and sentiment-driven market trends in its decision-making process.

In Figure 8, we observe the agent's trading decisions. The number of "buy" actions, totaling 475, slightly surpassed the number of "sell" actions, which accounted for 414. This distribution reflects the agent's strategic balance in action selection, informed by a broad spectrum of market data.

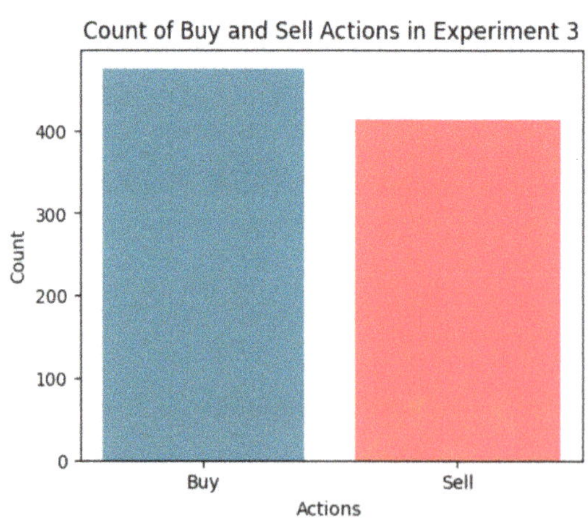

Figure 8. Experiment 3—buy/sell actions.

Figure 9 illustrates the cumulative profit trajectory over 300 training episodes within the DDQN model. The graph shows an ascending profit curve, demonstrating the DDQN agent's effective learning process. This ascending trend suggests the agent's increasing adeptness at securing profitable transactions within the given market simulation. Toward the training's conclusion, cumulative profits exceed USD 3500, indicating an optimal performance level achieved by the agent.

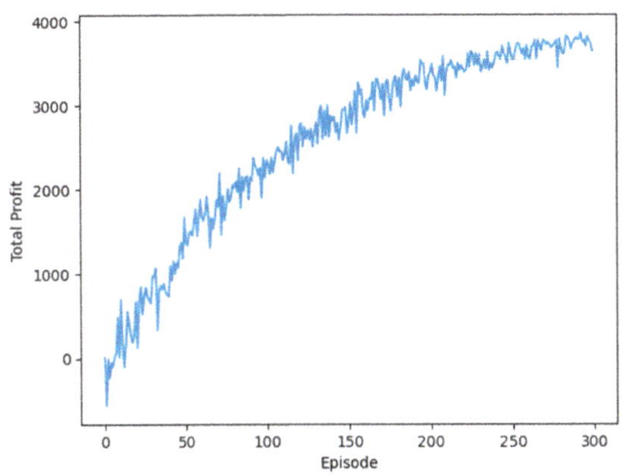

Figure 9. Experiment 3—evolution of total profits per episode.

The execution of 300 episodes proved satisfactory for the agent to refine and optimize its policy. Notably, the profit graph does not plateau, suggesting the potential for further improvements in agent performance with additional training episodes. However, this scenario also raises concerns about overfitting. The final episodes show profits reaching USD 4000, signifying the agent's expedited learning and application of optimal actions within the enriched environment.

This experiment's stable profit trajectory, without significant fluctuations or downturns, signifies a consistent and effective learning process. In the context of reinforcement learning, especially within volatile financial markets such as stock trading, such stability is crucial. This implies the agent's ability to learn, adapt, and proficiently apply this knowledge effectively. The steady increase in total profits further indicates that the training reward function is aptly designed to align with the goal of profit maximization.

5.3. Evaluation Phase

The evaluation phase is essential, as it assesses the model's proficiency in applying its acquired strategies to unseen datasets, a critical attribute for a resilient trading algorithm. Following the training of the DDQN agent within three distinct environments, each reflecting distinct market dynamics or asset behaviors, a real test of its utility coverage was conducted during the evaluation phase.

Spanning 47 trading days, the evaluation phase is designed to cover a timeframe not previously encountered by the agent in its training, offering a thorough examination of the agent's adaptability across varying market conditions. This duration is selected to provide an insightful analysis of the agent's capability through multiple market situations, from short-term volatilities to more extended market trends, confirming the effectiveness of the DDQN model in real-world trading settings. Currently, the agent's performance serves as a reliable measure of its practical value and adaptability in dynamic trading environments, where estimating accordingly to new information is crucial.

In financial time series analysis, an innovative normalization technique known as adaptive/dynamic normalization [82,83] has emerged, particularly aimed at tackling the challenges of nonstationary data. Traditional normalization methods, such as min–max scaling and z score normalization, often do not efficiently address the variable nature of financial time series characterized by frequent shifts in scale and distribution.

The dynamic window-based normalization method [84] bypasses these issues by adjusting normalization parameters in alignment with the latest available data, ensuring that test data are normalized contextually appropriately. This approach is especially relevant for financial time series forecasting, where it is vital to incorporate recent market trends and volatilities into the normalization process.

This methodology selects a recent "window" of data points from the training set, with the window's size reflecting the data's volatility and frequency—typically the past few weeks or months—for daily stock prices. Normalization parameters, such as the mean and standard deviation, are derived from this window and applied to the test data. For our study, we considered the most recent 30 days of data for this purpose. A significant benefit of this approach is its sensitivity to recent market conditions, enabling a more realistic and flexible data processing framework. This is particularly beneficial in fast-changing environments such as the stock market.

Nevertheless, this technique also presents challenges, including the selection of window size and normalization metrics, which can affect model performance. Moreover, if the window size is too small, there is a risk of overfitting to short-term trends, potentially overlooking longer-term market behaviors. The following sections will present and discuss the results, highlighting these considerations.

5.3.1. Validation in a Closing Price Environment (Experiment 1)

Figure 10 shows the results from Experiment 1, where the agent was tested under three distinct random seeds—42, 75, and 93—introducing variability to its training conditions to evaluate the stability of its trading strategy. For seeds 42 and 75, the agent's trading actions (buys and sells) distribution remained notably uniform, with buys constituting 63.8% and sells constituting 36.2%. The introduction of seed 93 led to an altered distribution, with buys increasing to 68.1% and sells decreasing to 31.9%. This shift indicates that the agent's strategy has a certain level of robustness but remains sensitive to the influence of initial conditions determined by the random seed. The buying action preference may suggest an inherent learning bias or reflect the market conditions encountered during the experiment. The prominent difference with seed 93 underlines the importance of randomness in training to strengthen the strategy's adaptability to diverse market environments.

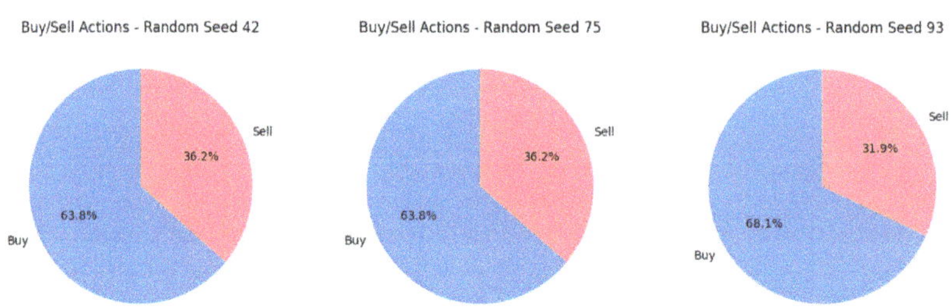

Figure 10. Experiment 1—buy/sell actions across three different random seeds.

Figure 11 presents the dynamics of positive and negative rewards by the agent for each test day, aligned with the training phase's random seeds. The outcomes illustrate minimal variation in the seed reward patterns, signifying a consistent mechanism for the agent's actions irrespective of the seeds' initial conditions. The rewards exhibit similar fluctuations across all seeds, denoting the stability of the agent's learning and decision-making framework against the randomness introduced at the training's outset.

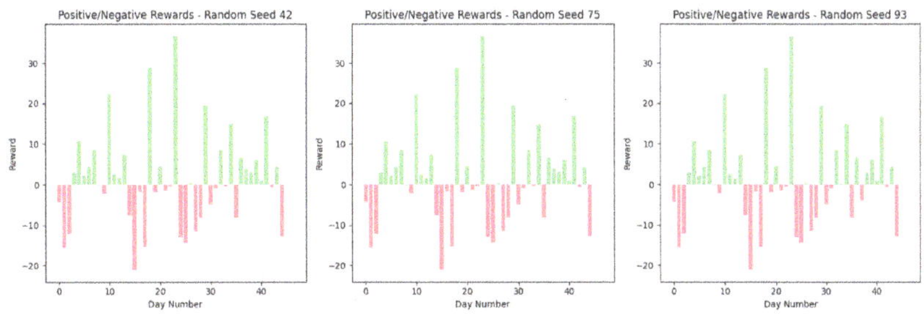

Figure 11. Experiment 1—daily profits (green) and losses (red) across three different random seeds.

The agent can navigate and identify advantageous actions despite the environment's simplicity, focused exclusively on the stock's closing price. The reward distribution represents the agent's proficient decision-making capabilities, consistently securing positive and negative rewards across various seeds and days. This consistent performance underscores the agent's aptitude for recognizing and leveraging profitable ventures within a limited informational framework. This signifies the efficacy of the underlying learning algorithm in distilling valuable insights from a constrained dataset, indicating the model's utility in practical settings well.

5.3.2. Validation of the Closing Price with the Technical Indicator Environment (Experiment 2)

Figure 12 presents the division of buy and sell decisions made by the agent in Experiment 2, where technical indicators are integrated alongside closing price data within the trading framework. For Seed 42, buy actions accounted for 68.1%, and sell actions accounted for 31.9%. Seed 75 demonstrated a more equitable distribution, with 59.6% of the participants exhibiting buy actions and 40.4% exhibiting sell actions. Moreover, 93 seeds exhibited 63.8% of buy actions and 36.2% of sell actions.

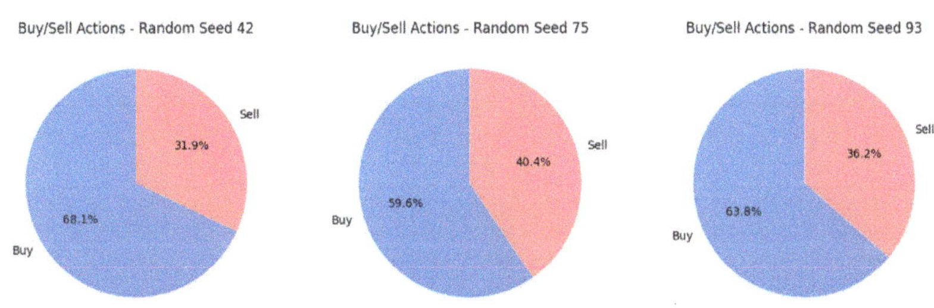

Figure 12. Experiment 2—buy/sell actions across three different random seeds.

The analysis depicted in Figure 13 shows the daily rewards, both positive and negative, leveraging similar random seeds. This experiment's findings, compared to those of Experiment 1, which solely relied on closing price information for the agent's decisions, illustrated a significant evolution in trading behavior. Including technical indicators has prompted the agent to adopt a more evenly distributed trading approach, particularly with Seed 75. The agent's previous predilection for buying actions seen in Experiment 1 decreased, indicating a moderate bias in Experiment 2.

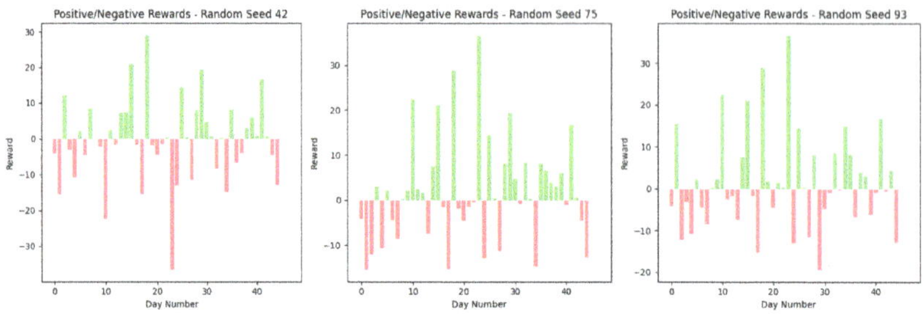

Figure 13. Experiment 2—daily profits (green) and losses (red) across three different random seeds.

Moreover, the reward patterns in Experiment 2 show a reduction in extreme losses, indicating that the extended data from technical indicators enabled more informed and profitable trading decisions. This addition has expanded the agent's capability beyond tracking short-term price movements, enabling it to discern and act on wider market indicators.

The integration of technical indicators has enriched the agent's informational environment, facilitating more sophisticated navigational and decision-making capabilities within the trading scenario, evident in both the action distribution and the daily reward pattern, where the agent exhibits an enhanced ability to secure rewards and execute balanced trading decisions. Such improvements suggest a more in-depth understanding of the market and a strengthened trading strategy, which can be attributed to the inclusion of complex input data.

5.3.3. Validation of the Closing Price with Technical Indicators and the Sentiment Environment (Experiment 3)

In Experiment 3, the trading environment is enriched with sentiment analysis from the StockTwits platform, introducing an additional layer to the already utilized closing prices and technical indicators from Experiment 2. This inclusion aims to provide a holistic view of market dynamics by combining quantitative data with qualitative sentiment insights.

Figure 14 displays the distribution of buy and sell actions by the trading agent, showcasing a nearly even split: 53.2% of buys and 46.8% of sells. This balanced action distribution is consistently observed across all three evaluated random seeds—42, 75, and 93. This indicates that including sentiment data might have allowed the agent to adopt a more unbiased stance in its trading decisions, moving away from the pronounced buy or sell bias observed in earlier experiments.

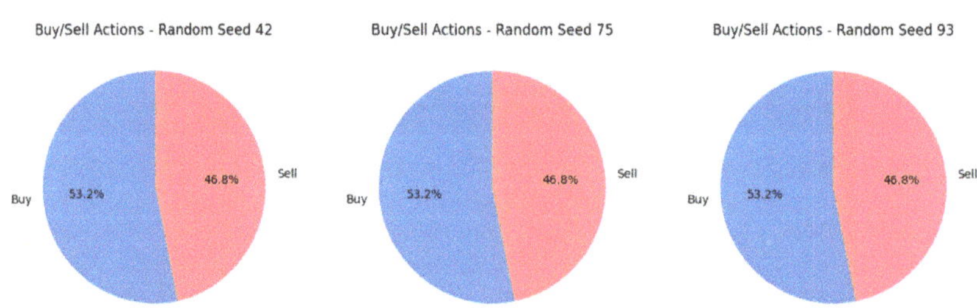

Figure 14. Experiment 3—buy/sell actions across three different random seeds.

Figure 15 compares the daily rewards, both positive and negative, across the random seeds. Differing from Experiment 2, the integration of sentiment analysis has refined the agent's reward dynamics, potentially tempering the extremities of gains or losses and offering a deeper comprehension of the market factors influencing trading choices.

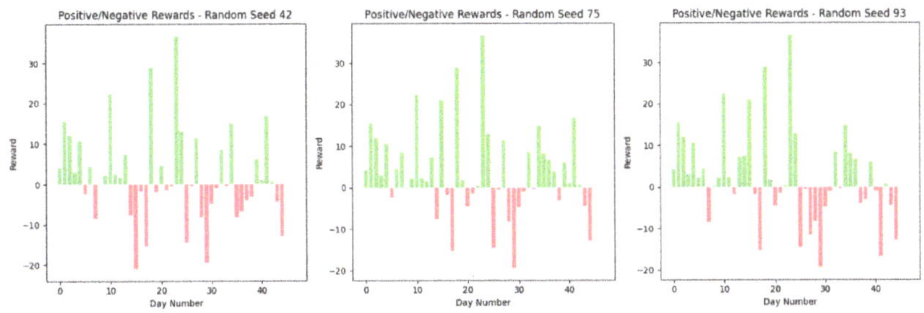

Figure 15. Experiment 3—daily profits (green) and losses (red) across three different random seeds.

By analyzing the findings from Experiment 2, it is evident that sentiment analysis contributes significantly to the agent's trading strategy. While Experiment 2 marked a progression in the agent's capability to balance buy and sell actions beyond the fundamental model, Experiment 3 showcases a further refined trading method, as reflected by the equitable distribution of actions. Additionally, the patterns of rewards imply that sentiment integration provides the agent with an added layer of market insight, enriching its decision-making process and leading to steadier performance under various market scenarios.

Nonetheless, Experiment 3's increased complexity also brings about a degree of variability among the outcomes derived from the three distinct random seeds. Despite achieving higher overall profits compared to Experiment 2, the daily actions exhibited variability across seeds, suggesting the introduction of fluctuations within this enriched environment.

6. Discussion

The ascending trajectory in average profits and outcome variability from Experiments 1 through 3 indicates a progressive increase in the complexity of the training environment. This escalation likely provided the DDQN model with a more diverse array of data points and scenarios, enhancing its ability to make informed and profitable decisions in real-world trading situations. Figure 16 compares outcomes from three distinct experiments utilizing the DDQN model to forecast stock market movements. The outcomes from each experiment are illustrated through a range of results (minimum to maximum) depicted by blue boxes, with the mean outcome of each experiment marked by a red line.

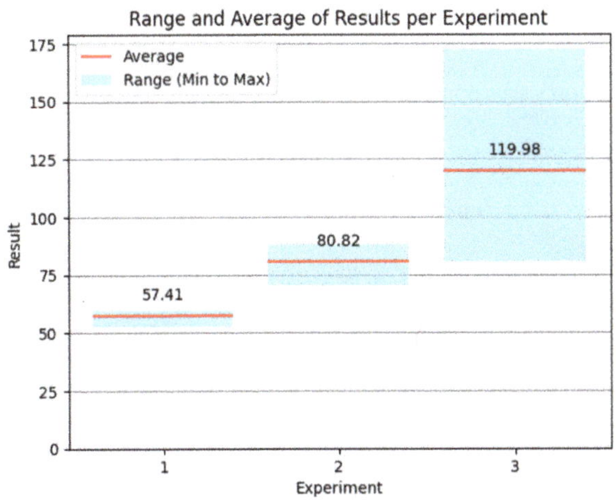

Figure 16. Comparison of total profit range across experiments and random seeds.

Experiment 1's average profit is 57.41, with outcomes showing limited variability. This consistency points to uniform performance across the board, although the average profit is lower than that in the latest experiments. The minimal variability highlights the simplistic nature of this initial experiment, which focused solely on the day's closing price.

Experiment 2 records an enhanced average profit of 80.82 along with a wider spread of outcomes, presenting exposure to a more complex trading environment (comprising closing prices + technical indicators). Despite the enlarged outcome range, consistency remains across the three random seeds used.

Experiment 3 shows a notable increase, with an average profit of 119.98, which significantly increased from the initial experiments. This experiment also exhibited the most considerable spread in outcomes, indicating a highly dynamic environment enriched with closing prices, technical indicators, and sentiment analysis. This wide range suggests that while the model achieved higher performance peaks, it also faced substantial troughs, reflecting the environment's increased complexity and the exogenous factors affecting stock market predictions.

The trend of growing average profits based on the trajectory of experiments suggests that the DDQN model is continually refining its predictive process and decision-making strategies. The expansion in both average outcomes and their ranges indicates an improved capability of the model to navigate the stock market, leveraging a richer dataset for its trading decisions. Nevertheless, the extensive variability observed in Experiment 3 also highlights a greater degree of performance unpredictability. This suggests that while the DDQN model has the capacity for high returns, it is also exposed to significant losses, reflecting the dual edge of engaging with a more complex and variable trading environment.

It is worth mentioning that while the model developed for NVIDIA stock demonstrated effectiveness in a volatile market, its application to other datasets requires careful consideration. The DDQN presented performance is tailored to the specific dynamics of NVIDIA stock and could potentially limit its transferability to stocks with different characteristics. For experiments with broader applicability, the model could be retrained or fine-tuned with new data to accommodate dissimilar market conditions or sector-specific factors. Additionally, robustness checks by back-testing on diverse datasets could benefit from assessing their generalizability. Lastly, adjustments and validations are essential to confirm the model's effectiveness across varying market scenarios for reproducibility in other stock dynamics.

7. Conclusions

This research focuses on developing and optimizing a DDQN model to examine the impact of progressively adding layers of information on its stock market prediction capabilities, specifically focusing on volatile and significant NVIDIA stocks. Initiated with a basic setup that only considered the stock's closing prices, this research established a performance baseline for the DDQN model without complex market variables, allowing for a step-by-step evaluation of additional information layers (technical indicators and sentiment analysis). Then, we expanded the model's environment by incorporating technical indicators to enhance market insight and assess their influence on forecasting accuracy. A vital factor of the investigation was integrating sentiment analysis to quantify the influence of public opinion on stock performance, utilizing social media commentary from the StockTwits platform to estimate investor sentiment toward NVIDIA stocks.

The DDQN model's performance was comprehensively evaluated across each stage, aiming to compare the environment's complexity with its trading efficacy. The initial experiment, which relied only on closing prices, involved setting the groundwork. Furthermore, in the second experiment with technical indicators, a significant improvement in the model's decision making was observed, denoted by a more balanced distribution of buy and sell actions and an increase in cumulative profits. This progression was finalized in the third experiment, where sentiment analysis introduced a more profound layer of market understanding, subsequently enhancing profitability. However, this increase in profitability was accompanied by heightened complexity in the model environment. Every additional layer of information not only broadened the model's analytical and predictive scope, but also introduced more variability in outcomes. This complexity, resulting in a wider range of potential outcomes, suggests that while added information can boost profits, it necessitates a thorough consideration of the environment's intricacies and the resilience of the underlying trading strategies.

The exploration of the DDQN model in forecasting NVIDIA's stock movements over a volatile period has yielded significant insights into the benefits of layered data integration in algorithmic trading strategies. From a simple model based on closing prices to gradually incorporating technical indicators and sentiment analysis, the study's approach has demonstrated a clear trajectory of strategic evolution and improved profitability. The initial model's tendency towards buy actions underscored the need for a more comprehensive approach to decision making within the trading algorithm. The integration of technical indicators marked the first step toward achieving this, leading to a more balanced distribution of trading actions and an initial increase in profitability. The subsequent incorporation of sentiment analysis, capturing market participants' collective mood and outlook, further refined the model's trading strategies.

Comparative analysis across the three stages revealed increased profitability, demonstrating the significant impact of combining sentiment analysis with traditional financial metrics. From an average profit of 57.41 in the simplest model setup to 119.98 with full data integration, the findings underscore the potential for sophisticated data synthesis to enhance predictive accuracy and trading performance. This incremental improvement, however, came with increased variability in outcomes, suggesting a more complex environment for the model to navigate. The research concludes that while adding data sources can substantially boost the model's profitability, it also necessitates a deeper understanding of the underlying complexities and a careful consideration of the robustness of the trading strategies. The insights gained from this study establish the value of integrating sentiment analysis alongside traditional financial metrics, increasing the sophistication and effectiveness of algorithmic trading strategies in the face of fluctuating market conditions.

Finally, by addressing off-market days such as weekends and holidays, which were excluded from the dataset for continuity, this approach might overlook critical events that could significantly affect stock sentiment and prices. Future research could explore methods such as linear interpolation [85] to effectively bridge this data gap, potentially allowing for a more refined stock performance analysis. Moreover, the sentiment analysis methodology, based on average daily social media sentiment, could be used in future studies to include weighted sentiment scores that reflect the influence of individual posts, enhancing the depth of market sentiment analysis.

Investigating hyperparameter optimization and architectural enhancements presents opportunities for further refinement of stock market predictions with the DDQN model. With no standardized approach for tuning reinforcement learning models to financial tasks, future research could explore adjustments in neural network architecture and other model components to discover more subtle market patterns. In conclusion, exploring advanced time series forecasting techniques beyond sliding window normalization [86], such as "differencing", could be an alternative approach for handling financial data, potentially leading to more accurate and robust forecasting models in future studies.

Author Contributions: Conceptualization: G.P. and D.G.; methodology: G.P. and D.G.; software: G.P. and D.G.; validation: C.T., G.P. and D.G.; formal analysis: G.P. and D.G.; investigation: G.P. and D.G.; resources: C.T., G.P. and D.G.; data curation: G.P. and D.G.; writing—original draft preparation: G.P. and D.G.; writing—review and editing: C.T., G.P. and D.G.; visualization: G.P. and D.G.; supervision: C.T.; project administration: C.T. and G.P. All authors have read and agreed to the published version of the manuscript.

Funding: This research received no external funding.

Data Availability Statement: The data presented in this study are openly available in GitHub at https://github.com/gpapageorgiouedu/Enhancing-Stock-Market-Forecasts-with-Double-Deep-Q-Network-in-Volatile-Stock-Market-Environments.

Conflicts of Interest: The authors declare no potential conflicts of interest with respect to the research, authorship, and/or publication of this article. This manuscript is according to the guidelines and complies with the Ethical Standards.

References

1. Taylor, M.P.; Allen, H. The Use of Technical Analysis in the Foreign Exchange Market. *J. Int. Money Financ.* **1992**, *11*, 304–314. [CrossRef]
2. Strader, T.J.; Rozycki, J.J.; Root, T.H.; Huang, Y.-H.J. Machine Learning Stock Market Prediction Studies: Review and Research Directions. *J. Int. Technol. Inf. Manag.* **2020**, *28*, 63–83. [CrossRef]
3. Khan, W.; Ghazanfar, M.A.; Azam, M.A.; Karami, A.; Alyoubi, K.H.; Alfakeeh, A.S. Stock Market Prediction Using Machine Learning Classifiers and Social Media, News. *J. Ambient. Intell. Humaniz. Comput.* **2022**, *13*, 3433–3456. [CrossRef]
4. Koukaras, P.; Nousi, C.; Tjortjis, C. Stock Market Prediction Using Microblogging Sentiment Analysis and Machine Learning. *Telecom* **2022**, *3*, 358–378. [CrossRef]
5. Batra, R.; Daudpota, S.M. Integrating StockTwits with Sentiment Analysis for Better Prediction of Stock Price Movement. In Proceedings of the 2018 International Conference on Computing, Mathematics and Engineering Technologies (iCoMET), Sukkur, Pakistan, 3–4 March 2018; pp. 1–5.
6. Qiu, Y.; Song, Z.; Chen, Z. Short-Term Stock Trends Prediction Based on Sentiment Analysis and Machine Learning. *Soft Comput.* **2022**, *26*, 2209–2224. [CrossRef]
7. Nousi, C.; Tjortjis, C. A Methodology for Stock Movement Prediction Using Sentiment Analysis on Twitter and StockTwits Data. In Proceedings of the 2021 6th South-East Europe Design Automation, Computer Engineering, Computer Networks and Social Media Conference (SEEDA-CECNSM), Preveza, Greece, 24–26 September 2021; pp. 1–7.
8. Islam, S.; Ab Ghani, N.; Ahmed, M. A Review on Recent Advances in Deep Learning for Sentiment Analysis: Performances, Challenges and Limitations. *Compusoft* **2020**, *9*, 3775–3783.
9. Kumbure, M.M.; Lohrmann, C.; Luukka, P.; Porras, J. Machine Learning Techniques and Data for Stock Market Forecasting: A Literature Review. *Expert Syst. Appl.* **2022**, *197*, 116659. [CrossRef]
10. Chalkias, I.; Tzafilkou, K.; Karapiperis, D.; Tjortjis, C. Learning Analytics on YouTube Educational Videos: Exploring Sentiment Analysis Methods and Topic Clustering. *Electronics* **2023**, *12*, 3949. [CrossRef]
11. Hasselt, H. Double Q-Learning. In *Proceedings of the Advances in Neural Information Processing Systems*; Lafferty, J., Williams, C., Shawe-Taylor, J., Zemel, R., Culotta, A., Eds.; Curran Associates, Inc.: Glasgow, UK, 2010; Volume 23.
12. Yen, G.; Lee, C. Efficient Market Hypothesis (EMH): Past, Present and Future. *Rev. Pac. Basin Financ. Mark. Policies* **2008**, *11*, 305–329. [CrossRef]
13. Van Horne, J.C.; Parker, G.G.C. The Random-Walk Theory: An Empirical Test. *Financ. Anal. J.* **1967**, *23*, 87–92. [CrossRef]
14. Bakar, S.; Yi, A.N.C. The Impact of Psychological Factors on Investors' Decision Making in Malaysian Stock Market: A Case of Klang Valley and Pahang. *Procedia Econ. Financ.* **2016**, *35*, 319–328. [CrossRef]
15. Huang, W.; Nakamori, Y.; Wang, S.-Y. Forecasting Stock Market Movement Direction with Support Vector Machine. *Comput. Oper. Res.* **2005**, *32*, 2513–2522. [CrossRef]
16. Yadav, A.; Jha, C.K.; Sharan, A. Optimizing LSTM for Time Series Prediction in Indian Stock Market. *Procedia Comput. Sci.* **2020**, *167*, 2091–2100. [CrossRef]
17. Chen, K.; Zhou, Y.; Dai, F. A LSTM-Based Method for Stock Returns Prediction: A Case Study of China Stock Market. In Proceedings of the 2015 IEEE International Conference on Big Data (Big Data), Santa Clara, CA, USA, 29 October–1 November 2015; pp. 2823–2824.
18. Awad, A.L.; Elkaffas, S.M.; Fakhr, M.W. Stock Market Prediction Using Deep Reinforcement Learning. *Appl. Syst. Innov.* **2023**, *6*, 106. [CrossRef]
19. Kabbani, T.; Duman, E. Deep Reinforcement Learning Approach for Trading Automation in the Stock Market. *IEEE Access* **2022**, *10*, 93564–93574. [CrossRef]
20. Lima, M.L.; Nascimento, T.P.; Labidi, S.; Timbó, N.S.; Batista, M.V.L.; Neto, G.N.; Costa, E.A.M.; Sousa, S.R.S. Using Sentiment Analysis for Stock Exchange Prediction. *Int. J. Artif. Intell. Appl.* **2016**, *7*, 59–67.
21. Fama, E.F. Efficient Capital Markets A Review of Theory and Empirical Work. In *Selected Papers of Eugene F. Fama*; Cochrane, J.H., Moskowitz, T.J., Eds.; University of Chicago Press: Chicago, IL, USA, 2017; pp. 76–121. ISBN 9780226426983.
22. Roberts, H. Statistical versus Clinical Prediction of the Stock Market. 1967; 252, *unpublished manuscript*.
23. Wafi, A.S.; Hassan, H.; Mabrouk, A. Fundamental Analysis Models in Financial Markets—Review Study. *Procedia Econ. Financ.* **2015**, *30*, 939–947. [CrossRef]
24. Malkiel, B.G. The Efficient Market Hypothesis and Its Critics. *J. Econ. Perspect.* **2003**, *17*, 59–82. [CrossRef]

25. Bachelier, L. Théorie de La Spéculation. In *Annales Scientifiques de l'École Normale Supérieure*; Gauthier-Villars: Paris, France, 1900; Volume 17, pp. 21–86.
26. Fama, E.F. The Behavior of Stock-Market Prices. *J. Bus.* **1965**, *38*, 34–105. [CrossRef]
27. Lo, A.W.; MacKinlay, A.C. *A Non-Random Walk Down Wall Street*; Princeton University Press: Princeton, NJ, USA, 2011; ISBN 9781400829095.
28. Fontanills, G.A.; Gentile, T. *The Stock Market Course*; John Wiley & Sons: Hoboken, NJ, USA, 2002; Volume 117.
29. Thomsett, M.C. *Getting Started in Fundamental Analysis*; John Wiley & Sons: Hoboken, NJ, USA, 2006.
30. Bauman, M.P. A Review of Fundamental Analysis Research in Accounting. *J. Account. Lit.* **1996**, *15*, 1.
31. Lev, B.; Ohlson, J.A. Market-Based Empirical Research in Accounting: A Review, Interpretation, and Extension. *J. Account. Res.* **1982**, *20*, 249. [CrossRef]
32. Lev, B. On the Usefulness of Earnings and Earnings Research: Lessons and Directions from Two Decades of Empirical Research. *J. Account. Res.* **1989**, *27*, 153. [CrossRef]
33. Bernard, V.L. *Accounting-Based Valuation Methods, Determinants of Market-to-Book Ratios, and Implications for Financial Statement Analysis*; Working Paper; University of Michigan: Ann Arbor, MI, USA, 1994.
34. Sureshkumar, K.K.; Elango, N.M. An Efficient Approach to Forecast Indian Stock Market Price and Their Performance Analysis. *Int. J. Comput. Appl.* **2011**, *34*, 44–49.
35. Anbalagan, T.; Maheswari, S.U. Classification and Prediction of Stock Market Index Based on Fuzzy Metagraph. *Procedia Comput. Sci.* **2015**, *47*, 214–221. [CrossRef]
36. Dash, R.; Dash, P.K.; Bisoi, R. A Self Adaptive Differential Harmony Search Based Optimized Extreme Learning Machine for Financial Time Series Prediction. *Swarm Evol. Comput.* **2014**, *19*, 25–42. [CrossRef]
37. Bisoi, R.; Dash, P.K. A Hybrid Evolutionary Dynamic Neural Network for Stock Market Trend Analysis and Prediction Using Unscented Kalman Filter. *Appl. Soft. Comput.* **2014**, *19*, 41–56. [CrossRef]
38. Murphy, J.J. *Technical Analysis of the Financial Markets: A Comprehensive Guide to Trading Methods and Applications*; Penguin: London, UK, 1999.
39. Box, G.E.P.; Jenkins, G.M.; Reinsel, G.C.; Ljung, G.M. *Time Series Analysis: Forecasting and Control*; John Wiley & Sons: Hoboken, NJ, USA, 2015.
40. Jegadeesh, N.; Titman, S. Returns to Buying Winners and Selling Losers: Implications for Stock Market Efficiency. *J. Financ.* **1993**, *48*, 65–91. [CrossRef]
41. Moskowitz, T.J.; Grinblatt, M. Do Industries Explain Momentum? *J. Financ.* **1999**, *54*, 1249–1290. [CrossRef]
42. Chan, L.K.C.; Jegadeesh, N.; Lakonishok, J. Momentum Strategies. *J. Financ.* **1996**, *51*, 1681–1713. [CrossRef]
43. Andreassen, P.B.; Kraus, S.J. Judgmental Extrapolation and the Salience of Change. *J. Forecast.* **1990**, *9*, 347–372. [CrossRef]
44. Kim, K. Financial Time Series Forecasting Using Support Vector Machines. *Neurocomputing* **2003**, *55*, 307–319. [CrossRef]
45. Das, S.P.; Padhy, S. Support Vector Machines for Prediction of Futures Prices in Indian Stock Market. *Int. J. Comput. Appl.* **2012**, *41*, 22–26.
46. Nelson, D.M.Q.; Pereira, A.C.M.; de Oliveira, R.A. Stock Market's Price Movement Prediction with LSTM Neural Networks. In Proceedings of the 2017 International Joint Conference on Neural Networks (IJCNN), Anchorage, AK, USA, 14–19 May 2017; pp. 1419–1426.
47. Kalva, S.; Satuluri, N. Stock Market Investment Strategy Using Deep-Q-Learning Network. In *International Conference on Multi-disciplinary Trends in Artificial Intelligence*; Springer Nature: Cham, Switzerland, 2023; pp. 484–495.
48. Chakole, J.; Kurhekar, M. Trend Following Deep Q-Learning Strategy for Stock Trading. *Expert Syst.* **2020**, *37*, e12514. [CrossRef]
49. Chinnamuniyandi, M.; Chandran, S.; Xu, C. Fractional Order Uncertain BAM Neural Networks with Mixed Time Delays: An Existence and Quasi-Uniform Stability Analysis. *J. Intell. Fuzzy Syst.* **2024**, *46*, 4291–4313. [CrossRef]
50. Yi, G.; Zhuang, X.; Li, Y. Probabilistic State Estimation in District Heating Grids Using Deep Neural Network. *Sustain. Energy Grids Netw.* **2024**, *38*, 101353. [CrossRef]
51. Xiao, Q.; Ihnaini, B. Stock Trend Prediction Using Sentiment Analysis. *PeerJ Comput. Sci.* **2023**, *9*, e1293. [CrossRef]
52. Praturi, S.S.G.; Ramakrishnan, A.; Deepthi, L.R. Stock Price Prediction Using Sentiment Analysis on Financial News. In *International Conference on Data Science and Applications*; Springer Nature: Singapore, 2024; pp. 551–567.
53. Pandey, M.; Nayak, S.; Rautaray, S.S. An Analysis on Sentiment Analysis and Stock Market Price Prediction. In Proceedings of the 2023 2nd International Conference on Automation, Computing and Renewable Systems (ICACRS), Pudukkottai, India, 11–13 December 2023; pp. 367–370.
54. Abdelfattah, B.A.; Darwish, S.M.; Elkaffas, S.M. Enhancing the Prediction of Stock Market Movement Using Neutrosophic-Logic-Based Sentiment Analysis. *J. Theor. Appl. Electron. Commer. Res.* **2024**, *19*, 116–134. [CrossRef]
55. Das, N.; Sadhukhan, B.; Chatterjee, R.; Chakrabarti, S. Integrating Sentiment Analysis with Graph Neural Networks for Enhanced Stock Prediction: A Comprehensive Survey. *Decis. Anal. J.* **2024**, *10*, 100417. [CrossRef]
56. Messner, W. Cultural and Individual Differences in Online Reviews. *J. Int. Consum. Mark* **2020**, *32*, 356–382. [CrossRef]

57. Kapoteli, E.; Koukaras, P.; Tjortjis, C. Social Media Sentiment Analysis Related to COVID-19 Vaccines: Case Studies in English and Greek Language. In *IFIP International Conference on Artificial Intelligence Applications and Innovations*; Springer: Cham, Switzerland, 2022; pp. 360–372.
58. Akritidis, L.; Bozanis, P. Low-Dimensional Text Representations for Sentiment Analysis NLP Tasks. *SN Comput. Sci.* **2023**, *4*, 474. [CrossRef]
59. Akritidis, L.; Bozanis, P. How Dimensionality Reduction Affects Sentiment Analysis NLP Tasks: An Experimental Study. In *IFIP International Conference on Artificial Intelligence Applications and Innovations*; Springer: Cham, Switzerland, 2022; pp. 301–312.
60. Friesen, G.C.; Weller, P.A.; Dunham, L.M. Price Trends and Patterns in Technical Analysis: A Theoretical and Empirical Examination. *J. Bank Financ.* **2009**, *33*, 1089–1100. [CrossRef]
61. Pagolu, V.S.; Reddy, K.N.; Panda, G.; Majhi, B. Sentiment Analysis of Twitter Data for Predicting Stock Market Movements. In Proceedings of the 2016 International Conference on Signal Processing, Communication, Power and Embedded System (SCOPES), Paralakhemundi, India, 3–5 October 2016; pp. 1345–1350.
62. Valle-Cruz, D.; Fernandez-Cortez, V.; López-Chau, A.; Sandoval-Almazán, R. Does Twitter Affect Stock Market Decisions? Financial Sentiment Analysis During Pandemics: A Comparative Study of the H1N1 and the COVID-19 Periods. *Cognit. Comput.* **2022**, *14*, 372–387. [CrossRef]
63. Ellis, C.A.; Parbery, S.A. Is Smarter Better? A Comparison of Adaptive, and Simple Moving Average Trading Strategies. *Res. Int. Bus. Financ.* **2005**, *19*, 399–411. [CrossRef]
64. Levy, R.A. Relative Strength as a Criterion for Investment Selection. *J. Financ.* **1967**, *22*, 595. [CrossRef]
65. Vaiz, J.S.; Ramaswami, M. A Study on Technical Indicators in Stock Price Movement Prediction Using Decision Tree Algorithms. *Am. J. Eng. Res. (AJER)* **2016**, *5*, 207–212.
66. Antonio Agudelo Aguirre, A.; Alfredo Rojas Medina, R.; Darío Duque Méndez, N. Machine Learning Applied in the Stock Market through the Moving Average Convergence Divergence (MACD) Indicator. *Invest. Manag. Financ. Innov.* **2020**, *17*, 44–60. [CrossRef]
67. Mitchell, D.; Białkowski, J.; Tompaidis, S. Volume-Weighted Average Price Tracking: A Theoretical and Empirical Study. *IISE Trans.* **2020**, *52*, 864–889. [CrossRef]
68. Albahli, S.; Nazir, T.; Mehmood, A.; Irtaza, A.; Alkhalifah, A.; Albattah, W. AEI-DNET: A Novel DenseNet Model with an Autoencoder for the Stock Market Predictions Using Stock Technical Indicators. *Electronics* **2022**, *11*, 611. [CrossRef]
69. Liu, Y.; Ott, M.; Goyal, N.; Du, J.; Joshi, M.; Chen, D.; Levy, O.; Lewis, M.; Zettlemoyer, L.; Stoyanov, V. RoBERTa: A Robustly Optimized BERT Pretraining Approach. *arXiv* **2019**, arXiv:1907.11692.
70. Hutto, C.; Gilbert, E. VADER: A Parsimonious Rule-Based Model for Sentiment Analysis of Social Media Text. In Proceedings of the International AAAI Conference on Web and Social Media, Ann Arbor, MI, USA, 1–4 June 2014; 2014; Volume 8, pp. 216–225. [CrossRef]
71. Loria, S. Textblob Documentation. *Release 0.15* **2018**, *2*, 269.
72. Barbieri, F.; Camacho-Collados, J.; Espinosa Anke, L.; Neves, L. TweetEval: Unified Benchmark and Comparative Evaluation for Tweet Classification. *arXiv* **2020**, arXiv:2010.12421.
73. Wu, N.; Ke, Z.; Feng, L. Stock Price Forecast Based on LSTM and DDQN. In Proceedings of the 2022 14th International Conference on Advanced Computational Intelligence (ICACI), Wuhan, China, 15–17 July 2022; pp. 182–185.
74. Zhang, H.; Qu, C.; Zhang, J.; Li, J. Self-Adaptive Priority Correction for Prioritized Experience Replay. *Appl. Sci.* **2020**, *10*, 6925. [CrossRef]
75. Pedregosa, F.; Varoquaux, G.; Gramfort, A.; Michel, V.; Thirion, B.; Grisel, O.; Blondel, M.; Prettenhofer, P.; Weiss, R.; Dubourg, V.; et al. Scikit-Learn: Machine Learning in Python. *J. Mach. Learn. Res.* **2011**, *12*, 2825–2830.
76. Zejnullahu, F.; Moser, M.; Osterrieder, J. Applications of Reinforcement Learning in Finance—Trading with a Double Deep Q-Network. *arXiv* **2022**, arXiv:2206.14267.
77. Sowerby, H.; Zhou, Z.; Littman, M.L. Designing Rewards for Fast Learning. *arXiv* **2022**, arXiv:2205.15400.
78. Mnih, V.; Kavukcuoglu, K.; Silver, D.; Graves, A.; Antonoglou, I.; Wierstra, D.; Riedmiller, M. Playing Atari with Deep Reinforcement Learning. *arXiv* **2013**, arXiv:1312.5602.
79. Lin, L.-J. Self-Improving Reactive Agents Based on Reinforcement Learning, Planning and Teaching. *Mach. Learn.* **1992**, *8*, 293–321. [CrossRef]
80. Gu, W.; Wang, S. An Improved Strategy for Blood Glucose Control Using Multi-Step Deep Reinforcement Learning. *arXiv* **2024**, arXiv:2403.07566.
81. Kaleel, P.B.; Sheen, S. Focused Crawler Based on Reinforcement Learning and Decaying Epsilon-Greedy Exploration Policy. *Int. Arab. J. Inf. Technol.* **2023**, *20*, 819–830. [CrossRef]
82. Liu, C.; Gao, Y.; Lv, J. Dynamic Normalization. *arXiv* **2021**, arXiv:2101.06073.
83. Gupta, V.; Hewett, R. Adaptive Normalization in Streaming Data. In Proceedings of the 2019 3rd International Conference on Big Data Research, Cergy-Pontoise, France, 20–22 November 2019; ACM: New York, NY, USA; pp. 12–17.
84. Shi, Y.; Li, W.; Zhu, L.; Guo, K.; Cambria, E. Stock Trading Rule Discovery with Double Deep Q-Network. *Appl. Soft Comput.* **2021**, *107*, 107320. [CrossRef]

85. Lepot, M.; Aubin, J.-B.; Clemens, F. Interpolation in Time Series: An Introductive Overview of Existing Methods, Their Performance Criteria and Uncertainty Assessment. *Water* **2017**, *9*, 796. [CrossRef]
86. Ogasawara, E.; Martinez, L.C.; de Oliveira, D.; Zimbrao, G.; Pap, G.L.; Mattoso, M. Adaptive Normalization: A Novel Data Normalization Approach for Non-Stationary Time Series. In Proceedings of the 2010 International Joint Conference on Neural Networks (IJCNN), Barcelona, Spain, 18–23 July 2010; pp. 1–8.

electronics

MDPI

Review

Sentiment Dimensions and Intentions in Scientific Analysis: Multilevel Classification in Text and Citations

Aristotelis Kampatzis *, Antonis Sidiropoulos *, Konstantinos Diamantaras and Stefanos Ougiaroglou

Department of Information and Electronic Engineering, International Hellenic University (IHU), 57400 Thessaloniki, Greece; kdiamant@ihu.gr (K.D.); stoug@ihu.gr (S.O.)

* Correspondence: kampatzistelis@gmail.com (A.K.); asidirop@ihu.gr (A.S.)

Abstract: Sentiment Analysis in text, especially text containing scientific citations, is an emerging research field with important applications in the research community. This review explores the field of sentiment analysis by focusing on the interpretation of citations, presenting a detailed description of techniques and methods ranging from lexicon-based approaches to Machine and Deep Learning models. The importance of understanding both the emotion and the intention behind citations is emphasized, reflecting their critical role in scientific communication. In addition, this study presents the challenges faced by researchers (such as complex scientific terminology, multilingualism, and the abstract nature of scientific discourse), highlighting the need for specialized language processing techniques. Finally, future research directions include improving the quality of datasets as well as exploring architectures and models to improve the accuracy of sentiment detection.

Keywords: natural language processing (NLP); machine learning; deep learning; sentiment analysis; scientometrics; sentiment analysis of scientific citations

1. Introduction

Starting with the definition, sentiment analysis is a growing field of science that intersects with fields such as Artificial Intelligence (AI), Statistical Analysis (SA), and Natural Language Processing (NLP). Its central goal is to identify and evaluate the emotional expressions contained in texts. This approach uses various methods of data analysis to identify and evaluate the different nuances of the emotions and subjective elements expressed. Key work in this field includes the detection of emotion polarity (positive, negative, neutral), extraction of opinion elements, and overall emotional perception of texts [1].

In recent years, the problem of emotion analysis has attracted the interest of the scientific community, and the ability to assess people's preferences quickly and reliably for a topic has lead many companies and organizations to invest in this process. According to M. Wankhade et al. [1], applications of sentiment analysis are very useful in areas such as companies (product and service evaluations), the health sector for categorizing medical data, art (music, movie reviews, etc.), and social networks for monitoring public opinion. In addition, Sentiment Analysis has been explored at different levels, such as the Document Level, Sentence Level, Phrase Level and Aspect Level, as shown in Figure 1.

The Document Level focuses on evaluating the emotional charge of a whole text, with the purpose being to determine whether the document has positive, negative, or neutral emotional connotations. Both supervised and unsupervised learning approaches can be used. However, this type is not often used, mainly due to the large number of ideas and conflicting emotions. The Sentence Level focuses on assessing the emotion conveyed by each individual sentence. This method allows for a more detailed analysis compared to the Document Level, as it separates the text into sentences to evaluate the sentiment of each one individually. The Phrase Level focuses on specific expressions within a sentence and identifies the emotion present in smaller sections of the text. This level of analysis can reveal subtle variations in emotion that may be lost in a more generalized analysis at the

Document or Sentence Levels. Aspect Level analysis focuses on understanding the emotion associated with specific features of a product or service. For example, in mobile phone reviews, aspects may include design, durability, performance, battery life, camera, etc.

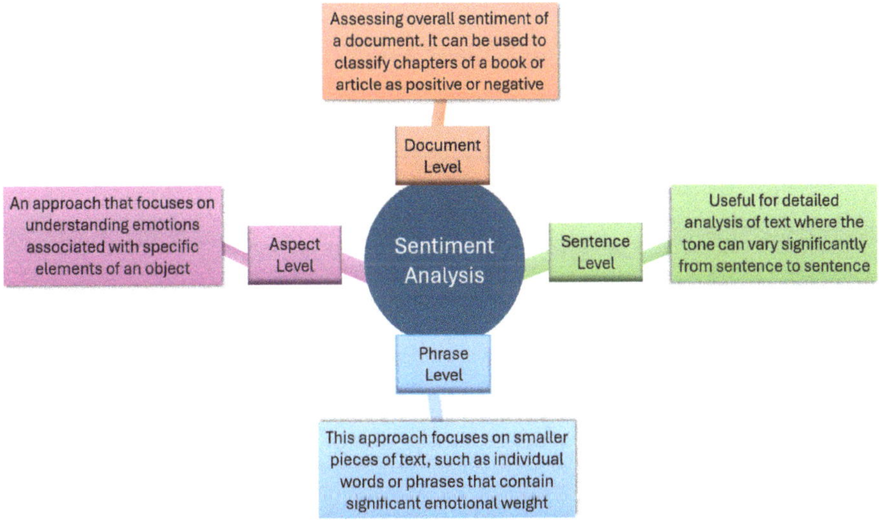

Figure 1. Sentiment Analysis Approaches.

The importance of literature references in the world of scientific research is a long-lasting and dynamic phenomenon. As the scientific community grows and evolves in the digital age, citations continue to be a vital link between research papers, allowing for interaction, acknowledgement, and critique between researchers. In this context, digital libraries and analytical services provide a rich source of information, facilitating access to, and evaluation of, scientific papers [2]. In fact, a citation is a textual element in a scientific publication that highlights and links to previous work for various reasons. It can be used to compare or highlight and identify different sources or previous work, thus contributing to academic discussion and scientific debate [2].

According to Alvarez et al. [3], in the field of citation analysis, qualitative evaluation is as important as quantitative evaluation, with the latter focusing on the frequency of citations. It is also argued that citations present different weights depending on the influence of the works that cite them, with it being thought that sentiment analysis can enhance the evaluation of the influence of scientific works by considering the author's disposition towards the cited work. Similarly, in [4,5], the authors provide a detailed examination of both quantitative and qualitative evaluation of citations. The quantitative evaluation concerns the frequency of citations and how this correlates with various aspects of the research work. On the other hand, the qualitative evaluation focuses on the quality of the citations, examining their importance, relevance, and weight within the text, and it is considered to be more critical than a quantitative evaluation. Therefore, by considering both quantity and quality, researchers can gain a more complete picture of both the influence and importance of a work in the scientific field.

Many research papers define a text that includes citations to a publication as a "citation context". They classify citations into being either explicit and implicit, with an explicit citation involving one or more sentences around a citation position in a document. This means that explicit citations are those that directly and clearly mention a source or previous work within the text of the article, usually stating the names of the authors. In contrast, an implicit or implied citation is a sentence that is not directly linked to the cited article and is usually quoted within the text following an explicit citation [2,6,7]. For example, in the following text:

> *"Gregori et al. [19] introduced an innovative algorithm for sentiment analysis, leveraging a revolutionary methodology that enables the identification of nuanced emotional nuances within textual data. This state-of-the-art approach provides an adaptable, user-defined, and context-independent framework for sentiment analysis, thereby enhancing accuracy and efficiency in natural language processing tasks".*

The first sentence, *"Gregori et al. [19] introduced . . . within textual data"*, is an explicit citation, while the second sentence, *"This state-of-the-art ... natural language processing tasks"*, is an implicit citation.

Athar and Teufel [7] examine the detection of implicit citations in sentiment analyses of scientific texts. They emphasize the importance of including such citations to improve the quality of the overall polarity assignment. Finally, they point out the weakness of many recognition techniques, which usually ignore implicit citations by focusing only on citations that contain a direct reference to the author's name and publication date.

As the above demonstrates, the citation framework is an important resource for a variety of applications that need to identify the purpose or thematic objective of a citation, the reasons for citing a particular idea, as well as the critique of concepts that have preceded it in the academic literature. It is very important for new researchers to be able to understand the perspective of a project in a particular field; therefore, they will be able to discover any gaps in the literature if they identify a citation with a negative polarity or acknowledge the researchers' contribution by identifying citations with a positive sentiment [2]. The development of methods to evaluate citations with a deeper understanding and accuracy, focusing on both quality and quantity, has proven to be challenging. Sentiment analysis, as part of this approach, reveals new dimensions in evaluating the impact and contribution of a scientific project, thus helping to better understand the value of scientific communication as it impacts the academic community.

Recognizing that scientific texts hide a wealth of affective cues that are often overlooked, this study aims to provide a framework for analyzing these affective data. The aim of this review is therefore to highlight the importance of the emotional expressions that emerge in texts and scientific publications. The study aims to reveal patterns in the ways that emotions influence scientific discourse and the judgments that are formed around research results. Using modern Natural Language Processing and Neural Network techniques, it encourages the development of advanced systems capable of detecting and analyzing both the emotional connotations and the intensity of the reactions behind citations. The aim is to enhance transparency and accuracy in scientific communication, as well as to ensure a framework that encourages critical thinking and the constant review of research methods.

2. Research Methodology

The continuous development and evolution of research in each field makes it necessary to carry out extensive literature reviews to summarize and evaluate existing knowledge. In this context, previous work in the field of NLP and Sentiment Analysis has focused on the analysis of specific areas and other specific subject areas while also remaining limited in terms of methodology and scope. In contrast, this paper aims to provide a broader and more systematic literature review using the PRISMA (Preferred Reporting Items for Systematic Reviews and Meta-Analyses) methodology [8]. The PRISMA methodology, which is based on rigorous criteria for selecting and evaluating items, allows for the development of a transparent and reproducible literature review, thus providing significant added value to the field. Therefore, to conduct our systematic review, we followed the below steps:

- Defining the research questions.
- Searching for literature in reliable repositories.
- Setting criteria for rejecting certain papers.

- Removal of duplicate documents.

2.1. Research Questions

Below are the research questions that will be addressed in this study in order to explain the importance of classification in texts. Through these questions, we will examine how classification can contribute to exploring the role of each citation, highlighting the complexity of scientific discourse. In addition, these questions will seek to highlight the challenges faced by Sentiment Analysis while also exploring the contribution of advanced Machine Learning techniques that improve the evaluation of scientific research.

- *RQ1.* What algorithms and models have been developed for Sentiment Analysis in texts and how do they compare with traditional methods?
- *RQ2.* What preprocessing methods and classification accuracy metrics are applied in Sentiment Analysis?
- *RQ3.* In which cases do Machine Learning models perform better compared to Deep Learning models?
- *RQ4.* Which types of learning are most often used in classification problems in Sentiment Analysis?
- *RQ5.* How can Sentiment Analysis improve the understanding and evaluation of scientific communication?
- *RQ6.* What are the challenges in Sentiment Analysis in scientific texts?
- *RQ7.* What classifications are generally applied in the analysis of reporting frameworks?
- *RQ8.* Are there datasets available for Sentiment Analysis in citation contexts?
- *RQ9.* What is the role of emotions in communicating scientific results and how do they affect the acceptance of information?

All research questions will be answered in Section 5 (Discussion) after presenting the literature review.

2.2. Search Strategy and Selection Criteria

To find articles covering Sentiment Analysis in text and citations, we selected eight (8) databases: Springer, Google Scholar, Semantic Scholar, Science Direct, Association for Computing Machinery (ACM), MDPI, ACL Anthology, and IEEE Xplore. In each database, we performed several search queries to identify articles related to our review topic. The search queries were defined based on the requirements of each database, selecting and combining keywords to match the scientific and research focus of each platform. In general, we did not apply strict temporal search filters. In some of the queries, there was a need to restrict results, resulting in us activating a filter for the year of publication. Table 1 lists the queries that returned the most relevant results. In some platforms, however, it took more than one query before we found results that covered the scope of our work, while in others, such as IEEE, we identified relevant results with just one query. We also identified criteria for including and excluding articles in order to focus on the topic of the review. The included papers were screened to meet the following selection criteria:

- Be Conference Papers or Journal Articles.
- Apply NLP and Machine Learning methods.
- Apply Sentiment Analysis methods in citation contexts.
- Be Research Papers.
- The full text is available.
- Be published in reputable Journals or Conferences that show high-quality research.

Additional reasons for rejecting articles are as follows:

- *Rejection due to contradictions.* If there are contradictions in the data or results presented, the article may not be credible.
- *Rejection based on content.* If the screening process finds that the content of the article is not relevant to the topic of our study, we reject it.

Table 1. Search queries.

Digital Repositories/Databases	Number of Query	Query
Springer	1	with the exact phrase: Sentiment Analysis Challenges. with at least one of the words: sentiment analysis challenges methods [Filters] year: 2021–2022
	2	with at least one of the words: Scientometrics Citation. where the title contains: "Citation Context" OR "Citation Function Classification"
	3	with at least one of the words: Polarity Classification. where the title contains: "Polarity Classification" AND "Twitter"
	4	with all the words: Automatic Content Extraction. with the exact phrase: Named-entity Recognition. with at least one of the words: Sentiment Analysis Polarity Detection. where the title contains: "Sentiment Analysis" AND "Mining" [Filters] year: 2014–2019
	5	with at least one of the words: Scientific Citation Sentiment Function BERT. where the title contains: "Scientific Citations" OR "BERT" AND "Formal Citation"
Google Scholar	1	("sentiment analysis" AND "emotions") AND ("Word2Vec") AND "lexicon" AND ("word embeddings") AND "NLP" AND "machine learning" AND "online user reviews"
	2	("Text Classification" AND "Product Reviews") AND ("Sentiment Analysis" OR ("Support Vector Machines" AND "TF-IDF" AND "Naive Bayes" AND "BERT")
	3	"sentiment classification" AND "comparative experiments" AND "product reviews" OR "text reviews"
	4	"Patterns" AND "Scientometrics" AND "Scientometrics Analysis" AND "Citation Analysis"
	5	"Sentiment Analysis" AND "Natural Language Toolkit" AND ("Twitter Messages" OR "tweets") AND "Word2Vec" AND ("CBOW" AND "Skip-Gram")
	6	"Sentiment Analysis" OR "Scientometric Analysis" AND "Convolutional Neural Networks" AND "CNN" AND "KNN" AND "Explicit Features"
	7	"Scientometrics" AND "citation function" AND "citation role"
	8	"Role" AND "Negative Citations" AND "natural language processing" AND "objective citations"
	9	Bibliometric AND "Analysis Methods" AND PageRank AND "Author citation"
	10	"Conditional random fields" AND "Extracting citation metadata" AND "citation indexing" AND "CiteSeer" AND "Extracting Citation Contexts"
	11	"BERT" AND "Attention Layer" AND "Sentiment Classification" AND "Attention" AND "Classification" AND "Citation" AND "Dictionary"

Table 1. *Cont.*

Digital Repositories/Databases	Number of Query	Query
Semantic Scholar	1	"Basic Emotions" AND "Detection of Implicit Citations" [Filters] Fields of Study: Psychology, Computer Science Date Range: 1990–2012, Has PDF = ON
	2	"Characteristics" AND "Citing Paper" AND "Cited and Citing" [Filters] Fields of Study: Computer Science Date Range: 1980–2007, Has PDF = ON
	3	"citation identification" AND "text citations" AND "Citation sentiment analysis" AND "Analysis Using Word2vec" AND "CBOW" OR "Skip-Gram" [Filters] Fields of Study: Computer Science, Has PDF = ON
Science Direct	1	("Sentiment Analysis" AND "word embeddings" AND "Machine Learning") AND ("Sentiment lexicon" OR emotions OR "lexicon-based") AND "Supervised Machine Learning"
	2	("Sentiment Analysis" AND "Reviews") AND ("LSTM" OR "Word2vec" AND ("RNN" OR "CNN") AND ("CBOW" OR "Skip-gram")
Association for Computing Machinery (ACM)	1	[[[Full Text: tweets] AND [Full Text: hashtags]] OR [[Full Text: "hashtag sentiment"] AND [Full Text: "sentiment lexicon"]]] AND [Title: tweets hashtags] AND [[Title: sentiment] OR [Title: lexicon]]
	2	[All: "citation recommendation system"] AND [All: "citation recommendation"]
MDPI	1	(Title: Sentiment Analysis) AND (Title: Social Media) OR (Title: Scientometric Analysis) AND (Title: Convolutional Neural Networks) AND (Full Text: CNN) OR (Full Text: NER) [Filters] year: 2021–2022, Journals: Electronics and Information, Article Types: Article
ACL Anthology	1	"Sentiment Detection" AND "Polarity" AND "Citation" AND "Implicit Citations" OR "Survey in Sentiment"
	2	"HMM" AND "Hidden Markov Models" AND "CRF" AND "Conditional Random Fields" AND "Information Extraction"
	3	Dataset Bibliographic Research
	4	Citation Analysis AND Neural networks
	5	"Conditional Random Fields" OR "CRF" AND "Function" AND "Analysis" AND "Citation"
	6	"Sentiment Analysis" AND "Citations" AND "Polarity Features" AND "Sentence Splitting"
	7	"scientific papers" AND "citation intent classification" AND "sentence extractions" OR "citation intent classification"
IEEE Xplore	1	("Document Title": Citing Sentences) AND ("Document Title": Research Papers) OR ("Full Text Only": Citation Analysis) AND ("Document Title": Challenges) OR ("Document Title": Applications) AND ("Document Title": Sentiment Analysis) [Filters] year: 2010–2022

By applying the search queries, we obtained a total of 6801 articles. Due to the large volume of results, we decided to discard many papers. We applied the following approach: When a query returned more than 50 results, we saved the papers on the first results page; otherwise we saved all returned papers. We then discarded more papers, duplicates, and those that did not match the selection criteria we set. Table 2 shows the search results for each query in each database, as well as the articles we saved for further analysis. Most of the queries were performed on Google Scholar (11 queries). Table 3 shows the total number of papers found per database, the total number of papers we saved, and the total number of papers we finally included in our review. Of the 6801 articles initially found, we saved 468 and finally included 37. A very large volume of papers was found via Google Scholar and ACL Anthology.

Table 2. Papers found and saved by search query.

Digital Repositories/Databases	Number of Query	Papers Found	Papers Saved
Springer	1	16	16
	2	43	43
	3	17	17
	4	15	15
	5	10	10
Google Scholar	1	53	10
	2	768	10
	3	651	10
	4	508	10
	5	305	10
	6	51	10
	7	17	17
	8	6	6
	9	62	10
	10	10	10
	11	246	10
Semantic Scholar	1	783	10
	2	62	10
	3	12	12
Science Direct	1	205	25
	2	353	25
ACM	1	36	36
	2	21	21
MDPI	1	30	30
ACL Anthology	1	6	6
	2	585	10
	3	782	10
	4	67	10
	5	702	10
	6	4	4
	7	51	10
IEEE Xplore	1	324	25

Table 3. Papers found, saved, and included in the review by Database/Digital Repository.

Digital Repositories/Databases	Papers Found	Papers Saved	Papers Included
Springer	101	101	8
Google Scholar	2677	113	10
Semantic Scholar	857	32	3
ScienceDirect	558	50	1
ACM	57	57	3
MDPI	30	30	2
ACL Anthology	2197	60	8
IEEE Xplore	324	25	2
Total	**6801**	**468**	**37**

In the process of systematically reviewing the existing literature, in addition to using reliable scientific databases, we also included papers discovered through citations of the included articles as well as work-projects from relevant websites. The selection of these papers was shaped by their contribution to strengthening and deepening our review. This approach guarantees transparency in the methodology and source selection, ensuring that each incorporated paper or source contributes substantially to the understanding and interpretation of the research area of interest. At this point, we should mention that papers found via citations (as well as websites) are not considered in the PRISMA methodology, although we did include them in our review.

Figures 2 and 3 show the number of papers found, saved, and finally evaluated (bar graph), as well the percentages of papers included in the review (pie graph). Table 4 shows the number of all types of publications included in the review (Journal Article, Conference Paper, Website). Table 5 shows the publication types of only the papers found in the databases we used.

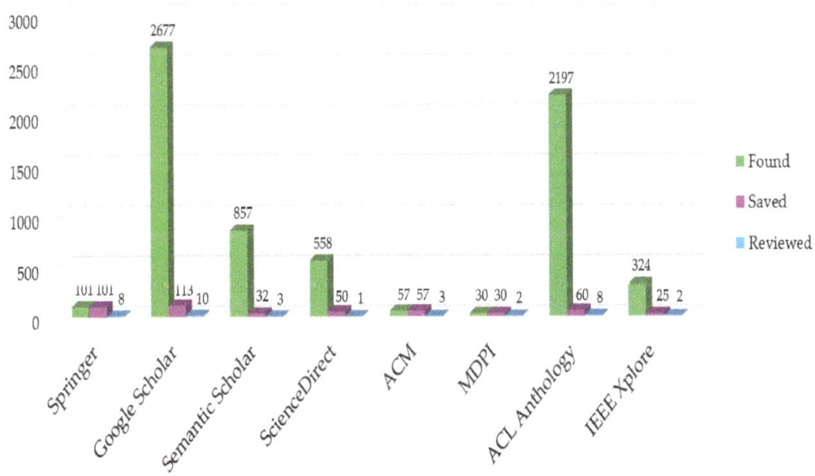

Figure 2. Articles found, saved, and included in the review.

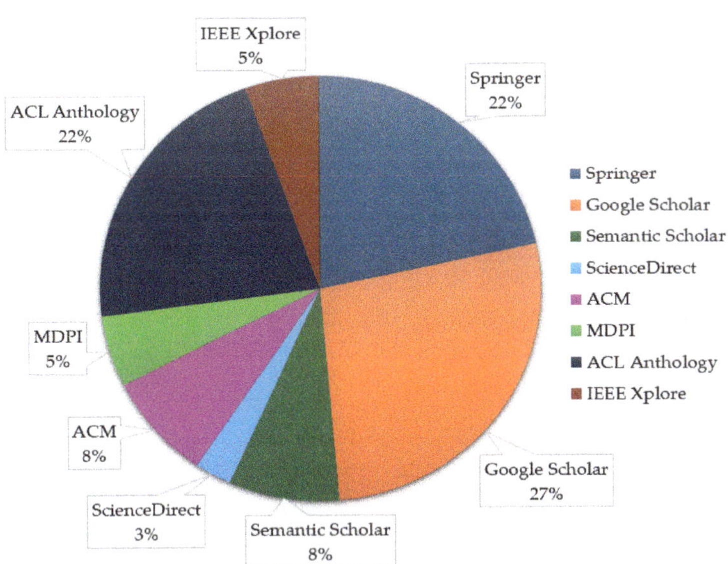

Figure 3. Percentage of papers included in our review by Digital Repository.

Figure 4 shows the percentages of publication types, with websites taking the smallest share. An equal number of papers are published in conferences and journals. Figure 5 shows the percentages of papers found in databases. Most of the papers are publications in conference proceedings.

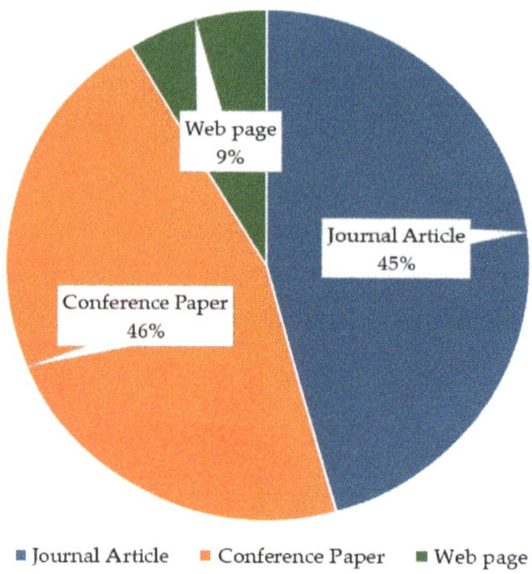

Figure 4. All types of publications of reviewed papers (includes papers found in papers we included in the review from the Digital Repositories).

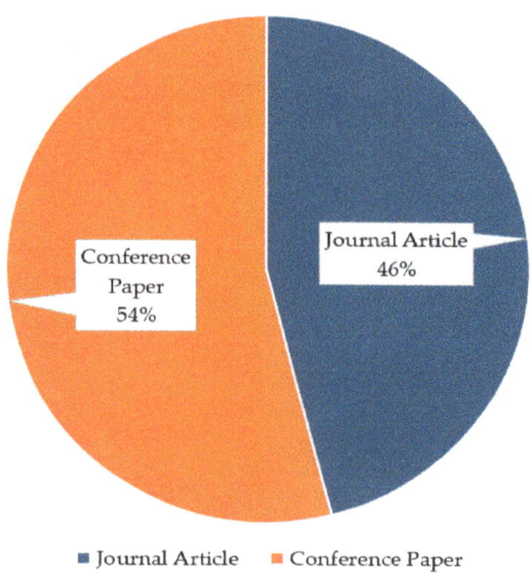

Figure 5. Publication types of reviewed papers (only in Digital Repositories).

Table 4. All types of publications included in the review.

Publication Type	Number of Papers
Journal Article	21 [1]
Conference Paper	21 [1]
Website	4
Total	**46**

[1] Four (4) Journal Articles and one (1) Conference Paper were found in the papers we have included in the review from the Digital Repositories.

Table 5. Publication types of only the papers found in the Databases/Digital Repositories.

Publication Type	Number of Papers
Journal Article	17
Conference Paper	20
Total	37

Figure 6 shows in detail the steps we followed according to the PRISMA Search Methodology. All steps were recorded, from the identification of papers found in digital libraries to the inclusion of the final papers in our review. At intermediate stages, we recorded the reasons for rejecting the papers.

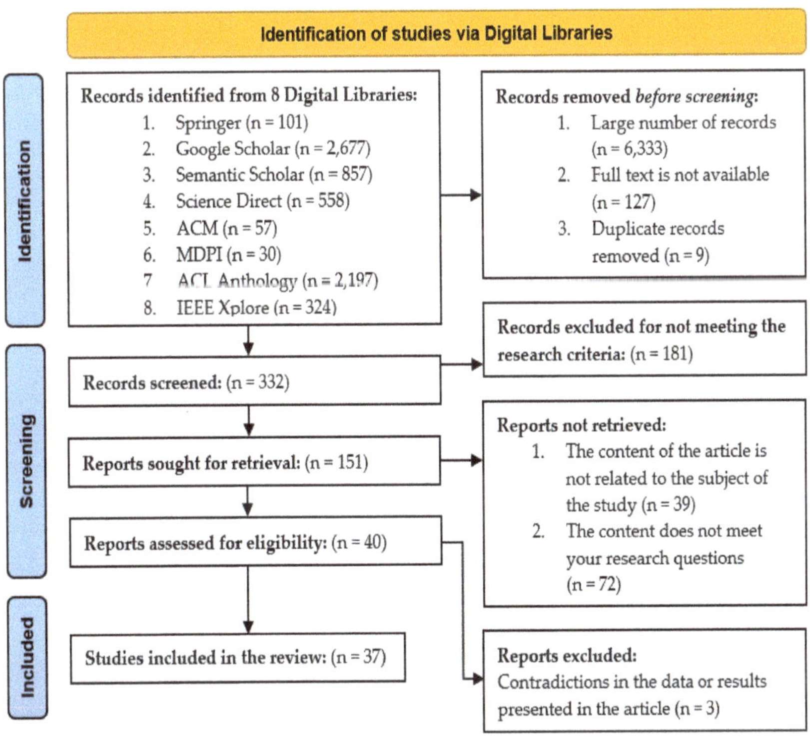

Figure 6. Papers retrieval steps (PRISMA Searching Methodology).

3. Literature Review

In this section, we focus on Sentiment Analysis and Scientometrics, presenting significant works conducted in these fields. Subsequently, we examine studies on scientific publication analysis related to classification and citation recommendation.

3.1. Sentiment Analysis

Before the introduction of Machine Learning and the so-called Transformer models in NLP, the process of detecting and understanding emotions in texts relied mainly on the use of specific dictionaries containing words with specific emotional values or tendencies. A prominent benchmark is the dictionary created by the researchers [9], which includes more than 2000 words categorized according to emotion polarization (positive, negative, or neutral emotion), objectivity, and Ekman's six basic emotions [10]. In addition, [9] used the Twitter API over a two-day period in March 2014, collecting 250,000 tweets written in English and applying an ensemble Machine Learning algorithm that combines the predictions of several models to produce a more reliable prediction. In their experiments, this algorithm achieved an excellent average accuracy of 81.81%.

S. Symeonidis et al. [11] used the above dictionary to perform sentiment identification based on data from the social network Twitter in order to identify the sentiment emerging from the most popular topics (hashtags). The aim of this paper was to conduct an analysis of sentiment by covering Ekman's key emotions and not necessarily to identify polarity. They applied methodologies such as Arithmetic Mean, Quadratic Mean or Root Mean Square (RMS), Maximum, and CombMNZ. As statistical measures, they used the Pearson and Kendall correlation coefficients, where the highest Pearson score recorded was 0.26 for "Happiness" and the corresponding Kendall value was 0.22 for the same emotion.

Also, researchers P. Tsantilas et al. [12], utilized a different dictionary that consisted of at least 6000 words which are classified as positive or negative. In this case, the goal was reputation management, and a rule system was used to categorize sentiment in a dataset of more than 2000 texts; the accuracy of this methodology approached 64%. For polarity identification, they described an application for text analysis known as PaloPro, which combines several technologies, one of which is the OpinionBuster system, for extracting named entities. Finally, data were collected from a wide range of sources, including news from two Greek newspapers (Real News and Kathimerini), and posts on Facebook and Twitter.

More advanced methods use Machine Learning algorithms, while many different approaches can be found in the literature. The main divergences lie in the creation of so-called word embeddings, as well as in the choice of architecture and model parameters.

The resources [13,14] trace sentiment in a database of reviews in stores on the Skroutz platform, and they are an additional important source. In these sources, Neural Networks are used, where in [13], the researcher creates a Deep Neural Network by introducing an embedding layer, which transforms the multidimensional input into smaller dimensional vectors and achieves 92% accuracy. In [14], a version of the Bidirectional Encoder Representations from the Transformer (BERT) model is used, with 96% accuracy being achieved.

Similarly, the study [15] uses a Dataset for sentiment analysis of product reviews written in Greek, which includes less than 500 sentences classified as positive or negative, taken from the Skroutz website. This researcher uses two traditional Machine Learning algorithms: Support Vector Machine (SVM) and Naïve Bayes (NB). He combines SVM with Unigram features and the Term Frequency-Inverse Document Frequency (TF-IDF) technique. He also uses Unigram and Bigram features with NB by applying and deleting Stopwords. In addition, the researcher also considers a variant of the BERT model. With this small dataset, the researcher manages to achieve an excellent 97% accuracy with BERT over four training epochs. Regarding the SVM and NB models, in the case where all words were used as features, SVM scored 87% accuracy, followed by NB with 86%. When using Unigrams, SVM again prevailed with 86% accuracy, while NB achieved 84% accuracy. As for the Bigrams features, only the NB algorithm was used, featuring an accuracy of 89%. To improve the accuracy of NB, the paper tested its use with the help of the Stopwords deletion technique, where, in combination with Unigrams and Bigrams, they achieved 87% and 89% accuracy, respectively. Finally, another experiment was conducted in which SVM was used in combination with the technique of estimating the importance of a word in a text (TF-IDF). The result was satisfactory, as the accuracy reached 92%. From the experiments conducted in [15], a clear picture emerges of the dynamics that Transformer models, such as BERT, incorporate in regard to sentiment analysis.

The contribution of [16] to the research community is also important. In this paper, we consider another Machine Learning methodology using the SVM algorithm on datasets expressing people's opinions in different languages. More specifically, the researchers consider a hybrid approach for sentiment prediction in which they use the Word2Vec methodology to generate word embeddings in combination with the use of dictionaries. Finally, by applying different combinations, they achieve an accuracy of 83.60% on a set of user ratings (Dataset MOBILE-PAR: includes 1976 ratings for training and 3329 for testing), a performance that significantly stands out from the unsupervised methods of other researchers, where, according to [16], they achieved an accuracy of 78.05%. Due to its great potential, the Word2Vec model has been used in many NLP research projects, offering remarkable results.

Cui et al. [17] conducted research on product reviews online and classified them as either positive or negative. They examined at least 100,000 product reviews collected from Froogle (an early name of Google's product search service; it was renamed Google Shopping in 2007) and trained Passive—Aggressive (PA) algorithms, which are variations of SVM models, and Language Modeling (LM) algorithms, which calculate the probability of a text appearing based on the n-gram occurrence frequency. The best accuracy achieved was reported using the PA Classifier with n-gram features for n = 6, where the overall F1-score approached 90%. The use of more complex features, such as higher-order n-grams, seems to confirm that the accuracy of sentiment classification in product reviews can be improved, providing more detailed and satisfactory content analysis.

The paper [18] presents and discusses the use of the Word2Vec model for sentiment classification in Twitter posts about US airlines. The models used in this research are Logistic Regression (LR), Gaussian Naïve Bayes (GNB), Bernoulli Naïve Bayes (BNB), and SVM. In addition, the CBOW and Skip-Gram methods, two key approaches to Word2Vec, were examined. Skip-Gram attempts to predict neighboring words given a central word, while CBOW attempts to predict a central word based on its neighboring words. The best accuracy obtained by CBOW is for the SVM classifier at 70%, while Skip-Gram achieves a higher accuracy of 72% when combined with SVM and LR.

The research paper [19] discusses sentiment analysis of hotel reviews in the Indonesian language retrieved from the Traveloka website using Selenium and Scrapy detection libraries. This research achieved an average accuracy of 85.96% on 2500 review texts using a combined approach featuring Word2Vec and the Long Short-Term Memory (LSTM) model. More specifically, Word2Vec was used to generate the word embeddings from the hotel reviews, and these embeddings were then fed into the input of the LSTM model to classify them with a positive or negative polarity. The LSTM architecture has the advantage of being able to maintain an internal state (cell state) which acts as a memory that allows information to be stored for long periods of time while having the ability to forget information that is not useful.

Another very important contribution to the research community is the work of [20]. In this study, the researchers use a dataset that includes at least 7900 negative comments, more than 7000 positive comments, and over 44,000 neutral comments of varying length, all originating from different social media platforms. They perform tests on binary (2 classes: negative and positive) and three-class (3 classes: negative, positive, and neutral) classification, using Transformers models and other advanced architectures. They are particularly interested in three-class classification, with which they train a GreekBERT model, a PaloBERT model based on the Robustly Optimized BERT Pretraining Approach (RoBERTa), and a GreekSocialBERT model, which is an extension of GreekBERT. Although the dataset does not have balanced class-clusters, the researchers achieve an excellent performance, scoring 99% accuracy while using a Generative Pre-trained Transformer (GPT) model for binary classification. On the other hand, in the three-class case, the GreekSocialBERT model shows the highest performance, achieving 80% accuracy.

3.2. Scientometrics

An important branch of research dealing with the measurement, analysis, and evaluation of scientific activity is Scientometrics [21], which is often considered the science of science. The main difference between Scientometrics and Sentiment Analysis is that it uses mainly quantitative methods. The goal of Scientometrics is to evaluate the development of a field and the influence of scientific publications. It essentially monitors research, evaluating the scientific contribution of author-researchers, journals, and specific papers, as well as evaluating the development and dissemination of scientific knowledge [22]. The researchers González-Alcaide et al. [23] used scientometric methods to identify the main research interests and directions regarding cardiomyopathy in the MEDLINE Database, one of the most well-known and authoritative databases in the field of medicine and health, which is under the auspices of the National Library of Medicine (NLM) of the United States. They identify research patterns and trends in Chagas' cardiomyopathy. Similarly, Mosallaie et al. [24] used scientometrics approaches to identify trends in cancer research, while Wahid et al. [25] applied scientometric methods and a comparative analysis to a group of authors to determine their scientific productivity. Additionally, [26] presented an alternative approach by mainly applying Convolutional Neural Networks (CNNs) to classify scientific literature. The model they proposed performed better compared to classical Machine Learning methods in terms of accuracy.

3.3. *Scientific Citation Analysis (SCA)*

3.3.1. Citation Contribution

In the world of scientific research, no research work is exclusively independent, as it is necessarily embedded in the literature of the respective research field. Citation-referencing, a vital element of this embedded structure, reveals the relationships and interactions between research articles, confirming the interactivity and ongoing debate within the scientific community. Beyond being just a reference method, citations have a critical role in the scientific literature, contributing to the ranking of various aspects, such as the ranking of research institutions and authors [5]. Citation analysis is at the core of bibliometrics, functioning as the science that studies these complex relationships between research articles. This systematic process through which authors cite the works of others creates a dense network of citations that is essential for the maintenance and advancement of scientific knowledge [5,27].

As mentioned above, sentiment analysis identifies and classifies opinions expressed in documents. Sentiment analysis of citations has attracted particular attention for two main reasons: First, to improve bibliometric metrics by focusing primarily on the quality rather than quantity of citations, with the aim of reducing bias and providing evidence-based support for writing. Second, to detect non-reproducible research, i.e., the identification of research papers or results that cannot be replicated or verified by other researchers, especially in the biomedical field, where unfavorable attitudes may be early indicators of the non-reproducibility of research, thus saving time and resources [28]. Therefore, although positive polarity citations have a significant impact on science, as they can enhance the validity and reliability of findings and even promote the reputation and career of researchers, the study by Catalini et al. [29], however, equally highlights that negative citations can also play an important role in science. Indeed, in some cases these citations can help to improve initial findings and aid in the development of a field, indicating the multidimensional importance of emotion analysis in scientific research. Often, however, due to their nature, such citations may simply not attract attention, and the information they offer may take some time to become widely known [29]. Therefore, observing the trajectory of negative citations, as well as the various motivations that lead to the citation of prior literature, is a very important process [29].

3.3.2. Text and Citation Preprocessing

Text Preprocessing before classification is a critical step in the process of extracting useful information and knowledge from the data. This process usually involves techniques such as tokenization, whereby a text is broken down into tokens; cleaning the text of unwanted elements, such as punctuation and other special characters; removing words without significant meaning (Stopwords); and converting to lower case. In addition, there are other important techniques, such as Lemmatization, where words in various forms are converted to their basic form (known as lemma), and Entity Recognition, where a system attempts to identify and categorize the names of people, organizations, places, etc.

within the text. Entity Recognition or Named Entity Recognition (NER) is particularly useful for structured organization of information, as it helps to further analyze the data and therefore is also part of the preliminary steps that prepare the text for more specialized Machine Learning techniques [5,18]. In addition, the Term Frequency-Inverse Document Frequency (TF-IDF) and Word2Vec techniques are also part of the broader text processing process. They refer to the phase of representing words in the form of vectors, which usually follows basic pre-processing. TF-IDF is a statistical method used in NLP to evaluate how important a word is in a document. The more often a word appears in a document, the greater its importance. Word2Vec is also a technique that generates word vectors using Deep Neural Networks. These vectors represent words in a continuous-dimensional space where words with similar semantic properties are close to each other. This allows the models to understand words based on their context of use and their relationship with other words [5,18].

At this point, it should be emphasized that there are significant differences in preprocessing plain text compared to a scientific text. These differences stem from the nature of the vocabulary, the structure of the text, and the complexity of the information. Scientific texts include technical terminology, so preprocessing must manage these concepts appropriately and preserve relevant terms rather than removing them as noise. Scientific texts include citations to other works that need to be recognized and managed differently from the plain text. To effectively preprocess scientific texts, there are several steps that can help to better manage and analyze the data. In terms of special character management, characters that are important in scientific terminology, such as mathematical formulas, should be preserved. In addition, in terms of identifying citation contexts, keywords should be kept that identify semantic citations such as expressions of the form "according to <author>" or the form "author et al.". This depends on the citation style used. Finally, in scientific texts, an excellent preprocessing technique is the NER procedure mentioned above. NER can improve the way words are represented within a document, identify entities, and extract information from a large volume of scientific articles. Finally, NER systems are very often combined with ontologies to identify categories of entities, moving beyond general labels such as "person" to more specific and scientifically relevant labels.

3.3.3. Citation Context Retrieval Methods and Classification

Retrieving citation context from scientific articles aims to understand and analyze the content. The process starts with the identification and extraction of sentences containing citations. This is usually achieved using NLP models and Machine Learning algorithms, such as SVM or Conditional Random Fields (CRFs), which analyze the text and identify areas that may contain citations. Once these areas are identified, the next phase is to interpret the content to apply further analysis techniques depending on the research objectives, such as the polarity assessment discussed in the previous sections. Figure 7 shows the basic steps of text classification.

Many researchers have used open-source tools or other techniques to retrieve and analyze citations. Awais Athar [30], in his research in 2011, studied Supervised Learning by applying the SVM model with n-grams, length 1–3, and other features to analyze citations. He chose the ACL Anthology Network [30–32] for data collection and analyzed a total of 8736 citation frames from 310 scientific articles via manual labelling methods, classifying each sentence into a category: positive, negative, or neutral. In addition, he separated the data into 1472 samples for training and 7264 samples for control, of which 6277 were classified as neutral, 743 as positive, and 244 as negative. Thus, an unbalanced data set was formed. The results of his experiments showed that applying such an approach is useful for identifying only explicit citations [2]. As evaluation metrics he reported macro-F1 and micro-F1 using 10-fold Cross Validation. The best results obtained were 76.40% and 89.80% for macro-F1 and micro-F1, respectively [30].

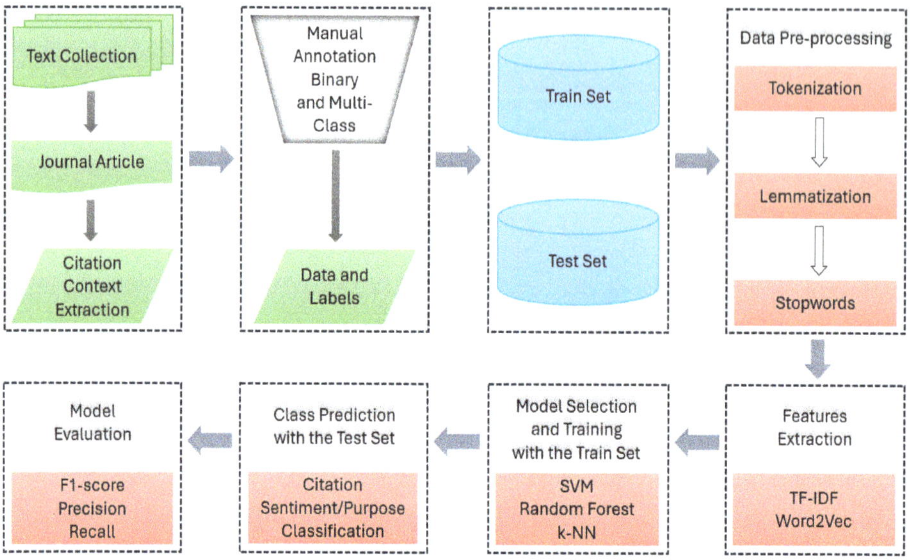

Figure 7. The basics steps for Text Classification with a focus on Citation Contexts.

Councill et al. [33], in their 2008 research, describe ParsCit, an open-source software tool for retrieving the citation context from research papers and analyzing literature strings. To enable comparison with other related tools, the researchers focused on literature analysis, meaning that they examined the references typically listed in the last section of a scientific article, ignoring the contextual contexts within the text. At the core of ParsCit is a pre-trained CRF model that is used to label the tokens of strings. Furthermore, it offers additional functionality using state-of-the-art Machine Learning models and heuristics to achieve high accuracy in text segmentation, as well as in string recognition and retrieval. Also, the software comes with utilities to run as a standalone or as a Web service. One of the key works of [33] was the comparison of ParsCit with an older CRF-based system proposed by Peng and McCallum in 2004 [34]. This system was the source of the research of [33]. The dataset they used was Cora [35], which is one of the earliest works in text analysis. This dataset created a template with 200 reference samples collected from a variety of scientific publications in the field of computer science [33]. Each of these references was divided into thirteen distinct categories: "author", "book title", "date", "publisher", "organization", "journal", "location", "notes", "pages", "publisher", "technology", "project title", and "volume" [33]. The results showed the superiority of ParsCit (with Average F1-score: 95%) over Peng CRF (with Average F1-score: 91%) [33].

Due to the effectiveness and widespread use of the SVM algorithm, the team of Ezra et al. [36] successfully applied this algorithm to classify citation sentences within the text. According to them, existing bibliometric measures usually provide quantitative indicators of how good a scientific paper is. However, this does not necessarily mean that they reflect the level of quality of the work exposed in the research. For example, when calculating a researcher's h-index, every incoming citation is considered in the same way, ignoring the possibility that some of them might be negative [36]. Thus, researchers [36] proposed the use of NLP techniques to add a qualitative aspect to bibliometrics. Specifically, they analyzed the citation contexts of scientific articles obtained from the ACL Anthology Network [32] and applied supervised Machine Learning methods to determine the purpose and polarity of the citations. To categorize purpose, they used six category-classes: "Critique", "Comparison", "Use", "Documentation", "Base", and "Other". For their experiments, they applied several classification models, including LR, Naïve Bayes Classifier, and SVM. The researchers do not present the results of all the algorithms; however, they do highlight SVM, which achieved the highest Accuracy of 70.50%, while macro-F1 reached 58%. For the citation polarity classification, only the results for the SVM model are also presented. Two experiments were conducted: in the first one, only explicit citations were used without considering any other context of the text, while in contrast, the second experiment used the wider context surrounding a sentence. This broader context does not exclusively involve implicit citations; it simply includes those sentences that are close to the referencing sentence and are considered important or relevant by human evaluators for understanding the meaning of the citation. The results noted with SVM are Accuracy 74.20% and 84.20% and macro-F1 62.10% and 74.20% for the first and second experiments, respectively [36]. The findings of the study point out that incorporating the wider context of the citation significantly contributes to improving classification accuracy (especially in the categories with subjective nature, and particularly in the negative category). This can be seen through the improvement in the Recall metric of the negative category, which, while only reaching 71.10% in the first experiment, improves by 10 points to approach 81.10% in the second experiment [36].

A different approach from the above papers that focuses on literature analysis and the purpose/polarity classification of citations is the research by Kumar et al. [37], who applied Supervised Learning using Maximum Entropy (ME) and SVM classifiers. Their goal was to determine whether a sentence in an article is a citation to another article or not, thereby making it a Binary Classification problem. They used the ACL Anthology Reference Corpus (ACL ARC) [32,38] for their experiments. The ACL ARC numbered about 10,921 articles by February 2007, and the researchers were able to retrieve features from a total of 955,755 sentences. Then, for citation identification, they identified 112,533 sentences as instances containing citations (positive samples), followed by subsequent processing to remove citation markers (e.g., IEEE styles such as [1,2] or APA such as Schmidt, 2017) from them. The remaining 843,222 sentences were classified as sentences that did not constitute citations (negative samples) [37]. Thus, they formed a dataset and applied the 10-fold Cross Validation evaluation method by separating the data into two parts: 90% for training and 10% for testing. This procedure was repeated 10 times to obtain the results of the evaluation [37]. According to their results, the lowest accuracy was noted in the "Bigram" feature for both models. ME achieved an accuracy of 82.70%, while SVM reached 85.10%. On the other hand, the highest accuracy was achieved on the features "Proper Noun" and "Previous and Next Sentence". Both ME and SVM achieved the same maximum accuracy of 88.20% in both the above features [37]. Also noteworthy is the conclusion drawn about the size of the training data. By changing the volume of this data, variations in the performance of the models can be discerned; however, the ME shows more variation mainly in the accuracy of the "Unigram", "Bigram" and "All" features. This means that the accuracy of these features depends on the volume of training data, and it follows that, the larger the size of these data, the higher the classification accuracy that can be achieved [37].

The features retrieved by [37] to construct their classifiers are presented in more detail below:

- *Unigram*. Unigram refers to a model of language analysis where the key element is the individual word. In this framework, each word in a sentence is considered an independent element or feature. In NLP, Unigrams are used to analyze and understand texts based on the individual words that make up the texts [37].
- *Bigram*. Bigram is a linguistic unit consisting of two consecutive words. In NLP, Bigrams are used to understand the relationships and structures created between two consecutive words in a sentence. This helps in analyzing the language flow and word combinations that are frequent in each text [37].
- *Proper Nouns*. These are nouns that describe the names of people, places, and organisms. These features are of great importance in the detection of referential sentences, as it is known that such sentences tend to focus on different institutions, specific scientists, and the systems they have developed [37].

- *Previous and Next Sentence.* This is information about neighboring sentences. For example, if a sentence follows a sentence with a citation, it may continue the discussion of the same topic, so it is less likely to include an additional citation [37].
- *Position.* The position attribute provides information about the part of the document in which a sentence appears. These attributes are important, as sentences appearing in certain sections have different probabilities of containing a citation. For example, sentences in the middle or at the end of a research article are more likely to discuss authors' works, evaluations, or experiment results, so they are considered less likely to be areas with citation compared to the beginning of the article, where authors often discuss and acknowledge previous work [37].
- *Orthographic.* This group of features looks at various morphological elements in sentences, including the specific orthographic forms used. Sentences that include numbers or single capital letters tend to be more suggestive of citation sentences, as they may indicate comparative figures or the initial letters of the name of the authors of the papers being referenced [37].
- *All.* Includes all the above features.

One of the main difficulties in Machine Learning approaches is their dependence on the correct choice of features [2], at least as far as Sentiment Analysis in texts and scientific citations are concerned. Therefore, feature extraction methods are not effective in some cases, as is the case with recognizing the negation or opposite meaning of a sentence. For example, the sentence "I hate violence" might not elicit any negative emotion; however, a Machine Learning model might, due to the presence of two negative words, classify it as a sentence with a negative polarity. These are the limitations that Deep Learning models are called upon to address, as they can produce semantic representations. According to [2], not much research has been conducted regarding the Sentiment Analysis of scientific citations with Deep Learning models; however, they propose the implementation of Recurrent Neural Networks (RNNs) to test the effectiveness, as they show good performances in regard to interpreting semantic content.

One research that examines Neural Networks for Sentiment Analysis in citations is the work of Munkhdalai et al. [39]. Their study describes the development of a new Neural Network model called Compositional Attention Network (CAN). They use data from PubMed Central, focusing on function categorization and sentiment analysis in four classes: "Negational", "Confirmative", "Neutral", and "Do Not know". Specifically, they selected 5000 citation sentences from 2500 random articles, then organized a tagging scheme for these sentences where each sentence was tagged by five human annotators. Finally, they constructed two datasets for training and evaluation. The first dataset consisted of labels on which at least three of the five annotators agreed (Three Label Matching). This resulted in 3624 citations for sentiment analysis. To construct the second dataset, most of the opinions of the five commentators were relied upon. In other words, a label was chosen for each citation text only if that label was decided by a majority of the five commentators (Majority Voting). This means that, even if only two commentators agreed on a label, it would be entered into the dataset because it represented a clear majority, as the other three labels differed. As a result, a total of 4423 citation suggestions for sentiment classification were entered into the second dataset. It becomes obvious from the above that the Majority Voting approach is more lenient compared to the Three Label Matching method. In addition, the researchers applied models such as LSTM, Bi-LSTM, and attention models. CAN shows significant improvement in accuracy, especially when additional sentence context information is included. For sentiment analysis, the LSTM model combined with CAN achieves the highest accuracy compared to the other models (76.04% for Majority Voting and 78.10% for Three Label Matching), showing its superiority in handling more information and providing better representations of the data. It should also be mentioned that the study of [39] also used the SVM model, which showed low generalization to new data as it scored the lowest accuracy in both methods (75% for Majority Voting and 71.95% for Three Label

Matching) compared to the Neural Network models, which highlights the superiority of Deep Learning.

Progress in the field of Deep Learning led to the creation of the Transformer language models. These models are a powerful class and have proven their effectiveness in many AI applications. These models were originally introduced to solve problems in the NLP domain, such as text generation and entity recognition. The main feature of Transformers is their ability to consider the semantic dependencies between words in a text without the use of traditional recursive architectures. This is achieved through mechanisms that focus on parallel processing of information in large sequences of data, such as the Attention Mechanism. Important research on sentiment recognition using Transformer models was conducted by researchers Dahai Yu and Bolin Hua [40]. In their study, they emphasized the importance of pre-trained models such as BERT, which was trained on general texts from the internet, and SCIBERT, which is a variant of BERT and was trained using scientific articles. According to [40], SCIBERT is considered more suitable for applications related to the scientific and academic community, such as the classification of scientific texts and the recognition of emotions in them. After a detailed investigation, it was found that several sentiment analysis studies did not disclose the datasets, while, in other cases, the available datasets proved to be of low quality [40]. To further improve the accuracy of content-level training, the researchers decided to use the SCICite dataset proposed by Arman and colleagues [41]. This dataset included a training set of about 10,000 citations and a control set of about 1000 citations, which were classified into three categories in terms of intent: "Method", "Background" and "Result" [40]. They also considered the dataset proposed by Athar in [30] and, after extracting about 1000 citations from SCICite, they enhanced Athar's dataset. Finally, the aggregated dataset consisted of 7912 suggestions, including 1237 positive, 347 negative, and 6328 neutral [40]. To perform their experiments, in addition to the two pre-trained models (BERT, SCIBERT) used as a basis, they designed and proposed the DictSentiBERT model, which adapts the Dictionary-based Attention Mechanism and applies emotion categorization of scientific citations [40]. In addition, four other models, LSTM, FeedForward NN (FNN), TextCNN, and Self-Attention, were tested. The models were trained on an RTX A4000 processor with 16 GB of memory and a maximum number of epochs of 50. During an epoch, the data was split into an 80% for the training set and a 20% for the test set. The Batch Size and Learning Rate parameters were set to 32 and 5×10^{-6}, respectively. AdamW was used as the optimizer, and cross-entropy was used as the loss function [40]. From the data presented in Table 6, the FNN, LSTM, TextCNN, Self-Attention, and DictSentiBERT models based on both BERT and SCIBERT showed high Accuracy, with DictSentiBERT achieving the highest accuracy (BERT 93.49% and SCIBERT 95.20%). Additionally, the BERT model showed an average accuracy of 91.23% and an average macro-F1 value of 74.60%. In contrast, SCIBERT showed even better results, with an average accuracy of 94.80% and an average macro-F1 value of 85.20%. This finding suggests that SCIBERT, which, as mentioned, was specifically trained on scientific texts, is more suitable for analyzing and categorizing emotions in citation texts. Furthermore, the improved performance of DictSentiBERT indicates the advantage of incorporating a sentiment lexicon into the model [40].

Table 6. Experimental results. Accuracy and macro-F1 (%) [40].

	BERT		SCIBERT	
Models	**Accuracy**	**Macro-F1**	**Accuracy**	**Macro-F1**
FNN	93.05	80	95.14	86
LSTM	93.11	80	94.63	84
TextCNN	83.20	52	94.57	86
Self-ATTENTION	93.30	80	94.44	84
DictSentiBERT	**93.49** [1]	81	**95.20** [1]	86

[1] Max Accuracy for DictSentiBERT.

The dynamics of Transformer models were also highlighted in the study by Ning Yang et al. [42], which analysed the effectiveness of BERT-based methods for identifying scientific data citations while focusing on information extraction from bioinformatics texts and citation recognition as a Binary Classification problem. The texts were obtained from PubMed Central (PMC), where 35 journals were collected as data sources and 38,931 full-text documents were retrieved. The paper classified the diverse forms of text citations into the categories of "scientific data citations" and "non-scientific data citations"; these two categories were treated as positive and negative, respectively (Binary Classification). In the end, 3067 citations (positive samples) and 12,869 citations (negative samples) were obtained. The study compared the performance of some models, such as SCIBERT discussed above, with classical Machine and Deep Learning models. The study also found that BERT-based models, especially BioBERT, perform better compared to other models. For their experiments, in addition to SCIBERT, BERT and BioBERT, classical models such as, Decision Tree model, Random Forest model, TextCNN, and TextRCNN were used. In Table 7, we present the results, which show the superiority of the BERT based models. Precision, Recall, and F1-score metrics are also shown. Of significant interest is the BioBERT model proposed by Lee et al. [43], which is based on BERT and applied to the biomedical domain (which is closely related to the field of bioinformatics). This makes it a high-performance model which, in the study of [42], scores the highest Recall.

Table 7. Models and Metrics. Precision (%), Recall (%), F1-score (%) [42].

	METRICS		
Models	**Precision**	**Recall**	**F1-Score**
Random Forest	82.80	71.60	75.20
Decision Tree	75	75.40	75.20
TextCNN	86.40	75.60	79.40
TextRCNN	84.20	76.50	79.50
BERT	86.90	82.70	84.60
SCIBERT	86.70	84.10	85.30
BioBERT	85.70	**84.90** [1]	85.30

[1] Max Recall for BioBERT.

Finally, this research [42] demonstrates that Machine and Deep Learning techniques are successful in detecting and classification scientific citations. Moreover, the findings of this study support that Deep Learning outperforms traditional models by achieving higher generalization and performances, as it considers the semantic features of a document. The capability of these models makes them an important tool in natural language analysis and processing, offering significant potential for accurate interpretations of information.

3.3.4. Citation Recommendation

The development of a Citation Recommendation System (CRS) can help researchers discover additional research relevant to their topic. Through sophisticated algorithms and Machine Learning models, such a system can recommend citations that are closely related to the content of the article. By highlighting the most relevant citations, researchers can enhance the validity and relevance of their work. When writing research articles, there are often instances where previous research needs to be referenced, but there is no certainty in selecting cited sources. In their study, He et al. [44] propose a context-aware CRS. Creating high-quality citation proposals can be significantly challenging as the citations proposed must be relevant to the topic of the article and adapted to the specific contexts where they are used. The main idea of [44] is therefore to design a new non-parametric probabilistic model that can evaluate the relevance of a citation context and a paper. Similarly, the issue of citation recommendation was also addressed by Silvescu et al. [45]. In their research, they examined the challenges of discovering relevant citations by focusing on the use of the Singular Value Decomposition (SVD) technique compared to Collaborative Filtering (CF) methods. The results of their experiments showed the superiority of the proposed SVD approach, which achieved significant success compared to CF methods. Their paper also discussed the creation of a new dataset from the CiteSeer Digital Library [46] for experimentation and evaluation on more advanced recommendation models.

The above research highlights the importance of the evolution in citation recommendation technology, offering more interesting, comprehensive, and relevant information to researchers.

4. Challenges in Sentiment Analysis

Sentiment Analysis in text, in general, faces several challenges that range mainly from technical issues to semantic aspects. Some of the most basic challenges are discussed below:

- *Syntax errors.* Natural language is complex, and people often make syntactic errors which can make it difficult to process language automatically.
- *Multiple meaning.* Words can have multiple meanings depending on the context in which they are used, which can create confusion and misinterpretation. The use of complex vocabulary usually makes it difficult to understand the information. For example, in a text containing the phrase "It was terribly good", the word "terrible" usually has a negative connotation; however, in this phrase it is used to reinforce a positive adjective, "good", which can confuse automated sentiment analysis systems.
- *Variety and style.* Texts in general can include various types of written expression, such as literature, essay, narrative, journalism, and many others, each with its own style and mode of expression.
- *Complexity.* Natural language in general is complex and multidimensional, with sarcasm, allegory, hyperbole, and other elements adding considerable complexity to the analysis of emotions [47]. Irony and innuendo often escape analysis by automatic systems, which can lead to misunderstandings and misinterpretations of emotional tones in research.
- *Subjectivity.* As the understanding of emotions is subjective, different people may interpret the same texts differently [47].
- *Ambiguity.* Dealing with vague or contradictory statements in texts is a very important challenge.
- *Cultural differences.* Cultural and dialectal differences can affect the way emotions are expressed, making analysis difficult for systems not trained in different languages or cultures [47]. For example, in some cultures, the expression of anger may be less direct or intense compared to others. This may affect the accuracy of emotion analysis models that have not been trained to recognize such variations.
- *Spam detection.* The content present in messages can be complex, which makes it difficult to identify as spam. Moreover, the amount of data to be analyzed is huge, making spam detection resource intensive [47].
- *Language evolution.* Natural language is dynamic and constantly evolving, requiring a corresponding evolution of methods and systems for emotion analysis.

There are significant differences in the challenges encountered when analyzing emotions in texts compared to those encountered in scientific publications. When examining scientific citations, emotion identification is a complex challenge due to the specialized nature of language, the need to accurately understand emotional nuances, and the complexity of scientific concepts. This requires the development of advanced algorithms that can adapt to the constant changes in the field of linguistic and scientific development. Some of the fundamental challenges are discussed below:

- *Complexity and complex vocabulary.* Scientific citations often include specialized vocabulary and technical terms that may not express emotions in the traditional way.
- *Abstraction.* The use of language is often more abstract and less direct, resulting in a lack of strong feelings towards the reported research [2].

- *Multilingualism.* Citations can be written in multiple languages, increasing the complexity of sentiment analysis due to differences in grammar, syntax, and affective expressions that are specific to each language [2].
- *Context and social environment.* Understanding the context and social environment in which a scientific article was written is essential for accurate analysis of emotions.
- *NLP methods.* The development of algorithms that can recognize and interpret polarity in scientific texts requires advanced NLP techniques.
- *Lack of datasets.* There are not many datasets available that are labeled either for purpose or for citation polarity [2]. The creation of a database that is enriched with citation contexts to serve later in the training of a model capable of recognizing citations in scientific texts (while, at the same time, distinguishing their polarity) emerges as a significant challenge.
- *Stop words.* As mentioned, these are a category of words that are usually removed from the data in NLP applications. These words often include prepositions, links, and other common words that do not add significant meaning to the essence of a document. However, in scientific texts, the absence of some of these words can negatively affect classification performance [2].
- *Exporting a citation context.* Identifying the right context is an important issue. The contexts derived are varied. Some researchers focus on extracting a single sentence, while others extract entire paragraphs. This diversity makes accurate extraction an important and complex process [2].
- *Citation label.* How a class is assigned to a citation sentence is of great importance. In many cases this process is undertaken manually, making it difficult to label large datasets. Therefore, the process of automatic tagging in such texts is a very important challenge [2].
- *Words of denial.* The role of negation words is crucial in determining the emotional direction of a citation context. Identifying and handling negation is a difficult process and continues to be a significant challenge, as it can result in reverse polarity [2].

Below, we present a concise table that compiles and examines the primary challenges encountered, the Machine Learning models, the management of available resources and datasets, as well as the performance analysis through the experiments of the studies investigated (Table 8). Papers that do not provide enough information, such as models, datasets, and experimental results, were not included in the table.

Table 8. Comprehensive Overview of Machine Learning Challenges, Data Management, and Performance Insights.

Authors, Year	Challenges	Models, Techniques	Datasets, Data Sources	Experimental Results
H. Cui et al., 2006 [17]	Sentiment Analysis in Product Reviews	Passive-Aggressive (PA) Language Modeling (LM)	Froogle	Accuracy: 90%
I. G. Councill et al., 2008 [33]	References Extraction, ParsCit vs. Peng CRF Comparison	ParsCit, Peng	CORA Dataset	ParsCit micro-F1: 95% Peng CRF macro-F1: 91%
K. Sugiyama et al., 2010 [37]	Citation Recognition, Binary Classification	Max Entropy (ME), Support Vector Machine (SVM)	ACL Anthology	Min Accuracy (Bigram Feature) ME: 82.70% SVM: 85.10%, Max Accuracy (Proper Noun and Previous and Next Sentence) ME and SVM: 88.20%

Table 8. *Cont.*

Authors, Year	Challenges	Models, Techniques	Datasets, Data Sources	Experimental Results
A. Athar, 2011 [30]	Polarity Analysis in Explicit Citations	SVM, WEKA	ACL Anthology and Resources [1]	macro-F1: 76.40% micro-F1: 89.80%
A. A. Jbara et al., 2013 [36]	Citation Context Analysis, Citation Purpose Classification, Citation Polarity Classification	SVM, Logistic Regression (LR), Naïve Bayes (NB)	ACL Anthology	SVM only Purpose Class. Accuracy: 70.50% macro-F1: 58%, Polarity Class. Explicit Accuracy: 74.20% macro-F1: 62.10%, Polarity Class. Wide Content Accuracy: 84.20% macro-F1: 74.20%
A. Tsakalidis et al., 2014 [9]	Tweets Extraction, Polarity Analysis, Feature Extraction	TBR, FBR, LBR, CR, Twitter API, Ensemble Algorithm	Resources [2]	Accuracy: 81.81%
P. Tsantilas et al., 2014 [12]	Sentiment Analysis, Named Entity Recognition	PaloPro [3] OpinionBuster [4]	Real News [5] Kathimerini [6] Facebook, Twitter	Accuracy: 64%
S. Symeonidis et al., 2015 [11]	Greek tweets Extraction, Sentiment Analysis	Maximum, CombMNZ, Arithmetic Mean, Quadratic Mean, Twitter Streaming API	Dataset with Greek tweets	Pearson Correlation 0.26 Kendall Correlation 0.22
T. Munkhdalai et al., 2016 [39]	Citation Function Classification, Citation Sentiment Classification	Compositional Attention Network (CAN)	PubMed Central (PMC) and Resources [7,8]	Citation Function F1-score Bi-LSTMs + CAN Majority Voting: 60.67% and Three Label Matching: 75.57%, Citation Sentiment F1-score LSTM + CAN Maj. Vot.: 76.04% and T. L. Matching: 78.10%
M. Giatsoglou et al., 2017 [16]	Sentiment Analysis	Word2Vec, Lexicon Based	Mobile—PAR	Accuracy: 83.60%
J. Acosta et al., 2017 [18]	Sentiment Analysis of Twitter Messages	LR, Gaussian Naïve Bayes (GNB), Bernoulli Naïve Bayes (BNB), SVM, CBOW, Skip-Gram, Word2Vec	Twitter, Kaggle [9]	Accuracy CBOW + SVM: 70% Skip-Gram + SVM: 72% Skip-Gram + LR: 72%
P. Muhammad et al., 2021 [19]	Sentiment Analysis	Word2Vec, LSTM, Selenium, Scrapy	Traveloka Travel Platform [10]	Accuracy: 85.96%
G. Alexandridis et al., 2021 [20]	Polarity Analysis in Greek Social Media	Transformers, GreekBERT, PaloBERT, RoBERTa, GreekSocialBERT, GPT	Greek Social Media	Binary Classification GPT Accuracy: 99% Multi Classification GreekSocialBERT Accuracy: 80%
N. Avgeros, 2022 [13]	Sentiment Analysis	Neural Networks	Database from Skroutz	Accuracy: 92%
N. Fragkis, 2022 [14]	Sentiment Analysis	BERT Model	Database from Skroutz	Accuracy: 96%

Table 8. *Cont.*

Authors, Year	Challenges	Models, Techniques	Datasets, Data Sources	Experimental Results
D. Bilianos, 2022 [15]	Sentiment Analysis	SVM, NB, TF-IDF, BERT	Resources [11]	NB + Bigrams + Stopwords Accuracy: 89%, SVM + TF-IDF Accuracy: 92%, BERT Accuracy: 97%
M. Daradkeh et al., 2022 [26]	Scientometrics	CNNs Models	Unknown	Accuracy: 81%
D. Yu et al., 2023 [40]	Sentiment Classification of Scientific Citation	BERT, SCIBERT, DictSentiBERT, LSTM, FNN, TextCNN, Self-Attention	Resources [12,13]	DictSentiBERT (BERT) Accuracy: 93.49%, DictSentiBERT (SCIBERT) Accuracy: 95.20%
N. Yang et al., 2023 [42]	Entity Citation Recognition, Binary Classification	Random Forest, Decision Tree, TextCNN, TextRCNN, BERT, SCIBERT, BIOBERT	PubMed Central (PMC)	SCIBERT and BIOBERT F1-score: 85.30%

[1] Resources by Athar: "https://cl.awaisathar.com/citation-sentiment-corpus/ (accessed on 8 April 2024)"; [2] Resources by Tsakalidis (github): "https://github.com/socialsensor/sentiment-analysis/tree/master/src/main/resources (accessed on 10 April 2024)"; [3] Palo Digital Technologies Ltd. (Athens, Greece): "https://www.palo.gr/ (accessed on 10 April 2024)"; [4] OpinionBuster has been developed as part of the Ellogon Platform: "http://www.ellogon.org (accessed on 10 April 2024)"; [5] "https://www.real.gr/ (accessed on 11 April 2024)"; [6] "https://www.kathimerini.gr/ (accessed on 11 April 2024)"; [7] Yelp 2013: "https://www.yelp.com/dataset/documentation/main (accessed on 11 April 2024)"; [8] IMDb Movie Reviews: "https://paperswithcode.com/dataset/imdb-movie-reviews (accessed on 12 April 2024)"; [9] "https://www.kaggle.com/ (accessed on 12 April 2024)"; [10] Traveloka website: "https://www.traveloka.com/ (accessed on 13 April 2024)"; [11] Resources by Billianos (github): "https://github.com/DimitrisBil/greek-sentiment-analysis (accessed on 13 April 2024)"; [12] (github): "https://github.com/UFOdestiny/DictSentiBERT (accessed on 13 April 2024)"; [13] (github): "https://github.com/allenai/scibert/tree/master/data/text_classification/sci-cite (accessed on 14 April 2024)".

5. Discussion

This section will answer the Research Questions noted in Section 2.1.

- *RQ1.* Machine Learning based techniques, such as SVM, Naive Bayes, and Decision Tree, and advanced Machine Learning models, such as LSTM, BERT, RoBERTa, and BioBERT, have provided significant improvements in the accuracy of detection and the analysis of emotions. Deep Learning models have shown wonderful progress because they can identify semantic patterns in the data. However, Deep Learning requires significant computational resources and expertise, while traditional methods are often simpler and more accessible.
- *RQ2.* In our review, the researchers used several preprocessing methods, such as removing unimportant words (stopwords) from the text and converting words to vectors using TF-IDF and Word2Vec techniques. Additionally, precision, recall, and accuracy were used as evaluation metrics.
- *RQ3.* Machine Learning models, such as SVM, Naive Bayes, Decision Tree, etc., may perform better in applications where data is limited or where parameters need to be slightly modified. In contrast, Deep Learning models, such as CNN, LSTM, BERT, etc., are more suitable in cases of large and complex datasets. This is confirmed in [15], where a small dataset was used and the SVM achieved excellent classification accuracy, coming very close to the BERT model.
- *RQ4.* In Sentiment Analysis, and classification tasks in general, the two main types of learning used are Supervised Learning and Unsupervised Learning. Supervised Learning is particularly popular because of its ability to provide accurate predictions based on labelled data, which is critical in Sentiment Analysis. Unsupervised Learning is a type of Machine Learning where models are trained on previously unlabeled data.

Its goal is to discover hidden patterns in the data. In our review, we observed the implementation of Supervised Learning.

- *RQ5*. Sentiment Analysis allows for the identification of both positive and negative emotions in scientific citations, increasing the ability to critique and understand the motivations behind scientific findings. By understanding the emotion conveyed through scientific texts, researchers can improve communication and collaboration among themselves. Recognizing the emotional cues in texts can help avoid misinterpretations and create more constructive communication.
- *RQ6*. Challenges include dealing with complex scientific terminology, multilingualism, and the abstract nature of discussions that require specialized language processing techniques.
- *RQ7*. In addition to polarity detection, many researchers, as we observed in our review, apply classification based on the purpose of the citation. For example, a frame of reference can be supportive (supportive type) and reinforce an idea or viewpoint presented in the text, critique another research (critique type), be used to compare research results of papers (comparison type), document important previous studies that support or influence the current research (documentation type), or even refer to a paper that forms the theoretical background of the current study (base type).
- *RQ8*. The availability of public datasets is still limited. Although there are some sources that offer access to scientific articles and their references, datasets that include labeled citation contexts are rare. One reason for this relates to the copyright that protects scientific documents. Moreover, in the case of Supervised Learning it is necessary to label citations manually, which makes it a complex process.
- *RQ9*. Emotions play a crucial role in communicating scientific results, as they influence the acceptance of information by the scientific community and the wider public. Emotions can strengthen or weaken the persuasiveness of arguments, and they can also encourage confidence in findings or, conversely, cause doubt. For example, a scientific article that receives more positive citations may stimulate more interest and active acceptance, while an article that receives negative citations may potentially raise reservations among other researchers.

6. Future Research

Some recommendations for improvement in future related work are as follows:

- *Increase data*. By increasing the amount of data, models become more accurate and achieve higher generalization. In addition, the ability to collect data from different platforms offers a more comprehensive approach to analyzing emotions.
- *Combination of different types of data*. Merging information, such as text, image, audio, and video, can improve the accuracy and completeness of sentiment analysis.
- *Pre-process methods*. Data processing prior to model training can have a major impact on the final performance. The choice of the most appropriate pre-processing method depends on the nature of the data and the goal of each application.
- *Model selection*. The process of selecting the appropriate model for solving a Machine Learning problem is also a very important process. Any model trained on specific data will perform well on such new data.
- *Architecture*. The use of more complex Neural Network architectures (number of layers and neurons) clearly affects the performance of the models.
- *Analysis of implicit and explicit citations*. Extensive studying of the distinction and interpretation of implicit and explicit citations within scientific texts for a better understanding of purpose and polarity.
- *Citation context retrieval methods*. Focus on developing and improving methods for retrieving, processing, and analyzing the citation context, including more advanced approaches to reveal its deeper meaning.

Having reviewed the current challenges in the field of research regarding the analysis of polarity in scientific texts, it is important to mention the prospects for future work. In the next stage of research, emphasis will be placed on the development of NLP and Machine Learning methods. An important goal is to create a new dataset for both experimentation and detecting polarity in scientific publications, as well as for comparing the results with those reported by the research studies reviewed in this paper. Also, the intention behind a citation in a scientific article will be investigated. Finally, there is the consideration of developing a Citation Recognition System using pre-trained language models based on BERT.

7. Conclusions

This research approached the analysis of emotions in text and scientific publications by combining techniques from the fields of Machine Learning and Deep Learning, highlighting the need for more advanced methods for detecting and evaluating emotional nuances. Through the analysis of the polarity of emotions and understanding the purpose of citations, their complexity and importance in scientific communication was revealed. With the help of the research papers reviewed, this study highlighted the need for further research and development in this area, enhancing the understanding of the value and influence of scientific papers.

Author Contributions: All authors have contributed to the review presented. Conceptualization, A.K. and A.S.; writing original draft preparation, A.K. and A.S.; writing review and editing A.K., A.S., K.D. and S.O.; visualization, A.K.; supervision, A.S., K.D. and S.O.; resources, A.S., K.D. and S.O.; All authors have read and agreed to the published version of the manuscript.

Funding: This review article has not received external funding.

Data Availability Statement: Data are contained within the review article.

Conflicts of Interest: The authors declare no conflicts of interest.

References

1. Wankhade, M.; Rao, A.C.S.; Kulkarni, C. A Survey on Sentiment Analysis Methods, Applications, and Challenges. *Artif. Intell. Rev.* **2022**, *55*, 5731–5780. [CrossRef]
2. Yousif, A.; Niu, Z.; Tarus, J.K.; Ahmad, A. A Survey on Sentiment Analysis of Scientific Citations. *Artif. Intell. Rev.* **2019**, *52*, 1805–1838. [CrossRef]
3. Hernández, M.; Gómez, J.M. Survey in Sentiment, Polarity and Function Analysis of Citation. In Proceedings of the First Workshop on Argumentation Mining, Baltimore, MD, USA, 26 June 2014; Association for Computational Linguistics: Stroudsburg, PA, USA, 2014; pp. 102–103.
4. Bonzi, S. Characteristics of a Literature as Predictors of Relatedness Between Cited and Citing Works. *J. Am. Soc. Inf. Sci.* **1982**, *33*, 208–216. [CrossRef]
5. Aljuaid, H.; Iftikhar, R.; Ahmad, S.; Asif, M.; Tanvir Afzal, M. Important Citation Identification Using Sentiment Analysis of In-Text Citations. *Telemat. Inform.* **2021**, *56*, 101492. [CrossRef]
6. Small, H. Interpreting Maps of Science Using Citation Context Sentiments: A Preliminary Investigation. *Scientometrics* **2011**, *87*, 373–388. [CrossRef]
7. Athar, A.; Teufel, S. Detection of Implicit Citations for Sentiment Detection. In Proceedings of the Workshop on Detecting Structure in Scholarly Discourse, Jeju, Republic of Korea, 25 May 2012; Association for Computational Linguistics: Stroudsburg, PA, USA, 2012; pp. 18–26.
8. Page, M.J.; McKenzie, J.E.; Bossuyt, P.M.; Boutron, I.; Hoffmann, T.C.; Mulrow, C.D.; Shamseer, L.; Tetzlaff, J.M.; Akl, E.A.; Brennan, S.E.; et al. The PRISMA 2020 Statement: An Updated Guideline for Reporting Systematic Reviews. *J. Clin. Epidemiol.* **2021**, *134*, 178–189. [CrossRef] [PubMed]
9. Tsakalidis, A.; Papadopoulos, S.; Kompatsiaris, I. An Ensemble Model for Cross-Domain Polarity Classification on Twitter. In Proceedings of the Web Information Systems Engineering–WISE 2014: 15th International Conference, Thessaloniki, Greece, 12–14 October 2014; Springer International Publishing: Berlin/Heidelberg, Germany, 2014; Volume 8787, pp. 168–177.
10. Ekman, P. An Argument for Basic Emotions. *Cogn. Emot.* **1992**, *6*, 169–200. [CrossRef]
11. Kalamatianos, G.; Mallis, D.; Symeonidis, S.; Arampatzis, A. Sentiment Analysis of Greek Tweets and Hashtags Using a Sentiment Lexicon. In Proceedings of the PCI '15: Proceedings of the 19th Panhellenic Conference on Informatics, Athens, Greece, 1–3 October 2015; Association for Computing Machinery: New York, NY, USA, 2015; pp. 63–68.
12. Petasis, G.; Spiliotopoulos, D.; Tsirakis, N.; Tsantilas, P. Sentiment Analysis for Reputation Management: Mining the Greek Web. In Proceedings of the Artificial Intelligence: Methods and Applications: 8th Hellenic Conference on AI, SETN 2014, Ioannina, Greece, 15–17 May 2014; Springer International Publishing: Berlin/Heidelberg, Germany, 2014; Volume 8445 LNCS, pp. 327–340.

13. Avgeros Nikos Skroutz Sentiment Analysis. Available online: https://www.kaggle.com/code/nikosavgeros/skroutz-sentiment-analysis (accessed on 7 February 2024).
14. Fragkis Nikos Skroutz Sentiment Analysis with BERT (Greek). Available online: https://www.kaggle.com/code/nikosfragkis/skroutz-sentiment-analysis-with-bert-greek (accessed on 7 February 2024).
15. Bilianos, D. Experiments in Text Classification: Analyzing the Sentiment of Electronic Product Reviews in Greek. *J. Quant. Linguist.* **2022**, *29*, 374–386. [CrossRef]
16. Giatsoglou, M.; Vozalis, M.G.; Diamantaras, K.; Vakali, A.; Sarigiannidis, G.; Chatzisavvas, K.C. Sentiment Analysis Leveraging Emotions and Word Embeddings. *Expert. Syst. Appl.* **2017**, *69*, 214–224. [CrossRef]
17. Cui, H.; Mittal, V.; Datar, M. Comparative Experiments on Sentiment Classification for Online Product Reviews. In Proceedings of the 21st National Conference on Artificial Intelligence, Boston, MA, USA, 16–20 June 2006; Association for the Advancement of Artificial Intelligence (AAAI): Washington, DC, USA, 2006; pp. 1–6.
18. Acosta, J.; Lamaute, N.; Luo, M.; Finkelstein, E.; Cotoranu, A. Sentiment Analysis of Twitter Messages Using Word2Vec. In Proceedings of the Student-Faculty Research Day, Pleasantville, NY, USA, 5 May 2017; CSIS, Pace University: White Plains, NY, USA, 2017; pp. 1–7.
19. Muhammad, P.F.; Kusumaningrum, R.; Wibowo, A. Sentiment Analysis Using Word2vec and Long Short-Term Memory (LSTM) for Indonesian Hotel Reviews. *Procedia Comput. Sci.* **2021**, *179*, 728–735. [CrossRef]
20. Alexandridis, G.; Varlamis, I.; Korovesis, K.; Caridakis, G.; Tsantilas, P. A Survey on Sentiment Analysis and Opinion Mining in Greek Social Media. *Information* **2021**, *12*, 331. [CrossRef]
21. Jha, R.; Jbara, A.A.; Qazvinian, V.; Radev, D.R. NLP-Driven Citation Analysis for Scientometrics. *Nat. Lang. Eng.* **2017**, *23*, 93–130. [CrossRef]
22. Mercer, R.E.; Di Marco, C. The Importance of Fine-Grained Cue Phrases in Scientific Citations. In Proceedings of the Conference of the Canadian Society for Computational Studies of Intelligence, Canadian AI 2003, Advances in Artificial Intelligence, Halifax, NS, Canada, 11–13 June 2003; Springer: Berlin/Heidelberg, Germany, 2003; pp. 550–556.
23. González-Alcaide, G.; Salinas, A.; Ramos, J.M. Scientometrics Analysis of Research Activity and Collaboration Patterns in Chagas Cardiomyopathy. *PLoS Negl. Trop. Dis.* **2018**, *12*, e0006602. [CrossRef]
24. Mosallaie, S.; Rad, M.; Schiffaeurova, A.; Ebadi, A. Discovering the Evolution of Artificial Intelligence in Cancer Research Using Dynamic Topic Modeling. *COLLNET J. Scientometr. Inf. Manag.* **2021**, *15*, 225–240. [CrossRef]
25. Wahid, N.; Warraich, F.; Tahira, M. Group Level Scientometric Analysis of Pakistani Authors. *COLLNET J. Scientometr. Inf. Manag.* **2021**, *15*, 287–304. [CrossRef]
26. Daradkeh, M.; Abualigah, L.; Atalla, S.; Mansoor, W. Scientometric Analysis and Classification of Research Using Convolutional Neural Networks: A Case Study in Data Science and Analytics. *Electronics* **2022**, *11*, 2066. [CrossRef]
27. Smith, L.C. Citation Analysis. *Libr. Trends* **1981**, *30*, 83–106.
28. Budi, I.; Yaniasih, Y. Understanding the Meanings of Citations Using Sentiment, Role, and Citation Function Classifications. *Scientometrics* **2022**, *128*, 735–759. [CrossRef]
29. Catalini, C.; Lacetera, N.; Oettl, A. The Incidence and Role of Negative Citations in Science. *Proc. Natl. Acad. Sci. USA* **2015**, *112*, 13823–13826. [CrossRef]
30. Athar, A. Sentiment Analysis of Citations Using Sentence Structure-Based Features. In Proceedings of the ACL 2011 Student Session, Portland, OR, USA, 19 June 2011; Association for Computational Linguistics: Stroudsburg, PA, USA, 2011; pp. 81–87.
31. Radev, D.R.; Joseph, M.T.; Gibson, B.; Muthukrishnan, P. A Bibliometric and Network Analysis of the Field of Computational Linguistics. *J. Assoc. Inf. Sci. Technol.* **2016**, *67*, 683–706. [CrossRef]
32. ACL Welcome to the ACL Anthology. Available online: https://aclanthology.org/ (accessed on 9 February 2024).
33. Councill, I.G.; Giles, C.L.; Kan, M.-Y. ParsCit: An Open-Source CRF Reference String Parsing Package. In Proceedings of the Sixth International Conference on Language Resources and Evaluation (LREC' 08), Marrakech, Morocco, 26 May–1 June 2008; European Language Resources Association (ELRA): Paris, France, 2008; pp. 661–667.
34. Peng, F.; Mccallum, A. Accurate Information Extraction from Research Papers Using Conditional Random Fields. In Proceedings of the Human Language Technology Conference of the North American Chapter of the Association for Computational Linguistics: HLT-NAACL, Boston, MA, USA, 2 May 2004; Association for Computational Linguistics: Stroudsburg, PA, USA, 2004; pp. 329–336.
35. Seymore, K.; Mccallum, A.; Rosenfeld, R. Learning Hidden Markov Model Structure for Information Extraction. In Proceedings of the Workshop Paper, AAAI '99 Workshop on Machine Learning for Information Extraction, Pittsburgh, PA, USA, 31–36 July 1999; pp. 37–42.
36. Abu-Jbara, A.; Ezra, J.; Radev, D. Purpose, and Polarity of Citation: Towards NLP-Based Bibliometrics. In Proceedings of the Proceedings of the North American Association for Computational Linguistics (NAACL-HLT), Atlanta, GA, USA, 9–14 June 2013; Association for Computational Linguistics: Stroudsburg, PA, USA, 2013; pp. 596–606.
37. Sugiyama, K.; Kumar, T.; Kan, M.-Y.; Tripathi, R.C. Identifying Citing Sentences in Research Papers Supervised Learning. In Proceedings of the International Conference on Information Retrieval & Knowledge Management (CAMP), Shah Alam, Malaysia, 17 March 2010; IEEE: New York, NY, USA, 2010; pp. 67–72.

38. Bird, S.; Dale, R.; Dorr, B.J.; Gibson, B.; Joseph, M.T.; Kan, M.-Y.; Lee, D.; Powley, B.; Radev, D.R.; Fan Tan, Y. The ACL Anthology Reference Corpus: A Reference Dataset for Bibliographic Research in Computational Linguistics. In Proceedings of the 6th International Conference on Language Resources and Evaluation, LREC 2008, Marrakech, Morocco, 26 May–1 June 2008; European Language Resources Association (ELRA): Paris, France, 2008; pp. 1755–1759.
39. Munkhdalai, T.; Lalor, J.; Yu, H. Citation Analysis with Neural Attention Models. In Proceedings of the Seventh International Workshop on Health Text Mining and Information Analysis, Austin, TX, USA, 5 November 2016; Association for Computational Linguistics: Stroudsburg, PA, USA, 2016; pp. 69–77.
40. Yu, D.; Hua, B. Sentiment Classification of Scientific Citation Based on Modified BERT Attention by Sentiment Dictionary. In Proceedings of the Joint Workshop of the 4th Extraction and Evaluation of Knowledge Entities from Scientific Documents and the 3rd AI + Informetrics (EEKEAII 2023), Santa Fe, NM, USA, 26 June 2023; CEUR Workshop Proceedings: Aachen, Germany, 2023; pp. 59–64.
41. Cohan, A.; Ammar, W.; Van Zuylen, M.; Cady, F. Structural Scaffolds for Citation Intent Classification in Scientific Publications. In Proceedings of the NAACL-HLT 2019, Minneapolis, MN, USA, 2 June 2019; Association for Computational Linguistics: Stroudsburg, PA, USA, 2019; pp. 3586–3596.
42. Yang, N.; Zhang, Z.; Huang, F. A Study of BERT-Based Methods for Formal Citation Identification of Scientific Data. *Scientometrics* **2023**, *128*, 5865–5881. [CrossRef]
43. Lee, J.; Yoon, W.; Kim, S.; Kim, D.; Kim, S.; So, C.H.; Kang, J. BioBERT: A Pre-Trained Biomedical Language Representation Model for Biomedical Text Mining. *Bioinformatics* **2020**, *36*, 1234–1240. [CrossRef] [PubMed]
44. He, Q.; Pei, J.; Kifer, D.; Mitra, P.; Giles, L. Context-Aware Citation Recommendation. In Proceedings of the 19th International Conference on World Wide Web, WWW '10, Raleigh, NC, USA, 26 April 2010; Association for Computing Machinery (ACM): New York, NY, USA, 2010; pp. 421–430.
45. Caragea, C.; Silvescu, A.; Mitra, P.; Giles, L. Can't See the Forest for the Trees? A Citation Recommendation System. In Proceedings of the 13th ACM/IEEE-CS joint conference on Digital libraries (JCDL '13), Indianapolis, IN, USA, 22 July 2013; Association for Computing Machinery (ACM): New York, NY, USA, 2013; pp. 111–114.
46. CiteSeerX About CiteSeerX. Available online: https://csxstatic.ist.psu.edu/home (accessed on 24 February 2024).
47. Devi, V.; Sharma, A. Sentiment Analysis Approaches, Types, Challenges, and Applications: An Exploratory Analysis. In Proceedings of the PDGC 2022—2022 7th International Conference on Parallel, Distributed and Grid Computing, Solan, Himachal Pradesh, India, 25 November 2022; IEEE: New York, NY, USA, 2022; pp. 34–38.

electronics

MDPI

Article

On Embedding Implementations in Text Ranking and Classification Employing Graphs

Nikitas-Rigas Kalogeropoulos *, Dimitris Ioannou, Dionysios Stathopoulos and Christos Makris *

Department of Computer Engineering and Informatics, University of Patras, University Campus, Rio, 26504 Patras, Greece; diioannou@ceid.upatras.gr (D.I.); stath@ceid.upatras.gr (D.S.)

* Correspondence: kalogeropo@ceid.upatras.gr (N.-R.K.); makri@ceid.upatras.gr (C.M.)

Abstract: This paper aims to enhance the Graphical Set-based model (GSB) for ranking and classification tasks by incorporating node and word embeddings. The model integrates a textual graph representation with a set-based model for information retrieval. Initially, each document in a collection is transformed into a graph representation. The proposed enhancement involves augmenting the edges of these graphs with embeddings, which can be pretrained or generated using Word2Vec and GloVe models. Additionally, an alternative aspect of our proposed model consists of the Node2Vec embedding technique, which is applied to a graph created at the collection level through the extension of the set-based model, providing edges based on the graph's structural information. Core decomposition is utilized as a method for pruning the graph. As a byproduct of our information retrieval model, we explore text classification techniques based on our approach. Node2Vec embeddings are generated by our graphs and are applied in order to represent the different documents in our collections that have undergone various preprocessing methods. We compare the graph-based embeddings with the Doc2Vec and Word2Vec representations to elaborate on whether our approach can be implemented on topic classification problems. For that reason, we then train popular classifiers on the document embeddings obtained from each model.

Keywords: information retrieval models; set-based model; graphical document representation; embeddings; text classification

1. Introduction

The primary focus in information retrieval lies in developing models that are both effective and efficient, aligning with the information-seeking needs expressed by users through unstructured queries. That process is conducted via information retrieval models separated into three categories, set-theoretic, algebraic, and probabilistic; moreover, numerous hybrid models have been developed, integrating a complexity that spans multiple scientific domains beyond the scope of classical approaches [1].

One of the previously mentioned areas pertains to the field of graph theory. The inception of graph-theoretic models for information retrieval can be traced back to approximately 1957, as highlighted by Firth [2]. Subsequently, numerous graphical formalisms have been applied to represent textual data in the format of these graphs. Blanco and Lioma [3] introduced two distinct aspects of co-occurrence text graphs. The first aspect involves an undirected structure, where an edge connects two nodes (terms) if they are found within a specified window of terms. Term weights are computed using a methodology similar to TextRank [4], a variant of PageRank [5], or with a degree-based metric known as TextLink. The second aspect entails a directed co-occurrence graph incorporating grammatical constraints, expressed through part-of-speech (PoS) tagging.

Classical information retrieval models generate sparse document representations, giving rise to the concept of "Sparse Retrieval". However, the evolution of information retrieval has integrated machine learning algorithms to generate document vectors containing term scores learned from the documents, akin to traditional term frequency. This integration of machine learning, primarily based on neural networks, has led to the emergence of Neural Information Retrieval [6].

Previously, models were trained on documents to learn sparse vector representations. However, with the advent of transformers and attention mechanisms in 2017 [7], models with dense vector representations have become prevalent in the literature. Consequently, depending on the shape of the document vectors, the retrieval method can be categorized as "learned sparse" [8–12] or "dense" [13–15]. Many dense retrieval models leverage representations derived from BERT [16], which may introduce latency issues in delivering final results. Hence, it is common practice to employ a two-stage pipeline comprising an initial ranking stage followed by a re-ranking stage. A sparse model, such as the BM25, is commonly implemented as a first-stage ranker.

This study adopts the methodology introduced by Kalogeropoulos et al. [17] and seeks to augment the extension of the Set-Based model [18,19] proposed by them. The primary objective of this research is to introduce a robust initial ranking approach, integrating graphs with the set-based model, enriched with word and node vector representations, commonly referred to as embeddings. In a general sense, embeddings are real-valued vectors containing semantic or structural information about the term. Each document will be represented as a graph, a structure exploitable for various tasks, including keyword detection, summarization, and classification.

Another contribution of our work is that, besides addressing the information retrieval aspect, it also tackles the text classification task, which involves organizing text documents into predetermined categories or classes. The primary objective is to automatically assign a label or category to a given piece of text based on its content. This task holds significance for various applications, including spam detection, sentiment analysis, and topic modeling. Textual data can be represented as numerical features, which will serve as input for machine learning algorithms. Common techniques encompass bag-of-words representations such as tf-idf (Term Frequency–Inverse Document Frequency) and word embeddings. These embeddings can be generated either through contextualized pretrained models like BERT [16] or from count-based models such as Word2Vec or GloVe [20,21].

The foundation of the graph-based extension of the set-based model's [17] scheme rests on the assumption that every term in a document shares an equal bidirectional relationship with all others, creating a complete graph for each document. Terms are depicted as nodes and their connections as edges in this graph. However, linguistically, it is evident that the initial hypothesis is overly simplistic. Therefore, it becomes crucial to limit the relationships within a document, which will be considered in our experimental evaluation.

A similar method, known as Graph of Words (GoW), waws proposed by Rousseau and Vazirgiannis [22]. They proposed a degree-based evaluation scheme based on the BM25 model [23,24], which implements an overlapping sliding window to limit the correlation of terms in a sentence on the graph creation process. Their graph algorithm is implemented with minor variations on multiple applications. The implementation of directed graphs proved beneficial in applications like document summarization or phrasal indexing.

Furthermore, when addressing the keyword detection problem, they [25] employed core decomposition [26]. The identification of document keywords was achieved by preserving nodes within the main core of each textual graph. Subsequently, the authors introduced techniques for estimating crucial nodes by considering dense subgraphs beyond the main core. In their initial exploration, they concentrated on dense cores or trusses [27], ultimately suggesting a node ranking based on the sum of core numbers to which each neighbor belongs for a given node [28]. These methods have the ability to isolate significant components within a large graph, often as dense subgraphs. Therefore, they can be applied as edge removal techniques, and they are also useful in tasks like identifying important nodes.

The remainder of this paper is structured into five sections. The second section (Section 2) will delve into a theoretical analysis of significant methods and models that are pertinent to this study. Specifically, it will encompass discussions on the basic set-based model, its graph extensions, graph decomposition techniques, and embedding methodologies.

The third section (Section 3) will outline the contributions of the paper to ranking and classification tasks. Following this, the fourth section (Section 4) will delve into the results obtained from the proposed approach.

Concluding remarks, limitations, and future directions will be addressed in the fifth and final section (Section 5).

2. Preliminaries and Methods

This section outlines the baseline and introduces some novel concepts proposed by Kalogeropoulos et al. [17]. Prior to delving into the proposed model, it is imperative to elucidate and grasp the functioning of the simple set-based model along with its extension.

2.1. Set-Based Model

The set-based model is a combination of set theory with an algebraic influence on the way weights are computed. It introduces the concept of term sets, where if each term in a particular set exists in a text, then the text is defined as containing that set. Initially, the sets may appear to be very large, but in practice, this is not the case; it is proportional to the size of the query. Thus, a model is created with high accuracy in combination with the cost of equivalent efficient models.

Every term that appears in any document of the collection belongs to the collection's vocabulary V. Every subset of the vocabulary constitutes a set of terms n in size, where n is the number of terms it contains. A vocabulary of size m can potentially generate 2^m sets of terms. Naturally, several of these sets may not exist in any document of the collection. For this reason, the frequency of appearance of each set of terms in the texts, denoted as dS_i and defined as the cardinality of the set of documents for each term set, is the frequency of its occurrence.

The model decreases the number of term sets even more, by considering only the frequent sets in the termset creation process. A set of terms is called frequent if the number of occurrences of it is greater than a minimum threshold set by the model creator. Therefore, the Apriori algorithm is implemented for the process of term set creation in the simplest form of the model [29]. The Apriori algorithm is a popular algorithm used for association rule mining in data mining and machine learning. By considering the text as a transaction database and the terms as an item, the algorithm can discover frequent itemsets from the database. It is important to notice that in our approach, we implemented the Eclat algorithm [30] as it will result in similar itemsets with lower time complexity.

The model utilizes, as previously mentioned, term sets as structural elements for representing text queries. Specifically, each text and query is represented as a vector that includes the weight of each set in that particular text or query. The term sets are determined by the terms of the query. The calculation of the weight for each frequent term set is influenced by the number of occurrences of the entire set in the text, the rarity of the set in the collection texts, and the size of the referenced text. Naturally, a set that appears in many texts has less semantic value than a rarer one. Additionally, large texts may contain more than one term set from the query, which, if not addressed, could provide an advantage in the retrieval process. Therefore, an algebraic weight calculation scheme similar to the Vector Space Model (tf-idf) is followed (Equation (1) and (2)). Notably, the reference is to sets of terms rather than individual terms of the query. Thus, the term frequency is replaced by the set frequency Sf_{ij} for text j and set S_i, and similarly, the inverse document frequency in the collection pertains to the corresponding set idS_i. The variable N represents the total number of texts, while dS_i expresses the number of texts in which the set S_i appears.

$$W_{set-based_{S_{ij}}} = (1 + \log Sf_{ij}) \cdot \log\left(1 + \frac{N}{dS_i}\right) \quad (1)$$

$$W_{S_{iq}} = \log\left(1 + \frac{N}{dS_i}\right) \tag{2}$$

Finally, the document ($\overrightarrow{d_j}$) and query ($\overrightarrow{Q}$) vectors are formed with a size of at most 2^n elements, where n is the number of unique terms that the query contains (Equation (3)).

$$\begin{aligned} \vec{d_j} &= (W_{S_1 j}, W_{S_2 j}, \cdots, W_{S_{2^n} j}) \\ \vec{Q} &= (W_{S_1 q}, W_{S_2 q}, \cdots, W_{S_{2^n} q}) \end{aligned} \tag{3}$$

It is imperative to notice that a collection-wise termset calculation would be non-realistic, since it is computationally expensive because the lexicon size N is vastly larger than the number of query terms ($N \gg n$). As the set-based model dictates, the ranking scheme is expressed as the ordered cosine similarity between the collection documents and the query.

$$sim(Q, d_j) = \frac{\overrightarrow{d_j} \cdot \overrightarrow{Q}}{\|\overrightarrow{d_j}\| \times \|\overrightarrow{Q}\|} \tag{4}$$

2.2. Core Decomposition

Core Decomposition was proposed by Seidman [26] and is used in many applications of important node estimation, or subgraph mining.

Let $G = (V, E)$ be a graph, and let $S = (V_k, E(V_k))$ be its subgraph. The k-core (order k) of graph G is a subgraph S where each node $u \in V_k$ has a degree greater than k. The set of all k-core cores constitutes the core decomposition of graph G. The decomposition based on core numbers (K-core decomposition) has been proposed as a tool for studying graphs, aiming to identify vertices of particular significance that exert a more substantial influence on the graph. The absence of these vertices could potentially lead to issues with connectivity.

Qualitatively describing the above definition, we observe that a subgraph has the order K if and only if every node within it has a degree greater than or equal to K. Meanwhile, a node has a core number of K if it belongs to the K-core but not to the (K + 1)-core. In graphs with weighted edges, the degree order of a node is the sum of the weights of its edges. For small values of K, the K-core tends to be large, and its cohesion increases as K grows.

2.3. Graphs and Set-Based Model

Kalogeropoulos et al. [17] proposed a novel extension to the simple set-based model (GSB), which accumulates structural information about the text and the collection using graphs. Figure 1 illustrates the model architecture. At first, their approach considers a fully connected graph (complete graph) for each document that, in the most naive approach, is combined in a collection-wide graph. Each node represents a document term, and the edge weight among terms is calculated multiplicatively by the nodes' respective term frequency.

To elaborate further, the document graph referred to as the Rational Path Graph is a co-occurrence graph characterized by two types of edges: in-edges and out-edges. An in-edge is a self-loop on a node N with a weight W_{in_n} equal to $\frac{TF_n \cdot (TF_n + 1)}{2}$ and the out-edge is an edge between two nodes N, M with weight $W_{out_{n,m}} = TF_n \cdot TF_m$, where TF_n or TF_m is the term frequency of the respective term in the document.

They introduced the graph union operation [31] as a graph merge method. That operator (Equation (5)) will accumulate all document graphs into one graph. Each term is considered a node, and the resulting edge weight is calculated by the sum of the weights that the edge has in every graph that exists.

$$G_D = \bigcup_{i=1}^{n} G_i \tag{5}$$

Thereafter, for each node/term, a graph derived from the union is calculated (Equation (6)) and indexed. It is important to note that the parallelization of the graph construction and union and the weight parallelisation are feasible tasks.

$$nw_k = \log\left(1 + a\frac{W_{out_k}}{(W_{in_k}+1)(Cn_k+1)}\right)\log\left(1 + b\frac{1}{Cn_k+1}\right) \quad (6)$$

The aforementioned weights will be implemented on the set-based weighting scheme, with the variable tnw_{S_i}. That variable is the product of the nw_k weights for every term k that the termset contains.

$$W_{S_{ij}} = W_{set-based_{S_{ij}}} \cdot tnw_{S_i} \quad (7)$$

The nw_k is a compilation of the sum of the out-edges related to node k (W_{out_k}), the weight of the self-loop (W_{in_k}), and the number of the node's k neighbors (Cn_k).

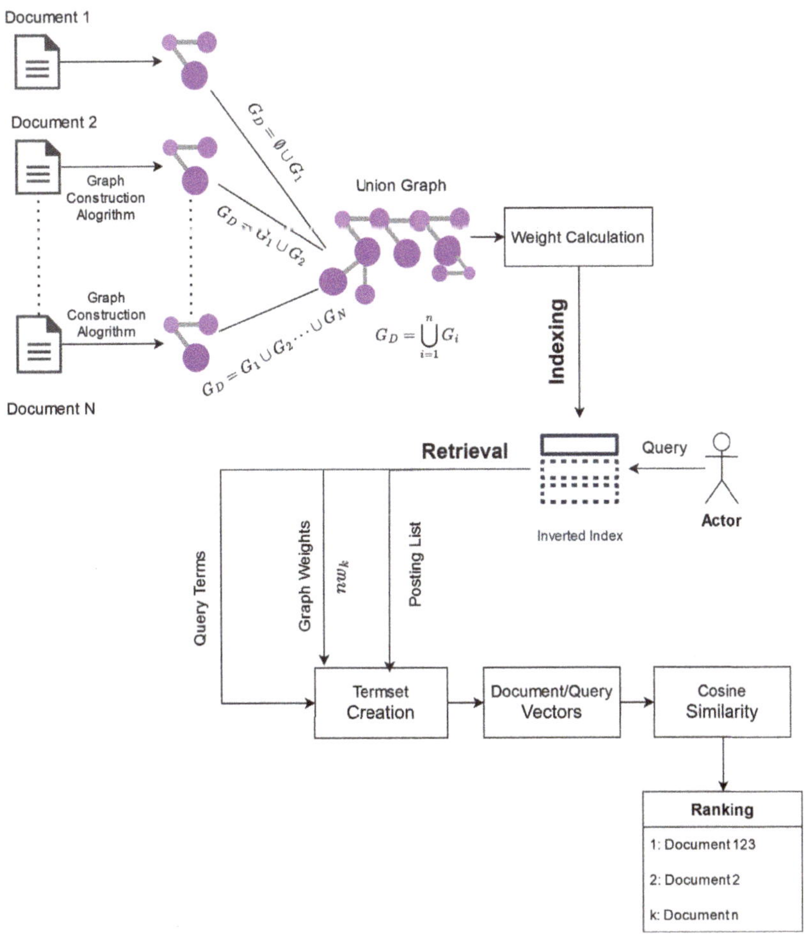

Figure 1. Graph-based extension of the set-based model.

However, unlike the naive approach, they include a level of document graph processing before the graph union operation. At first, a running method can be used to reduce the number of edges, keeping only the important ones, which are expressed by the respective edge weight. Therefore, the model removes edges to an extent that is less than the percentage of the average edge weight. Furthermore, following the work of Rousseau and Vazirgiannis [25] and Tixier et al. [28], they amplify the keyword-related edges by an importance variable h. Such keywords have been located that implement methods and algorithms that include core decomposition. This process assists the model in identifying and handling noisy data, without any performance loss. On the contrary, the ranking process in many cases supersedes the simple set-based model.

2.4. Word Embeddings

Word2Vec [20] efficiently captures semantic relationships by mapping words to high-dimensional vector spaces. The fundamental idea behind Word2Vec is that it learns distributed representations for words based on their contextual usage in a given corpus. The model is trained to predict the likelihood of words appearing together in a given context, enabling it to create dense vectors where words with similar meanings or contexts are geometrically closer. This not only preserves semantic relationships but also allows mathematical operations on word vectors to produce intriguing results, such as analogies.

Node2Vec [32] is a powerful graph embedding algorithm designed to represent nodes in a network as continuous vectors in a multi-dimensional space. Developed to capture intricate structural and semantic relationships within graphs, Node2Vec extends the concept of Word2Vec to network data. It navigates through the graph by employing a flexible biased random walk strategy, allowing it to balance between exploring local neighbourhoods and jumping to more distant nodes. This nuanced exploration approach enables Node2Vec to generate embeddings that preserve the network's topology and community structure.

GloVe [21] is designed to transform words into continuous vector representations, capturing the semantic relationships between them based on their co-occurrence patterns in a given corpus. The underlying principle involves constructing a word–word co-occurrence matrix from the corpus, followed by training the model to learn word embeddings. The objective function of GloVe is carefully crafted to maximize the dot product of word vectors for frequently co-occurring words while minimizing it for those that rarely co-occur.

3. Proposed Methods

In our approach, we will explore the enhancement of the graph-based extension of the set-based model with embedding vectors on two different problems, a ranking one and a classification one. We will try to gauge in our experimental approach whether the information retrieval model is capable of categorizing documents or not as a byproduct of the ranking process. If the model exhibits good performance on the classification task, we can imply that the produced graphs contain and retain semantic and structural information derived from the document.

3.1. Ranking

In the ranking problem, which is an information-retrieval task, we will mainly expand the graph-based extension of the set-based model to include semantic or structural information from embedding vectors. Such vectors will be considered on the edge weights, which will later affect the ranking schema of the graph-based extension of the set-based model. The gist of our approach is to generate embeddings or implement pretrained embedding vectors for each term of a collection of documents. Such vectors will be applied to the graph construction algorithm on the edge weight scheme.

The graph construction algorithm is similar to preliminary work [17], but as a pruning method, we consider the notion of a text window, which is a segment of the document that the graph construction algorithm will regard as an input. In our experiments, we will explore the complete document case, an overlapping sliding windowed case, and lastly, a fixed sliding window one. The base model implements a pruning method that removes edges with a weight less than a user-defined percentage of the graph's average weight. However, this creates a computationally expensive revision step, which will cost time $O(m)$, where m stands for the total number of edges. It is important to note that in a large document corpus, such a method might deteriorate the model's performance.

3.1.1. Word Embeddings on Graphs

To incorporate semantic information in our graph representation, we used word embeddings derived from Word2Vec [20] or GloVe [21]. Pretrained embeddings are generated by training the Word2Vec model or GloVe on a large corpus of text data, such as Wikipedia articles, news articles, Twitter, or other web pages. After training, the final learned word embeddings are extracted and made available for downstream tasks such as natural language understanding, sentiment analysis, and machine translation through the Gensim framework [33] or Stanford's website for the GloVe case. We explored either pretrained options or generated on a specific collection option, but the results were pretty similar. Therefore, we decided to follow the first option for complexity and generalization purposes. The embeddings inclusion framework is outlined in Figure 2.

After the graph creation process is finished, an element-wise summation operation is conducted for each edge between the embedding vectors of the respective nodes, resulting in an edge vector. The vector quantification is achieved through a straightforward averaging of the values it encompasses. The most simple approach is the complete windowed, which is shown in Equation (8).

$$W_{edge_{n,k}} = TF_{n,j} \cdot TF_{k,j} \cdot mean(emb_{1,n} + emb_{1,k}, \cdots, emb_{M,n} + emb_{M,k}) \quad (8)$$

In the windowed case, the above equation is transformed into Equation (9).

$$W_{edge_{n,k}} = \Big(\sum_{w=0}^{N} (TF_{n,j,w} \cdot TF_{k,j,w})\Big) \cdot mean(emb_{1,n} + emb_{1,k}, \cdots, emb_{M,n} + emb_{M,k}) \quad (9)$$

The edge weight, before implementing the embeddings in the windowed graph, is calculated as the sum of the term frequency inside a text segment for each segment. This notion is expressed by the variable w in the above equation. For symbolism, the $TF_{i,j}$ or $TF_{i,j,w}$ is the term frequency of a word in the whole text or a segment, and the constant $emb_{i,k}$ is the embedding vector value for the term k.

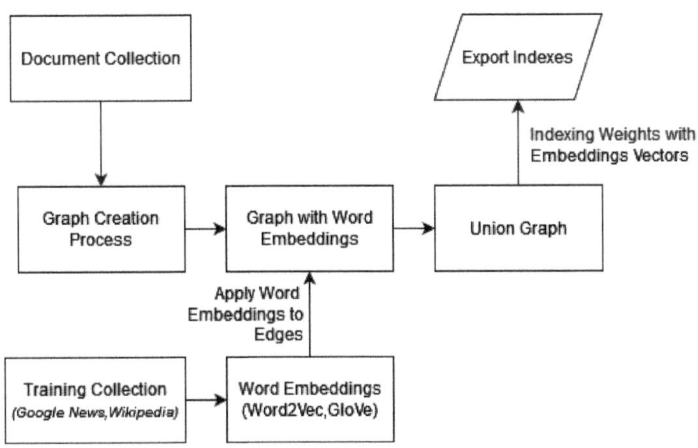

Figure 2. Word embedding on ranking.

For notation purposes in Equation (8), the $TF_{n,j}$ is the term frequency of term n in document j, and $TF_{n,j,w}$ is the term frequency of node n in the window w of document j in Equation (9). The element-wise summation of embedding value, denoted as $emb_{i,n} + emb_{z,k}$, generates an edge embedding vector that is subsequently consolidated into a single value through the mean operation on the edge vector.

From this point, the model continues its functionality identical to Section 2.3. After each document is represented as a graph, the union graph is created, and the nw_k is calculated. The necessary values are indexed alongside the terms in an inverted index, which will later be used in the termset-document weighting scheme of the extension.

3.1.2. Node Embedding on Ranking

A node-embedding vector can offer the model structural information about the nodes on the collection. Such pretrained vectors do not contain meaningful information, since they are created from a different collection. The graph-based extension of the set-based model constructs a collection-wide graph (Figure 3). Thus algorithms that produce graph or node embeddings can be applied. Subsequently, vectors with structural information can be formulated.

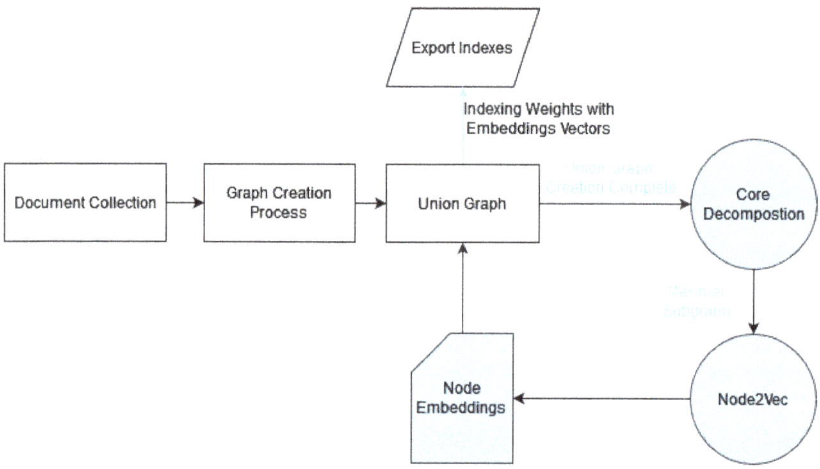

Figure 3. Node embeddings on ranking.

In our approach, we utilize the Node2Vec algorithm [32] to generate vector representations for nodes in the union graph. However, this approach is somewhat naive and computationally intensive. To address this, we leverage insights from the keyword detection findings of Rouseau and Vazirgiannis [28], Tixier et al. [25], and Kalogeropoulos et al. [17]. Specifically, we focus solely on the main core subgraph as input for the embedding algorithm. This introduces another challenge: many nodes may not exist in this maximal subgraph, resulting in vector representations consisting of ones for such nodes. Finally, by normalizing the existing values to 1, our model combines structural knowledge with important node amplification methods.

Both approaches for integrating word or node embeddings into the graph-based extension of the set-based model, despite being computationally intensive tasks, can be concurrently applied, as depicted in Figure 4, although this may not represent the optimal solution or implementation.

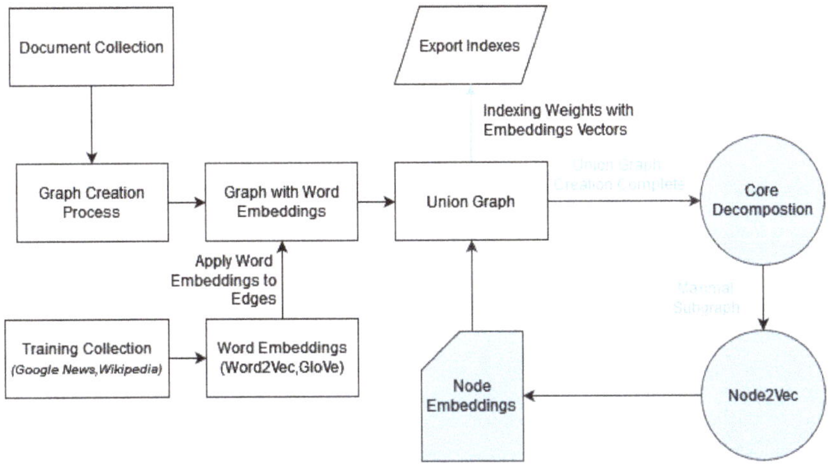

Figure 4. Node and word embeddings on ranking.

3.2. Text Classification

In the text classification problem, we implement the graph creation algorithms of the graph-based extension of the set-based model to assort textual data into different categories, using embedding vectors derived from the graph. The produced document graphs contain edges that function as bridges among cliques. Upon examining the graph construction algorithm, we will notice that the most common nodes that create such edges will be either stopwords or keywords. Therefore, we will enforce three independent preprocessing methods on the textual data.

3.2.1. Preprocessing

The proposed approach explores three different types of document preprocessing in order to estimate the effect of stopwords, stems, and lemmas not only on the graph process but also on the text classification task. Therefore, we implemented our model with documents preprocessed in three different ways.

- Basic preprocessing: removal of URLs/emails, punctuation marks, and digits; conversion of all letters to lowercase; and tokenization.
- Basic preprocessing and removal of stopwords, e.g., "a", "the", "is", "are". The total number of stopwords that we used in our approach following the Python NLTK library is 40.
- Basic preprocessing and application of stemming/lemmatization, meaning the removal of prefixes/suffixes and retaining the stem/lemma of each word.

3.2.2. Node Embeddings from Graphs

As a baseline of our approach, the Word2Vec [20] and Doc2Vec [34] algorithms will be used. The algorithms will be trained on our collection, due to the performance improvement achieved in comparison to the pretrained case.

As Figure 5 depicts, for each preprocessed case, the Word2Vec model generates embeddings for each term t in the vocabulary V. We index these embeddings, and for each document, we create a vector representation as the embedding vectors' element-wise average vector and use them as feature vectors on classification algorithms. These algorithms are Support Vector Machines, Logistic Regression, and multi-layer perception networks.

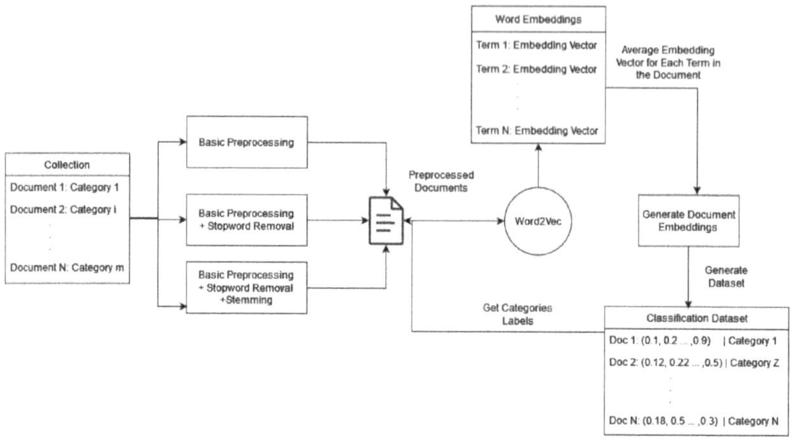

Figure 5. Word embedding on text classification.

Furthermore, the process on Doc2Vec is similar to that no Word2Vec without the need to merge word embedding vectors into one document vector. The algorithm will produce a document vector alongside the terms.

Figure 6 shows the node embedding process. The main difference in this approach is located in the Node2Vec training process. For each document, the respective graph is created. When the union graph is completed, the embedding process begins with that graph as an input. Later, the vectors are indexed and used, similar to the Word2Vec method, to create document vectors.

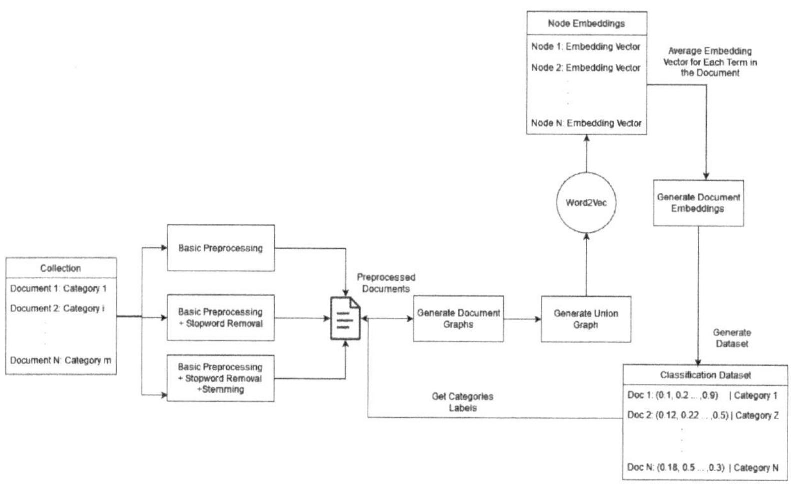

Figure 6. Node embedding on text classification.

4. Experiments

This section consider the results of our experiments regarding the two aforementioned tasks on multiple collections. Table 1 shows the collection name, size, and task that each collection was used for to evaluate the ranking and classification aspect. Those experiments aim to determine the ranking performance of our approach versus the complete extension of the set-based model, as well as the set-based model itself, while being a competent document classification method.

Table 1. Collections and types of experiments used on each one.

Name	Acronym	Docs	Queries/Categories	Task
Cystic Fibrosis	CFC	1.239	100	Ranking
20newsgroups	20news	20.000	20 (used 18)	Classification
BBC News	BBC	2.225	5	Classification
Spam/Ham emails	SP	5.728	2	Classification

The Cystic Fibrosis collection contains 1.239 abstracts regarding the disease. The collection is accompanied by 100 queries with respective expert-derived relevant document lists, which can be used to assess the ranking performance. The 20newsgroups collection contains 20 different categories. However, in our experiments, we tried to make our data set be balanced or fairly balanced; thus, two categories were omitted. It is important to notice here that the 20 labels can be merged into larger groups (Figure 7), thus creating dependencies among classes and rendering the task even more difficult.

The BBC News collection is a balanced five-category collection and the Spam/Ham Emails collection is an imbalanced binary collection, which will be used for the classification task. That way, we can estimate the performance on standard and difficult multi-class issues without disregarding the more simple binary task.

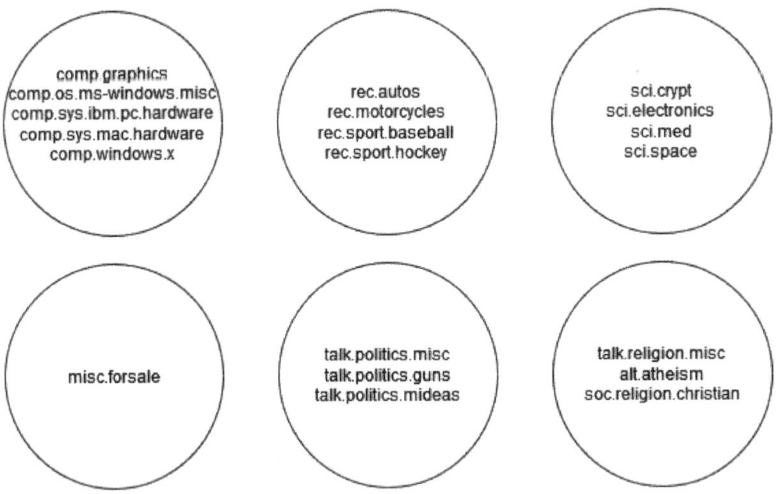

Figure 7. 20newsgroup categories.

4.1. Models' Performance on Ranking

In this subsection, we evaluate the performance of the proposed embedding method on a classical information retrieval application as depicted in Figure 8. Given a collection of documents, alongside the respective queries and relevant documents, we will apply each model separately. For each query–document pair, a similarity function will be implemented, resulting in a ranking that will be evaluated by employing the appropriate metrics (Average Precision per query and Mean Average Precision). The CF collection contains 100 queries on which our model will offer rankings. We will estimate the average precision of each approach and compare it with that of the simple set-based model, creating a metric that will express the number of queries each method supersedes in the set-based model. That method of validation will render the set-based model as our baseline, as shown in Figure 8.

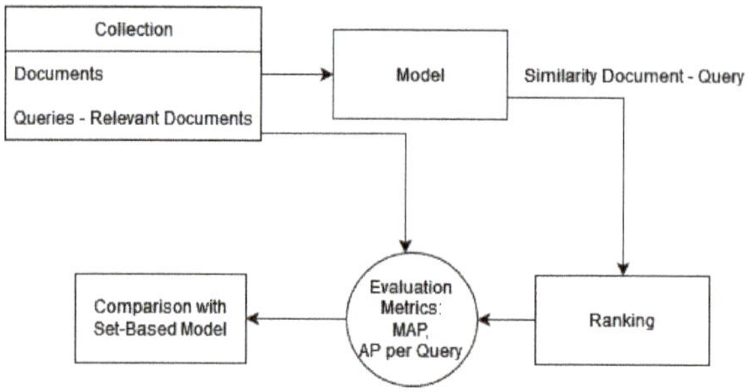

Figure 8. Ranking experiments.

First, we will evaluate the performance of the complete case [17] augmented with embeddings of Node2Vec, Word2Vec, and GloVe with embedding vector sizes of 50 and 200. Immediately, we can notice a substantial performance improvement versus the simple model. The best embedding technique in this approach seems to be the Word2Vec one, as shown in Figure 9.

Figure 9. Ranking performance on each approach.

At this point, instead of a pruning method, we will apply our graph creation algorithm on non-overlapping text segments—windows. We can notice a slight performance increase when implementing GloVe vectors. However, the most important observation lies in the stability of the performance regardless of the window size. This shows that our windowed approach is window-agnostic, which was a drawback of the simple model.

Finally, if we allow the text segments to overlap, we can notice a performance drop in the general model. However, the general stability of the model is increased. The GloVe vectors in this case also yield the best results. Table 2 depicts the best-noted results in each case.

Table 2. Best cases for each approach.

	w/o Embeddings	Word2Vec	GloVe 50	GloVe 200	Node2Vec
GSB	57	79	75	77	71
Constant Window	**82**	78	*81*	**82**	80
Overlapping Window	77	72	*81*	*81*	77

The complete extension is highly amplified by inducing embeddings on the edges. Although the overall highest performance on the windowed options is slightly impacted by our approach, the stability of each model's precision is greatly improved, as mentioned in the above figures.

Table 3 provides a concise overview of several state-of-the-art models, categorised based on their underlying principles. More information about BERT-based models and other variants of them can be found in the literature [15,35]. The first section of the table includes vector-space-probabilistic models, followed by BERT-based models in the second section, and graph-based models in the final section. We will compare the performance of the models in those categories in a later table. It is noteworthy that models like BM25, GoW, or GSB can be utilized as first-stage rankers. Contextual embeddings extracted from BERT are frequently employed as representations in both dense and sparse approaches. Later on, we will compare models from each category with our proposed methods.

In Table 4, we present a comparison of the Mean Average Precision (MAP) for each model concerning the 100 queries contained within the Cystic Fibrosis collection. The performance of the set-based model is enhanced through the incorporation of graphs, leading to the graph-based extension. This extension effectively captures structural information, particularly with the inclusion of windows. The results for the windowed case closely resemble those of the BM25 model (and in some queries improve it). The BM25 model is widely recognized as a foundational model that is frequently utilized for re-ranking purposes in the initial stage. Moreover, our approach is close to (and in some queries an improvement on) the colBERT model and, in conjunction with it, can yield better results, as observed in preliminary experiments (these experiments are the subject of future work). Overall, this outcome suggests that our approach could be effectively employed as a first-stage model alongside dense retrieval models.

Table 3. A theoretic comparison among models.

Model	Description
LSI [36]	Utilizes singular value decomposition to reduce the dimensionality of the term–document matrix and capture latent semantic relationships.
BM25 [37]	A probabilistic information retrieval model that calculates the relevance score of a document to a query based on the term frequencies and document lengths.

Table 3. *Cont.*

Model	Description
BERT [16]	Bidirectional Encoder Representations from Transformers (BERT) is a pre-trained language model that can be fine-tuned for various NLP tasks, including information retrieval, by considering the context of words in both directions.
SPLADE [10]	A self-supervised pretraining approach for dense retrieval that leverages positive and negative passages to learn dense representations of documents and queries.
ColBERT [13]	A late interaction model that employs cross-attention to compute the relevance score between a query and a document by simultaneously attending over the tokens of both query and document representations.
Deep Impact [9]	Utilizes pretrained contextualized representations to perform retrieval with fine-grained ranking based on deep semantic matching and a learnable re-ranking mechanism.
GoW [22]	Utilizes a graph-based representation of words with overlapping sliding windows to capture information for information retrieval tasks with a degree-based weighting scheme.
GSB [17]	Enhances the traditional set-based information retrieval model by incorporating graph-based representations. It employs graphical structures during indexing while maintaining the set-based approach for querying and document representations.

Table 4. Comparison of models on their best case at CFC.

	Model	MAP
1	Set Based Model	0.161875265
2	Graphical Extension of SB	0.186186087
3	BM25	0.222656198
4	Graph of Words	0.117287827
5	**Windowed Model + Word Embeddings**	0.221905122
6	**Windowed Model + Node Embeddings**	0.212273438
7	colBERT	0.226567975

4.2. Text Classification Performance

In this section, we present the results of our classification model trained on the dataset. We evaluate the performance of the model using various metrics and analyze its effectiveness in accurately predicting the target classes. The design of the experiment is depicted in Figure 10.

In Tables 5–7, we can observe that the Word2Vec embeddings are slightly better against the Node2Vec (Tables 8–10) in some cases, and Doc2vec (Tables 11–13) falls short as an embedding technique in the classification task; however, in general, the Node2Vec approach yields results that are competitive with those of Word2Vec. Therefore, we can conclude that our graph creation algorithm can be implemented and perform competitively on classification tasks, such as topic modeling. Furthermore, in each of the columns of the following tables, the preprocessing is more aggressive from left to right, as explained before. Regarding the preprocessing aspect of the textual data, we can conclude that a stemming/lemmatization process deteriorates the performance of the model due to the information loss that occurs. On the other hand, a stopword removal phase seems to increase the classifiers' performance.

From Tables 5–13, we can conclude that the Multilayer Perceptron (MLP) outperforms the rest of the classifiers on every task at hand. For the hard multi-class problem, the Node2Vec results dominates slightly amongst the embedding techniques. However, on easier tasks such as a simple multi-class or a binary classification case, Word2Vec yields better results as the number of classes dwindles. Eventually, Doc2Vec cannot compete equally with the under-discussion models and techniques with a substantial performance loss with respect to the Word2Vec–Node2Vec comparison.

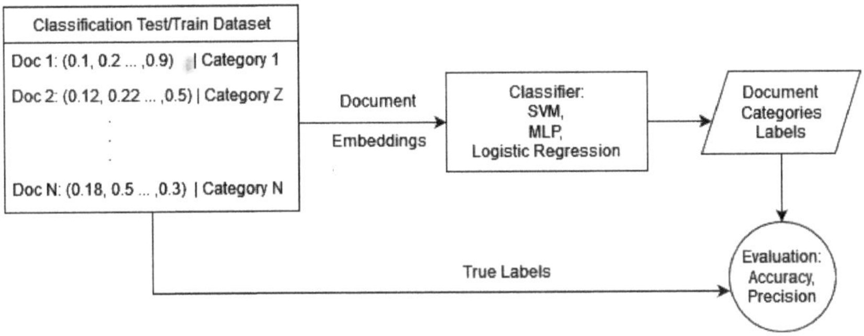

Figure 10. Classification experiment.

Table 5. Word2Vec Embeddings: 20newsgroups.

	20newsgroups 1		**20newsgroups 2**		**20newsgroups 3**	
	Accuracy	**Precision**	**Accuracy**	**Precision**	**Accuracy**	**Precision**
MLP	0.812	0.8153	0.8269	0.8275	0.81266	0.8148
SVC	0.8123	0.814	0.8395	0.8427	0.81	0.8149
Logistic Regression	0.8003	0.8014	0.8225	0.8244	0.7921	0.7947

Table 6. Word2Vec Embeddings: BBC News.

	BBC 1		**BBC 2**		**BBC 3**	
	Accuracy	**Precision**	**Accuracy**	**Precision**	**Accuracy**	**Precision**
MLP	0.9685	0.9687	0.9707	0.9709	0.9685	0.9685
SVC	0.964	0.964	0.964	0.9643	0.9617	0.9619
Logistic Regression	0.9595	0.96	0.9595	0.9597	0.9595	0.9597

Table 7. Word2Vec Embeddings: Spam/Ham Emails.

	Spam 1		**Spam 2**		**Spam 3**	
	Accuracy	**Precision**	**Accuracy**	**Precision**	**Accuracy**	**Precision**
MLP	0.9912	0.9913	0.9904	0.9903	0.9921	0.9921
SVC	0.9912	0.9912	0.9877	0.9878	0.9904	0.9905
Logistic Regression	0.986	0.986	0.986	0.986	0.9851	0.9852

Table 8. Node2Vec Embeddings: 20 Newsgroups.

	20newsgroups 1		**20newsgroups 2**		**20newsgroups 3**	
	Accuracy	**Precision**	**Accuracy**	**Precision**	**Accuracy**	**Precision**
MLP	0.8006	0.8002	0.8284	0.8287	0.7947	0.7925
SVC	0.7877	0.7971	0.8152	0.8201	0.7628	0.7709
Logistic Regression	0.7833	0.7859	0.8055	0.8075	0.7678	0.7705

Table 9. Node2Vec Embeddings: BBC News.

	BBC 1		**BBC 2**		**BBC 3**	
	Accuracy	**Precision**	**Accuracy**	**Precision**	**Accuracy**	**Precision**
MLP	0.8584	0.8605	0.9393	0.9393	0.7707	0.7721
SVC	0.7955	0.81	0.9101	0.9106	0.4584	0.2503
Logistic Regression	0.7865	0.8118	0.9258	0.9262	0.6404	0.7615

Table 10. Node2Vec Embeddings: Spam/Ham Emails.

	Spam 1 Accuracy	Precision	Spam 2 Accuracy	Precision	Spam 3 Accuracy	Precision
MLP	0.9773	0.9773	0.9799	0.9801	0.9703	0.9737
SVC	0.9624	0.9624	0.972	0.9733	0.9616	0.9641
Logistic Regression	0.9554	0.955	0.9712	0.9718	0.9563	0.956

Table 11. Doc2Vec Embeddings: 20 Newsgroups.

	20newsgroups 1 Accuracy	Precision	20newsgroups 2 Accuracy	Precision	20newsgroups 3 Accuracy	Precision
MLP	0.7276	0.7267	0.6964	0.6972	0.7288	0.7299
SVC	0.6866	0.6889	0.6815	0.6811	0.6725	0.6771
Logistic Regression	0.732	0.7318	0.7152	0.7145	0.7229	0.723

Table 12. Doc2Vec Embeddings: BBC News.

	BBC 1 Accuracy	Precision	BBC 2 Accuracy	Precision	BBC 3 Accuracy	Precision
MLP	0.8157	0.8201	0.8764	0.8808	0.8247	0.8243
SVC	0.8	0.7995	0.8606	0.8611	0.7775	0.7773
Logistic Regression	0.8	0.7994	0.8494	0.8498	0.7595	0.7591

Table 13. Doc2Vec Embeddings: Spam/Ham Emails.

	Spam 1 Accuracy	Precision	Spam 2 Accuracy	Precision	Spam 3 Accuracy	Precision
MLP	0.9284	0.9275	0.9415	0.94174	0.9389	0.9399
SVC	0.8368	0.8252	0.8246	0.8099	0.8333	0.8212
Logistic Regression	0.8455	0.8362	0.8202	0.8044	0.8263	0.8123

In terms of computational performance, it is evident that Doc2Vec can generate the required document vectors more efficiently than the Word2Vec model. This efficiency stems from the fact that Doc2Vec does not require the vector aggregations that the basic Word2Vec model needs to compute in order to merge term vectors into a single document vector. On the other hand, the Node2Vec model inherently involves computationally intensive tasks [32]. Initially, it must calculate transition probabilities for each node, followed by computing the necessary paths. This process inherently introduces computational complexity, which can be mitigated through pruning or subgraph mining techniques such as core decomposition, as implemented in this paper. Furthermore, akin to Word2Vec, Node2Vec also needs to transform term–node vectors into document vectors through aggregation, thereby potentially compromising the model's efficiency.

In the following figures, we will delve into the Word2Vec and Node2Vec methodologies through visualization, employing t-SNE, a potent technique for dimensionality reduction and data visualization. Figures 11–17 illustrate documents in a two-dimensional space, with each colored according to its respective class under different preprocessing techniques. Notably, we observe that Node2Vec yields more distinct clusters in this space. A similar trend is apparent in the BBC collection, as depicted in the figure.

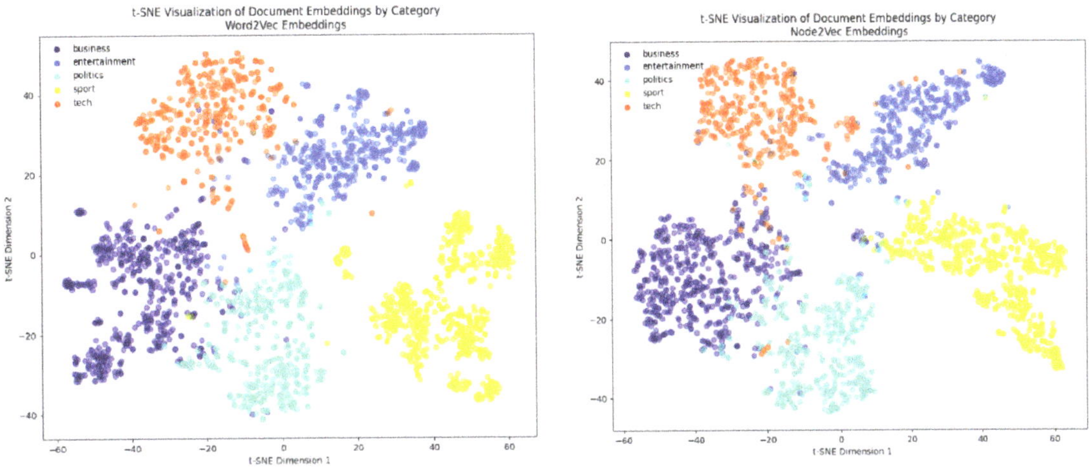

Figure 11. Visualizing embeddings on BBC.

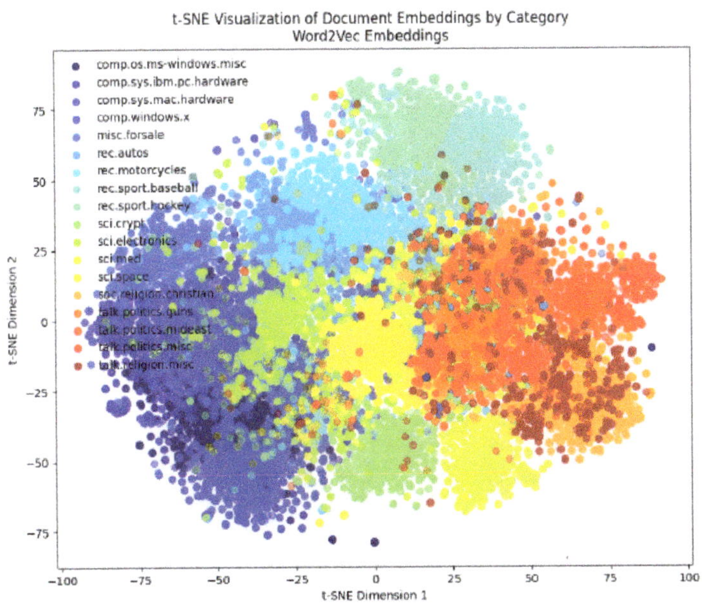

Figure 12. Preprocess Type 1: visualizing Word2Vec embeddings.

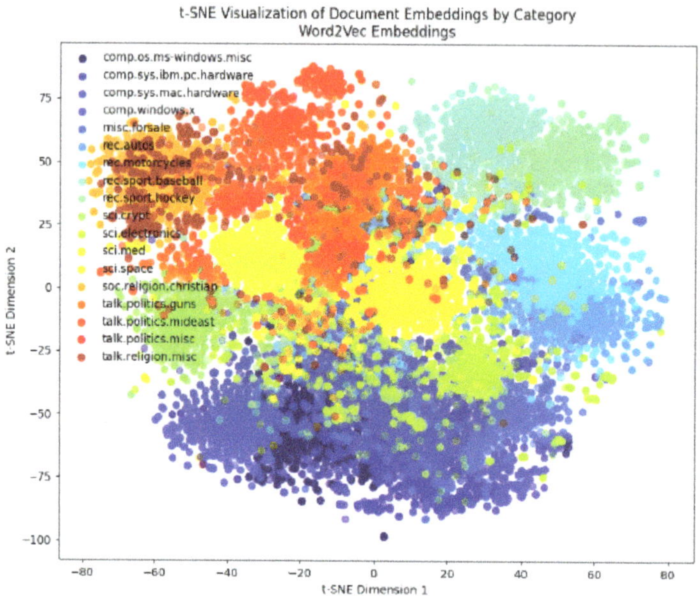

Figure 13. Preprocess Type 2: visualizing Word2Vec embeddings.

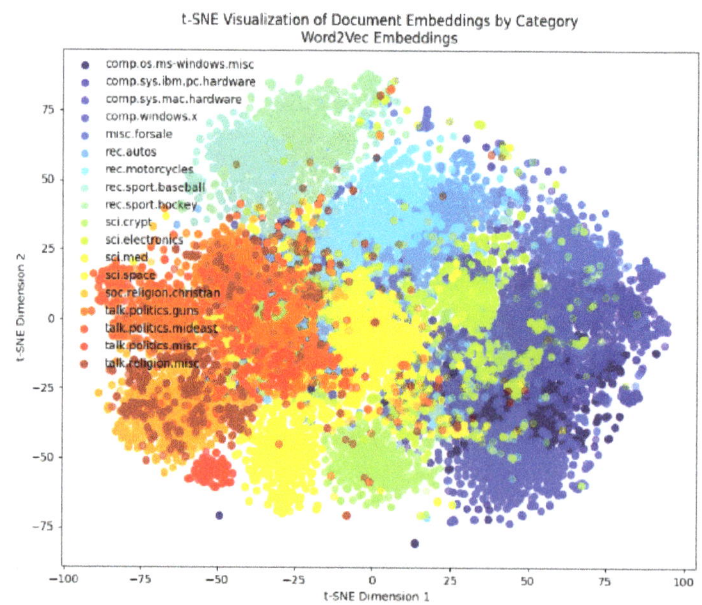

Figure 14. Preprocess Type 3: visualizing Word2Vec embeddings.

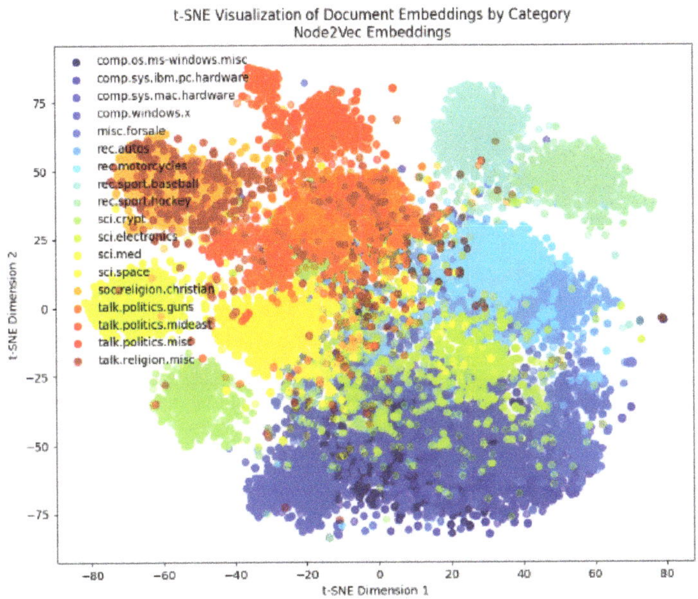

Figure 15. Preprocess Type 1: visualizing Node2Vec embeddings.

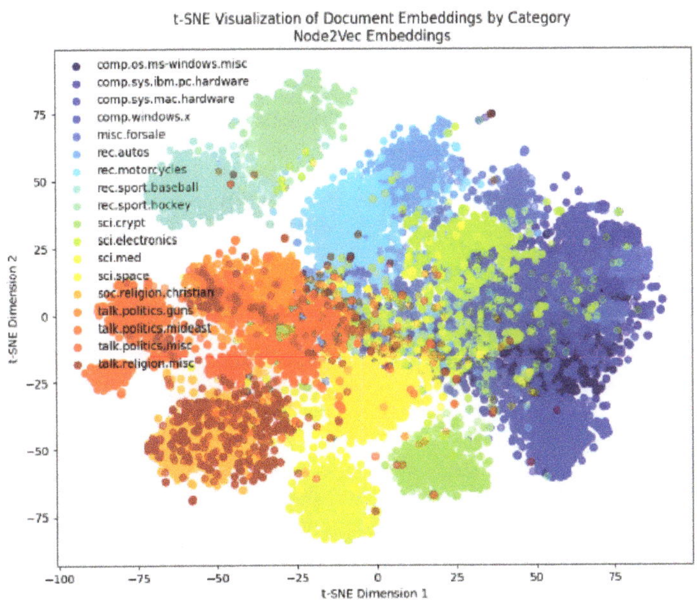

Figure 16. Preprocess Type 2: visualizing Node2Vec embeddings.

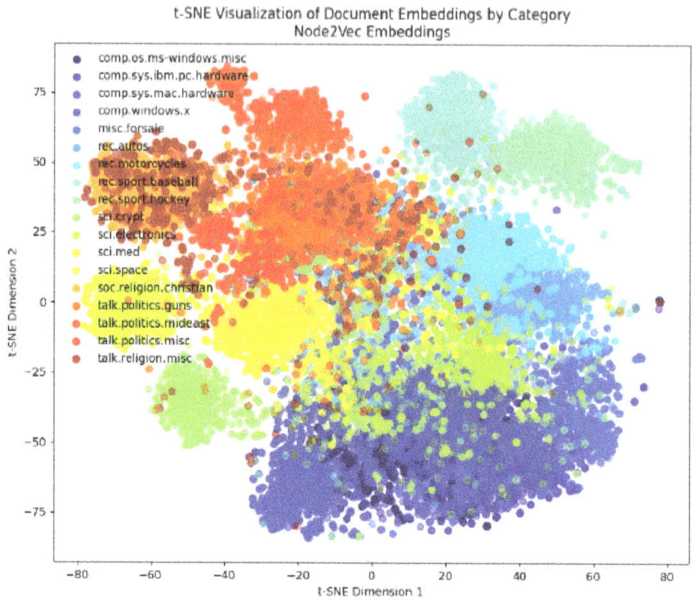

Figure 17. Preprocess Type 3: visualizing Node2Vec embeddings.

5. Conclusions and Future Work

In this paper, we proposed an initial ranking approach that can be implemented as a first-stage ranker in reranking schemes or, in some cases, as a standalone ranker. The model offers structures that can be exploited in various domains, such as in classification. In conclusion, the proposed extensions notably enhance the graph-based extension of the set-based model. The inclusion of text segments as windows for pruning has notably boosted the performance of the ranking model, particularly for larger window sizes, while the integration of embeddings ensures result stability, particularly for large window sizes. Therefore, the proposed model exhibits capability in addressing ranking tasks, whether as a standalone model or as a first-stage ranker.

Additionally, the proposed method contains intermediate structures that can be implemented for various tasks. The main task we explored in this paper was that of classifying documents into categories. We observed that the proposed graph methods contain information capable of categorizing documents on a binary problem, as well as on multiple classification problems regardless of the number of categories, leveraging node embeddings. Therefore, we offer a model that is capable of tackling the two main tasks of information retrieval and data mining.

The existence of an intermediate structure creates an increase in time and space complexity in the model's indexing stage. However, if the model is applied to an information retrieval task, document graphs and the collection union graph can be disregarded after the indexing phase. Although, to fully acknowledge the models' advantages, it is recommended that such structures be stored in appropriate databases (e.g., Neo4j [38]).

Another important aspect to consider pertains to the absence of embeddings. Despite the abundance of pretrained embeddings, we cannot guarantee the presence of a representation for every term, nor can we ensure its quality. The quality of embedding vectors is not solely determined by the model that generates them; rather, it is context-dependent. Consequently, there may be instances where fine-tuning or even training the model from scratch becomes necessary. While this process can increase computational complexity, such cases are rare.

In future research, a focal point of its direction should elaborate on the window aspect of the model, exploring linguistically sound window options that will also capture the notion of a paragraph. The windowed algorithm creates cliques connected with bridge edges. Such edges contain nodes that are important for graph cohesion. Exploratory research about the importance of those nodes in the document, as well as their role inside the text (i.e., keywords or stopwords), should be conducted as a keyword- or stopword-detection problem that can be applied in summarization tasks. Furthermore, for the computational aspect, the model contains algorithms that can be parallelized or computed for distributed implementation frameworks such as Apache Spark [39]. Finally, the collection union graph can be implemented as an online indexer. Each node can contain a label, which will store any information needed by the model to form a knowledge graph-like structure. When an edge information is changed, the respective nodes will recalculate the necessary weights.

Author Contributions: All authors contributed equally to the conceptualization, methodology, validation, formal analysis, investigation, and writing of this paper. The experimentation process was conducted mainly by N.-R.K., D.I. and D.S., while C.M. supervised and coordinated the design and overall experimentation process. All authors have read and agreed to the published version of the manuscript.

Funding: This research received no external funding.

Data Availability Statement: Data and Source code can be found on Github link 1 and Github link 2. The Cystic Fibrosis Collection can be found at Shaw, W.M. & Wood, J.B. & Wood, R.E. & Tibbo, H.R. The Cystic Fibrosis Database: Content and Research Opportunities. LISR 13, pp. 347–366, 1991 and the additional datasets can be found at 20newsgroups (http://qwone.com/~jason/20Newsgroups/), BBC News (http://mlg.ucd.ie/datasets/bbc.html), Spam/Ham emails (https://www.kaggle.com/datasets/maharshipandya/email-spam-dataset-extended). (All links accessed on 9 May 2024).

Conflicts of Interest: The authors declare no conflicts of interest.

References

1. Baeza-Yates, R.; Ribeiro-Neto, B. *Modern Information Retrieval*; ACM Press: New York, NY, USA, 1999; Volume 463.
2. Firth, J.R. A synopsis of linguistic theory 1930-55. In *Studies in Linguistic Analysis (Special Volume of the Philological Society)*; Basil Blackwell: Oxford, UK, 1957; Volume 1952-59, pp. 1–32, ISBN 0631113002/9780631113003.
3. Blanco, R.; Lioma, C. Graph-based term weighting for information retrieval. *Inf. Retr.* **2012**, *15*, 54–92. [CrossRef]
4. Mihalcea, R.; Tarau, P. TextRank: Bringing Order into Text. In Proceedings of the 2004 Conference on Empirical Methods in Natural Language Processing, Barcelona, Spain, 25–26 July 2004; pp. 404–411.
5. Page, L.; Brin, S.; Motwani, R.; Winograd, T. *The PageRank Citation Ranking: Bringing Order to the Web*; Technical Report 1999-66; Stanford InfoLab: Stanford, CA, USA, 1999.
6. Nguyen, T.; MacAvaney, S.; Yates, A. A unified framework for learned sparse retrieval. In Proceedings of the European Conference on Information Retrieval, Dublin, Ireland, 2–6 April 2023; Springer: Berlin/Heidelberg, Germany, 2023; pp. 101–116.
7. Vaswani, A.; Shazeer, N.; Parmar, N.; Uszkoreit, J.; Jones, L.; Gomez, A.N.; Kaiser, Ł.; Polosukhin, I. Attention is all you need. In *Advances in Neural Information Processing Systems*; Curran Associates, Inc.: Red Hook, NY, USA, 2017; Volume 30.
8. Dai, Z.; Callan, J. Context-Aware Document Term Weighting for Ad-Hoc Search. In Proceedings of the Web Conference 2020 (WWW '20), Taipei, Taiwan, 20–24 April 2020; Association for Computing Machinery: New York, NY, USA, 2020; pp. 1897–1907. [CrossRef]
9. Mallia, A.; Khattab, O.; Suel, T.; Tonellotto, N. Learning passage impacts for inverted indexes. In Proceedings of the 44th International ACM SIGIR Conference on Research and Development in Information Retrieval, New York, NY, USA, 11–15 July 2021; pp. 1723–1727.
10. Formal, T.; Piwowarski, B.; Clinchant, S. SPLADE: Sparse Lexical and Expansion Model for First Stage Ranking. In Proceedings of the 44th International ACM SIGIR Conference on Research and Development in Information Retrieval (SIGIR '21), New York, NY, USA, 11–15 July 2021; pp. 2288–2292. [CrossRef]
11. Formal, T.; Lassance, C.; Piwowarski, B.; Clinchant, S. SPLADE v2: Sparse lexical and expansion model for information retrieval. *arXiv* **2021**, arXiv:2109.10086.
12. Nogueira, R.; Yang, W.; Cho, K.; Lin, J. Multi-stage document ranking with BERT. *arXiv* **2019**, arXiv:1910.14424.
13. Khattab, O.; Zaharia, M. Colbert: Efficient and effective passage search via contextualized late interaction over bert. In Proceedings of the 43rd International ACM SIGIR Conference on Research and Development in Information Retrieval, Xi'an, China, 25–30 July 2020; pp. 39–48.

14. Sanh, V.; Debut, L.; Chaumond, J.; Wolf, T. DistilBERT, a distilled version of BERT: Smaller, faster, cheaper and lighter. *arXiv* **2019**, arXiv:1910.01108.
15. Lin, J.; Nogueira, R.; Yates, A. *Pretrained Transformers for Text Ranking: Bert and Beyond*; Springer Nature: Berlin/Heidelberg, Germany, 2022.
16. Devlin, J.; Chang, M.W.; Lee, K.; Toutanova, K. Bert: Pre-training of deep bidirectional transformers for language understanding. *arXiv* **2018**, arXiv:1810.04805.
17. Kalogeropoulos, N.R.; Doukas, I.; Makris, C.; Kanavos, A. A Graph-Based Extension for the Set-Based Model Implementing Algorithms Based on Important Nodes. In Proceedings of the Artificial Intelligence Applications and Innovations, AIAI 2020 IFIP WG 12.5 International Workshops, Neos Marmaras, Greece, 5–7 June 2020; Maglogiannis, I., Iliadis, L., Pimenidis, E., Eds.; Springer: Cham, Switzerland, 2020; pp. 143–154.
18. Possas, B.; Ziviani, N.; Meira, W., Jr.; Ribeiro-Neto, B. Set-based Model: A New Approach for Information Retrieval. In Proceedings of the 25th Annual International ACM SIGIR Conference on Research and Development in Information Retrieval (IGIR '02), Tampere, Finland, 11–15 August 2002; pp. 230–237. [CrossRef]
19. Pôssas, B.; Ziviani, N.; Meira, W.; Ribeiro-Neto, B.A. Set-based vector model: An efficient approach for correlation-based ranking. *ACM Trans. Inf. Syst.* **2005**, *23*, 397–429. [CrossRef]
20. Mikolov, T.; Chen, K.; Corrado, G.; Dean, J. Efficient estimation of word representations in vector space. *arXiv* **2013**, arXiv:1301.3781.
21. Pennington, J.; Socher, R.; Manning, C. GloVe: Global Vectors for Word Representation. In Proceedings of the 2014 Conference on Empirical Methods in Natural Language Processing (EMNLP), Association for Computational Linguistics, Doha, Qatar, 25–29 October 2014; Moschitti, A., Pang, B., Daelemans, W., Eds.; pp. 1532–1543. [CrossRef]
22. Rousseau, F.; Vazirgiannis, M. Graph-of-word and TW-IDF: New Approach to Ad Hoc IR. In Proceedings of the 22Nd ACM International Conference on Information and Knowledge Management (CIKM '13), San Francisco, CA, USA, 27 October–1 November 2013; ACM: New York, NY, USA, 2013; pp. 59–68. [CrossRef]
23. Robertson, S.E.; Sparck Jones, K. Relevance weighting of search terms. *J. Am. Soc. Inf. Sci.* **1977**, *27*, 129–146. [CrossRef]
24. Robertson, S.E.; Zaragoza, H.; Taylor, M. Simple BM25 extension to multiple weighted fields. In Proceedings of the 2004 ACM CIKM International Conference on Information and Knowledge Management, Washington, DC, USA, 8–13 November 2004; ACM: New York, NY, USA, 2004; pp. 42–49.
25. Rousseau, F.; Vazirgiannis, M. Main Core Retention on Graph-of-Words for Single-Document Keyword Extraction. In *Advances in Information Retrieval, Proceedings of the 37th European Conference on IR Research (ECIR 2015), Vienna, Austria, 29 March–2 April 2015;* Proceedings 37; Springer International Publishing: Berlin/Heidelberg, Germany, 2015; pp. 382–393.
26. Seidman, S.B. Network structure and minimum degree. *Soc. Netw.* **1983**, *5*, 269–287. [CrossRef]
27. Cohen, J. *Trusses: Cohesive Subgraphs for Social Network Analysis*; Technical Report; National Security Agency: Fort Meade, MD, USA, 2008; p. 16.
28. Tixier, A.; Malliaros, F.; Vazirgiannis, M. A Graph Degeneracy-based Approach to Keyword Extraction. In Proceedings of the 2016 Conference on Empirical Methods in Natural Language Processing, Austin, TX, USA, 1–5 November 2016; pp. 1860–1870. [CrossRef]
29. Agrawal, R.; Srikant, R. Fast Algorithms for Mining Association Rules in Large Databases. In Proceedings of the 20th International Conference on Very Large Data Bases (VLDB '94), San Francisco, CA, USA, 12–15 September 1994; pp. 487–499.
30. Zaki, M.; Parthasarathy, S.; Ogihara, M.; Li, W. New Algorithms for Fast Discovery of Association Rules. In *KDD*; University of Rochester: Rochester, NY, USA, 1997; pp. 283–286.
31. Sonawane, S.; Kulkarni, P. Graph based Representation and Analysis of Text Document: A Survey of Techniques. *Int. J. Comput. Appl.* **2014**, *96*, 1–8. [CrossRef]
32. Grover, A.; Leskovec, J. node2vec: Scalable feature learning for networks. In Proceedings of the 22nd ACM SIGKDD International Conference on Knowledge Discovery and Data Mining, San Francisco, CA, USA, 13–17 August 2016; pp. 855–864.
33. Řehůřek, R.; Sojka, P. Software Framework for Topic Modelling with Large Corpora. In Proceedings of the LREC 2010 Workshop on New Challenges for NLP Frameworks, Valletta, Malta, 22 May 2010; pp. 45–50. Available online: http://is.muni.cz/publication/884893/en (accessed on 9 May 2024).
34. Le, Q.; Mikolov, T. Distributed representations of sentences and documents. In Proceedings of the International Conference on Machine Learning, PMLR, Beijing, China, 22–24 June 2014; pp. 1188–1196.
35. Wang, J.; Huang, J.X.; Tu, X.; Wang, J.; Huang, A.J.; Laskar, M.T.R.; Bhuiyan, A. Utilizing BERT for Information Retrieval: Survey, Applications, Resources, and Challenges. *ACM Comput. Surv.* **2024**, *56*, 1–33. [CrossRef]
36. Deerwester, S.; Dumais, S.T.; Furnas, G.W.; Landauer, T.K.; Harshman, R. Indexing by latent semantic analysis. *J. Am. Soc. Inf. Sci.* **1990**, *41*, 391–407. [CrossRef]
37. Robertson, S.; Zaragoza, H. The Probabilistic Relevance Framework: BM25 and Beyond. *Found. Trends Inf. Retr.* **2009**, *3*, 333–389. [CrossRef]

38. Webber, J. A programmatic introduction to Neo4j. In Proceedings of the 3rd Annual Conference on Systems, Programming, and Applications: Software for Humanity (SPLASH '12), New York, NY, USA, 21–25 October 2012; pp. 217–218. [CrossRef]
39. Zaharia, M.; Chowdhury, M.; Das, T.; Dave, A.; Ma, J.; McCauley, M.; Franklin, M.J.; Shenker, S.; Stoica, I. Resilient distributed datasets: A fault-tolerant abstraction for in-memory cluster computing. In Proceedings of the 9th USENIX Conference on Networked Systems Design and Implementation (NSDI'12), San Jose, CA, USA, 25–27 April 2012; p. 2.

electronics

MDPI

Article

Raising the Bar on Acceptability Judgments Classification: An Experiment on ItaCoLA Using ELECTRA

Raffaele Guarasci [1], Aniello Minutolo [1,*], Giuseppe Buonaiuto [1], Giuseppe De Pietro [2] and Massimo Esposito [1]

[1] Institute for High Performance Computing and Networking (ICAR), National Research Council of Italy (CNR), 80100 Naples, Italy
[2] Department of Information Science and Technology, Pegaso Telematic University, 80143 Naples, Italy
* Correspondence: aniello.minutolo@icar.cnr.it

Abstract: The task of automatically evaluating acceptability judgments has relished increasing success in Natural Language Processing, starting from including the Corpus of Linguistic Acceptability (CoLa) in the GLUE benchmark dataset. CoLa spawned a thread that led to the development of several similar datasets in different languages, broadening the investigation possibilities to many languages other than English. In this study, leveraging the Italian Corpus of Linguistic Acceptability (ItaCoLA), comprising nearly 10,000 sentences with acceptability judgments, we propose a new methodology that utilizes the neural language model ELECTRA. This approach exceeds the scores obtained from current baselines and demonstrates that it can overcome language-specific limitations in dealing with specific phenomena.

Keywords: natural language processing; sentence classification; acceptability judgments; BERT; ELECTRA; low-resource languages

1. Introduction

In recent years [1], scholarly interest in acceptability judgments has been rekindled, sparked by the creation of the Corpus of Linguistic Acceptability (COLA) [2], the first large-scale resource collecting acceptability judgments designed specifically to be used for training neural models in the Natural Language Processing field. Such a resource has given rise to a strand of research on this task that started in English and has since expanded to various other languages. Acceptability judgment is a pivotal concept in theoretical linguistics. It can be defined as the assessment of how natural a sentence is perceived by a speaker in his or her native language. Although they are *de facto* recognized as the main source of linguistic data [3,4], there is still a heated debate about the methodologies for collecting and evaluating such judgments [5–7].

Concerning NLP, developing larger and more powerful Neural Language Models (NLMs) has led researchers to explore their capacity to encode various forms of linguistic information. Studies have ranged from investigating specific linguistic phenomena to general grammar knowledge [8–12]. In this context, acceptability judgments have emerged as a crucial domain for evaluating the linguistic knowledge acquisition of these models [13,14], mainly since COLA has been incorporated into the widely used GLUE evaluation benchmark [2]. Subsequently, similar resources have been released in different languages, including those belonging to very different language families: Russian [15], Japanese [16], Norwegian [17], Swedish [18], Spanish [19], and Italian [20], which is the language that is the subject of this work.

These datasets have been typically used with monolingual and cross-lingual approaches to assess the syntactic abilities of NLMs or to evaluate the goodness of models in natural language generation tasks [21]. Currently, BERT-based models are the ones that achieve the best performance.

This paper proposes an approach for the Italian language using ELECTRA [22] for the acceptability task, demonstrating that it can exceed the performance currently achieved in the literature. In recent years, ELECTRA has demonstrated that it can overcome BERT in different NLP tasks [23,24] with equal size and available resources, with a particular focus on its application in languages other than English [25,26]. The dataset on which the model is tested is ItaCoLA [20], the largest current resource in the Italian language for acceptability judgments. ItaCoLA includes around 9700 sentences from linguistic scientific literature spanning four decades. These sentences have been manually transcribed and converted into digital format [27].

Adhering to the prevailing methodology in this domain, the acceptability assessment is based on binary judgments, as determined by expert linguists. In addition to the quantitative analysis, which compares performance with the current ItaCoLA baseline, a qualitative analysis is also proposed, which takes advantage of the large number of linguistic phenomena covered by the corpus and the manual annotation [28,29].

Notice that the work's primary contribution is to demonstrate how applying a model like ELECTRA, whose main feature is to achieve superior performance to models such as BERT with lower computational cost and fewer examples, can improve performance on acceptability judgment tasks in the Italian language. Although the task of predicting acceptability judgments has been heavily discussed in recent years, and more resources are being released in other languages, often the time costs and complexity of the models used make it difficult to achieve a very satisfactory cost–benefit ratio [30], even if results are promising.

The paper's organization is the following: Section 2 briefly describes recent works on acceptability judgments. Section 3 describes the resources and models taken into account, along with the experiment setup. In Section 4, the results of the analyses, both from a quantitative and qualitative perspective, are presented and discussed. Finally, Section 5 summarizes the work and provides the conclusions.

2. Related Work

Accurately classifying acceptability judgments has always been a popular topic of discussion in linguistics because of its theoretical aspects related to cognitive science or issues concerning the connection between syntax and knowledge [31]. Concerning NLP, the task is at the heart of many applications, ranging from simple tasks such as grammar correction to more elaborate ones such as machine translation and evaluation of automated dialogue systems. Consequently, several challenges arise in this context. The first issue is the subjective nature of acceptability judgment, which can vary according to context and language and is influenced by syntactic or semantic features as well as pragmatic and dialogic ones. Therefore, models facing this task must be able to identify and capture complex linguistic structures [32] and exploit cross-lingual approaches to generalize between languages [33].

Moreover, an additional bottleneck is the cost and difficulty of obtaining annotated data that may suit these models. Often, it is necessary to rely on crowdsourcing or the support of domain experts.

The event that caused great traction for the assessment of acceptability tasks has been the public release of the CoLa corpus [2], the most extensive existing English acceptability corpus that includes over 10,000 sentences. Numerous neural network-based approaches were compared on the CoLA corpus, which was then incorporated into the widely known natural language understanding (NLU) benchmark dataset GLUE [34].

Regrettably, most studies within GLUE have reported accuracy instead of the Matthews Correlation Coefficient (MCC), making it challenging to determine the optimal approach. Nevertheless, it is noteworthy that top-ranking systems are transformer-based models, i.e., ALBERT [35] (69.1 Accuracy), and StructBERT [36] (69.2 Accuracy). Instead, another line of research has approached the task using entailment and exploiting small-scale models [37] showing promising results (86.4 Accuracy).

The methodology introduced in CoLA has been the starting point for several derivative resources developed recently and focused on languages other than English. Such languages include Italian [20], Norwegian [17], Swedish [18], Russian [15], Japanese [38], Chinese [39,40], and Spanish [19]. It is important to note, however, that since acceptability has always fascinated scholars, small datasets had already been released before CoLa, mainly focused on theoretical linguistics or cognitive science-related tasks [41–43]. In addition to English, informal acceptability judgments have been evaluated in Hebrew and Japanese [32], as well as in French [44] and Chinese [45]. A small Italian dataset focusing on complexity and acceptability has also been released [46]. Notice that—in the context of the newborn field of Quantum Natural Language Processing (QNLP)—ItaCola has been used to evaluate the feasibility of a quantum machine learning algorithm to classify acceptable/unacceptable sentences using the new distributional compositional models of language [47].

3. Materials and Methods

3.1. Dataset

The resource employed in this work is ItaCoLA, which stands for the Italian Corpus of Linguistic Acceptability [20]. ItaCoLA has been meticulously constructed to encompass a diverse spectrum of linguistic phenomena while making a clear distinction between sentences regarded as acceptable and those deemed unacceptable. The process used to curate this corpus has been closely modeled after the methodology applied in creating the original CoLA [2].

ItaCoLA consists of 9700 sentences whose origins vary. These sentences encompass a wide array of linguistic phenomena for comprehensive coverage of the linguistic literature. The acceptability assessment of each sentence comes from experts who authored the diverse data sources and is formulated as a binary score.

The sentences have been collected from a wide range of linguistic publications spanning four decades, meticulously transcribed by hand, and made available in digital format. A sample extracted from ItaCoLA with some acceptable sentences (label 1) and some unacceptable ones (label 0) is shown in Table 1.

As mentioned above, the annotation process lies in domain-expert judgments. This procedure, already known in corpus linguistics studies [48], has become the standard de facto for this type of task, shared by all the works in other languages derived from CoLa. The possibility of using crowdsourcing approaches and naive annotators is still debated in the literature [49], as well as creating deliberately unacceptable examples ad-hoc by compromising well-formed sentences [50], a procedure widely used in other NLP tasks, such as sentiment analysis or fake news detection [51–54].

Table 1. Sentences from ItaCoLA. The first column indicates the acceptability judgment (1 = acceptable, 0 = not acceptable).

Label	Sentence
0	Maria andava nella sua l'inverno passato città. (Maria went to her winter past city)
1	Max vuole sposare Andrea (Max want to marry Andrea)
0	Il racconto ti hanno colpito. (The story have impressed you)
1	Il racconto ti ha colpito. (The story has impressed you)

ItaCoLA is divided as follows: 7801 sentences compose the test set, the validation set includes 946 sentences, while the test set is 975. The ratio of acceptable to unacceptable sentences in each split is balanced.

3.2. Models

3.2.1. BERT

In the realm of NLMs, BERT has emerged in the literature as the most widely adopted model due to its remarkable efficiency [55]. BERT is based on a Transformer encoder [56], and it needs several non-annotated data for the training phase, articulated in two different training objectives, namely masked language modeling (MLM) and next sentence prediction.

MLM entails randomly masking a portion of words of the training dataset. This technique enables the model to capture information bidirectionally within sentences while simultaneously predicting the masked words. It is worth noting that two possible options for vocabulary (cased or uncased) imply two distinct pre-trained models. This bidirectional analytical adaptability allows the model to maintain a significant generative capacity through the inner layers of the network while also facilitating adaptation to specific tasks during the subsequent fine-tuning phase.

BERT operates by initiating each input word sequence with a special token, marked as *"[CLS]"*. This token is crucial in deriving an output vector of size H, corresponding to the hidden layers' dimensions and the whole input sequence. Furthermore, another unique token, *"[SEP]"*, needs to be correctly situated within the input sequence following each sentence. Starting from a sequence of input words denoted as $t = (t_1, t_2, \ldots, t_m)$, BERT produces an output represented as $h = (h_0, h_1, h_2, \ldots, h_m)$. In this representation, $h_0 \in \mathbb{R}^H$ is the ultimate hidden state of the special token *"[CLS]"*, acting as a comprehensive representation for the entire input sequence. Meanwhile, $h_1, h_2, \ldots, h_m$ signify the final hidden states of the remaining input tokens.

The context-dependent representation of sentences obtained from this training phase can be further customized to specific tasks by fine-tuning and modifying several hyper-parameters. The $BERT_{base}$ model has 110 million parameters (12 hidden layers, each composed of 768-dimensional states and 12 attention heads). Every layer of the model produces a unique embedded representation of the input words, whose dimension is limited to a maximum of 512 tokens.

For the fine-tuning of BERT in classifying input sequences of words into K distinct text categories, the final hidden state h_0 can serve as the input to a classification layer. Subsequently, a softmax operation [57] is employed to transform the scores corresponding to each text category into probabilities.

$$P = softmax(CW^T) \tag{1}$$

The parameter matrix of the classification layer as $W \in \mathbb{R}^{K \times H}$ is the one selected for this work. Concerning the BERT version, the *dbmdz* Italian BERT model (XXL, cased) [58] has been chosen. It is an Italian pre-trained version of BERT trained using different corpora [59,60]. The corpus used for the training is 81 GB and includes 13,138,379,147 tokens.

3.2.2. ELECTRA

The other NLM under consideration is ELECTRA, first introduced in [22]. ELECTRA has demonstrated superior proficiency in capturing contextual word representations, surpassing other models in downstream performance when subjected to identical model sizes, data, and computational resources, as noted by [61]. ELECTRA's pre-training includes two transformer models: the generator (G) and the discriminator (D), as shown in Figure 1. G is devoted to replacing some tokens in a sequence, typically trained as a masked language model. In contrast, the main focus in ELECTRA is on the discriminator model D, which aims to discern the tokens substituted by G in the sequence.

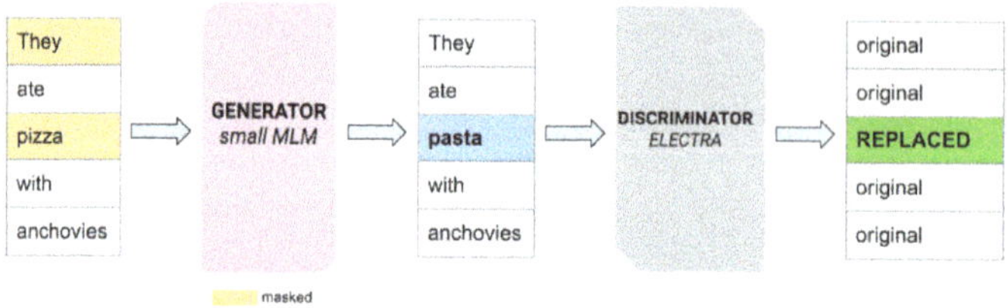

Figure 1. ELECTRA overview with replaced token detection.

In a specific scenario, when certain tokens within a given input sequence are randomly substituted with a unique "*[MASK]*" token, the aim of G is to predict the original tokens for all the masked instances. Following this, a sequence with fake tokens is generated for D, which is trained to distinguish genuine from fake tokens using a method called replaced token detection (RTD). The RTD offers the advantage of not compromising the model's overall performance while having fewer examples available.

Similarly to BERT, a version of the model used is *dbmdz* Italian ELECTRA [62]. Here are the details: starting from a sentence κ of raw text χ, made of a set of tokens $\kappa = w_1, w_2, \ldots, w_n$ where w_t $(1 \leq t \leq n)$ is a generic token, κ is encoded in a sequence of contextualized vector representations $h(\kappa) = h_1, h_2, \ldots, h_n$ by G and D. After that, using a softmax layer, G is the probability of generating a specific token w_t for each position t for which $w_t = [MASK]$.

$$p_G(w_t|\kappa) = \frac{r(w_t)^T h_G(\kappa)_t}{\sum_{w'} exp(r(w')^T h_G(\kappa)_t)} \tag{2}$$

The embedding function is represented by $r(\cdot) : w_t \in \kappa \rightarrow \mathbb{R}^{dim}$; *dim* is the chosen embedding size, while the prediction of whether w_t is original or fake is given by D. A sigmoid layer, σ, is used to perform this task:

$$D(\kappa, t) = \sigma(r(w_t)^T h_D(\kappa)_t) \tag{3}$$

During the pre-training, the combined loss function is minimized:

$$\min_{\eta_G, \eta_D} \sum_{\kappa \in \chi} \mathcal{L}_{Gen}(\kappa, \eta_G) + \lambda \mathcal{L}_{Dis}(\kappa, \eta_D) \tag{4}$$

Note that $\mathcal{L}_{\text{Gen}}$ represents the loss function of G and $\mathcal{L}_{\text{Dis}}$ that of D. Subsequently, only D is used for the fine-tuning.

Techniques like MLM, exemplified by BERT, introduce input corruption by substituting a masked token for an original one, which the trained model then retrieves. Such methods yield commendable results when applied to downstream NLP tasks; they typically demand substantial computational resources for optimal effectiveness.

By contrast, RTD provides a more efficient pre-training technique, corrupting a subset of input tokens with plausible alternatives using a generator network. ELECTRA's efficiency compared to models such as BERT lies in including the predictions of all input tokens, not only the masked ones. Therefore, D loss can also be computed on the whole set of tokens in the input sequence, allowing the use of examples in the training phase without compromising performance.

4. Results and Discussion

Two different types of analysis have been carried out: quantitative, which aims to verify the performance achieved by the tested models using metrics well known in the literature and the improvement from the baseline, and qualitative, which aims to deepen the analysis and estimate whether there are specific phenomena that impact performance the most.

4.1. Quantitative Analysis

According to previous studies approaching this task, two different metrics have been used for the analysis: accuracy and the Matthews Correlation Coefficient (MCC). Accuracy is the most commonly used basic metric and is also the one used to be able to compare with GLUE. MCC is a correlation metric increasingly used in binary classification tasks [63].

The Adam optimizer has been used for training (learning rate of 2×10^{-5}, epsilon of 10^{-8}), while batch size has been set to 32, with 2 labels, 0 warm-up steps, a maximum input sequence length of 64 words, categorical cross-entropy as the objective function. The number of epochs on which the model has been trained is 7.

As evidenced by the loss functions shown in Figure 2, ELECTRA is more efficient than BERT at loss-minimizing learning to perform classification.

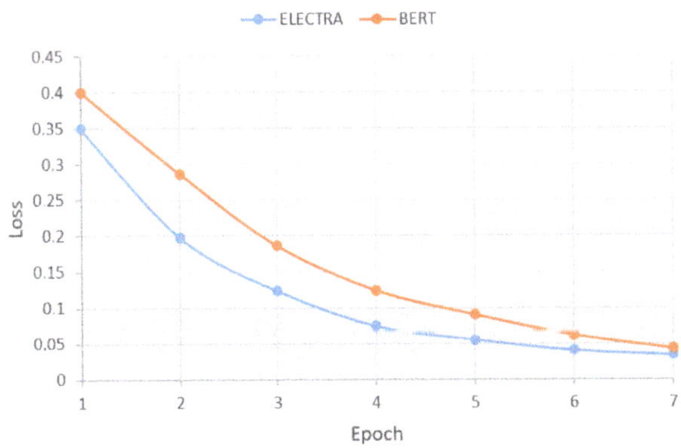

Figure 2. The loss functions for BERT and ELECTRA training.

Concerning NLMs tested, as shown in Table 2, it can be noted that both BERT and ELECTRA outperform the classic LSTM baseline.

Table 2. Classification results comparing LSTM, BERT, and ELECTRA.

Model	Accuracy	MCC
LSTM	0.794	0.278 ± 0.029
BERT	0.904	0.603 ± 0.022
ELECTRA	0.923 ± 0.008	0.690 ± 0.035

Notice that, although it is an outdated architecture [64], LSTM (Long Short-Term Memory) models have been used in several works for acceptability classification [2,65]. Their peculiarity is, in fact, their ability to adequately capture and handle long-term dependencies in sequential data. Furthermore, LSTM memory cells are able to maintain long-term information, unlike traditional RNNs.

In particular, experiments carried out using ELECTRA achieve the best results, reaching an accuracy of 0.923, while the BERT-Classic reaches a lower score, ending at 0.904. By using MCC as a metric, the result is even more significant.

This result is attributable to a more efficient use of available data. ELECTRA's pre-training strategy is not limited to learning only masked words, as with BERT. Unlike MLM, RTD produces a better contextual representation by learning from all input words and using a similar amount of data, model size, and computational cost [66]. Further confirmation of the validity of this approach is given by its application in similar binary classification tasks in different languages [53,67,68].

4.2. Qualitative Analysis

The evaluation has also been extended to a qualitative level to take advantage of fine-grained annotations provided along with ItaCoLA.

Since its release, around 30% of the sentences composing the corpus have been annotated using labels covering nine linguistic phenomena, as shown in Table 3. The phenomena combine some classes proposed for the AcComplit dataset [46] and other ones used in [69] for the English language.

Table 3. Overview of different phenomena collected in ItaCola.

Phenomenon	Sentences	Description	Example
Simple	365	One-verb sentences composed of only mandatory arguments.	"Marco ha baciato Alice" (En. *Marco kissed Alice.*)
Cleft constructions	136	Sentences in which a constituent is displaced from its typical position to give it emphasis.	"È Clara che Anna ha visto uscire" (En. *It is Clara whom Anna saw leaving.*)
Subject–verb agreement	406	Sentences lacking the agreement in gender or number between subject and verb.	"Maurizio sostiene che Lucia ha parlato di lui a casa con la moglie" (En. *Maurizio claims that Lucia talked about him at home with his wife.*)
Indefinite pronouns	312	Sentences with one or more indefinite pronouns referring to someone or something.	"Spero in qualcosa che arriverà" (En. *I am hoping for something to come.*)
Copular constructions	855	Sentences in which the subject is connected to a noun or an adjective with a copulative verb.	"Cicerone era un grande oratore" (En. *Cicero was a great speaker.*)
Auxiliary	398	Sentences containing the verb "essere" (to be) or "avere" (to have).	"Stavamo correndo nel pomeriggio" (En. *We were running in the afternoon.*)
Bind	27	Sentences in which anaphoric elements are grammatically associated with their antecedents.	"Cesare adula se stesso" (En. *Caesar flatters himself.*)
Wh-islands violations	53	Sentences at the beginning of which there is a Wh- clause.	"Che opera lirica avevi suggerito di andare a vedere stasera?" (En. *What opera did you suggest we see tonight?*)
Questions	177	Interrogative sentences.	"È tua quella bicicletta rossa?" (En. *Is that red bicycle yours?*)

Since only 2088 sentences are accompanied by a fine-grained linguistic annotation, the train, test, and validation splits have been altered to achieve this objective: the whole set comprising all the 2088 sentences is designated the test set. Therefore, the remaining 7632 sentences in the dataset have been divided into two subsets, training and validation, which are composed of 6833 and 800 sentences, respectively. ELECTRA has undergone fine-tuning using identical parameters to those in previous experiments.

Concerning accuracy, as reported in Figure 3, some uniformity can be seen with a significant gap only in sentences belonging to the bind class.

As expected, sentences involving pervasive constructions of the Italian language are simpler for the model to handle. This is true for copular constructions and questions. Such sentences achieve almost identical results (accuracy equal to 0.88 and 0.86, respectively). In the other phenomena, on the other hand, the deviation is very low, in the range of 3 points.

The only exception, as mentioned above, concerns the bind class, classified poorly using BERT (0.55) but which undergoes a significant increase using ELECTRA (0.70). This is a very interesting result since binding is a complex phenomenon studied in various languages, related to well-known concepts in theoretical linguistics such as anaphora and ergative verbs [70,71], which have often posed numerous critical issues in NLP [72].

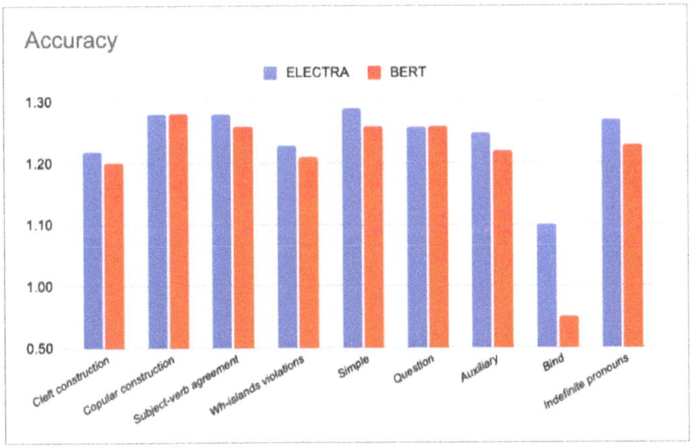

Figure 3. Comparison of performance in terms of accuracy between BERT and ELECTRA.

Unexpectedly, simple sentences do not yield the highest results. In contrast, this category achieves the best outcomes in the original English CoLA corpus [69]. This discrepancy can be attributed to English's extremely straightforward syntax and strict SVO (subject–verb–object) order [65], factors that contribute to sentences lacking any particular criticality.

The same is not true for Italian, where the syntax is often characterized by hypotaxis and the presence of pro-drop, and the free order of constituents constitute major critical factors that affect performance [73].

Furthermore, it is notable that ItaCoLA allows multiple annotations for the same sentence in case phenomena coexist.

Almost a third of the sentences in the dataset used for this experiment have multiple annotations. As for simple sentences, 77% have more than one annotation, which could be another reason they tend to be misclassified.

Overall, as shown in Table 4, the application of ELECTRA achieves values consistently better than or equal to BERT, both using accuracy and MCC in every phenomenon.

Table 4. Results of two models using MCC and Accuracy (ACC) with respect to each phenomenon taken into account.

Phenomenon	Model	
	ELECTRA	BERT
	MCC / ACC	
Cleft construction	0.53/0.82	0.48/0.80
Copular construction	0.56/0.88	0.36/0.88
Subject–verb agreement	0.54/0.88	0.41/0.86
Wh-islands violations	0.5 /0.83	0.46/0.81
Simple	0.54/0.89	0.35/0.86
Question	0.50/0.86	0.37/0.86
Auxiliary	0.47/0.85	0.30/0.82
Bind	0.43/0.70	0.18/0.55
Indefinite pronouns	0.51/0.87	0.28/0.83
Total	0.54/0.87	0.37/0.84

Considering the MCC as a metric, a major variability across phenomena can be observed (see Figure 4). An issue highlighted at the release of ItaCoLA was the low performance on the copula constructions and Wh-violations. This result strongly contrasted with the results obtained for English: in [69], a value of MCC > 0.50 was presented for both phenomena. This problem seems to be overcome using ELECTRA; in both cases, the values sharply increase, reaching MCC scores of 0.56 and 0.58, which is in line with English CoLa scores. Although interesting from a cross-linguistic perspective, it should be noted that many of these phenomena are highly language-specific. Therefore, a true Italian–English comparison for each phenomenon is not possible.

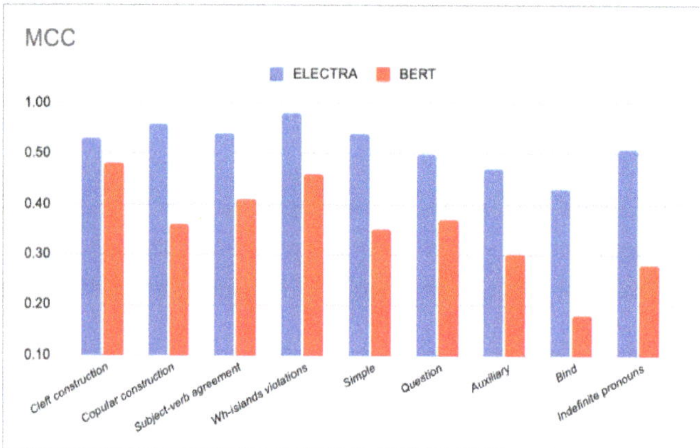

Figure 4. Comparison of performance in terms of MCC between BERT and ELECTRA.

5. Conclusions and Future Work

In this work, an approach that raises the bar for the performance of acceptability judgment tasks in Italian has been presented. In particular, using the ELECTRA model has enabled surpassing baselines and state-of-the-art BERT-based approaches.

ELECTRA performance has also been investigated in depth through a qualitative analysis that focused on specific linguistic phenomena, showing a generalized improvement, particularly regarding marginal phenomena poorly represented in the sample under analysis, in which BERT has been underperforming.

Following the insight already presented in [15], the work's future development consists of exploring the possibilities of cross-lingual approaches [74].

Obviously, many open issues cannot disregard the nature of the task itself, since the unacceptability of certain syntactic structures is strictly language-dependent. For this reason, it would be fruitless to compare global performance through cross-linguistic approaches; rather, it would be appropriate to focus on specific phenomena, as already demonstrated in other studies in the literature [75]. Concerning further experiments, additional models, such as decoder-only or encoder–decoder models, will be tested, and the effect of in-context learning and knowledge transfer from additional languages will be considered, following the most recent research trends in this topic.

Finally, given the recent interest in the syntactic evaluation of NLMs, to make the methodology more robust, a comparison with experienced and unskilled human annotators will be introduced, as proposed in [28,49], and a semi-automatic systematic evaluation system based on a set of minimal pairs, as has happened with English [76] and Japanese [38]. Furthermore, new lines of research will be investigated concerning the promising results in the area of QNLP obtained from the preliminary experiments [77] and the chance to also opt for different strategies based on zero or few-shot learning using other NLMs on this task [78].

Author Contributions: Conceptualization, R.G., A.M. and M.E.; Methodology, R.G., A.M., G.D.P. and M.E.; Software, A.M.; Validation, R.G.; Formal analysis, G.B.; Resources, R.G.; Writing—original draft, R.G. and A.M.; Writing—review & editing, G.B., G.D.P. and M.E.; Supervision, M.E.; Funding acquisition, M.E. All authors have read and agreed to the published version of the manuscript.

Funding: We acknowledge financial support from the H2IOSC Project—Humanities and Cultural Heritage Italian Open Science Cloud funded by the European Union—NextGenerationEU—NRRP M4C2—Project code IR0000029-CUP B63C22000730005.

Data Availability Statement: The data presented in this study are openly available in GitHub. [https://github.com/dhfbk/ItaCoLA-dataset] (accessed on 24 April 2024).

Conflicts of Interest: The authors declare no conflicts of interest.

References

1. Chen, S.Y.C.; Huang, C.M.; Hsing, C.W.; Kao, Y.J. Hybrid quantum-classical classifier based on tensor network and variational quantum circuit. *arXiv* **2020**, arXiv:2011.14651.
2. Warstadt, A.; Singh, A.; Bowman, S.R. Neural Network Acceptability Judgments. *Trans. Assoc. Comput. Linguist.* **2019**, *7*, 625–641. [CrossRef]
3. Chomsky, N. *Aspects of the Theory of Syntax*; MIT Press: New York, NY, USA, 1965.
4. Schütze, C.T. *The Empirical Base of Linguistics: Grammaticality Judgments and Linguistic Methodology*; University of Chicago Press: Chicago, IL, USA, 2016.
5. Gibson, E.; Fedorenko, E. The need for quantitative methods in syntax and semantics research. *Lang. Cogn. Process.* **2013**, *28*, 88–124. [CrossRef]
6. Sprouse, J.; Almeida, D. A quantitative defense of linguistic methodology. 2010, *Manuscript Submitted for Publication*.
7. Linzen, T. What can linguistics and deep learning contribute to each other? Response to Pater. *Language* **2019**, *95*, e99–e108. [CrossRef]
8. Hewitt, J.; Manning, C.D. A Structural Probe for Finding Syntax in Word Representations. In Proceedings of the 2019 Conference of the North American Chapter of the Association for Computational Linguistics: Human Language Technologies, Volume 1 (Long and Short Papers), Minneapolis, MN, USA, 2–7 June 2019; pp. 4129–4138. [CrossRef]
9. Manning, C.D.; Clark, K.; Hewitt, J.; Khandelwal, U.; Levy, O. Emergent linguistic structure in artificial neural networks trained by self-supervision. *Proc. Natl. Acad. Sci. USA* **2020**, *117*, 30046–30054. [CrossRef] [PubMed]
10. Jawahar, G.; Sagot, B.; Seddah, D. What does BERT learn about the structure of language? In Proceedings of the ACL 2019-57th Annual Meeting of the Association for Computational Linguistics, Florence, Italy, 28 July–2 August 2019.
11. Guarasci, R.; Damiano, E.; Minutolo, A.; Esposito, M.; De Pietro, G. Lexicon-grammar based open information extraction from natural language sentences in Italian. *Expert Syst. Appl.* **2020**, *143*, 112954. [CrossRef]
12. Esposito, M.; Damiano, E.; Minutolo, A.; De Pietro, G.; Fujita, H. Hybrid query expansion using lexical resources and word embeddings for sentence retrieval in question answering. *Inf. Sci.* **2020**, *514*, 88–105. [CrossRef]
13. Gulordava, K.; Bojanowski, P.; Grave, É.; Linzen, T.; Baroni, M. Colorless Green Recurrent Networks Dream Hierarchically. In Proceedings of the 2018 Conference of the North American Chapter of the Association for Computational Linguistics: Human Language Technologies, Volume 1 (Long Papers), New Orleans, LA, USA, 1–6 June 2018; pp. 1195–1205.
14. Lau, J.H.; Armendariz, C.; Lappin, S.; Purver, M.; Shu, C. How Furiously Can Colorless Green Ideas Sleep? Sentence Acceptability in Context. *Trans. Assoc. Comput. Linguist.* **2020**, *8*, 296–310. [CrossRef]
15. Mikhailov, V.; Shamardina, T.; Ryabinin, M.; Pestova, A.; Smurov, I.; Artemova, E. RuCoLA: Russian Corpus of Linguistic Acceptability. *arXiv* **2022**, arXiv:2210.12814.
16. Someya, T.; Sugimoto, Y.; Oseki, Y. JCoLA: Japanese Corpus of Linguistic Acceptability. *arXiv* **2023**, arXiv:2309.12676.
17. Jentoft, M.; Samuel, D. NocoLA: The norwegian corpus of linguistic acceptability. In Proceedings of the 24th Nordic Conference on Computational Linguistics (NoDaLiDa), Tórshavn, Faroe Islands, 22–24 May 2023; pp. 610–617.
18. Volodina, E.; Mohammed, Y.A.; Klezl, J. DaLAJ—A dataset for linguistic acceptability judgments for Swedish. In Proceedings of the 10th Workshop on NLP for Computer Assisted Language Learning, Online, May 2021; pp. 28–37.
19. Bel, N.; Punsola, M.; Ruíz-Fernández, V. EsCoLA: Spanish Corpus of Linguistic Acceptability. In Proceedings of the 2024 Joint International Conference on Computational Linguistics, Language Resources and Evaluation (LREC-COLING 2024), Torino, Italy, 20–25 May 2024; pp. 6268–6277.
20. Trotta, D.; Guarasci, R.; Leonardelli, E.; Tonelli, S. Monolingual and Cross-Lingual Acceptability Judgments with the Italian CoLA corpus. In Proceedings of the Findings of the Association for Computational Linguistics: EMNLP 2021, Punta Cana, Dominican Republic, 16–20 November 2021; pp. 2929–2940.
21. Volodina, E.; Mohammed, Y.A.; Berdičevskis, A.; Bouma, G.; Öhman, J. DaLAJ-GED-a dataset for Grammatical Error Detection tasks on Swedish. In Proceedings of the 12th Workshop on NLP for Computer Assisted Language Learning, Online, May 2023; pp. 94–101.
22. Clark, K.; Luong, M.T.; Le, Q.V.; Manning, C.D. ELECTRA: Pre-training Text Encoders as Discriminators Rather Than Generators. In Proceedings of the ICLR, Addis Ababa, Ethiopia, 26–30 April 2020.
23. Fang, H.; Xu, G.; Long, Y.; Tang, W. An Effective ELECTRA-Based Pipeline for Sentiment Analysis of Tourist Attraction Reviews. *Appl. Sci.* **2022**, *12*, 10881. [CrossRef]
24. Gargiulo, F.; Minutolo, A.; Guarasci, R.; Damiano, E.; De Pietro, G.; Fujita, H.; Esposito, M. An ELECTRA-Based Model for Neural Coreference Resolution. *IEEE Access* **2022**, *10*, 75144–75157. [CrossRef]

25. Guarasci, R.; Minutolo, A.; Damiano, E.; De Pietro, G.; Fujita, H.; Esposito, M. ELECTRA for neural coreference resolution in Italian. *IEEE Access* **2021**, *9*, 115643–115654. [CrossRef]
26. Kuo, C.C.; Chen, K.Y. Toward zero-shot and zero-resource multilingual question answering. *IEEE Access* **2022**, *10*, 99754–99761. [CrossRef]
27. Italian Corpus of Linguistic Acceptability (Repository). Available online: https://paperswithcode.com/dataset/itacola (accessed on 24 April 2024).
28. Bonetti, F.; Leonardelli, E.; Trotta, D.; Raffaele, G.; Tonelli, S. Work Hard, Play Hard: Collecting Acceptability Annotations through a 3D Game. In Proceedings of the Thirteenth Language Resources and Evaluation Conference, European Language Resources Association, Marseille, France, 20–25 June 2022; pp. 1740–1750.
29. Cho, H. Analyzing ChatGPT's Judgments on Nativelikeness of Sentences Written by English Native Speakers and Korean EFL Learners. *Multimed.-Assist. Lang. Learn.* **2023**, *26*, 9–32.
30. Qiu, Z.; Duan, X.; Cai, Z.G. Grammaticality Representation in ChatGPT as Compared to Linguists and Laypeople. *arXiv* **2024**, arXiv:2406.11116.
31. Ranaldi, L.; Pucci, G. Knowing knowledge: Epistemological study of knowledge in transformers. *Appl. Sci.* **2023**, *13*, 677. [CrossRef]
32. Linzen, T.; Oseki, Y. The reliability of acceptability judgments across languages. *Glossa J. Gen. Linguist.* **2018**, *3*, 100.
33. Cherniavskii, D.; Tulchinskii, E.; Mikhailov, V.; Proskurina, I.; Kushnareva, L.; Artemova, E.; Barannikov, S.; Piontkovskaya, I.; Piontkovski, D.; Burnaev, E. Acceptability judgements via examining the topology of attention maps. *arXiv* **2022**. arXiv:2205.09630.
34. Wang, A.; Singh, A.; Michael, J.; Hill, F.; Levy, O.; Bowman, S. GLUE: A Multi-Task Benchmark and Analysis Platform for Natural Language Understanding. In Proceedings of the 2018 EMNLP Workshop BlackboxNLP: Analyzing and Interpreting Neural Networks for NLP, Brussels, Belgium, 1 November 2018; pp. 353–355.
35. Lan, Z.; Chen, M.; Goodman, S.; Gimpel, K.; Sharma, P.; Soricut, R. ALBERT: A Lite BERT for Self-supervised Learning of Language Representations. In Proceedings of the 8th International Conference on Learning Representations, ICLR 2020, Addis Ababa, Ethiopia, 26–30 April 2020.
36. Wang, W.; Bi, B.; Yan, M.; Wu, C.; Xia, J.; Bao, Z.; Peng, L.; Si, L. StructBERT: Incorporating Language Structures into Pre-training for Deep Language Understanding. In Proceedings of the 8th International Conference on Learning Representations, ICLR 2020, Addis Ababa, Ethiopia, 26–30 April 2020.
37. Wang, S.; Fang, H.; Khabsa, M.; Mao, H.; Ma, H. Entailment as Few-Shot Learner. *arXiv* **2021**, arXiv:2104.14690.
38. Someya, T.; Oseki, Y. JBLiMP: Japanese Benchmark of Linguistic Minimal Pairs. In Proceedings of the Findings of the Association for Computational Linguistics: EACL 2023, Toronto, ON, Canada, 9–14 July 2023; pp. 1536–1549.
39. Xiang, B.; Yang, C.; Li, Y.; Warstadt, A.; Kann, K. CLiMP: A Benchmark for Chinese Language Model Evaluation. In Proceedings of the 16th Conference of the European Chapter of the Association for Computational Linguistics: Main Volume, Online, 19–23 April 2021; pp. 2784–2790. [CrossRef]
40. Hu, H.; Zhang, Z.; Huang, W.; Lai, J.Y.K.; Li, A.; Patterson, Y.; Huang, J.; Zhang, P.; Lin, C.J.C.; Wang, R. Revisiting Acceptability Judgements. *arXiv* **2023**, arXiv:2305.14091.
41. Sprouse, J.; Almeida, D. The empirical status of data in syntax: A reply to Gibson and Fedorenko. *Lang. Cogn. Processes* **2013**, *28*, 222–228. [CrossRef]
42. Lau, J.H.; Clark, A.; Lappin, S. Measuring gradience in speakers' grammaticality judgements. In Proceedings of the Annual Meeting of the Cognitive Science Society, Quebec City, QC, Canada, 23–26 July 2014; Volume 36.
43. Marvin, R.; Linzen, T. Targeted Syntactic Evaluation of Language Models. *arXiv* **2019**, arXiv:1808.09031.
44. Feldhausen, I.; Buchczyk, S. Testing the reliability of acceptability judgments for subjunctive obviation in French. In Proceedings of the Going Romance 2020, Online, 25–27 November 2020.
45. Chen, Z.; Xu, Y.; Xie, Z. Assessing introspective linguistic judgments quantitatively: The case of The Syntax of Chinese. *J. East Asian Linguist.* **2020**, *29*, 311–336. [CrossRef]
46. Brunato, D.; Chesi, C.; Dell'Orletta, F.; Montemagni, S.; Venturi, G.; Zamparelli, R. AcCompl-it @ EVALITA2020: Overview of the Acceptability & Complexity Evaluation Task for Italian. In Proceedings of the Seventh Evaluation Campaign of Natural Language Processing and Speech Tools for Italian. Final Workshop (EVALITA 2020), Online Event, 17 December 2020; Basile, V., Croce, D., Maro, M.D., Passaro, L.C., Eds.; CEUR Workshop Proceedings; Volume 2765.
47. Guarasci, R.; Buonaiuto, G.; De Pietro, G.; Esposito, M. Applying Variational Quantum Classifier on Acceptability Judgements: A QNLP experiment. *Numer. Comput. Theory Algorithms NUMTA* **2023**, 116.
48. Sprouse, J.; Schütze, C.; Almeida, D. Assessing the reliability of journal data in syntax: Linguistic Inquiry 2001–2010. *Lingua* **2013**, *134*, 219–248. [CrossRef]
49. Snow, R.; O'connor, B.; Jurafsky, D.; Ng, A.Y. Cheap and fast–but is it good? Evaluating non-expert annotations for natural language tasks. In Proceedings of the 2008 Conference on Empirical Methods in Natural Language Processing, Honolulu, HI, USA, 25–27 October 2008; pp. 254–263.
50. Lau, J.H.; Clark, A.; Lappin, S. Grammaticality, acceptability, and probability: A probabilistic view of linguistic knowledge. *Cogn. Sci.* **2017**, *41*, 1202–1241. [CrossRef] [PubMed]
51. Fornaciari, T.; Cagnina, L.; Rosso, P.; Poesio, M. Fake opinion detection: How similar are crowdsourced datasets to real data? *Lang. Resour. Eval.* **2020**, *54*, 1019–1058. [CrossRef]

52. Ott, M.; Cardie, C.; Hancock, J.T. Negative deceptive opinion spam. In Proceedings of the 2013 Conference of the north American Chapter of the Association for Computational Linguistics: Human Language Technologies, Atlanta, GA, USA, 9–14 June 2013; pp. 497–501.
53. Guarasci, R.; Catelli, R.; Esposito, M. Classifying deceptive reviews for the cultural heritage domain: A lexicon-based approach for the Italian language. *Expert Syst. Appl.* **2024**, *252*, 124131. [CrossRef]
54. Ruan, N.; Deng, R.; Su, C. GADM: Manual fake review detection for O2O commercial platforms. *Comput. Secur.* **2020**, *88*, 101657. [CrossRef]
55. Devlin, J.; Chang, M.W.; Lee, K.; Toutanova, K. BERT: Pre-training of Deep Bidirectional Transformers for Language Understanding. In Proceedings of the 2019 Conference of the North American Chapter of the Association for Computational Linguistics: Human Language Technologies, Volume 1 (Long and Short Papers), Minneapolis, MN, USA, 2–7 June 2019; pp. 4171–4186. [CrossRef]
56. Vaswani, A.; Shazeer, N.; Parmar, N.; Uszkoreit, J.; Jones, L.; Gomez, A.N.; Kaiser, Ł.; Polosukhin, I. Attention is all you need. *Adv. Neural Inf. Processing Syst.* **2017**, *30*.
57. Sun, C.; Qiu, X.; Xu, Y.; Huang, X. How to fine-tune bert for text classification? In Proceedings of the China national conference on Chinese computational linguistics, Kunming, China, 18–20 October 2019; Springer: Cham, Switzerland, 2019; pp. 194–206.
58. dbmdz BERT and ELECTRA Models. Available online: https://huggingface.co/dbmdz/bert-base-italian-xxl-cased (accessed on 20 June 2024).
59. Open Source Project on Multilingual Resources for Machine Learning (OSCAR). Available online: https://traces1.inria.fr/oscar/ (accessed on 20 June 2024).
60. OPUS Corpora Collection. Available online: http://opus.nlpl.eu/ (accessed on 20 June 2024).
61. Rogers, A.; Kovaleva, O.; Rumshisky, A. A primer in bertology: What we know about how bert works. *Trans. Assoc. Comput. Linguist.* **2020**, *8*, 842–866. [CrossRef]
62. Electra Base Iitalian XXL Cased. Available online: https://huggingface.co/dbmdz/electra-base-italian-xxl-cased-discriminator (accessed on 20 June 2024).
63. Peters, M.; Neumann, M.; Iyyer, M.; Gardner, M.; Clark, C.; Lee, K.; Zettlemoyer, L. Deep Contextualized Word Representations. In Proceedings of the 2018 Conference of the North American Chapter of the Association for Computational Linguistics: Human Language Technologies, Volume 1 (Long Papers), New Orleans, LA, USA, 1–6 June 2018; pp. 2227–2237.
64. Hochreiter, S.; Schmidhuber, J. Long short-term memory. *Neural Comput.* **1997**, *9*, 1735–1780. [CrossRef] [PubMed]
65. Liu, H. Dependency direction as a means of word-order typology: A method based on dependency treebanks. *Lingua* **2010**, *120*, 1567–1578. [CrossRef]
66. Di Liello, L.; Gabburo, M.; Moschitti, A. Efficient pre-training objectives for transformers. *arXiv* **2021**, arXiv:2104.09694.
67. Margiotta, V. Modeling and Classifying Textual Data through Transformer-Based Architecture: A Comparative Approach in Natural Language Processing. Ph.D. Thesis, Politecnico di Torino, Turin, Italy, 2021.
68. Tepecik, A.; Demir, E. Emotion Detection with Pre-Trained Language Models BERT and ELECTRA Analysis of Turkish Data. *Intell. Methods Eng. Sci.* **2024**, *3*, 7–12.
69. Warstadt, A.; Bowman, S.R. Grammatical Analysis of Pretrained Sentence Encoders with Acceptability Judgments. *arXiv* **2019**, arXiv:1901.03438.
70. Burzio, L. *Italian Syntax: A Government-Binding Approach*; Springer Science & Business Media: Berlin/Heidelberg, Germany, 1986; Volume 1.
71. Manning, C.D.; Sag, I.A. Argument structure, valence, and binding. *Nord. J. Linguist.* **1998**, *21*, 107–144. [CrossRef]
72. Chesi, C. An efficient Trie for binding (and movement). *Comput. Linguist. Clic-It* **2018**, 105.
73. Brunato, D.; De Mattei, L.; Dell'Orletta, F.; Iavarone, B.; Venturi, G. Is this Sentence Difficult? Do you Agree? In Proceedings of the 2018 Conference on Empirical Methods in Natural Language Processing, Brussels, Belgium, 31 October–4 November 2018; pp. 2690–2699.
74. Varda, A.G.d.; Marelli, M. Data-driven Cross-lingual Syntax: An Agreement Study with Massively Multilingual Models. *Comput. Linguist.* **2023**, *49*, 261–299. [CrossRef]
75. Marulli, F.; Pota, M.; Esposito, M.; Maisto, A.; Guarasci, R. Tuning syntaxnet for pos tagging italian sentences. *Lect. Notes Data Eng. Commun. Technol.* **2018**, *13*, 314–324. [CrossRef]
76. Warstadt, A.; Parrish, A.; Liu, H.; Mohananey, A.; Peng, W.; Wang, S.F.; Bowman, S.R. BLiMP: The benchmark of linguistic minimal pairs for English. *Trans. Assoc. Comput. Linguist.* **2020**, *8*, 377–392. [CrossRef]
77. Buonaiuto, G.; Guarasci, R.; Minutolo, A.; De Pietro, G.; Esposito, M. Quantum transfer learning for acceptability judgements. *Quantum Mach. Intell.* **2024**, *6*, 13. [CrossRef]
78. Li, L.; Li, Z.; Chen, Y.; Li, S.; Zhou, G. Prompt-Free Few-Shot Learning with ELECTRA for Acceptability Judgment. In Proceedings of the CCF International Conference on Natural Language Processing and Chinese Computing, Foshan, China, 12–15 October 2023; Springer: Cham, Switzerland, 2023; pp. 43–54.

electronics

MDPI

Article

Self-HCL: Self-Supervised Multitask Learning with Hybrid Contrastive Learning Strategy for Multimodal Sentiment Analysis

Youjia Fu [1], Junsong Fu [1,*], Huixia Xue [1] and Zihao Xu [2]

[1] College of Computer Science and Engineering, Chongqing University of Technology, Chongqing 400054, China; youjia_fu@cqut.edu.cn (Y.F.); xue_xue@stu.cqut.edu.cn (H.X.)
[2] Liangjiang Institute of Artificial Intelligence, Chongqing University of Technology, Chongqing 401135, China; xu139@stu.cqut.edu.cn
* Correspondence: juns_fu@stu.cqut.edu.cn

Abstract: Multimodal Sentiment Analysis (MSA) plays a critical role in many applications, including customer service, personal assistants, and video understanding. Currently, the majority of research on MSA is focused on the development of multimodal representations, largely owing to the scarcity of unimodal annotations in MSA benchmark datasets. However, the sole reliance on multimodal representations to train models results in suboptimal performance due to the insufficient learning of each unimodal representation. To this end, we propose Self-HCL, which initially optimizes the unimodal features extracted from a pretrained model through the Unimodal Feature Enhancement Module (UFEM), and then uses these optimized features to jointly train multimodal and unimodal tasks. Furthermore, we employ a Hybrid Contrastive Learning (HCL) strategy to facilitate the learned representation of multimodal data, enhance the representation ability of multimodal fusion through unsupervised contrastive learning, and improve the model's performance in the absence of unimodal annotations through supervised contrastive learning. Finally, based on the characteristics of unsupervised contrastive learning, we propose a new Unimodal Label Generation Module (ULGM) that can stably generate unimodal labels in a short training period. Extensive experiments on the benchmark datasets CMU-MOSI and CMU-MOSEI demonstrate that our model outperforms state-of-the-art methods.

Keywords: contrastive learning; feature optimization; multitask learning; multimodal sentiment analysis

1. Introduction

The rapid development of neural network modeling has brought diverse techniques and methods to the field of human–computer interaction. Long Short-Term Memory Networks (LSTMs) [1] have effectively solved the limitations of traditional Recurrent Neural Networks (RNNs) [2] in dealing with long-term dependencies by introducing a gating mechanism, which is especially suitable for analyzing and predicting time series data. The Transformer model based on the self-attention mechanism is able to deal with long-range dependencies and is now widely used in various sequence modeling tasks. In addition, "Knowing knowledge: Epistemological study of knowledge in transformers [3]" investigates the role of neural models in human–computer interaction, thus providing new perspectives for understanding how neural networks facilitate knowledge exchange.

Multimodal sentiment analysis (MSA) plays a crucial role in the field of human–computer interaction and has become a hot research topic in recent years [4]. MSA has received much attention in recent years compared to traditional unimodal sentiment analysis methods, MSA has demonstrated significant advantages in terms of robustness, and it has made breakthroughs in processing social media data in particular. With the explosive growth of user-generated content, MSA has been used in a wide range of domains, including social monitoring, consumer services, and the transcription of video content. By integrating information from different modalities, such as textual, audio, and visual data, this analytic approach is able to capture and parse the user's affective state more comprehensively, thus improving the accuracy and reliability of sentiment recognition.

Today, research in MSA mainly focuses on how to effectively learn joint representations. Researchers have evolved their work from tensor-based approaches [5] to approaches based on attention mechanisms [6,7], and they have continuously worked on designing modules that capture crossmodal information interactions and utilize multimodal representations to train models. However, relying solely on multimodal representations to train models often leads to suboptimal performance [8]. This is mainly due to the lack of unimodal annotations in the MSA benchmark dataset, thereby making it difficult for models to capture unimodal-specific information. As shown in Figure 1, uniform multimodal labels are not always appropriate for unimodal learning, which limits the model's ability to understand each unimodal state in depth. A number of attempts have been made by some researchers to solve this problem. Yu et al. [9] proposed the Self-MM, which calculates the distance between the modal representation and the category centroid to quantify the degree of similarity. Han et al. [10] designed the MMIM, which enhances the effect of multimodal fusion by increasing the mutual information between unimodal representations and the shared information between fusion embedding and unimodal representations. Furthermore, Hwang et al. [11] presented SUGRM using recalibration information to generate unimodal annotations with dynamically adjusted features. However, how to better learn unimodal feature representations and optimize multimodal feature representations in the absence of unimodal annotations remains to be further explored.

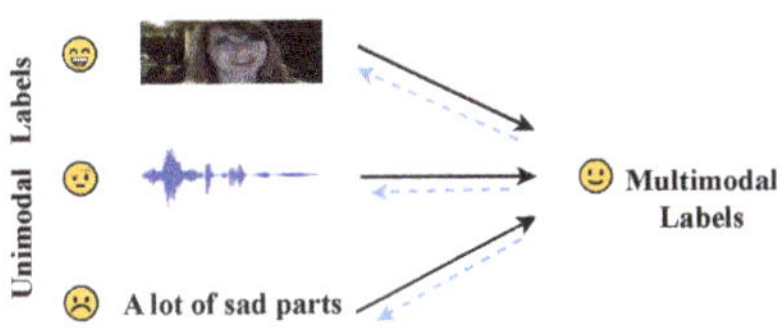

Figure 1. An example of unimodal labels and multimodal labels. The blue dotted lines represent the process of backpropagation.

In order to address the above problems, we designed an innovative Multimodal Sentiment Analysis framework called Self-HCL. The framework initially employs the Unimodal Feature Enhancement Module (UFEM) to optimize the learning of unimodal features. Specifically, the UFEM computes and assigns attentional weights to modal features in the channel and spatial dimensions by using the Convolutional Block Attention Module (CBAM) [12]. It then uses these weights to optimize the representation of unimodal features by finely tuning the original features and selectively reinforcing them through gating mechanisms and elemental multiplication. Next, the Sparse Phased Transformer (SPT) [13] is used to capture and integrate the final feature representations for each modality. In addition, Self-HCL integrates a Hybrid Contrastive Learning (HCL) strategy to optimize the representation learning process for multimodal data. On the one hand, we adopt the principle of Unsupervised Contrast Learning (UCL) [14], which enhances the extraction of interrelated information between the fused features and each unimodal modality through iterative operations so as to reveal the deep relationships between modalities and optimize the spatial layout of fused features. On the other hand, to address the problem of the scarcity of unimodal annotation data, we introduce a Supervised Comparative Learning (SCL) strategy. We map the features of different modalities into the same high-dimensional feature space to facilitate the aggregation of samples with the same emotion label in the embedding space while ensuring the differentiation of differently labeled samples. Finally, we improve the Unimodal Label Generation Module (ULGM) proposed by Hwang et al. [11]. We constructed a new UCL space based on it and combined with the properties of UCL, which enables the ULGM to output unimodal labels stably in a shorter period of time. The improved ULGM not only fully utilizes the advantages of contrast learning in mining feature differences and uniqueness, but it also successfully overcomes the limitations encountered by Hwang et al. [11] in dealing with the modal feature similarity puzzle. To summarize, the primary contributions of this work are as follows:

- We construct a novel MSA framework called Self-HCL, which improves the identification of salient features in the absence of unimodal annotation using the UFEM and optimizes the features by combining the gating mechanism with element multiplication, which effectively improves the representation learning of unimodal features.
- A hybrid contrastive learning strategy is designed for the purpose of deep exploration of the fused multimodal features and the inherent relationship between each single modal feature and emotional labels.
- We propose an improved ULGM, which reveals the deep relationship between different modalities and optimizes the spatial distribution of modal features by constructing a new unsupervised contrastive learning space, thus achieving the stable generation of unimodal labels within a short training cycle.

2. Related Work

2.1. Multimodal Sentiment Analysis

Multimodal Sentiment Analysis (MSA) is an approach for identifying and understanding emotions by analyzing speech, facial expressions, voice, music, and body movements. The discipline has advanced using publicly available datasets, including CMU-MOSI, CMU-MOSEI, and IEMOCAP [15]. There are three main MSA research directions: (1) Initially, multimodal fusion used techniques like tensor fusion networks [6] and low-rank multimodal fusion [16] with LSTM [1] to create high-dimensional tensors for integrating diverse data sources. (2) Modal interaction modeling [17] explores complex interactions between modalities using MCTN [18] and MulT [4], which enhance intermodal transformations using cyclic consistency loss and the Transformer architecture encoder/decoder, respectively. Sun et al. [19] offered deep normalized correlation analysis for improved intermodal consistency in high-dimensional nonlinear spaces. (3) Mode consistency and disparity techniques, which seek coherence and highlight discrepancies between modalities, have garnered attention. For example, Yu et al. [9] created a self-supervised learning module for label generation in multimodal and unimodal training tasks, thus minimizing mode differences. Han et al. [10] used mutual information in MSA and proposed a learning framework to preserve task-relevant information. In their model MISA [5], modal vectors were mapped into two spaces, and regularization was added to aid in learning shared and distinct modal properties.

2.2. Multitask Learning

Multitask learning is a key branch of machine learning that focuses on optimizing the connections between multiple related tasks simultaneously [20]. It falls under the migrating learning framework, which aims to extract and apply domain-specific knowledge from training data for various related tasks. In multitask learning, model parameters act as a sharing mechanism during training, thus allowing the model to extract common feature representations from different tasks to improve its generalization across various tasks. There are two main types of parameter sharing: soft sharing, where model parameters are adjusted for different tasks, and hard sharing, where fixed global parameters aid in learning all tasks. In the field of MSA, multitask learning has been widely used to integrate information from different modalities like text, speech, and image, thus leading to improved sentiment recognition and emotion analysis [21,22].

2.3. Contrastive Learning

Contrastive learning, based on the InfoNCE theory [23], uses a loss function to increase the mutual information between feature representations of the same object from different perspectives or conditions while reducing it between unrelated objects (negative sample pairs). This approach helps the model develop more distinct feature representations. Recent methodologies like SimCLR [24] and MoCo [25] have advanced the practical applications and theoretical exploration of contrastive learning in computer vision, thus improving learning outcomes in unsupervised settings through data augmentation and queuing mechanisms. As deep learning techniques have evolved, contrastive learning has expanded beyond visual data like images to fields such as natural language processing and multimodal learning. It has been successful in extracting unified representations from various data types, including text, images, and audio. For example, Khosla et al. [26] extended contrastive learning by incorporating supervised information into the unsupervised framework, thus allowing for multiple positive samples to be associated with the same anchor sample. Moreover, Han et al. [10] enhanced contrastive learning by maximizing mutual information across different aspects of a single input instance, thus filtering and amplifying feature information relevant to the target task.

2.4. ULGM

Designed and developed by Yu et al. [9], ULGM aims to automatically generate unimodal labels for multimodal tasks. The module relies on the assumption that label differences between categories are directly related to differences in the distances of modal eigenvectors from category centers. Labels from unimodal data should align with those from multimodal fusion information. However, close interclass distances and indistinguishable category centers can lead ULGM to produce unstable or inaccurate labels, thus impacting learning stability and causing the model to converge to a local optimum. Hwang et al. [11] proposed an enhancement based on Yu et al. [9] to address this issue. The enhancement scheme generates unimodal labels based on distances between the feature space and label space. ULGM proposes that the distances between feature points in a semantic space are linked to the distances of their corresponding labels. By calculating feature distances using multimodal tag information, ULGM infers and generates unimodal tags. It considers offset size and direction, thereby determining the offset by comparing distances between multimodal and unimodal features with the maximum tag space distance and analyzing positive and negative tag center positions relative to multimodal features.

3. Approach

3.1. Problem Definition

MSA is a technique that combines multiple modal signals such as text, audio, and visual to accurately determine sentiment states. In this study, the input to the model is defined as I_s, where $s \in \{t, a, v\}$. And this composite input consists of three key components: textual modality, audio modality, and video modality. The core task of the model is to predict the corresponding sentiment intensity value $\hat{y}_m \in \mathbb{R}$ after receiving inputs such as I_s. To optimize the learning process of the model, in the training phase, we generate the corresponding labels $y_s \in \mathbb{R}$ for each modality separately. Although the model can produce multiple potential outputs, in practical applications, we only select $\hat{y}_m \in \mathbb{R}$ as the final sentiment prediction index.

3.2. Overall Architecture

Self-HCL facilitates the sharing of fundamental modal representations by incorporating multimodal tasks, unimodal activities, and hybrid contrastive learning tasks. When faced with problems that involve several modes of input and various types of unimodal tasks, we employ a hard sharing method to construct a shared underlying learning network. Figure 2 depicts the comprehensive structure of Self-HCL, thus showcasing how modal representation information may be efficiently exchanged and utilized across activities. In Figure 2, y_s is the unimodal annotation generated by ULGM based on the manually annotated multimodal labels y_m for supervised learning of the unimodal task. $\hat{y}_s$ and $\hat{y}_m$

are the predicted sentiments for the unimodal task and the multimodal task, respectively, where $s \in \{t, a, v\}$.

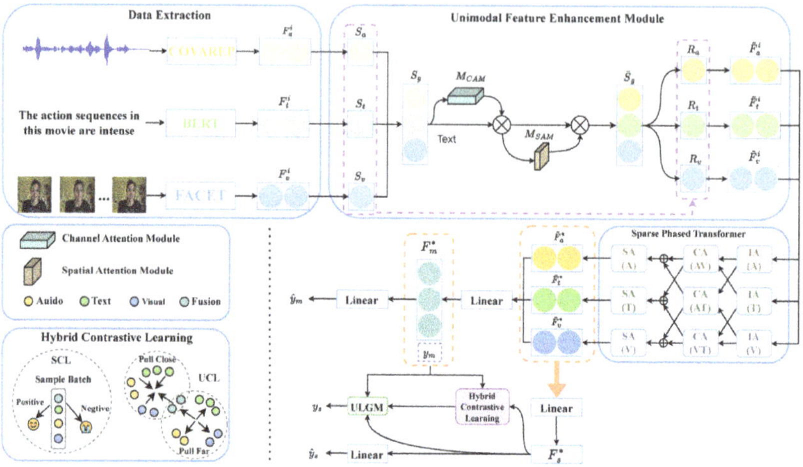

Figure 2. Overall architecture of Self-HCL.

3.3. Multimodal Task

For the multimodal task, we extract modality features F_s^i from pretrained BERT [27], COVAREP [28], and FACET [29] models for textual, acoustic, and visual input, respectively. Subsequently, the Unimodal Feature Enhancement Module (UFEM) is employed to optimize the extracted features for each modality type, and the Sparse Phased Transformer (SPT) is utilized to capture and integrate the final feature representation for each modality.

Unimodal Feature Enhancement Module: The UFEM primarily utilizes the Convolutional Block Attention Module (CBAM) [12], a specialized attention mechanism module designed for Convolutional Neural Networks (CNNs) [30], thus aiming to enhance the network's expressiveness and performance in processing visual tasks by strengthening the attention to key features. The CBAM comprises two primary modules: the Channel Attention Module (CAM) and the Spatial Attention Module (SAM). Here, we show how the CBAM can be applied to the UFEM. The UFEM receives $F_s^i \in \mathbb{R}^{l_s \times d_s}$ as input, where l_s is the length of the sequence, and d_s is the modal feature dimension, and we squeeze the input along the sequence length using global average pooling:

$$S_s(d) = \frac{1}{l_s} \sum_{l=1}^{l_s} F_s^i(l, d) \tag{1}$$

where $s \in \{t, a, v\}$, and $d = 1, 2, .., ds$. The compression feature S_s is then connected and fed into a series of fully connected networks and ReLU to learn the global multimodal embedding S_g:

$$S_g = ReLU(W_g[S_t; S_a; S_v] + b_g) \tag{2}$$

where $[;]$ denotes the feature concatenate, W_z is a 3×3 weight matrix, and b_z is a bias term. The global multimodal embedding S_g is then fed into the channel attention module, which is compressed into two one-dimensional vectors by average pooling and maximum pooling, which are then passed through a shared Multilayer Perceptron (MLP) and finally normalized to the interval [0,1] by the sigmoid function to obtain the M_{CAM}:

$$M_{CAM} = \sigma(MLP(\eta(S_g)) + MLP(\gamma(S_g))) \tag{3}$$

where $\sigma(\cdot)$ denotes the sigmoid function, and η and γ represent average pooling and maximum pooling, respectively. Similarly, in the SAM, average pooling and maximum pooling are again performed to aggregate the feature information and generate the 2D spatial attention map M_{SAM} using a convolutional layer of size 7×7:

$$M_{SAM} = \sigma(f^{7\times7}([\eta(M_{CAM}); \gamma(M_{CAM})])) \tag{4}$$

where $f^{7\times7}$ represents a convolutional layer of size 7×7, and η and γ represent average pooling and maximum pooling, respectively. Accordingly, the augmented feature S_g adjusted by CAM and SAM weighting is denoted as follows:

$$\bar{S}_g = M_{SAM} \otimes M_{CAM} \tag{5}$$

where $\otimes$ denotes the elemental multiplication. The dimensions are then restored to the original modal features using a fully connected layer:

$$R_s = W_s \bar{S}_g + b_s \tag{6}$$

where W_s and b_s represent the fusion weight matrices and bias terms of the fully linked network. Finally, the original input features are recalibrated using a gating mechanism:

$$\tilde{F}_s^i = 2 \times \sigma(R_s) \otimes F_s^i \tag{7}$$

where $\sigma(\cdot)$ denotes the sigmoid function, $f^{7\times7}$ denotes the elemental multiplication, and the coefficient 2 in Equation (7) serves as an amplification factor to further enhance the impact of the important features and ensure that the important features can receive more attention during the feature importance adjustment process. Overall, the textual, acoustic, and visual features after UFEM augmentation can be described as follows:

$$\tilde{F}_s^i = UFEM(F_s^i; \theta^{UFEM}) \in \mathbb{R}^{l_s \times d_s} \tag{8}$$

where θ^{UFEM} represents all the learnable parameters in the UFEM.

Sparse Phased Transformer: In the multimodal task, we use the Sparse Phased Transformer, SPT [13], architecture to extract the respective final feature representations from the data of different modalities. For any unimodal feature $\tilde{F}_s^i$, the final feature representation obtained after applying the SPT can be expressed as follows:

$$\tilde{F}_s^* = SPT(\tilde{F}_s^i; \theta^{spt}) \tag{9}$$

where θ^{spt} is the learnable parameter of the SPT, and $s \in \{t, a, v\}$. To obtain the fused feature representation, we first concatenate each unimodal feature representation and then project each one into a lower-dimensional feature space $\mathbb{R}^{d_c}$. This process can be specifically expressed through linear transformation:

$$F_m^* = ReLU(W_1^m[\tilde{F}_t^*; \tilde{F}_a^*; \tilde{F}_v^*] + b_1^m) \tag{10}$$

where $\tilde{F}_t^*; \tilde{F}_a^*; \tilde{F}_v^*$ denote the final eigenvectors of the text, audio, and visual modalities, respectively, and W_1^m and b_1^m are the corresponding fusion weight matrices and bias terms. Finally, sentiment prediction based on the fused multimodal feature vectors is implemented:

$$\hat{y}_m = W_2^m F_m^* + b_2^m \tag{11}$$

where F_m^* is the fused multimodal eigenvector, W_2^m and b_2^m represent the weight matrix and bias term of the sentiment prediction output layer, respectively, and $\hat{y}_m$ is the predicted sentiment label.

3.4. Unimodal Task

In the three unimodal tasks, we adopt the same modal characterization approach as the multimodal task, thus mapping each feature representation to the common semantic feature space $\mathbb{R}^{d_c}$ as follows:

$$F_s^* = ReLU(W_1^s \tilde{F}_s^* + b_1^s) \tag{12}$$

where $s \in \{t, a, v\}$. Next, the feature representations for each modality are further processed through their respective independent fully connected layer networks to obtain the corresponding sentiment prediction output for each modality:

$$\hat{y}_s = W_2^s F_s^* + b_2^s \tag{13}$$

In order to facilitate the training process of the unimodal task, we have developed a novel ULGM, which is capable of generating unimodal labels. A detailed description of the specific architecture of the ULGM and its working principle will be provided in Section 3.6. The ULGM is calculated as follows:

$$y_s = ULGM(y_m, F_m^*, F_s^*, \theta^{ULGM}) \tag{14}$$

where y_m stands for multimodal labels, and θ^{ULGM} stands for ULGM learnable parameters. Finally, we adopted a joint learning strategy that combines the manually annotated multimodal label y_m and the automatically generated single modal label y_s to jointly train a multimodal task and three unimodal subtasks that are only relevant during the training phase. It is important to emphasize that these unimodal tasks only exist during the training period. Consequently, we utilize $\hat{y}_m$ as the ultimate result.

3.5. Hybrid Contrastive Learning

Unsupervised Contrastive Learning: Although the SPT successfully improves the expressiveness of fused features, it does not deeply explore the intrinsic connections between unimodal features F_s^i and fused features F_m^*. Therefore, we use Unsupervised Contrastive Learning (UCL) with the aim of strengthening these connections and further optimizing the quality of fusion features. The goal of our design is to maximize the mutual information between the fused features and the inputs of each unimodal modality, which is optimized through repeated iterative optimization; thus, the network can effectively transition from each independent modality to the fusion features. Given that the current Self-HCL has obtained the multimodal fusion result F_m^* via the SPT network, an effective mapping from the fusion feature F_m^* back to each unimodal input F_s^i has not yet been established. Therefore, we follow the operation of [10] and adopt a strategy to measure the correlation between them using a function $Corr(\cdot)$ with normalized prediction vectors and true vectors, which is defined as follows:

$$\bar{G}_\varphi(F_m^*) = \frac{G_\varphi(F_m^*)}{||G_\varphi(F_m^*)||_2}, \bar{F}_s^i = \frac{F_s^i}{||F_s^i||_2} \tag{15}$$

$$Corr(F_s^i, F_m^*) = exp(\bar{F}_s^i(\bar{G}_\varphi(F_m^*))^T) \tag{16}$$

where G_φ is a neural network with parameter φ that generates the prediction of F_s^i from F_m^*, and $||\cdot||_2$ is the $L2$ normalization. The loss between individual modalities and fused features is computed by treating all other modal representations as negative samples in the same batch of samples:

$$\mathcal{L}_{F_m^*, F_s^i} = -\mathbb{E}_s \left[log \frac{Corr(F_m^*, F_s^i)}{\sum_j^N Corr(F_m^*, F_s^j)} \right] \tag{17}$$

where N is the number of samples in the batch, and $\mathcal{L}_{F_m^*,F_s^i}$ denotes the contrastive learning loss function between the two vectors F_m^* and F_s^i. Ultimately, the overall loss function of the UCL consists of the sum of the losses of the fused features F_m^* with respect to the textual, visual, and audio modalities:

$$\mathcal{L}_{UCL} = \mathcal{L}_{m,t} + \mathcal{L}_{m,a} + \mathcal{L}_{m,v} \tag{18}$$

where m represents the fusion feature F_m^*.

Supervised Contrastive Learning: By utilizing the label information to the fullest, Supervised Contrastive Learning (SCL) treats all samples in the collection with the same label as positive samples and those with different labels as negative samples, thus presuming that attention will be paid to specific key labels. In particular, when dealing with datasets such as CMU-MOSI and CMU-MOSEI, which are only labeled with multimodal labels but not unimodal labels, the SCL approach can skillfully utilize the label information to achieve efficient feature learning and expression enhancement. Specifically, the model first encodes the different modal features (e.g., text, audio, visual) corresponding to the samples within each batch into consistent high-dimensional vectors. Embeddings of similarly labeled samples will be close to each other during the comparison learning process, while dissimilarly labeled samples will be far away from each other. This facilitates Self-HCL to capture potential semantic associations between different modalities related to specific sentiment categories and to combine information from multiple modalities to accomplish effective sentiment recognition tasks despite the lack of unimodal fine-grained labeling. The SCL loss $\mathcal{L}_{SCL}$ is computed as follows:

$$Z = [F_t^i; F_a^i; F_v^i; F_m^*] \tag{19}$$

$$SIM(p,i) = log\frac{\exp((Z_i \cdot Z_p)/\tau)}{\sum_{a \in A(i)} \exp(Z_i \cdot Z_p/\tau)} \tag{20}$$

$$\mathcal{L}_{SCL} = \sum_{i \in I} \frac{-1}{|P(i)|} \sum_{p \in P(i)} SIM(p,i) \tag{21}$$

where $Z \in \mathbb{R}^{L \times d}$, $i \in I = \{1,2,...,L\}$ denotes the index of a batch of samples, $\tau \in \mathbb{R}^+$ denotes the temperature coefficient used to control the distances between the samples, $P(i) = I_{j=i} - \{i\}$ denotes the samples that share the same sentiment category as i but exclude i itself, $P(i)$ denotes the number of samples, and $A(i) = I - \{i\}$ denotes the samples in a batch of samples other than itself.

3.6. ULGM

The objective of the ULGM is to generate labels for each unimodality by applying multimodal labels and modality representations. Our ULGM design has been extended and optimized based on the work of Hwang et al. [11], whose design concept is that the distance between two features in the common semantic feature space is proportional to the distance between the corresponding labels in the Label Space. Based on this concept, and combining the features of unsupervised contrastive learning, we propose the Unsupervised Contrastive Learning Space (UCL Space). In the UCL Space, we map the data of different modalities into a unified representation space. In this space, if data points have similar attributes, they tend to be close to each other and form tight clusters, thus reflecting the similarity between data points. In contrast, data points that belong to different categories or have significant differences will be mapped to the far end of the space, thus highlighting the differences between them. The architecture of these three feature spaces is illustrated in Figure 3. In summary, the ULGM scheme is based on two key assumptions and mechanisms:

(1) The Common Semantic Feature Space is consistent with Label Space: The distance $D^F_{m\to s}$ between the eigenvectors of Fusion feature F^*_m and the eigenvectors of the unimodal feature F^*_s should be proportional to the semantic or categorical distance $D^L_{m\to s}$ between the labels of the two modalities corresponding to the two modalities in the Label Space.

(2) The Common Semantic Feature Space is associated with the UCL Space: The distance $D^F_{m\to s}$ within the feature space matches the relative position $D^C_{m\to s}$ between the fusion feature F^*_m and unimodal feature F^*_s embodied in the unsupervised contrastive learning. In summary, the design philosophy of the ULGM can be summarized as follows:

$$D^F_{m\to s} \propto D^L_{m\to s}, D^F_{m\to s} \propto D^C_{m\to s} \tag{22}$$

where $s \in \{t, a, v\}$. The ULGM method proposed in this work determines the amount of deviation of a unimodal label y_s with respect to a multimodal label y_m by measuring the distance from the multimodal feature to each unimodal feature. In the process of calculating the deviation, we focus on two core elements: the magnitude and the direction.

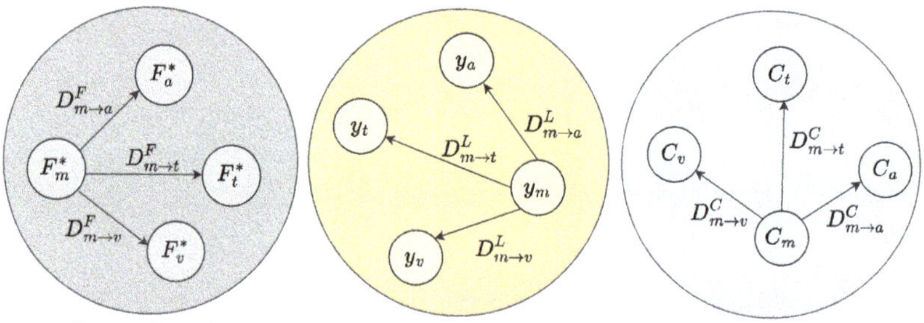

Figure 3. Schematic representation of the Common Semantic Feature Space, the Label Space, and the UCL Space.

Magnitude of Offset: To compute the offset, we argue that the greatest distance inside the common semantic feature space is proportional to the maximum distance within the Label Space. In the CMU-MOSI and CMU-MOSEI datasets, the multimodal labels vary from −3 to +3. This means that the distance between multimodal features with labels −3 (F^{*-3}_m) and +3 (F^{*+3}_m) must be the largest within the common same semantic feature space. Therefore, any $D^F_{m\to s}$ higher than the maximum distance is clipped to $D^F_{max} = ||\overline{F^{*+3}_m} - \overline{F^{*-3}_m}||$:

$$D^F_{m\to s} = \begin{cases} ||F^*_m - F^*_s||, & \text{if } D^F_{m\to s} \le D^F_{max}, \\ D^F_{max}, & \text{otherwise,} \end{cases} \tag{23}$$

where $\overline{F^{*+3}_m}$ and $\overline{F^{*-3}_m}$ are the mean values of F^{*+3}_m and F^{*-3}_m, respectively, and $||\cdot||_2$ is the $L2$ normalization. Based on the concepts and points mentioned, we can consider the following relations to calculate the offset magnitude from multimodal to unimodal labels:

$$D^F_{m\to s}/D^F_{max} = D^L_{m\to s}/D^L_{-3\to+3} \tag{24}$$

$$D^L_{m\to s} = \frac{D^F_{m\to s}}{D^F_{max}} D^L_{-3\to+3} \tag{25}$$

Under the current conditions, the unimodal labels y_s can be estimated as follows:

$$y_s = y_m + D^L_{m\to s} \tag{26}$$

For the results of UCL, due to its wider range, it is necessary to define a maximum distance that is consistent with the previous setting. Therefore, we set $D^{C}_{max} = ||\overline{F^{*+3}_{m}} - \overline{F^{*-3}_{m}}||$. In order to establish the connection between $D^{F}_{m\to s}$, $D^{C}_{m\to s}$, and y_s, y_m, we consider the following two relations:

$$\frac{y_s}{y_m} \propto \frac{D^{c}_{m\to s}}{D^{c}_{max}} \Rightarrow \frac{y_s}{y_m} = \frac{D^{c}_{m\to s}}{D^{c}_{max}} \Rightarrow y_s = \frac{D^{c}_{m\to s}}{D^{c}_{max}} y_m \tag{27}$$

$$y_s - y_m \propto D^{c}_{m\to s} - D^{c}_{max} \Rightarrow y_s = D^{c}_{m\to s} - D^{c}_{max} + y_m \tag{28}$$

Combining the above relations, the unimodal label y_s in this condition is obtained using equal weight summation:

$$y_s = y_m + \varphi_{cm} \tag{29}$$

where $\varphi_{cm} = y_m(\frac{D^{c}_{m\to s} - D^{c}_{max}}{2D^{c}_{max}}) + \frac{D^{c}_{m\to s} - D^{c}_{max}}{2}$.

Direction of Offset: In order to determine the direction of the offset, the spatial location of the unimodal features relative to the multimodal features is first analyzed. This process first involves obtaining the average of the multimodal features with positive annotations $\overline{F^{*+}_{m}}$ and negative annotations $\overline{F^{*-}_{m}}$ as a reference datum. Then, with reference to this benchmark, the multimodal features and unimodal features are localized in the feature space, as shown in Figure 4. By calculating the $L2$ distances from various types of modal representations (e.g., $F^{*}_{x\in\{m,t,a,v\}}$) to $\overline{F^{*+}_{m}}$ and $\overline{F^{*-}_{m}}$, the directions of the offsets can be deduced and determined accordingly:

$$Direction = \begin{cases} +, & \text{if } \frac{D^{p}_{s}}{D^{n}_{s}} < \frac{D^{p}_{m}}{D^{n}_{m}}, \\ -, & \text{if } \frac{D^{p}_{s}}{D^{n}_{s}} > \frac{D^{p}_{m}}{D^{n}_{m}}, \\ 0, & \text{if } \frac{D^{p}_{s}}{D^{n}_{s}} = \frac{D^{p}_{m}}{D^{n}_{m}}. \end{cases} \tag{30}$$

where $D^{p}_{s} = ||F^{*}_{s} - \overline{F^{*+}_{m}}||$, $D^{n}_{s} = ||F^{*}_{s} - \overline{F^{*-}_{m}}||$, $D^{p}_{m} = ||F^{*}_{s} - \overline{F^{*+}_{m}}||$, $D^{n}_{m} = ||F^{*}_{m} - \overline{F^{*-}_{m}}||$, and $||\cdot||$ are the $L2$ normalizations. Finally, the unimodal label y_s is obtained as follows:

$$y_s = \begin{cases} y_m + \alpha \times D^{L}_{m\to s} + \beta \times \varphi_{cm}, & \text{if direction is +}, \\ y_m - \alpha \times D^{L}_{m\to s} - \beta \times \varphi_{cm}, & \text{if direction is } -, \\ y_m, & \text{if direction is 0}. \end{cases} \tag{31}$$

where α and β represent the Label Space weight coefficients and the UCL Space weight coefficients, respectively.

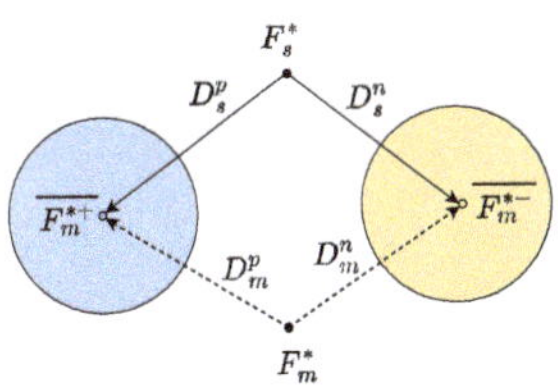

Figure 4. An illustration of the position of modality representations relative to the mean of multimodal representations with $\overline{F^{*+}_{m}}$ and $\overline{F^{*-}_{m}}$.

3.7. Objective Function for Training

We use the $\mathcal{L}_1$ loss as the main optimization objective of the model. In the unimodal task s, we use the difference between the automatically generated unimodal labels and the manually annotated multimodal labels as the weight of the loss function. This design means that the network will pay more attention to samples with large label differences, thereby improving the model's sensitivity to key differences. In addition, the unimodal task s provides an independent unimodal supervision signal and assists in multimodal task learning, thereby helping the model learn more discriminative modality-specific representations. The specific calculation formula is as follows:

$$\begin{aligned}\mathcal{L}_0 &= \mathcal{L}_1 + \frac{1}{N}\sum_{i}^{N}\sum_{s}^{\{t,a,v\}}(W_s^i \times |\hat{y}_s^i - y_s^i|) \\ &= \frac{1}{N}\sum_{i}^{N}(|\hat{y}_m^i - y_m^i|) + \frac{1}{N}\sum_{i}^{N}\sum_{s}^{\{t,a,v\}}(W_s^i \times |\hat{y}_s^i - y_s^i|) \\ &= \frac{1}{N}\sum_{i}^{N}(|\hat{y}_m^i - y_m^i| + \sum_{s}^{\{t,a,v\}} W_s^i \times |\hat{y}_s^i - y_s^i|)\end{aligned} \tag{32}$$

where N is the number of training samples. $W_s^i = \tanh(|y_s - y_m|)$ is the weight of the ith sample for the unimodal task s. The overall loss function $\mathcal{L}$ of Self-HCL combines the above components and is computed as follows:

$$\mathcal{L} = \lambda_0\mathcal{L}_0 + \lambda_1\mathcal{L}_{SCL} + \lambda_2\mathcal{L}_{UCL} \tag{33}$$

where λ_0 is the weight of the $\mathcal{L}_0$ loss, and λ_1 and λ_2 are the weights of $\mathcal{L}_{SCL}$ and $\mathcal{L}_{UCL}$, respectively, which are used to balance the contribution of different loss terms to model optimization.

4. Experimental Settings

4.1. Datasets

In this work, we conduct extensive experiments on two benchmark datasets in MSA. We give a brief introduction to each of them and summarize their basic statistics in Table 1.

CMU-MOSI: The CMU-MOSI dataset, introduced by [31], is widely acknowledged as a notable benchmark dataset for MSA. The dataset contains samples that have been annotated by human annotators with sentiment scores ranging from −3 (indicating strongly negative sentiment) to +3 (indicating very positive sentiment).

CMU-MOSEI: In contrast to CMU-MOSI, the CMU-MOSEI dataset [32] comprises a greater quantity of utterances, a more diverse sample of speakers, and a greater range of topics. In the same manner as MOSI, the CMU-MOSEI dataset is annotated with a sentiment score of −3 to +3 for each sample.

Table 1. Dataset statistics of CMU-MOSI and CMU-MOSEI.

Dataset	Train	Valid	Test	Total
CMU-MOSI	1284	229	686	2199
CMU-MOSEI	16,326	1871	4659	22,856

4.2. Baselines

In order to fully ensure the validity of Self-HCL, we provide a fair comparison between the baseline and state-of-the-art methods in the Multimodal Sentiment Analysis:

- **TFN** [6]: The Tensor Fusion Network (TFN) applies a subnetwork for modality embedding, along with tensor fusion, to understand both the intra- and intermodality dynamics.
- **LMF** [16]: Low-Rank Multimodal Fusion (LMF) carries out the fusion of multiple modalities by utilizing low-rank tensors, thus enhancing computational efficiency.

- **RAVEN** [33]: The Recurrent Attended Variation Embedding Network (RAVEN) captures the detailed structure of nonverbal subword sequences and adapts word representations in response to nonverbal signals.
- **MulT** [4]: The Multimodal Transformer (MulT) employs a crossmodal transformer with crossmodal attention to facilitate modality translation.
- **MISA** [5]: The Modality-Invariant and -Specific Representations (MISA) projects features into two separate spaces with specific constraints and performs fusion on these features.
- **MAG-BERT** [34]: The Multimodal Adaptation Gate for BERT (MAG-BERT) designs an alignment gate and inserts that into a vanilla BERT model to refine the fusion process.
- **Self-MM** [9]: Learning Modality-Specific Representations with Self-Supervised Multitask Learning (Self-MM) assigns each modality a unimodal training task with automatically generated labels, thus aiming to adjust the gradient backpropagation.
- **MMIM** [10]. Multimodal InfoMax (MMIM) uses the first implementation of the InfoMax principle on an MSA task, where the fusion representation is learned by maximizing its mutual information with unimodal representations.
- **SUGRM** [11]: The Self-Supervised Unimodal Label Generation Model (SUGRM) leverages recalibrated information to produce unimodal annotations by adaptively tuning features, thus postulating that the distance between two representations in a shared space should correspondingly reflect the distance between their associated labels in the label space.

4.3. Implementation Details

Experimental Details: Self-HCL was implemented on the Pytorch framework. For training the model, we used the Adam optimizer and implemented an early stopping strategy with eight cycles to monitor the performance of the model. To find the best combination of hyperparameters, we performed a stochastic search. Table 2 shows the detailed configuration of the CMU-MOSI and CMU-MOSEI datasets. All training and testing procedures were performed on a single NVIDIA GeForce RTX 3060 Ti GPU.

Evaluation Metrics: Following the previous works [9] , we report our experimental results in two forms: classification and regression. For classification, we report the weighted F1 score (F1-Score) and binary classification accuracy (Acc2). Specifically, for the CMU-MOSI and CMU-MOSEI datasets, we calculated the Acc-2 and F1-Score in two ways: negative/non-negative (nonexclude zero) and negative/positive (exclude zero). For the regression, we report the mean absolute error (MAE) and Pearson correlation (Corr). Except for the MAE, higher values denote better performance for all metrics.

Table 2. Main hyperparameters used in CMU-MOSI and CMU-MOSEI.

Hyperparameter	CMU-MOSI	CMU-MOSEI
Early Stop	8	8
Batch Size	32	32
LR for BERT	5×10^{-5}	5×10^{-5}
LR for Others	1×10^{-2}	1×10^{-3}
Encoder Layer	4	4
Num Heads	8	4
Output Dropout	0.3	0.1
Attn Dropout	0.3	0.1

5. Results and Analysis

5.1. Quantitative Results

The comparative results for the Multimodal Sentiment Analysis on the CMU-MOSI and CMU-MOSEI datasets are presented in Table 3. In this table, † means the results provided by MMIM [10], and ‡ is from SUGRM [11]. Models with * have been reproduced under the same conditions. Bold numbers indicate the best performance. Based on the various types of datasets, they can be categorized as aligned or unaligned. Generally, models using aligned datasets will achieve superior performance [4]. In this work, we conducted experiments using unaligned datasets on our model. As described in Table 3, we achieved significant improvements in all the assessment metrics compared to the unaligned models (TFN and LMF). Even when compared with aligned models (RAVEN, MulT, MISA, and MAG-BERT), our approach achieved competitive results. In addition, we reproduced the three best baselines Self-MM, MMIM, and SUGRM under the same conditions. We found that our model outperformed them in most of the evaluations. Specifically, in the CMU-MOSI dataset, only MMIM outperformed our model in the evaluation metric of the MAE, which we analyze as a result of the fact that MMIM uses a historical data memory mechanism for entropy estimation, which ensures the stability and accuracy of the training process. And on the CMU-MOSEI dataset, our model successfully exceeded all baseline metrics and reached the optimal level.

Table 3. Experimental results on CMU-MOSI and CMU-MOSEI.

Model				CMU-MOSI				CMU-MOSEI	Data State
	Acc-2	F1-Score	MAE	Corr	Acc-2	F1-Score	MAE	Corr	
TFN †	- /80.8	- /80.7	0.970	0.698	- /82.5	- /82.1	0.593	0.700	Unaligned
LMF †	- /82.5	- /82.4	0.917	0.695	- /82.0	- /82.1	0.623	0.677	Unaligned
RAVEN ‡	-/78.0	-/76.6	0.915	0.691	-/79.1	-/79.5	0.614	0.662	Aligned
MulT †	81.5/84.1	80.6/83.9	0.861	0.711	- /82.5	- /82.3	0.580	0.703	Aligned
MISA †	80.79/82.10	80.77/82.03	0.804	0.764	82.59/84.23	82.67/83.97	0.568	0.724	Aligned
MAG-BERT ‡	82.5/84.0	82.4/84.0	0.778	0.766	81.3/84.8	81.7/84.7	0.567	0.742	Aligned
Self-MM	84.00/85.98	84.42/85.95	0.713	0.798	82.81/85.17	82.53/85.30	0.530	0.765	Unaligned
MMIM	84.14/86.06	84.00/85.98	0.700	0.800	82.24/85.97	82.66/85.94	0.526	0.772	Unaligned
SUGRM	84.4/86.3	84.3/86.3	0.703	0.800	83.7/84.4	83.6/84.0	0.544	0.748	Unaligned
Self-MM *	82.60/84.67	82.52/84.66	0.726	0.786	82.51/84.99	82.57/85.02	0.535	0.769	Unaligned
MMIM *	82.94/**84.91**	82.81/84.84	**0.707**	0.785	82.89/85.34	82.75/85.48	0.552	0.768	Unaligned
SUGRM *	82.36/83.99	82.35/84.04	0.727	0.776	82.85/83.81	82.94/83.83	0.542	0.742	Unaligned
Ours *	**83.14/84.91**	**83.17/84.96**	0.711	**0.788**	**83.12/85.91**	**83.19/85.93**	**0.531**	**0.775**	Unaligned

5.2. Ablation Study

Unimodal Task Analysis: To evaluate the contribution of unimodal tasks in Self-HCL, we conducted experiments to test the effects of different unimodal task combinations. As shown in Table 4, the overall performance of the model was improved after integrating unimodal tasks, and M, T, A, and V represent multimodal, text, audio and visual tasks, respectively. In the CMU-MOSI dataset, the model performance improved regardless of which modality task was added individually. In particular, the "M, A, T" and "M, V, T" combinations performed better than the "M, A, V" combination. A comparable phenomenon can be observed in the CMU-MOSEI dataset. To summarize, unimodal tasks have a positive effect on enhancing model performance. Specifically, text and audio modal tasks have been demonstrated to have a more significant influence on improving performance.

UFEM: To examine the efficiency of our proposed UFEM in improving unimodal features, we performed an ablation experiment using the baseline model SUGRM [11]. We made adjustments to SUGRM: we removed its modal feature calibration (MRM) component and implanted the UFEM for feature enhancement while keeping the other modules unchanged. The same adjustment was applied to the Self-HCL to compare the performance differences between the UFEM and MRM. Table 5 shows the performance comparison results of the two models on the unaligned datasets CMU-MOSI and CMU-MOSEI. The underlined numbers indicate improved performance compared to the baseline model. As can be seen in Table 5, when our model adopted MRM , its performance generally showed a downward trend. In contrast, when the SUGRM adopted our proposed UFEM, its overall performance showed a significant improvement. This is attributed to the fact that the UFEM enhances the focus on key features and improves the expressiveness of the features, thus improving the performance of the model.

Table 4. Ablation study of unimodal task dominance using the unaligned datasets CMU-MOSI and CMU-MOSEI.

	CMU-MOSI				CMU-MOSEI			
Task	**Acc-2**	**F1-Score**	**MAE**	**Corr**	**Acc-2**	**F1-Score**	**MAE**	**Corr**
M	81.78/83.73	81.80/83.91	0.729	0.775	82.19/84.15	82.70/84.42	0.548	0.757
M, T	82.13/83.93	82.07/83.99	0.737	0.783	82.40/84.70	82.42/84.15	0.538	0.758
M, A	82.20/84.06	82.19/84.13	0.748	0.772	82.70/84.77	82.90/84.60	0.543	0.762
M, V	81.47/84.23	82.51/84.06	0.742	0.769	82.23/83.52	82.36/83.73	0.546	0.751
M, A, V	82.99/84.77	82.55/84.56	0.722	0.782	82.23/84.23	82.68/85.29	0.544	0.761
M, A, T	83.02/84.92	**83.21**/84.95	0.728	0.783	**83.20**/85.43	83.07/85.51	0.543	0.762
M, V, T	82.92/**85.08**	82.72/84.86	0.718	0.775	82.23/85.23	82.68/**86.10**	**0.529**	0.757
M, T, A, V	**83.14**/84.91	83.17/**84.96**	**0.711**	**0.788**	83.12/**85.91**	**83.19**/85.93	0.531	**0.775**

Table 5. UFEM ablation study on the unaligned datasets CMU-MOSI and CMU-MOSEI.

		CMU-MOSI				CMU-MOSEI			
Model	**Module**	**Acc-2**	**F1-Score**	**MAE**	**Corr**	**Acc-2**	**F1-Score**	**MAE**	**Corr**
SUGRM	MRM	82.36/83.99	82.35/84.04	0.727	0.776	82.85/83.81	82.94/83.83	0.542	0.742
	UFEM	82.47/84.23	82.45/84.27	0.723	0.779	83.02/84.23	83.11/84.43	0.538	0.756
Ours	MRM	82.84/84.52	82.93/84.47	0.718	0.780	82.94/85.63	82.96/85.71	0.536	0.762
	UFEM	**83.14/84.91**	**83.17/84.96**	**0.711**	**0.788**	**83.12/85.91**	**83.19/85.93**	**0.531**	**0.775**

HCL: In order to explore the impact of Hybrid Contrastive Learning (HCL) on our model performance, we conducted an ablation study on the unaligned datasets CMU-MOSI and CMU-MOSEI. Since HCL contains both Unsupervised Contrastive Learning (UCL) and Supervised Contrastive Learning (SCL) mechanisms, our ablation design was specified as follows:

- Employ w/o UCL: Remove only unsupervised contrastive learning from Self-HCL while leaving the rest unchanged.
- Employ w/o SCL: Remove only supervised contrastive learning from Self-HCL while keeping the remaining parts unaltered.

Table 6 shows the results of this ablation experiment. It is observed that when UCL was removed, the model showed a slight decrease in all the metrics, thus indicating that the UCL has a positive impact on improving the model's accuracy, F1-score, and Corr, as well as contributes to reducing the MAE. A similar trend can be observed when SCL was removed, thus confirming the effectiveness of HCL in enhancing the model in complex sentiment analysis tasks.

ULGM: The unique feature of our proposed ULGM is the introduction of a new unsupervised contrastive learning space, which is missing in the baseline model SUGRM [11]. Therefore, we did not directly apply the ULGM to the SUGRM, but we instead chose to perform ablation experiments within the Self-HCL framework. The specific settings are the following: $ULGM_{Ours}$ represents using our proposed ULGM in Self-HCL while ensuring that all other component configurations remain unchanged. For comparison, $ULGM_{SUGRM}$ represents the ULGM proposed using the SUGRM in Self-HCL while also keeping other components constant. Table 7 shows the results of the two processing methods on the unaligned CMU-MOSI and CMU-MOSEI datasets. We can observe from the table that when Self-HCL adopted the $ULGM_{SUGRM}$, various performance indicators of the model declined to varying degrees. This is because $ULGM_{SUGRM}$ faces challenges when dealing with similarity modal features, while $ULGM_{Ours}$ takes full advantage of contrastive learning in mining feature differences by introducing a new UCL Space, thereby successfully solving the limitations of $ULGM_{SUGRM}$ and ultimately improving the overall performance of the model.

Table 6. Ablation study of HCL on the unaligned datasets CMU-MOSI and CMU-MOSEI.

				CMU-MOSI				**CMU-MOSEI**
Model	**Acc-2**	**F1-Score**	**MAE**	**Corr**	**Acc-2**	**F1-Score**	**MAE**	**Corr**
w/o UCL	82.55/84.26	82.60/84.25	0.728	0.769	82.62/85.45	82.60/85.38	0.558	0.759
w/o SCL	82.78/84.23	82.86/84.57	0.722	0.773	82.87/85.68	82.86/85.68	0.546	0.762
Ours	**83.14/84.91**	**83.17/84.96**	**0.711**	**0.788**	**83.12/85.91**	**83.19/85.93**	**0.531**	**0.775**

Table 7. Ablation study of ULGM on the unaligned datasets CMU-MOSI and CMU-MOSEI.

				CMU-MOSI				**CMU-MOSEI**
Model	**Acc-2**	**F1-Score**	**MAE**	**Corr**	**Acc-2**	**F1-Score**	**MAE**	**Corr**
$ULGM_{SUGRM}$	82.49/84.30	82.58/84.33	0.727	0.768	82.50/85.47	82.66/85.58	0.552	0.760
$ULGM_{Ours}$	**83.14/84.91**	**83.17/84.96**	**0.711**	**0.788**	**83.12/85.91**	**83.19/85.93**	**0.531**	**0.775**

5.3. Case Study

HCL: To facilitate a qualitative examination of the Hybrid Contrastive Learning (HCL), we employed t-SNE [35] to visualize the preliminary distribution of some data and the hidden layer dynamics of the model subsequent to the application of HCL. As shown in Figure 5, the data without HCL processing had random distribution characteristics with no clear boundaries or clustering tendencies. In contrast, after applying HCL, the correlation between data points was optimized, the data points of the same category were aggregated to form a tight structure, and the separation between different categories was improved, thus showing stronger structure and recognizability. This shows that HCL plays a key role in improving model learning efficiency by strengthening feature fusion and contrastive learning, in addition to using multimodal label information to guide model training. Nevertheless, some data points may still be misclassified due to factors such as noise interference, modal mismatch, and sample complexity. Despite these problems, overall, HCL significantly improved the model's representation and classification performance for multimodal data. This finding prompts us to further optimize the learning strategy of the model to reduce misclassification.

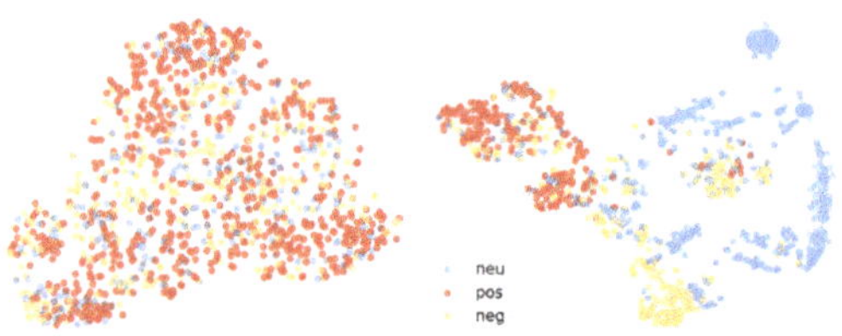

(a) Before HCL **(b)** After HCL

Figure 5. T-SNE visualization of the embedding space.

ULGM: To evaluate the performance of the ULGM, we conducted experiments on the unaligned CMU-MOSI dataset. Figure 6 shows the trajectory of the unimodal labels, which gradually stabilized as the number of training iterations increased. After approximately

12 training epochs, the unimodal label distribution generated by the ULGM showed significant stability. Furthermore, to quantitatively evaluate the quality of the multimodal labels generated by our model, we compared it with two baseline models: the Self-MM and SUGRM. Table 8 shows a detailed comparison of the fit between multimodal labels generated by different models and real labels. The results show that the multimodal labels generated by our proposed model fit the real labels more closely, which further proves the effectiveness and advancement of the ULGM.

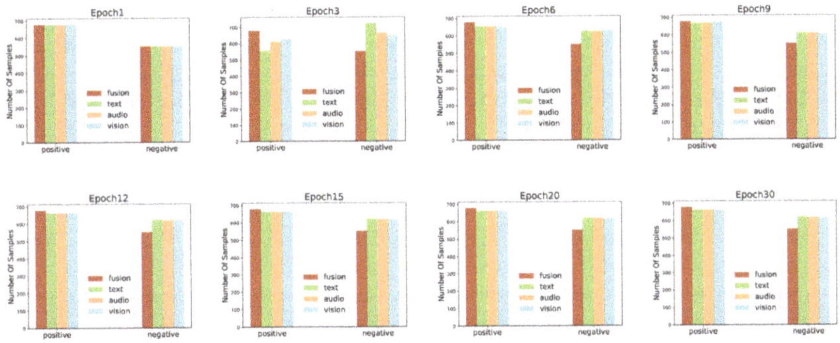

Figure 6. Visualization of the generated unimodal labels update process across epochs on the CMU-MOSI dataset.

Table 8. Case study for the Self-MM, SUGRM, and our model on the CMU-MOSI dataset.

Example	Annotation	Self-MM	SUGRM	Ours
Save your money wait till it comes out on rental. 	−2.0	−2.0	−1.9	−2.0
And I liked the first movie. I thought the first movie was really good. 	1.5	1.6	1.5	1.5
And I guess normally Shrek is for adults. 	0.0	0.1	0.1	0.0

6. Conclusions

In this work, we have presented a novel Multimodal Sentiment Analysis framework: Self-HCL. This framework optimizes the learning of unimodal feature representations in the absence of unimodal labeling by applying the Unimodal Feature Enhancement Module (UFEM), and it utilizes the Sparse Phased Transformer to capture and integrate the final feature representations for each modality. Furthermore, we implemented a Hybrid

Contrastive Learning (HCL) strategy to enhance the representation of multimodal data and proposed a novel Unimodal Label Generation Module (ULGM) to generate stable unimodal labels in a brief timeframe. Although Self-HCL introduces multiple optimization mechanisms, this may result in increased complexity and computational requirements for the model. However, we acknowledge that the introduction of multiple optimization mechanisms has increased the model's complexity and computational demands. This tradeoff between performance and computational efficiency is a critical consideration, especially in resource-constrained environments.

In light of these findings, we have identified avenues for future research. The primary focus will be on simplifying the model's architecture while striving to maintain or enhance its performance. This endeavor will involve exploring more lightweight components and algorithms that can offer comparable or superior results with reduced computational overhead. Moreover, we will delve deeper into the analysis of the results obtained, thus examining the impact of each component of Self-HCL on the overall performance. This comprehensive evaluation will provide valuable insights into the strengths and limitations of our framework, thus guiding further refinements and optimizations. Finally, we are committed to extending the applicability of Self-HCL to diverse domains and datasets, thus ensuring its robustness and versatility in real-world scenarios. By doing so, we aim to contribute to the broader field of sentiment analysis and pave the way for more sophisticated and efficient multimodal frameworks.

Author Contributions: Conceptualization, Y.F.; Funding acquisition, Y.F.; Investigation, Y.F. and J.F.; Methodology, Y.F. and J.F.; Project administration, Y.F.; Software, J.F.; Supervision, H.X.; Validation, J.F.; Visualization, J.F.; Writing—original draft, J.F.; Writing—review and editing, Y.F., J.F., H.X. and Z.X. All authors have read and agreed to the published version of the manuscript.

Funding: This work was supported by the Chongqing Basic Research and Frontier Exploration Project (Chongqing Natural Science Foundation) [grant number: CSTB2022NSCQ-MSX0918], the Humanities and Social Sciences Project of Chongqing Education Commission [grant number: 23SKGH252] and the Chongqing University of Technology Graduate Education High-Quality Development Action Plan Funding Results [grant number: gzlcx20242041].

Data Availability Statement: This study utilized publicly available datasets from references [31,32].

Conflicts of Interest: The authors declare no conflicts of interest.

References

1. Hochreiter, S.; Schmidhuber, J. Long short-term memory. *Neural Comput.* **1997**, *9*, 1735–1780. [CrossRef] [PubMed]
2. Grossberg, S. Recurrent neural networks. *Scholarpedia* **2013**, *8*, 1888. [CrossRef]
3. Ranaldi, L.; Pucci, G. Knowing knowledge: Epistemological study of knowledge in transformers. *Appl. Sci.* **2023**, *13*, 677. [CrossRef]
4. Tsai, Y.H.H.; Bai, S.; Liang, P.P.; Kolter, J.Z.; Morency, L.P.; Salakhutdinov, R. Multimodal transformer for unaligned multimodal language sequences. In Proceedings of the 57th Annual Meeting of the Association for Computational Linguistics, Florence, Italy, 28 July–2 August 2019 ; Volume 2019, p. 6558.
5. Hazarika, D.; Zimmermann, R.; Poria, S. Misa: Modality-invariant and-specific representations for multimodal sentiment analysis. In Proceedings of the 28th ACM International Conference on Multimedia, Seattle, WA, USA, 12–16 October 2020; pp. 1122–1131.
6. Zadeh, A.; Chen, M.; Poria, S.; Cambria, E.; Morency, L.P. Tensor Fusion Network for Multimodal Sentiment Analysis. In Proceedings of the Conference on Empirical Methods in Natural Language Processing, Copenhagen, Denmark, 7–11 September 2017.
7. Zadeh, A.; Liang, P.P.; Mazumder, N.; Poria, S.; Cambria, E.; Morency, L.P. Memory fusion network for multi-view sequential learning. In Proceedings of the AAAI Conference on Artificial Intelligence, New Orleans, LA, USA, 2–7 February 2018; Volume 32.
8. Poria, S.; Hazarika, D.; Majumder, N.; Mihalcea, R. Beneath the tip of the iceberg: Current challenges and new directions in sentiment analysis research. *IEEE Trans. Affect. Comput.* **2020**, *14*, 108–132. [CrossRef]
9. Yu, W.; Xu, H.; Yuan, Z.; Wu, J. Learning modality-specific representations with self-supervised multi-task learning for multimodal sentiment analysis. In Proceedings of the AAAI Conference on Artificial Intelligence, Virtual, 2–9 February 2021; Volume 35, pp. 10790–10797.
10. Han, W.; Chen, H.; Poria, S. Improving multimodal fusion with hierarchical mutual information maximization for multimodal sentiment analysis. *arXiv* **2021**, arXiv:2109.00412.

11. Hwang, Y.; Kim, J.H. Self-supervised unimodal label generation strategy using recalibrated modality representations for multimodal sentiment analysis. In Proceedings of the Findings of the Association for Computational Linguistics: EACL 2023, Dubrovnik, Croatia, 2–6 May 2023; pp. 35–46.
12. Woo, S.; Park, J.; Lee, J.Y.; Kweon, I.S. Cbam: Convolutional block attention module. In Proceedings of the European Conference on Computer Vision (ECCV), Munich, Germany, 8–14 September 2018; pp. 3–19.
13. Cheng, J.; Fostiropoulos, I.; Boehm, B.; Soleymani, M. Multimodal phased transformer for sentiment analysis. In Proceedings of the 2021 Conference on Empirical Methods in Natural Language Processing, Punta Cana, Dominican Republic, 7–11 November 2021; pp. 2447–2458.
14. Belghazi, M.I.; Baratin, A.; Rajeshwar, S.; Ozair, S.; Bengio, Y.; Courville, A.; Hjelm, D. Mutual information neural estimation. In Proceedings of the International Conference on Machine Learning, PMLR, Stockholm, Sweden, 10–15 July 2018; pp. 531–540.
15. Kaur, R.; Kautish, S. Multimodal sentiment analysis: A survey and comparison. In *Research Anthology on Implementing Sentiment Analysis across Multiple Disciplines*; IGI Global: Hershey, PA, USA, 2022; pp. 1846–1870.
16. Liu, Z.; Shen, Y.; Lakshminarasimhan, V.B.; Liang, P.P.; Zadeh, A.; Morency, L.P. Efficient low-rank multimodal fusion with modality-specific factors. *arXiv* **2018**, arXiv:1806.00064.
17. Liang, P.P.; Liu, Z.; Zadeh, A.; Morency, L.P. Multimodal language analysis with recurrent multistage fusion. *arXiv* **2018**, arXiv:1808.03920.
18. Pham, H.; Liang, P.P.; Manzini, T.; Morency, L.P.; Póczos, B. Found in translation: Learning robust joint representations by cyclic translations between modalities. In Proceedings of the AAAI Conference on Artificial Intelligence, Honolulu, HI, USA, 27 January–1 February 2019; Volume 33, pp. 6892–6899.
19. Sun, Z.; Sarma, P.; Sethares, W.; Liang, Y. Learning relationships between text, audio, and video via deep canonical correlation for multimodal language analysis. In Proceedings of the AAAI Conference on Artificial Intelligence, New York, NY, USA, 7–12 February 2020; Volume 34, pp. 8992–8999.
20. Zhang, Y.; Yang, Q. A survey on multi-task learning. *IEEE Trans. Knowl. Data Eng.* **2021**, *34*, 5586–5609. [CrossRef]
21. Yang, B.; Wu, L.; Zhu, J.; Shao, B.; Lin, X.; Liu, T.Y. Multimodal sentiment analysis with two-phase multi-task learning. *IEEE/ACM Trans. Audio Speech Lang. Process.* **2022**, *30*, 2015–2024. [CrossRef]
22. Chauhan, D.S.; Dhanush, S.; Ekbal, A.; Bhattacharyya, P. Sentiment and emotion help sarcasm? A multi-task learning framework for multi-modal sarcasm, sentiment and emotion analysis. In Proceedings of the 58th Annual Meeting of the Association for Computational Linguistics, Online, 5–10 July 2020; pp. 4351–4360.
23. Oord, A.v.d.; Li, Y.; Vinyals, O. Representation learning with contrastive predictive coding. *arXiv* **2018**, arXiv:1807.03748.
24. Chen, T.; Kornblith, S.; Norouzi, M.; Hinton, G. A simple framework for contrastive learning of visual representations. In Proceedings of the International Conference on Machine Learning, PMLR, Virtual, 13–18 July 2020; pp. 1597–1607.
25. He, K.; Fan, H.; Wu, Y.; Xie, S.; Girshick, R. Momentum Contrast for Unsupervised Visual Representation Learning. In Proceedings of the IEEE/CVF Conference on Computer Vision and Pattern Recognition (CVPR), Seattle, WA, USA, 13–19 June 2020.
26. Khosla, P.; Teterwak, P.; Wang, C.; Sarna, A.; Tian, Y.; Isola, P.; Maschinot, A.; Liu, C.; Krishnan, D. Supervised contrastive learning. *Adv. Neural Inf. Process. Syst.* **2020**, *33*, 18661–18673.
27. Devlin, J.; Chang, M.W.; Lee, K.; Toutanova, K. Bert: Pre-training of deep bidirectional transformers for language understanding. *arXiv* **2018**, arXiv:1810.04805.
28. Degottex, G.; Kane, J.; Drugman, T.; Raitio, T.; Scherer, S. COVAREP—A collaborative voice analysis repository for speech technologies. In Proceedings of the 2014 IEEE International Conference on Acoustics, Speech and Signal Processing (ICASSP), Florence, Italy, 4–9 May 2014; IEEE: Piscataway, NJ, USA , 2014; pp. 960–964.
29. iMotions, A. Facet iMotions Biometric Research Platform, 2013. Available online: https://imotions.com/products/imotions-lab/modules/fea-facial-expression-analysis/ (accessed on 16 July 2024).
30. Rakhlin, A. Convolutional neural networks for sentence classification. *GitHub* **2016**, *6*, 25.
31. Zadeh, A.; Zellers, R.; Pincus, E.; Morency, L.P. Mosi: Multimodal corpus of sentiment intensity and subjectivity analysis in online opinion videos. *arXiv***2016**, arXiv:1606.06259.
32. Zadeh, A.B.; Liang, P.P.; Poria, S.; Cambria, E.; Morency, L.P. Multimodal language analysis in the wild: Cmu-mosei dataset and interpretable dynamic fusion graph. In Proceedings of the 56th Annual Meeting of the Association for Computational Linguistics, Melbourne, Australia, 15–20 July 2018; Volume 1, pp. 2236–2246.
33. Wang, Y.; Shen, Y.; Liu, Z.; Liang, P.P.; Zadeh, A.; Morency, L.P. Words can shift: Dynamically adjusting word representations using nonverbal behaviors. In Proceedings of the AAAI Conference on Artificial Intelligence, Honolulu, HI, USA, 27 January–1 February 2019; Volume 33, pp. 7216–7223.
34. Rahman, W.; Hasan, M.K.; Lee, S.; Zadeh, A.; Mao, C.; Morency, L.P.; Hoque, E. Integrating multimodal information in large pretrained transformers. In Proceedings of the 58th Annual Meeting of the Association for Computational Linguistics, Online, 5–10 July 2020; Volume 2020, p. 2359.
35. Hinton, G.E.; Roweis, S. Stochastic neighbor embedding. *Adv. Neural Inf. Process. Syst.* **2002**, *15*, 857–864. [CrossRef]

electronics

MDPI

Article

Named Entity Recognition for Equipment Fault Diagnosis Based on RoBERTa-wwm-ext and Deep Learning Integration

Feifei Gao [1], Lin Zhang [1], Wenfeng Wang [1], Bo Zhang [1,*], Wei Liu [1], Jingyi Zhang [1] and Le Xie [2]

1 Air and Missile Defense College, Air Force Engineering University, Xi'an 710051, China; m18031827043@163.com (F.G.)
2 Electronic Information School, Xijing University, Xi'an 710123, China
* Correspondence: zhb8706@163.com

Abstract: Equipment fault diagnosis NER is to extract specific entities from Chinese equipment fault diagnosis text, which is the premise of constructing an equipment fault diagnosis knowledge graph. Named entity recognition for equipment fault diagnosis can also provide important data support for equipment maintenance support. Equipment fault diagnosis text has complex semantics, fuzzy entity boundaries, and limited data size. In order to extract entities from the equipment fault diagnosis text, this paper presents an NER model for equipment fault diagnosis based on RoBERTa-wwm-ext and Deep Learning network integration. Firstly, this model uses the RoBERTa-wwm-ext to extract context-sensitive embeddings of text sequences. Secondly, the context feature information is obtained through the BiLSTM network. Thirdly, the CRF is combined to output the label sequence with a constraint relationship, improve the accuracy of sequence labeling task, and complete the entity recognition task. Finally, experiments and predictions are carried out on the constructed dataset. The results show that the model can effectively identify five types of equipment fault diagnosis entities and has higher evaluation indexes than the traditional model. Its precision, recall, and F1 value are 94.57%, 95.39%, and 94.98%, respectively. The case study proves that the model can accurately recognize the entity of the input text.

Keywords: equipment fault diagnosis; named entity recognition; RoBERTa-wwm-ext; deep learning; knowledge graph

1. Introduction

With the extensive application of advanced science and technology in the military field, weapons and equipment continue to develop with a focus on information and intelligence. Complex high-tech equipment is constantly used in modern warfare and training, and high-level equipment's support capability is a key factor in the operational effectiveness of equipment and can determine the outcome of a war. However, the continuous application of new technology makes the complexity of equipment and the difficulty of support increase rapidly. The task of equipment support is to ensure the normal operation and use of equipment, so the main focus of equipment support is the maintenance of equipment to prevent failure. Equipment fault maintenance refers to the methods, techniques, skills, and means used for the maintenance and repair of equipment after failure. Equipment in the process of use will encounter a variety of failures, and troubleshooting and maintenance personnel mainly rely on their accumulated experience and technical specifications. In the troubleshooting process, the methods, processes, skills, and means adopted by maintenance personnel are usually recorded in the form of unstructured text, and these maintenance experiences are difficult to be effectively reused. Therefore, it is of great significance to efficiently use the data accumulated in equipment maintenance failure records, deeply mine the knowledge and potential relationship in the fault log text, and assist the maintenance personnel to quickly complete the fault analysis and troubleshooting in the process of equipment support.

Knowledge graph (KG) technology provides a better method for industry knowledge mining, representation, and management by mining the entities and relationships in the information and presenting them in the form of a visual semantic network [1]. By using the method of a knowledge graph, fault knowledge can be effectively mined from equipment fault texts. Through the integration and association of knowledge, combined with reasoning analysis, the equipment fault maintenance plan is formulated to assist maintenance personnel to quickly find, locate, diagnose, and repair faults [2]. At present, an increasing number of scholars have introduced KGs into fault diagnosis practice. For example, Deng et al. [3] explored strategies for building a KG for the fault diagnosis of robotic transmission systems. The BiLSTM network is used to capture the context information features in the fault text, the self-attention is used to accurately extract the interdependence features between characters in the multi-dimensional subspace, and the CRF is used to realize the effective identification of key entities, which plays a vital role in promoting the autonomous fault diagnosis. Tang et al. [2] used Deep Learning technology to extract the entity, relationship, and attribute information from aircraft fault diagnosis data to build a KG in the field of aircraft faults. Liu et al. [4] constructed an electrical equipment fault KG based on the text of the electrical equipment operation and maintenance records, showing the correlation of faulty equipment and components. In the process of constructing the KG of equipment fault diagnosis, NER plays a vital role. With the continuous accumulation and increase in equipment fault record data, it is unrealistic to rely on manual methods to extract the required information from a large number of texts. Deep Learning technologies have shown great potential in the task of NER for equipment fault diagnosis, which provides strong support for automatically extracting fault information and constructing KGs [5]. At present, there is little research in the field of equipment fault diagnosis NER, but researchers have carried out a lot of research and achieved certain results in the field of power equipment, aircraft, railway equipment, and the recognition of other named entities. For example, Gong et al. [6] introduced BiLSTM and CRF models on the basis of BERT, and entities related to High-Voltage Isolating circuit breakers and thermal faults are identified from power grid fault texts. Through the joint recognition model based on the sequence and TreeBiLSTM, Meng et al. [7] extracted the interdependence between the related entities and relationships in the area of aircraft health management. Using the fault reports provided by China Railway Administration as the data source, Yang et al. [8] fuses BERT, BiLSTM, and CRF to perform text mining on the fault reports of Chinese railway operation equipment and extract relevant entities.

The relevant entities in the equipment fault diagnosis text include equipment name, fault part, fault phenomenon, fault reason, and troubleshooting way. Compared with entity recognition in other fields such as finance, tourism, medicine, agriculture, culture and so on, the characters of equipment fault diagnosis entities are longer and include more proper names. In addition, there is also the phenomenon that different entity types nest with each other. At present, there is a lack of public datasets in the field of equipment fault diagnosis, and it will be a challenging work to carry out an equipment fault diagnosis NER.

In order to complete the work of NER for an equipment fault diagnosis, this study will propose an NER model based on the fusion of RoBERTa-wwm-ext and Deep Learning. Based on the equipment fault database, we extracted entities such as equipment name, fault part, fault phenomenon, fault reason, and troubleshooting way according to the fault text characteristics. Referring to NER models in other fields, this paper proposes a RoBERTa-wwm-ext-BiLSTM-CRF NER model for equipment fault diagnosis and proves the effectiveness of the model through experiments.

The main contributions of this paper are as follows:

(1) We collected and sorted out the fault diagnosis text from the equipment fault database; constructed a dedicated Chinese corpus in the field of equipment fault diagnosis; cleaned the data carefully, implemented sentence segmentation; labeled the entity labels of equipment name, fault location, phenomenon, cause, and elimination method; and completed the text preprocessing task.

(2) We use RoBERTa-wwm-ext to process the labeled fault diagnosis text, and a neural network combining BiLSTM and CRF is used to extract the context feature information of the text to obtain the optimal prediction sequence and complete the NER task.
(3) Through experiments, the performance of different models is compared, and the effectiveness of the presented NER model for equipment fault diagnosis is verified. The precision, recall, and F1 value of the model reach 94.57%, 95.39%, and 94.98%, respectively.
(4) Through experiments, the influence of different entity types on the model is evaluated, the hyperparameters of the model are explored, and the performance of NER is improved. The case study proves that the model can accurately recognize the entity of the input text.

2. Related Work

Early entity recognition is mostly based on rule templates, which are often reasonably designed by domain experts, but the expansibility of rule templates is poor and the cost of system migration is high [9]. Later, traditional Machine Learning technologies are widely applied in entity recognition. The commonly used models include ME [10], HMM [11], and CRF [12], etc. In recent years, as the core technology driving the vigorous development of AI, Deep Learning has also been widely applied in the field of natural language processing and KG and has gradually become the mainstream method of entity recognition. Compared with the early manual methods based on dictionary matching and templates, the Deep Learning model can learn features and patterns from sample data and does not need to manually select features. It has a better effect, higher efficiency, and stronger universality and is suitable for solving sequence labeling problems. RNN is suitable for processing and predicting sequence data, but it is prone to the problem of vanishing gradients when facing very long sequences. Hochreiter and Schmidhuber [13] proposed LSTM network to solve the problem of the insufficient reflux of error information and gradient attenuation. Huang et al. [14] presented a variety of sequence labeling models based on an LSTM network and proved that the BiLSTM-CRF model can effectively use forward and backward text input features through experiments. Miao et al. [15] presented a model consisting of LSTM and fully connected layers for short-term fog prediction. An et al. [16] applied a MUSA-BiLSTM-CRF model in the field of Chinese clinical NER, which greatly improved the entity recognition performance.

In 2018, Google introduced the BERT pre-training model, which quickly became a popular model in the field of NLP due to its powerful structural and semantic understanding capabilities. Since then, scholars have continuously applied pre-trained language models to named entity recognition tasks. Devlin et al. [17] utilize BERT and a bidirectional Transformer model to generate word embedding vectors containing positional information and contextual features, achieving excellent performance on sentence-level and token-level tasks. Guo et al. [18] used BERT-BiLSTM-CRF to identify case entities in Chinese domestic legal texts. Lin et al. [19] presented an entity extraction method for fault information of railway signaling equipment based on RoBERTa-wwm and Deep Learning. RoBERTa-wwm was used to generate word vectors of text sequences, and BiLSTM and CNN were used to obtain contextual features and local feature information. Liang et al. [20] proposed ALBERT fault pre-training model with fault data embedding for communication equipment faults of industrial Internet of Things. Kong et al. [21] presented a NLP algorithm based on a dictionary, language technology platform tools, and a BERT-CRF hybrid to perform entity recognition on electrical equipment fault texts in power systems and optimized the context relationship and preferred word labels. Chen et al. [22] used BERT-BiLSTM-CRF to recognize entities in the fault diagnosis text of air compressor and proved that the model showed an excellent performance in extracting entities in the field of compressor fault diagnosis by comparing with other sequence labeling models. Zhang et al. [23] used BERT-CRF to realize the recognition of power equipment fault entities and proved through experiments that the model can extract a wider range of power equipment fault entities from a small corpus. Zhou et al. [24] used the BERT model to extract the initial semantic information in the text of power equipment defects and then further extracted the context and local semantic features through BiLSTM-CNN, which provided a reference for the intelligent extraction of power equipment text information.

At present, there are relatively few studies on named entity recognition in the field of equipment fault diagnosis. In this paper, an equipment fault diagnosis corpus is constructed, the RoBERTa-wwm-ext-BiLSTM-CRF model is applied to recognize the named entities in the equipment fault diagnosis text, and the five types of equipment fault diagnosis entities are effectively extracted: equipment name, fault part, fault phenomenon, fault reason, and troubleshooting method.

3. Methodology

In this section, we will elaborate on the NER model for equipment fault diagnosis based on the fusion of RoBERTa-wwm-ext and BiLSTM-CRF architectures, and Figure 1 shows overall structure of model, including RoBERTa-wwm-ext, BiLSTM, and CRF layer. Firstly, RoBERTa-wwm-ext layer was used to convert the equipment fault diagnosis text data into word embedding vector representation. Then, the trained word vector sequence was input into BiLSTM network layer to fully extract the context feature information in text. Finally, dependency relationship between adjacent labels was learned in CRF layer, output results of BiLSTM layer were decoded, optimal label sequence with constraints was output, the entities in sequence were extracted and classified, and NER was completed.

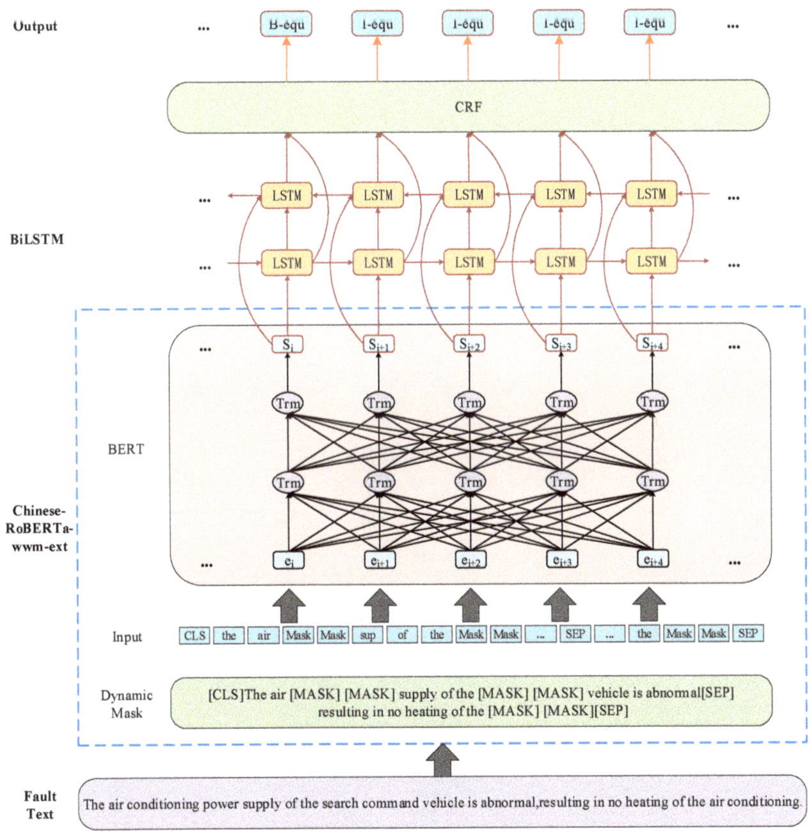

Figure 1. NER model based on RoBERTa-wwm-ext-BiLSTM-CRF network.

3.1. RoBERTa-wwm-ext Layer

RoBERTa-wwm-ext model is a Chinese pre-trained model released by HFL (HIT iFLYTEK Language Cognitive Computing Lab), which is a derivation and optimization of BERT model.

BERT model is built on the basis of the 12-layer encoder component of Transformer architecture. The deep bidirectional Transformer encoder is used to learn the rich semantic information in the text data. Figure 2 shows the framework structure of the Transformer. BERT learns the context information of the corpus through two pre-training tasks: MLM and NSP. Figure 3 shows the model structure of BERT. The input of model consists of two pieces of text concatenation, labels [CLS] for sentence classification tasks and labels [SEP] for two input sentence segmentation tasks.

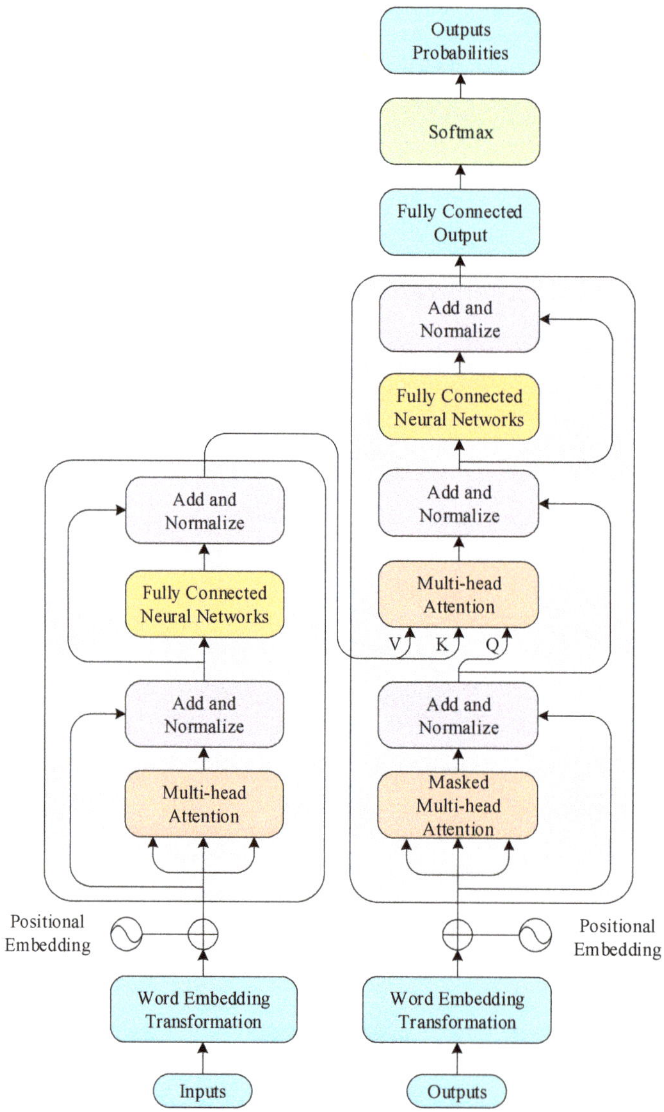

Figure 2. The structure of Transformer.

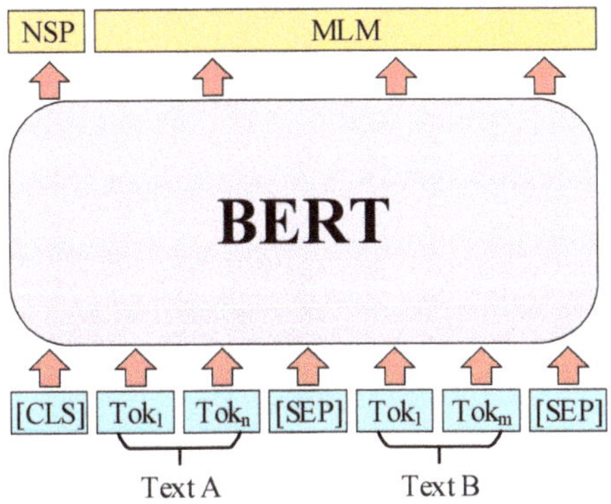

Figure 3. The structure of BERT.

Figure 4 shows the input representation of BERT, which consists of the sum of word vectors, block vectors, and position vectors [25]. The formula for computing the input representation v is as follows:

$$v = v^t + v^s + v^p \quad (1)$$

where v^t refers to the word vector, v^s refers to the block vector, and v^p refers to the position vector. The first layer of word vector represents transforming the words in the input text into 768-dimensional vectors, the second layer of block vector determines which sentence the current word belongs to, and the third layer of position vector encodes the absolute position of each word.

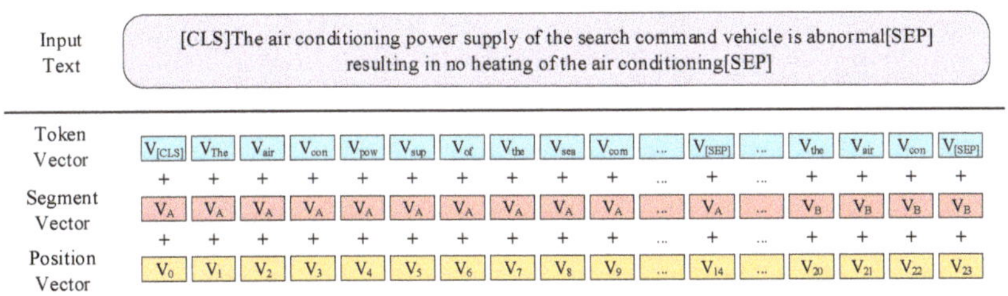

Figure 4. Input representation of BERT.

RoBERTa-wwm-ext model is an improved RoBERTa model, especially suitable for Chinese text processing. Compared with BERT model, the following improvements are made:

(1) Dynamic masking technology is introduced to ensure that the same text has different masking patterns under different training epochs, which improves the richness of training data and the efficiency of data reuse.
(2) NSP tasks are discarded to improve the efficiency of downstream tasks.
(3) Using the whole word mask technology, the context semantics can be better understood, and the accuracy and efficiency of Chinese text processing can be improved.
(4) Improving model performance by using larger batches, longer training steps, and larger data sizes.

Figure 5 shows the input representation of RoBERTa-wwm-ext model. The input text is first processed with labels [CLS] and [SEP] indicating where each text begins and ends, using a dynamic masking technique with labels [MASK] randomly masking characters in the text [19]. The input of the text consists of adding word vector, block vector, and position vector.

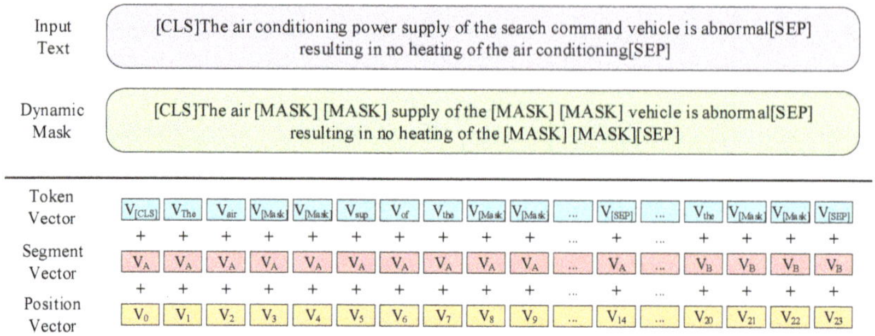

Figure 5. Input representation of RoBERTa-wwm-ext.

3.2. BiLSTM Layer

RNN is a neural network model specifically designed to process sequence data, which captures the contextual feature information of fault text through internal feedback links. However, the basic RNN has gradient explosion and gradient disappearance, which has drawbacks when dealing with long-distance dependence problems [26]. LSTM is an improvement of the basic RNN and is designed to solve the problem of long-distance dependence in sequence modeling. LSTM network consists of basic LSTM units. Figure 6 shows the internal structure of LSTM network unit.

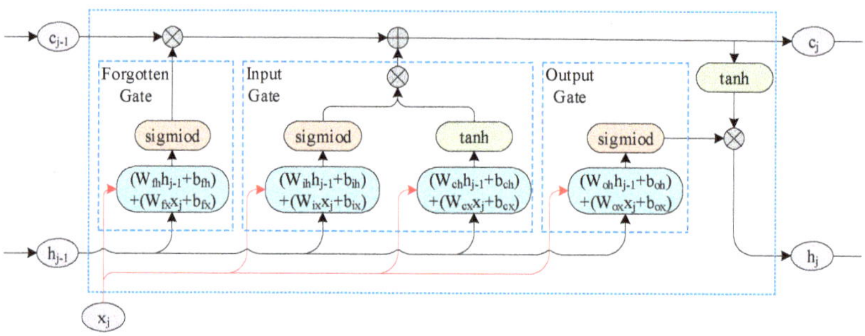

Figure 6. The internal structure of an LSTM network unit.

The mathematical expressions of LSTM network model are given by Equations (2)–(7).

$$f = sigmoid(W_{fx}x_j + b_{fx} + W_{fh}h_{j-1} + b_{fh}) \tag{2}$$

$$i = sigmoid(W_{ix}x_j + b_{ix} + W_{ih}h_{j-1} + b_{ih}) \tag{3}$$

$$g = \tanh(W_{cx}x_j + b_{cx} + W_{ch}h_{j-1} + b_{ch}) \tag{4}$$

$$o = sigmoid\hbar(W_{ox}x_j + b_{ox} + W_{oh}h_{j-1} + b_{oh}) \tag{5}$$

$$c_j = f \bigotimes c_{j-1} + i \bigotimes g \tag{6}$$

$$h_j = o \bigotimes \tanh(c_j) \tag{7}$$

The LSTM network unit processes the input data through forget gate, input gate, and output gate to realize the memory mechanism at long and short distances. Forget gate forgets the information in the memory and determines the unimportant and discarded information in the memory; Equation (2) represents its calculation process. Input gate processes the new information and decides information to be memorized; Equation (6) represents its calculation process, where Equation (3) calculates the brand new information to be memorized and Equation (4) calculates the update of the old information. Output gate processes input information, both by direct processing of the current input and by modifying these inputs based on previously memorized information, and Equations (5) and (7) represent their computation processes, respectively.

BiLSTM is a bidirectional LSTM network constructed based on LSTM units. BiLSTM connects the same input sequence into the forward and backward LSTMS [27], concatenates the hidden layers of LSTM network, and accesses output layer together for prediction. Figure 7 shows the structure of BiLSTM network. For NER task, BiLSTM network is used to extract context feature information, which can not only realize the dependence of backward text on forward text, but also realize the dependence of forward text on backward text, which can effectively solve the dependence problem of distant entities.

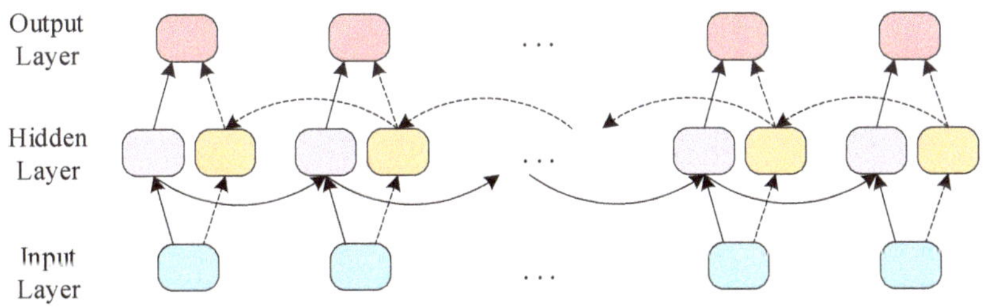

Figure 7. The structure of BiLSTM network.

3.3. CRF Layer

In NER task, BiLSTM layer extracts the context feature information of the fault text and obtains the probability of occurrence of each word on each label, but it lacks the ability to process the dependency between labels [28]. CRF can calculate the relationship between adjacent labels from a global perspective and obtain the optimal prediction sequence. CRF makes up for the BiLSTM layer's inability to deal with neighboring label dependencies and reduces the number of invalid predicted labels. The BiLSTM-CRF network model has been shown to significantly improve the precision of NER. Figure 8 shows the structure of CRF.

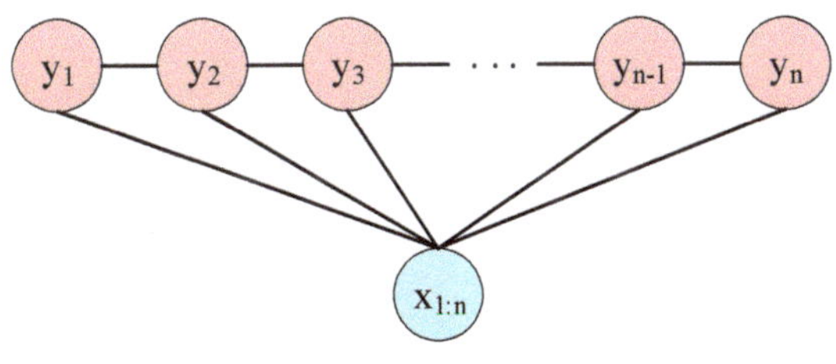

Figure 8. The structure of CRF.

In a given observation sequence $x = (x_1, x_2, x_3, \cdots, x_n)$, a label sequence $y = (y_1, y_2, y_3, \cdots, y_n)$ and Equation (8) calculates the corresponding $score(x, y)$, where λ_j denotes the corresponding weight and f_j denotes the characteristic function.

$$score(x, y) = \sum_j \sum_i \lambda_j f_j(y_{i-1}, y_i, x, i) \quad (8)$$

Softmax function is used to normalize all possible sequence paths, and the conditional probability distribution $p(y|x)$ of the predicted sequence is obtained according to Equation (9), where $\widetilde{y}$ represents the current predicted tag sequence, Y_x represents the set of all possible tag sequences, and $score(x, \tilde{y})$ represents the total score under the current predicted sequence. Taking the logarithm of both ends of Equation (9) yields the maximum likelihood probability function of the correct predicted label, as shown in Equation (10).

$$p(y|x) = \frac{exp\{score(x, y)\}}{\sum_{\tilde{y} \in Y_x} exp\{score(x, \tilde{y})\}} \tag{9}$$

$$\log p(y|x) = score(x, y) - \log\left(\sum_{\tilde{y} \in Y_x} score(x, \tilde{y})\right) \tag{10}$$

Finally, the maximum likelihood function $argmax()$ is used to decode, and optimal sequence is selected from all predicted label sequences, and the optimal sequence is the final label result, as shown in Equation (11).

$$y^* = argmax(score(x, \tilde{y})), (\tilde{y} \in Y_x) \tag{11}$$

4. Experiment and Analysis

This section introduces the experimental process of the equipment fault diagnosis text NER based on the fusion of the pre-trained model and Deep Learning model, including text preprocessing, text label, experimental environment setting, training parameter setting, result analysis, and the comparison of different model combination effects.

4.1. Text Preprocessing

The original data in this paper are 1302 fault records obtained from the equipment IETM fault database and the equipment user fault register, totaling about 50,000 words. These raw texts have many problems and cannot be directly utilized. For example, most of the content exists in the form of tables and flow charts, which cannot be recognized as text. In addition, when the text length is too long, the recognition precision is often affected and decreased. Therefore, it is crucial to pre-process the raw text. In this paper, text preprocessing mainly performs text cleaning, segmentation, and format conversion. In order to obtain text for entity annotation, the main work of text preprocessing includes correcting errors, filling in missing values, cutting long text, and converting tables and flow charts into text. The standardized sentences that only include words, numbers, and punctuation are obtained by text preprocessing.

4.2. Text Label

The text label is fundamental for building corpora and performing NER tasks. In this paper, the BIO format is used to annotate the entities in the text: "B-entity type" denotes the beginning of each entity, "I-entity type" denotes the rest of each entity, and "O" denotes non-entity words. A total of 3422 entities are annotated in this paper, including five main types of equipment fault diagnosis: equipment name, fault part, fault phenomenon, fault reason, and troubleshooting way, as shown in Table 1.

Table 1. Type and quantity of equipment fault diagnosis entity.

Label	Type	Number
Equipment	equipment name	67
Part	fault part	884
Phenomenon	fault phenomenon	977
Reason	fault reason	973
Way	troubleshooting way	521

The specific labeling work has the following steps: upload the text to the Label-Studio labeling tool, set the required labels, label each entity with the corresponding label, select the "json" format to export after the labeling is completed, and then convert the label format into the "BIO" format text through the format conversion program.

4.3. Training

In this paper, according to the allocation ratio of 80% training set, 10% test set, and 10% validation set, the dataset is divided into three parts containing 2737, 349, and 336 entities, respectively, for training, testing, and verifying model performance. The pre-trained models used in the experiments are "Chinese-RoBERTa-wwm-ext" and "Chinese-BERT-base", which contain 12 layers of transformers, 12 self-attention mechanisms, and 768 hidden layer dimensions. Word vectors output by model are the weighted average of the 12-layer network, and the final 768-dimensional word vector will be fed into the BiLSTM + CRF layer [5]. Table 2 shows experimental environment setup.

Table 2. Experimental environment.

Type	Configuration
Hardware configuration	CPU: 13th Gen Intel Core i7-13620H GPU: NVIDIA Tesla P40 OS: Windows 11 Video memory: 24 GB
Software environment	CUDA: 10.2 Python: 3.12.2 Tensorboard: 2.16.2 Transformers: 4.42.3 Tqdm: 4.66.4 Numpy: 1.26.4

To ensure reliability of results when conducting comparative experiments, it is necessary to use fixed hyperparameters for training, and the specific hyperparameters of the model settings are shown in Table 3. "max_seq_length" specifies maximum length of the input sequence, "epoch" specifies number of training rounds, "batch_size" specifies size of the training round, "learning_rate" controls the weight update rate of the model, and "dropout" reduces overfitting during training. "bilstm_size" is used to specify number of hidden units of a BiLSTM layer.

Table 3. Hyper-parameters of models.

Hyper-Parameters	Parameter Values
max_seq_length	128
epoch	10
batch_size	32
learning_rate	3×10^{-5}
dropout	0.1
bilstm_size	128

4.4. Evaluation Metrics

This paper evaluates the precision (P), recall (R), and F_1 value of all models in NER task of equipment fault diagnosis text, and these three evaluation indicators are widely used in NER tasks [29]. The formulas for the calculation of these three evaluation indicators are given in Equations (12)–(14).

$$P = \frac{TP}{TP + FP} \tag{12}$$

$$R = \frac{TP}{TP + FN} \tag{13}$$

$$F_1 = \frac{2 \times P \times R}{P + R} \tag{14}$$

where TP refers to entities identified from texts, FP refers to incorrectly identifying non-entities as entities, and FN refers to failure to identify real entities [19]. Precision represents the fraction of objects identified as entities by the NER system that are truly entities. Recall represents the proportion of all entities that actually exist that are correctly identified by the NER system. F_1 is the harmonic mean of precision and recall, which is used to comprehensively evaluate the performance of NER systems.

4.5. Experimental Results and Analysis

In this paper, the NER task is implemented for five different models on the equipment fault diagnosis dataset, and the actual performance of models is evaluated on the test set. The results show that the model presented in this paper can effectively extract equipment fault diagnosis entities. Table 4 show examples of extracting entities from equipment fault diagnosis texts. In this section, the experimental results are analyzed in terms of models, hyper-parameters, and entities.

Table 4. The samples of NER in English.

Original Text	Entity Recognition
The transmitter of the search command vehicle has no output of high voltage radiation power.	Equipment: search command vehicle; Part: transmitter; Phenomenon: no output of high voltage radiation power
The auxiliary power supply combined with the cathode current leads to no output of the transmitter high voltage radiated power.	Reason: auxiliary power supply combined cathode current; Part: transmitter; Phenomenon: no output of high voltage radiation power
Replace the auxiliary power supply in the combination of modulator plug-in transmitter high voltage radiation power no output phenomenon eliminated.	Way: Replace the modulator plug-in in the auxiliary power supply combination; Part: transmitter; Phenomenon: no output of high voltage radiation power

4.5.1. Comparison of Different Models

Table 5 shows results of five NER models, and the results are analyzed as follows:

Table 5. Model experimental results.

Model	Precision	Recall	F_1-Value
RoBERTa-wwm-ext-BiLSTM-CRF	0.9457	0.9539	0.9498
BERT-BiLSTM-CRF	0.9347	0.9481	0.9413
RoBERTa-wwm-ext-CRF	0.9259	0.9366	0.9312
BERT-CRF	0.9157	0.9395	0.9275
BiLSTM-CRF	0.8068	0.8251	0.8158

(1) The P, R, and F_1 values of BiLSTM-CRF and BERT-BiLSTM-CRF reach 0.8068, 0.8251, 0.8158 and 0.9347, 0.9481, 0.9413, respectively. Through comparison, it is found that the introduction of the pre-trained model can effectively improve the P, R, and F_1 value of NER.

(2) The F_1 values of RoBERTa-wwm-ext-BiLSTM-CRF and RoBERTa-wwm-ext-CRF are 0.9498 and 0.9312, respectively. The results show that the introduction of BiLSTM layer is able to improve the F_1 value, which verifies the effectiveness of adding the BiLSTM layer to the NER task.

(3) The P, R, and F_1 value of RoBERTa-wwm-ext-BiLSTM-CRF and BERT-BiLSTM-CRF are 0.9457, 0.9539, 0.9498 and 0.9374, 0.9481, 0.9413, respectively. The results show that, compared with the basic BERT model, RoBERTa-wwm-ext performs better in NER tasks by introducing dynamic masking technology, discarding NSP tasks, adopting the full-word masking strategy, and increasing the training batch, training step, and training dataset size.

(4) The P, R, and F_1 value of the RoBERTa wwm-ext-BiLSTM-CRF model reach 0.9457, 0.9539, and 0.9498, respectively, which is the best performance among all models, proving that the model presented in this paper has superior performance in the NER task of equipment fault diagnosis.

4.5.2. Effect of Type and Number of Entities

The entities belonging to five types of equipment fault diagnosis, namely equipment name, fault part, fault phenomenon, fault reason, and troubleshooting way, are identified. The recognition results of all models are shown in Table 6, and the experimental results are analyzed as follows.

Table 6. Experimental results of models for the recognition of different entity types and numbers.

Model	Evaluate	Equipment	Part	Phenomena	Reason	Way
RoBERTa-wwm-ext-BiLSTM-CRF	P	0.9855	0.9275	0.8873	0.9296	1.0000
	R	0.9855	0.9275	0.9130	0.9565	0.9859
	F_1	0.9855	0.9275	0.9000	0.9429	0.9929
BERT-BiLSTM-CRF	P	0.9855	0.9412	0.8493	0.9028	1.0000
	R	0.9855	0.9275	0.8986	0.9420	0.9859
	F_1	0.9855	0.9343	0.8732	0.9220	0.9929
RoBERTa-wwm-ext-CRF	P	1.0000	0.9091	0.8219	0.9041	1.0000
	R	1.0000	0.8696	0.8696	0.9565	0.9859
	F_1	1.0000	0.8889	0.8451	0.9296	0.9929
BERT-CRF	P	1.0000	0.8400	0.8571	0.8889	1.0000
	R	1.0000	0.9130	0.8696	0.9275	0.9859
	F_1	1.0000	0.8750	0.8633	0.9078	0.9929
BiLSTM-CRF	P	0.8855	0.8129	0.7333	0.7667	0.8806
	R	0.8855	0.8006	0.7696	0.8420	0.8551
	F_1	0.8855	0.8067	0.7511	0.8028	0.8676

In the recognition of the five types of entities, all models show that the recognition effect of equipment name and troubleshooting way entities are good, and the F_1 score is close to 1. The reason is that the equipment name type entities and the troubleshooting way type entities have relatively fixed formats in the equipment fault diagnosis text, high repeatability in each paragraph of fault text, and are easier to identify than other types of entities. Secondly, the effect of fault part and fault reason entity recognition is also good because these entity types have a large number of labels. In addition, the effect of entity recognition for fault phenomena is relatively low because different personnel will have certain differences in the description and record of fault phenomena, and the difficulty of recognition will be increased.

4.5.3. The Effect of Model Hyper-Parameters

Setting different values for the model hyperparameters sometimes affects the performance of the model, and the most appropriate hyperparameters can be found through experiments. Learning rate and training epochs are important parameters in the model. Learning rate determines the step size of the model parameters update, and affects the training effect and convergence speed of the model. For the adjustment of the model learning rate, the experimental results are shown in Table 7. When the learning rate is set to 3×10^{-5}, the model achieves the best performance.

Table 7. Model performance at different learning rates.

Learning Rate	Precision	Recall	F_1-Value
1×10^{-5}	0.8851	0.8876	0.8863
2×10^{-5}	0.9316	0.9424	0.9370
3×10^{-5}	0.9457	0.9539	0.9498
4×10^{-5}	0.9468	0.9468	0.9468
5×10^{-5}	0.9409	0.9381	0.9395

As the number of iterations grows, Figure 9 illustrates the trend in the F1 score of the model. RoBERTa-wwm-ext-BiLSTM-CRF has lower F_1 values than RoBERTa-wwm-ext-CRF and BERT-CRF in the first two epochs. The F_1 values of all models become stable after the fourth to fifth epoch, among which RoBERTa-wwm-ext-BiLSTM-CRF and BERT-BiLSTM-CRF have the best results, and RoBERTa-wwm-ext-BiLSTM-CRF maintains the largest F_1 value after the third epoch.

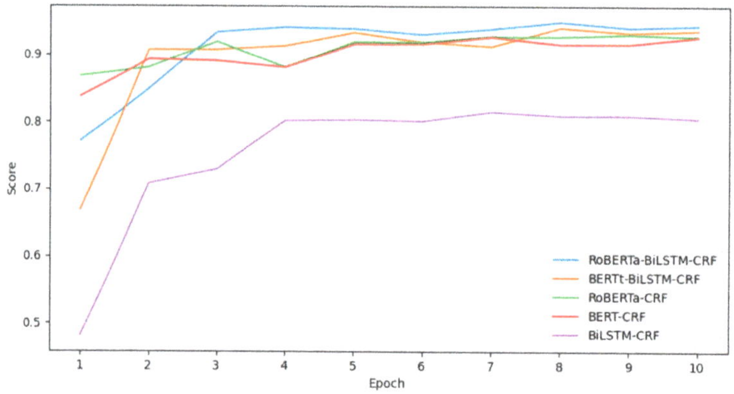

Figure 9. Variation of F1 value as the number of training epochs increases.

4.6. Case Study

The trained RoBERTa-wwm-ext-BiLSTM-CRF equipment fault diagnosis NER model can be directly invoked to recognize the entity of the input text. In order to verify the recognition effect of the model, we conducted a specific case study, and the results are shown in Figure 10.

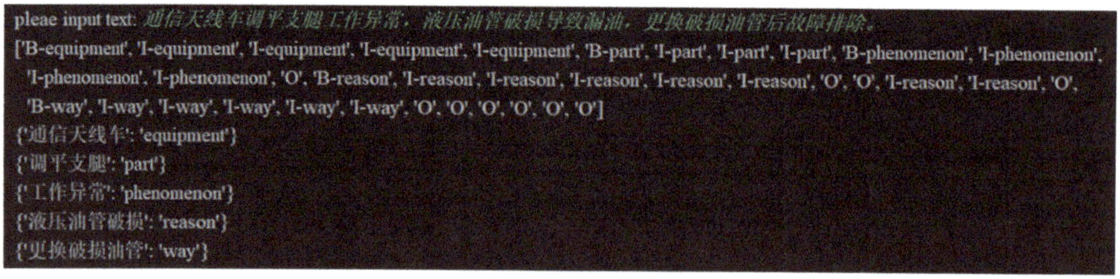

Figure 10. Entity recognition of the input text by the model.

In this example, the input text is "the communication antenna car leveling leg is working abnormally, the hydraulic oil pipe is damaged, and the oil leakage is caused, and the problem is solved after replacing the damaged oil pipe". The model marks the token in the text with their corresponding labels, and then outputs according to the "BIO" labeling rule. It can be seen that the model recognizes "communication antenna vehicle" in the text as "equipment", that is, "communication antenna vehicle" as the equipment name; "leveling leg" is identified as "part", that is, the "leveling leg" is the fault part; "abnormal work" is identified as "phenomenon", that is, " abnormal work" is the fault phenomenon. "the hydraulic oil pipe is damaged" is identified as "reason", that is, "the hydraulic oil pipe is damaged" is the fault reason. "replace the damaged oil pipe" is identified as "way", that is, "replace the damaged oil pipe" is the troubleshooting way. The recognition results confirm the effectiveness of our proposed model.

5. Conclusions

This paper establishes an NER model for equipment fault diagnosis based on the fusion of RoBERTa-wwm-ext and Deep Learning, aiming to automatically extract named entities from a massive set of equipment fault diagnosis text data. This paper then provides a solid data foundation and support for the construction of equipment fault diagnosis KGs. The model proposed in this paper is used to extract five types of entities from equipment fault diagnosis texts. The average P, R, and F_1 value are 0.9457, 0.9539, and 0.9498, respectively. Based on the experimental results, we draw the following conclusions: (1) After introducing the pre-trained model into NER task, the precision, recall, and F_1 value can be significantly improved. (2) Adding BiLSTM layer can boost model performance. (3) Comparative experiments show that the model proposed in this paper performs well in equipment fault diagnosis NER tasks. (4) When the meaning of entities is clear, the format is fixed, the repeatability is high, and the effect of entity extraction is better.

Although this study is effective for equipment fault diagnosis and named entities recognition, there are still some aspects worthy of improvement and in-depth exploration in future work: (1) For the recognition of fault phenomenon entities, the recognition effect is relatively poor due to the differences in description and record. (2) Due to the small amount of equipment fault diagnosis text data collection and imperfect performance indicators, we plan to build a high-quality equipment fault diagnosis corpus with a larger volume of data and richer entities. (3) The rapid progress of Deep Learning requires us to continuously optimize our model in pursuit of higher performance standards. (4) We plan to carry out related algorithm development work in order to effectively improve the P, R, and F1 values of named entity recognition in the field of equipment fault diagnosis. (5) We plan to apply the model to extract entities from a larger equipment fault diagnosis text and carry out the task of entity relation extraction from fault diagnosis text to build a domain knowledge graph. (6) We will further study the application effect of the model in other fields, such as the structural composition of equipment and other general fields, to further prove the effectiveness of the model.

Author Contributions: Conceptualization, F.G. and L.Z.; methodology, F.G. and B.Z.; software, L.X.; validation, W.W. and W.L.; formal analysis, W.L. and J.Z.; resources, F.G., L.X., and J.Z.; writing—original draft preparation, F.G. and W.L.; writing—review and editing, L.Z. and B.Z.; supervision, W.W.; funding acquisition, B.Z. All authors have read and agreed to the published version of the manuscript.

Funding: This work was supported in part by the National Social Science Foundation of China (2022-SKJJ-C-037).

Data Availability Statement: The data that support the findings of this study are available from the corresponding author upon reasonable request.

Conflicts of Interest: The authors declare no conflicts of interest.

References

1. Ji, S.; Pan, S.; Cambria, E.; Marttinen, P.; Yu, P.S. A Survey on Knowledge Graphs: Representation, Acquisition, and Applications. *IEEE Trans. Neural Netw. Learn. Syst.* **2022**, *33*, 494–514. [CrossRef] [PubMed]
2. Tang, X.; Chi, G.; Cui, L.; Ip, A.W.H.; Yung, K.L.; Xie, X. Exploring Research on the Construction and Application of Knowledge Graphs for Aircraft Fault Diagnosis. *Sensors* **2023**, *23*, 5295–5313. [CrossRef] [PubMed]

3. Deng, J.; Wang, T.; Wang, Z.; Zhou, J.; Cheng, L. Research on Event Logic Knowledge Graph Construction Method of Robot Transmission System Fault Diagnosis. *IEEE Access* **2022**, *10*, 17656–17673. [CrossRef]
4. Liu, L.; Wang, B.; Ma, F.; Zheng, Q.; Yao, L.; Zhang, C.; Mohamed, M.A. A Concurrent Fault Diagnosis Method of Transformer Based on Graph Convolutional Network and Knowledge Graph. *Front. Energy Res.* **2022**, *10*, 837553. [CrossRef]
5. Yu, Y.; Wang, Y.; Mu, J.; Li, W.; Jiao, S.; Wang, Z.; Lv, P.; Zhu, Y. Chinese Mineral Named Entity Recognition Based on BERT Model. *Expert Syst. Appl.* **2022**, *206*, 117727. [CrossRef]
6. Gong, Z.; Cao, Z.; Zhou, S.; Yang, F.; Shuai, C.; Ouyang, X.; Luo, Z. Thermal Fault Detection of High-Voltage Isolating Switches Based on Hybrid Data and BERT. *Arab. J. Sci. Eng.* **2024**, *49*, 6429–6443. [CrossRef]
7. Meng, X.; Jing, B.; Wang, S.; Pan, J.; Huang, Y.; Jiao, X. Fault Knowledge Graph Construction and Platform Development for Aircraft PHM. *Sensors* **2024**, *24*, 231–252. [CrossRef]
8. Yang, X.; Li, H.; Xu, Y.; Shen, N.; He, R. A Text Mining-Based Approach for Comprehensive Understanding of Chinese Railway Operational Equipment Failure Reports. 2024; *preprint*. [CrossRef]
9. Hettne, K.M.; Stierum, R.H.; Schuemie, M.J.; Hendriksen, P.J.M.; Schijvenaars, B.J.A.; van Mulligen, E.M.; Kleinjans, J.; Kors, J.A. A Dictionary to Identify Small Molecules and Drugs in Free Text. *Bioinformatics* **2009**, *25*, 2983–2991. [CrossRef]
10. Chieu, H.L.; Ng, H.T. Named Entity Recognition with a Maximum Entropy Approach. In Proceedings of the Seventh Conference on Natural Language Learning at HLT-NAACL 2003, Edmonton, AB, Canada, 31 May and 1 June 2003; pp. 160–163.
11. Zhao, S. Named Entity Recognition in Biomedical Texts Using an HMM Model. In Proceedings of the International Joint Workshop on Natural Language Processing in Biomedicine and Its Applications (NLPBA/BioNLP), Geneva, Switzerland, 28–29 August 2004; Collier, N., Ruch, P., Nazarenko, A., Eds.; COLING: Geneva, Switzerland, 2004; pp. 87–90.
12. Wang, C.; Ma, X.; Chen, J.; Chen, J. Information Extraction and Knowledge Graph Construction from Geoscience Literature. *Comput. Geosci.* **2018**, *112*, 112–120. [CrossRef]
13. Hochreiter, S.; Schmidhuber, J. Long Short-Term Memory. *Neural Comput.* **1997**, *9*, 1735–1780. [CrossRef]
14. Huang, Z.; Xu, W.; Yu, K. Bidirectional LSTM-CRF Models for Sequence Tagging. *arXiv* **2015**, arXiv:1508.01991.
15. Miao, K.; Han, T.; Yao, Y.; Lu, H.; Chen, P.; Wang, B.; Zhang, J. Application of LSTM for Short Term Fog Forecasting Based on Meteorological Elements. *Neurocomputing* **2020**, *408*, 285–291. [CrossRef]
16. An, Y.; Xia, X.; Chen, X.; Wu, F.-X.; Wang, J. Chinese Clinical Named Entity Recognition via Multi-Head Self-Attention Based BiLSTM-CRF. *Artif. Intell. Med.* **2022**, *127*, 102282. [CrossRef] [PubMed]
17. Devlin, J.; Chang, M.-W.; Lee, K.; Toutanova, K. BERT: Pre-Training of Deep Bidirectional Transformers for Language Understanding. *arXiv* **2018**, arXiv:1810.04805.
18. Guo, Z.X.; Deng, X.L. Intelligent Identification Method of Legal Case Entity Based on BERT-BiLSTM-CRF. *J. Beijing Univ. Posts Telecommun.* **2020**, *44*, 129–134. [CrossRef]
19. Lin, J.; Li, S.; Qin, N.; Ding, S. Entity Recognition of Railway Signal Equipment Fault Information Based on RoBERTa-Wwm and Deep Learning Integration. *Math. Biosci. Eng.* **2023**, *21*, 1228–1248. [CrossRef]
20. Liang, K.; Zhou, B.; Zhang, Y.; He, Y.; Guo, X.; Zhang, B. A Multi-Entity Knowledge Joint Extraction Method of Communication Equipment Faults for Industrial IoT. *Electronics* **2022**, *11*, 979–996. [CrossRef]
21. Kong, Z.; Yue, C.; Shi, Y.; Yu, J.; Xie, C.; Xie, L. Entity Extraction of Electrical Equipment Malfunction Text by a Hybrid Natural Language Processing Algorithm. *IEEE Access* **2021**, *9*, 40216–40226. [CrossRef]
22. Chen, T.; Zhu, J.; Zeng, Z.; Jia, X. Compressor Fault Diagnosis Knowledge: A Benchmark Dataset for Knowledge Extraction From Maintenance Log Sheets Based on Sequence Labeling. *IEEE Access* **2021**, *9*, 59394–59405. [CrossRef]
23. Zhang, Y.; Zhong, Y.; Luo, X. Power Equipment Fault Entity Recognition Based on BERT-CRF Model. In Proceedings of the Fifth International Conference on Artificial Intelligence and Computer Science, Wuhan, China, 26–28 July 2023; pp. 934–941.
24. Zhou, Z.; Zhang, C.; Liang, X.; Liu, H.; Diao, M.; Deng, Y. BERT-Based Dual-Channel Power Equipment Defect Text Assessment Model. *IEEE Access* **2024**, *12*, 134020–134026. [CrossRef]
25. Liu, T.; Liu, Q.; Fu, L. Automation of Book Categorisation Based on Network Centric Quality Management System. *Int. J. Adv. Comput. Sci. Appl. IJACSA* **2024**, *15*, 259. [CrossRef]
26. Zhuang, Y.; Cheng, S.; Kovalchuk, N.; Simmons, M.; Matar, O.K.; Guo, Y.-K.; Arcucci, R. Ensemble Latent Assimilation with Deep Learning Surrogate Model: Application to Drop Interaction in a Microfluidics Device. *Lab Chip* **2022**, *22*, 3187–3202. [CrossRef] [PubMed]
27. Liu, P.; Lv, S. Chinese RoBERTa Distillation For Emotion Classification. *Comput. J.* **2023**, *66*, 3107–3118. [CrossRef]
28. Li, D.; Yan, L.; Yang, J.; Ma, Z. Dependency Syntax Guided BERT-BiLSTM-GAM-CRF for Chinese NER. *Expert Syst. Appl.* **2022**, *196*, 116682. [CrossRef]
29. Liu, X.; Yang, N.; Jiang, Y.; Gu, L.; Shi, X. A Parallel Computing-Based Deep Attention Model for Named Entity Recognition. *J. Supercomput.* **2020**, *76*, 814–830. [CrossRef]

electronics

MDPI

Article

A Picture May Be Worth a Hundred Words for Visual Question Answering †

Yusuke Hirota [1,*], Noa Garcia [1], Mayu Otani [2], Chenhui Chu [3] and Yuta Nakashima [1]

1 Graduate School of Information Science and Technology, Osaka University, Osaka 565-0871, Japan; noagarcia@ids.osaka-u.ac.jp (N.G.); n-yuta@ids.osaka-u.ac.jp (Y.N.)
2 CyberAgent, Inc., Tokyo 150-0042, Japan; otani_mayu@cyberagent.co.jp
3 Department of Intelligence Science and Technology, Graduate School of Informatics, Kyoto University, Kyoto 606-8507, Japan; chu@i.kyoto-u.ac.jp
* Correspondence: y-hirota@is.ids.osaka-u.ac.jp

† This paper is an extended version of our paper published in a paper entitled "Visual Question Answering with Textual Representations for Images", which was presented at Proceedings of the IEEE/CVF International Conference on Computer Vision, Virtual, 11–17 October 2021.

Abstract: How far can textual representations go in understanding images? In image understanding, effective representations are essential. Deep visual features from object recognition models currently dominate various tasks, especially Visual Question Answering (VQA). However, these conventional features often struggle to capture image details in ways that match human understanding, and their decision processes lack interpretability. Meanwhile, the recent progress in language models suggests that descriptive text could offer a viable alternative. This paper investigated the use of descriptive text as an alternative to deep visual features in VQA. We propose to process description–question pairs rather than visual features, utilizing a language-only Transformer model. We also explored data augmentation strategies to enhance training set diversity and mitigate statistical bias. Extensive evaluation shows that textual representations using approximately a hundred words can effectively compete with deep visual features on both the VQA 2.0 and VQA-CP v2 datasets. Our qualitative experiments further reveal that these textual representations enable clearer investigation of VQA model decision processes, thereby improving interpretability.

Keywords: visual question answering; textual representations; data augmentation; interpretability; vision-and-language

1. Introduction

Understanding the visual world through language has been a fundamental challenge in artificial intelligence. Computer vision systems have made remarkable progress in tasks like object detection [1] and scene understanding [2,3], primarily relying on deep visual features—mathematical representations of images learned through neural networks. However, these features face two critical limitations [4–6]: they often struggle to capture complex semantic relationships in images, and their decision-making process remains opaque to humans [7].

The English proverb "A picture is worth a thousand words" suggests that visual information can convey meaning more efficiently than verbal descriptions. However, recent advances in natural language processing, particularly the emergence of powerful language models, such as Transformer [8] and Transformer-based models [9–12], have demonstrated remarkable capabilities in understanding and reasoning about textual information, suggesting that concise textual descriptions might serve as an effective alternative to image representation.

Current approaches to visual understanding tasks, such as Visual Question Answering (VQA), have explored various ways to represent images. Traditional systems rely on deep visual features extracted by object recognition models [1], while more recent approaches utilize Transformer-based models [13–20] like Vision Transformer [21] to learn representations from image–text pairs. Despite their widespread adoption, these visual representations often struggle to capture detailed semantic relationships and lack human interpretability, limiting their effectiveness in complex reasoning tasks like VQA.

In this paper, we explored a different approach to VQA that moves away from conventional visual feature-based methods. Instead of focusing on improving image feature extraction or visual processing techniques, we investigated the potential of using pure textual descriptions to represent image content. Specifically, we investigated whether well-crafted textual descriptions can serve as an effective alternative to traditional visual features, potentially offering benefits in both performance and interpretability.

To address these challenges, we propose a novel approach that replaces image–question pairs with image description–question pairs in VQA tasks. Our key research questions are as follows:

- Can textual representations compete with or outperform deep visual features in VQA tasks?
- How many words are actually necessary to effectively represent an image for machine understanding?
- Can data augmentation techniques enhance the performance of text-based image understanding?

We used RoBERTa [9], one of the most well-known Transformer-based language models, as our VQA model. The input description–question pairs were jointly fed into the model to predict an answer. In addition, with the success of data augmentation methods on both VQA and NLP tasks [22–26], we investigated the use of synthetic samples on language-only representations. As the aim of the study was to explore the viability of language-only representations in VQA, we relied on already annotated descriptions from two standard datasets [27,28]. Automatically generating the image descriptions, although a necessary future step, is out of the scope of this paper.

Our work makes three key contributions:

- We demonstrate that textual representations using approximately 100 words can match or exceed the performance of deep visual features on standard VQA benchmarks, challenging conventional wisdom about image representation.
- We introduce a more interpretable approach to VQA, where the system's decision-making process can be readily understood by examining the textual descriptions it uses.
- We present novel data augmentation techniques adapted for text-only VQA, including a particularly effective back translation method for questions that significantly improves performance.

The remainder of this paper is organized as follows: Section 2 reviews related work in VQA, image representation, and data augmentation. Section 3 details our proposed approach and methodology. Section 4 presents our experimental results and analysis. Section 5 provides qualitative analysis and discussion of our findings, Section 6 discusses the limitations of our approach and the benefits from our results, and Section 7 concludes with implications for future research.

2. Related Work

Image Representations for VQA. Image representation plays a crucial role in vision-and-language tasks. Traditional VQA approaches [29–34] rely on deep visual features extracted by object detectors like Faster R-CNN [1], where each feature vector captures information about a specific image region. Recent models utilizing Transformer-based architectures [21] have shown promising results [13–15,35]. However, these approaches face two key challenges: they often learn superficial correlations rather than true visual understanding [4–6], and their internal representations remain difficult for humans to interpret [7].

On the other hand, there has been a growing trend in studies utilizing textual representations of images [18–20,36–40]. These approaches offer several advantages: they can capture semantic relationships more explicitly, provide human-interpretable representations, and leverage recent advances in language understanding. Many works have adapted Transformer models to fuse visual and textual information [13,16–19,41], achieving high performance through pre-training with image–caption pairs. For example, Wu et al. [38] generates question-relevant captions to provide additional context for answering. While these approaches demonstrate the value of textual information, they typically treat text as supplementary to visual features rather than as the primary representation medium. This leaves open the question of whether textual descriptions alone could serve as effective image representations.

Recent works have shown promising solutions to various VQA challenges: SCLSM [42] effectively addresses language bias through contrastive learning, Atlantis [43] successfully integrates aesthetic features for sentiment analysis, and studies on out-of-distribution detection [44] improve system reliability. While these approaches advance VQA through different learning strategies, our work takes a fundamentally different direction by investigating the potential of pure textual representations for image understanding.

Data Augmentation for VQA. Data augmentation techniques for VQA have primarily focused on addressing language bias [4–6], where models tend to exploit superficial correlations between questions and answers in the training set. Chen et al. [23] demonstrated the effectiveness of counterfactual sample synthesis by manipulating critical parts of input images, while Gokhale et al. [22] showed that systematic manipulation of both images and questions can improve model robustness. While these approaches have proven effective, they require computationally expensive image manipulation.

Our work adapts these counterfactual generation principles to operate directly on textual descriptions, preserving the benefits of data augmentation while reducing computational costs. Furthermore, we extend these ideas by incorporating techniques from NLP-based data augmentation, creating a framework that leverages the strengths of both VQA-specific and text-specific augmentation methods.

Data Augmentation for NLP. The NLP community has developed diverse data augmentation strategies to enhance model performance. Back translation [25,26,45] stands as one of the fundamental techniques where text is transformed through intermediate languages to create semantically equivalent but linguistically diverse samples. Another significant approach is EDA (Easy Data Augmentation) [24], which has demonstrated success in various text classification scenarios [46–50], particularly when training data are limited. Recent methods have also explored contextual augmentation, where words are strategically replaced or inserted based on their semantic context.

Given the text-centric nature of our approach, we investigated how these established NLP augmentation techniques can benefit VQA tasks when applied to our textual representations. This novel integration of NLP-specific augmentation methods into VQA presents an opportunity to leverage well-studied text manipulation strategies in a new context.

Distinction from Previous Work. While previous studies have made significant progress in VQA, our approach differs in several key aspects. Unlike works that use textual information as supplementary input [38,39], we explored the potential of using text as the primary representation of visual content. Moreover, while existing data augmentation methods [22,23] focus on image manipulation, our approach uniquely combines VQA-specific and NLP-based augmentation techniques in a text-only setting. This not only reduces computational costs but also provides better interpretability, as all operations are performed in the human-readable text domain.

3. Approach

We present a text-based model to explore the potential of language-only representations for VQA, as shown in Figure 1. The input, comprising a question and a detailed image description, is processed by a Transformer model with multiple self-attention layers. The Transformer's output is then passed to a classifier to predict the answer. Additionally, we employ data augmentation techniques to expand and diversify the training set.

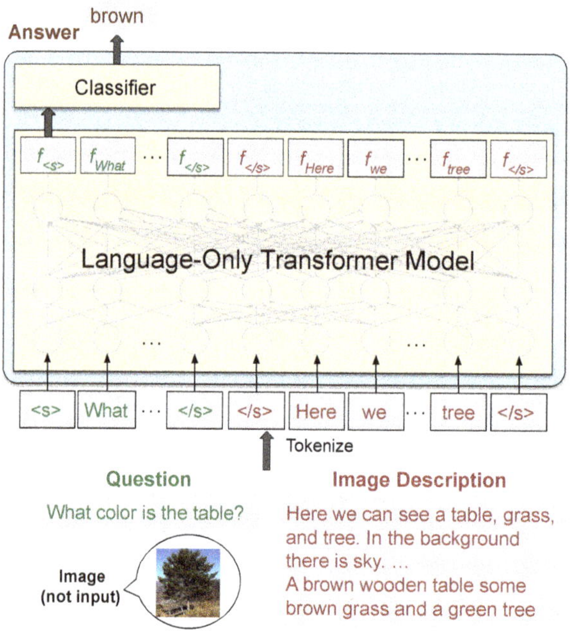

Figure 1. Model overview. Our language-only model takes a question and a description as the input of a language-only Transformer model and predicts an answer accordingly.

3.1. Language-Only Data

Our language-only VQA framework utilizes the following: (1) questions and answers from standard VQA datasets, (2) image descriptions representing the image content, and (3) synthetic data generated through data augmentation techniques.

Questions and Answers. We use the VQA-CP v2 [4] and VQA 2.0 [51] datasets for the questions and answers. VQA 2.0 consists of 1.1 M question–answer pairs across 204 K images, while VQA-CP v2 contains 603 K question–answer pairs from 219 K images. Both datasets use images from the MSCOCO dataset [52]. Although VQA 2.0 is a standard for natural image VQA, it has been shown to exhibit strong statistical biases in its training distribution [4–6], allowing models to achieve high accuracy by focusing on the first few words of a question. VQA-CP v2 mitigates this issue by reorganizing the training and validation splits.

Image Descriptions. We source image descriptions from two corpora: COCO captions [27] and Localized Narratives [28]. COCO captions provide five short captions per image in the MSCOCO dataset [52], with an average of 10.5 words per caption. These captions focus on describing key elements in the scene, omitting less important details. Localized Narratives, on the other hand, offer detailed image descriptions for several datasets, including MSCOCO. Annotators generate these narratives by describing the image aloud while highlighting the relevant regions with a mouse, capturing both prominent and minor objects. This results in more comprehensive descriptions, averaging 42.9 words per narrative.

Synthetic Data. To enhance the diversity of the training set in our language-only framework, we generate synthetic samples using data augmentation techniques, categorized into two types: Data Augmentation for VQA (Section 3.2) and Data Augmentation for Language (Section 3.3). For Data Augmentation for VQA (DAV), inspired by recent multimodal augmentation methods [22,23], which generate new images and questions by altering objects in an image or question, we adapt these methods for our text-only approach by creating synthetic descriptions instead of modifying images. For Data Augmentation for Language (DAL), we employ well-established NLP techniques to enhance language tasks, drawing from methods such as EDA, back translation, and others [24–26,45].

3.2. Data Augmentation for VQA

We utilize data augmentation methods for VQA [22,23] for our language-only input for two reasons: (1) to generate diverse training samples that force the model to focus on essential information rather than superficial patterns, and (2) to achieve this in a computationally efficient way by manipulating text rather than images. While previous approaches [22,23,53,54] required complex image manipulation through masking or GANs [55], our text-based methods achieve similar diversity through simple word-level operations.

Let s denote a training triplet, i.e., $s = (\mathbf{q}, \mathbf{d}, A)$, where $\mathbf{q} = [q_1, \cdots, q_Q]$ is a question sequence with Q tokens, associated with a question type t, and $\mathbf{d} = [d_1, \cdots, d_D]$ is a description sequence with D tokens. The set $A = \{a_1, \cdots, a_N\}$ contains N ground-truth answers, with N being at most 10 for VQA 2.0 and VQA-CP v2 datasets, varying across samples. We propose four data augmentation techniques: (1) hypernym and hyponym replacement, (2) color inversion, (3) adversarial replacement, and (4) counterfactual samples. Examples are illustrated in Figure 2.

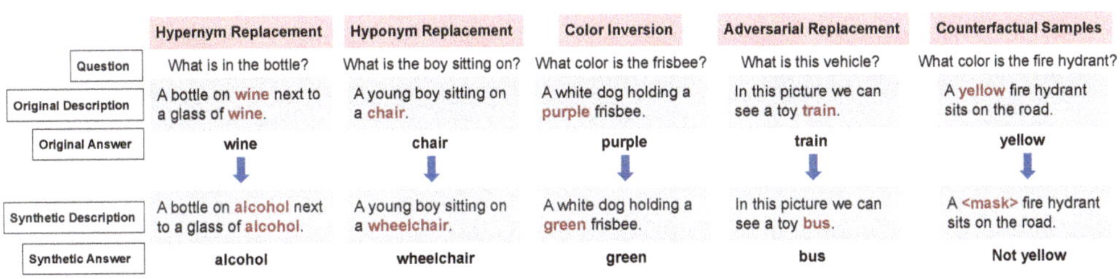

Figure 2. Examples of synthetic samples generated using our proposed data augmentation techniques for VQA.

Hypernym and Hyponym Replacement. Following [22], we use hypernym and hyponym replacement to create semantically meaningful variations in image descriptions while preserving their basic truth value. For example, replacing "fruit" with its hypernym "food" encourages the model to generalize across broader categories, while replacing it with its hyponym "apple" allows the model to handle specific instances. In a real-world scenario, if the description contains the word "car", it might be replaced with "vehicle" (hypernym) to generalize, or "sedan" (hyponym) to specialize. This technique forces the model to learn more abstract or specific concepts, which reduces reliance on narrow language patterns and helps in combating biases that arise from overfitting to common words in the training data.

To generate new samples, let $A_{\mathbf{d}}$ be the set of ground-truth answers a that appear in $\mathbf{d}$. We replace $a \in A_{\mathbf{d}}$ with its hypernym $h_e(a)$ (or hyponym $h_o(a)$) in both A and $\mathbf{d}$. The new triplet for hypernym replacement, s_{h}, is defined as follows:

$$s_{\mathrm{h}} = (\mathbf{q}, \mathbf{d}_{\mathrm{h}}, A_{\mathrm{h}}) \tag{1}$$

$$A_{\mathrm{h}} = A \setminus A_{\mathbf{d}} \cup \{h_e(a)\}_{a \in A_{\mathbf{d}}} \tag{2}$$

$$\mathbf{d}_{\mathrm{h}} = [d_1, \cdots, d_L] \quad \text{where } d_i = h_e(a) \text{ if } d_i = a, \quad \forall a \in A_{\mathbf{d}} \tag{3}$$

Similarly, $h_o(a)$ is used for hyponym replacement. If $h_e(a) \in A$ (or $h_o(a) \in A$), we skip generating s_{h} to avoid duplicates. Hypernyms and hyponyms are identified using WordNet [56].

Color Inversion. For color inversion [22], we substitute a color word in a description with another color word. For example, if the original description states that "the car is white", we replace "white" with "black", resulting in "the car is black". This method helps the model handle different color schemes and ensures that it does not overly rely on specific color cues, making it more robust in tasks that involve color-based questions or object recognition.

We define a set of K color words, $C = \{c_1, \cdots, c_K\}$, and a set of question types related to colors, T_C ($T_C = \{$"what color", "what color are the", "what color is", "what color is the"$\}$). For a training triplet s with question type t, if $t \in T_C$ and a ground-truth color answer $a \in A \cap C$ appears in the description (i.e., $d_i = a$ for some i), we randomly replace the color word a with a different color $c \neq a$. The new training triplet s_{c} is as follows:

$$s_{\mathrm{c}} = (\mathbf{q}, \mathbf{d}_{\mathrm{c}}, A_{\mathrm{c}}) \tag{4}$$

$$A_{\mathrm{c}} = A \setminus \{a\} \cup \{c\} \tag{5}$$

$$\mathbf{d}_{\mathrm{c}} = [d_1, \cdots, d_L] \text{ with } d_i = c \text{ if } d_i = a \tag{6}$$

Adversarial Replacement. For Yes/No samples, we replace object words in the description with adversarial words. For instance, if the original description states "the cat is on the sofa" and the question is "Is the cat on the sofa?", we might replace "sofa" with "chair", resulting in "the cat is on the chair", forcing the model to change the answer from "yes" to "no". This helps the model learn to better distinguish between subtle changes in object references and makes it more robust in answering questions accurately when similar but different objects are involved.

For Yes/No samples, i.e., $s = (\mathbf{q}, \mathbf{d}, A)$ where $\{\mathrm{yes}, \mathrm{no}\} \cap A \neq \emptyset$, we replace object words $o \in O$ in the description $\mathbf{d}$ with adversarial words. O is the set of 80 object classes in MSCOCO [52]. Following [22], we define an adversarial word, $w_{\mathrm{adv}}(o)$, as the word most similar to o but with a different meaning. If o (or its synonyms) appear in $\mathbf{q}$, the answer is switched from "yes" to "no"; otherwise, the answer remains unchanged. The new training triplet s_{a} is as follows:

$$s_{\mathrm{a}} = (\mathbf{q}, \mathbf{d}_{\mathrm{a}}, A_{\mathrm{a}}) \tag{7}$$

$$A_{\mathrm{a}} = \begin{cases} \{\mathrm{no}\} & \text{if } o \text{ is in } \mathbf{q} \\ A & \text{otherwise} \end{cases} \tag{8}$$

$$\mathbf{d}_{\mathrm{a}} = [d_1, \cdots, d_L] \text{ with } d_i = w_{\mathrm{adv}}(o) \text{ if } d_i = o, \tag{9}$$

where $w_{\mathrm{adv}}(o)$ is selected as the closest word to $o \in O$ based on the Euclidean distance between their GloVe embeddings [57].

Unlike [22], we avoid generating adversarial samples from questions, as altering a word in the question results in a new answer that cannot be automatically inferred, e.g., "How many bins?" $\rightarrow$"How many pens?".

Counterfactual Samples. Counterfactual samples [23] are generated by modifying parts of the question or description to create alternative scenarios. For example, if the original question is "What color is the car?", and the description states "The car is red", we modify the description to "The car is blue" to generate a counterfactual sample. This forces the model to understand changes in the input and adjust its predictions accordingly, improving its ability to handle ambiguous or altered situations.

Specifically, we generate counterfactual training samples (CSS) by adapting the method in [23] for language-only description–question pairs. For a given training triplet $s = (\mathbf{q}, \mathbf{d}, A)$, we create counterfactual samples s_{cssq} and $scss_d$ from the query and description.

$$s_{\text{css}_\text{q}} = (\mathbf{q}_{\text{css}_\text{q}}, \mathbf{d}, A_{\text{css}_\text{q}}) \tag{10}$$
$$s_{\text{css}_\text{d}} = (\mathbf{q}, \mathbf{d}_{\text{css}_\text{d}}, A_{\text{css}_\text{d}}) \tag{11}$$

To generate s_{cssq}, we input $\mathbf{q}$ and $\mathbf{d}$ into a trained Transformer VQA model $\mathcal{M}$ and use Grad-CAM [58] to find the contribution of each word in $\mathbf{q}$ to the answer set A. The top-D words with the highest contribution form the critical set Ωq. Two new questions, $\mathbf{q}^{+}_{\text{css}_\text{q}}$ and $\mathbf{q}^{-}_{\text{css}_\text{q}}$, are created by masking words not in Ω_q and masking the words in Ω_q, respectively.

$$\begin{aligned} \mathbf{q}^{+}_{\text{css}_\text{q}} &= [q_1, \cdots, q_L] \\ &\quad \text{with } q_i = \texttt{<mask>} \quad \text{for all } q_i \notin \Omega_\text{q} \end{aligned} \tag{12}$$
$$\begin{aligned} \mathbf{q}^{-}_{\text{css}_\text{q}} &= [q_1, \cdots, q_L] \\ &\quad \text{with } q_i = \texttt{<mask>} \quad \text{for all } q_i \in \Omega_\text{q}, \end{aligned} \tag{13}$$

where $\mathbf{q}^{-}_{\text{css}_\text{q}}$ serves as the question $\mathbf{q}_{\text{css}_\text{q}}$ for the CSS sample; the first few words that indicate the question type (e.g., "what color is") are not masked, as in [23].

To determine A_{css_q}, we feed $\mathbf{q}^{+}_{\text{css}_\text{q}}$ and $\mathbf{d}$ back into $\mathcal{M}$ to score each candidate answer. The top-J scoring answers are excluded from the original answer set. Specifically, letting $\mathcal{M}_J(\mathbf{q}^{+}_{\text{css}_\text{q}}, \mathbf{d})$ represent the top-J answers, the new ground-truth answers are given by

$$A_{\text{css}_\text{q}} = A \setminus \mathcal{M}_J(\mathbf{q}^{+}_{\text{css}_\text{q}}, \mathbf{d}). \tag{14}$$

For s_{css_d}, the values of Ω_d, $\mathbf{d}^{+}_{\text{css}_\text{d}}$, $\mathbf{d}^{-}_{\text{css}_\text{d}}$, and $M_N(\mathbf{q}, \mathbf{d}^{+}_{\text{css}_\text{d}})$ are determined using the same process.

3.3. Data Augmentation for Language

Given our text-only approach, we leverage established NLP augmentation techniques that have proven effective in maintaining semantic meaning while introducing linguistic diversity. We specifically select three complementary techniques: EDA for simple yet effective transformations, back translation for generating naturally varied paraphrases, and word replacement/insertion via contextual word embedding for ensuring semantic coherence. These methods work together to create a robust training set that helps the model better understand the relationship between textual descriptions and visual concepts. Each technique is applied to either the description or the question in the input triplet s to create new samples:

$$s_{\text{nlp}_\text{q}} = (\mathbf{q}_{\text{nlp}}, \mathbf{d}, A) \tag{15}$$
$$s_{\text{nlp}_\text{d}} = (\mathbf{q}, \mathbf{d}_{\text{nlp}}, A) \tag{16}$$

where $\mathbf{q}_{\text{nlp}}$ and $\mathbf{d}_{\text{nlp}}$ represent the question and description after applying one of the transformations below. Examples of generated synthetic samples are provided in Table 1.

EDA (Easy Data Augmentation) [24] includes the following four operations:

- Synonym Replacement randomly selects n words from the sentence and substitutes them with their synonyms.
- Random Insertion inserts a random synonym of a randomly chosen word into a random position in the sentence.
- Random Swap selects two words from the sentence and swaps their positions.
- Random Deletion removes words from the sentence with a probability of p.

Table 1. Examples of Data Augmentation for Language when applied to questions.

Original	Is This an Ocean Area?	What Is the Giraffe Standing Behind?
EDA (Synonym Replacement)	Is this an ocean region?	What is the camelopard standing behind?
EDA (Random Insertion)	Is this sea an ocean area?	What is the giraffe abide standing behind?
EDA (Random Swap)	Is this ocean an area?	What is the standing giraffe behind?
EDA (Random Deletion)	Is this an area?	What is the standing behind?
Back Translation	Is it a maritime area?	What's behind the giraffe?
Contextual Word Replacement	Is this an ocean top?	What is the giraffe tree behind?
Contextual Word Insertion	Is this an urban ocean area?	What is the giraffe standing silently behind?

For example, using synonym replacement, the sentence "The cat is sitting on the sofa" can become "The feline is sitting on the couch". This introduces variations in the input data while keeping the meaning intact, making the model more robust to paraphrases and improving its generalization across different language expressions. For each sample, one of these four operations is applied at random.

Back Translation [25,26] translates a sentence into another language and then translates it back into the original language. For instance, translating "The dog is playing in the garden" to German and back into English might produce "The dog plays in the yard." This method introduces linguistic variety while preserving meaning, which helps to reduce bias introduced by specific language patterns in the training data. By generating paraphrases that use different sentence structures and vocabulary, the model is exposed to a broader range of linguistic expressions, reducing overfitting to common phrases and thus mitigating language bias. For back translation, we implement it using the Python library nlpaug [59], which translates a sentence into German and back into English. If the sentence remains unchanged after translation, we discard it.

Contextual Word Replacement/Insertion replaces or inserts words based on the surrounding context. For example, if the original sentence is The dog is running in the park, the word "park" might be replaced with "field" or "garden" based on the context. This helps the model to generalize its understanding of different environments while maintaining the overall meaning of the sentence, making it more robust to variations in language and context. To obtain contextually appropriate words for replacement or insertion, we leverage the Python nlpaug library [59], selecting random words from the description or question and replace or insert the most contextually similar words. Pre-trained XLNet [60] is used for generating the contextual word embeddings needed for these transformations.

3.4. Language-Only VQA Model

Unlike most VQA models that take image–question pairs as input, our language-only VQA model uses description–question pairs. For the original VQA triplet $(\mathbf{q}, I, A)$, where I is the image related to the question, we generate the image description $\mathbf{d}$ by combining the narrative from Localized Narratives with the captions from COCO captions. Following the sequence format of the RoBERTa's implementation in Huggingface [61], the question and image description are then merged into a single sequence, $\mathbf{l}$, by inserting a classifier token <s> at the start, and sentence-ending tokens </s> as follows:

$$\mathbf{l} = \texttt{<s>} + \mathbf{q} + \texttt{</s>} + \texttt{</s>} + \mathbf{d} + \texttt{</s>} \quad (17)$$

where "+" denotes concatenation. The resulting input sequence is then fed into our Transformer-based language model $\mathcal{T}$, producing the sequence of embeddings $\mathbf{f}$, i.e.,

$$\mathbf{f} = \mathcal{T}(\mathbf{l}). \quad (18)$$

Then, the embedding corresponding to the classifier token <s> is passed into the classifier $\mathcal{C}$ to generate the final prediction:

$$\rho = \mathcal{C}(\mathbf{f}_{<s>}) \tag{19}$$

List of Abbreviations

We summarize the abbreviations used in our approach and its explanations.

- CSS: Counterfactual Samples Synthesizing;
- EDA: Easy Data Augmentation;
- VQA: Visual Question Answering;
- NLP: Natural Language Processing.

Summary: This section introduced our approach of using textual representations and a Transformer-based model, with the support of data augmentation techniques to enhance performance.

4. Experiments

We conducted five main experiments to evaluate the effectiveness of textual representations in VQA: (Section 4.1) comparing various image descriptions, (Section 4.2) assessing different data augmentation techniques, (Section 4.3) comparing textual representations with deep visual features, (Section 4.4) examining the effect of data augmentation on questions for models using deep visual features, and (Section 4.5) comparing different language-only Transformers.

Setup. We chose RoBERTa [9] as the primary Transformer model for our experiments due to its strong performance on a wide range of natural language processing tasks, including question answering and its improvements over BERT [10], such as better pre-training techniques and removal of the next sentence prediction objective. These optimizations lead to better generalization and higher accuracy, making RoBERTa well-suited for VQA tasks where both questions and image descriptions must be processed efficiently. While other models like BERT and XLNet were also viable, RoBERTa consistently showed superior results in our experiments (Section 4.5) . For RoBERTa hyperparameters, we used the large variant with 24 layers and 355 million parameters. The model was trained with a batch size of 32 and a learning rate of 1×10^{-5}, using the Adam optimizer with $\beta_1 = 0.9$ and $\beta_2 = 0.999$. The maximum sequence length for inputs was set to 512 tokens, and we used dropout with a rate of 0.1 for regularization. Training was performed for 10 epochs, with early stopping based on validation loss. As a classifier, we used a multi-layer perceptron with two fully-connected layers and the Swish activation function [62] between them. We used softmax cross entropy over the answer vocabulary for the loss function. The parameters for the data augmentation techniques were as follows: for counterfactual samples, we set $D = 10$ to select critical words and $J = 5$ to assign new answers. For EDA, the rate of words to be changed was set to 0.1, as recommended in the original paper [24]. Unless otherwise specified, the input to our model included the entire sequence of the question, narrative, and five captions. Results were presented in terms of accuracy, as in [51].

4.1. Describing an Image with Words

This experiment explored how different types and lengths of image descriptions impact VQA performance. The goal was to determine whether more detailed descriptions improve accuracy and to assess how much information is needed for optimal results. Understanding this helps to clarify the relationship between the richness of image descriptions and the model's ability to answer questions effectively.

Image descriptions. We began by evaluating the performance of different language-only inputs, including the following: only the question, the question with one to five randomly selected captions from COCO captions, the question with a narrative, and the entire input (question, narrative, and five captions). The results, reported in Table 2, also include the average sequence length.

The complete input, which combined the narrative with five captions, averaging 95.3 tokens per sample, achieved the highest performance, indicating that both datasets provided complementary information useful for VQA. When comparing captions with narratives, captions resulted in better accuracy with fewer words. For example, using just two captions surpassed the performance of narratives, even though the word count was nearly half. This suggests that the VQA dataset contains a large number of questions about general image content rather than specific details, as COCO captions tend to focus on prominent elements of the scene, unlike narratives. In other words, most questions that people ask about an image pertain to its key elements. This tendency for humans to emphasize the prominent parts while overlooking minor details is known as reporting bias [63,64].

Input length. We analyzed the relationship between input length and model accuracy by progressively truncating the image descriptions at test time. The model was trained with the full input (question, narrative, and five captions). To preserve context, we randomly shuffled the sentences before truncating them and then returned them to their original order. The question portion of the input remained intact throughout. The results, shown in Figure 3, indicate a steady decline in accuracy as more words were removed from the input.

Accuracy decreased consistently up to a 60% truncation rate, after which performance dropped more sharply. This suggests that while longer descriptions provided useful context, the model struggled to process the input effectively if too much information was lost. This trend aligns with the concept of diminishing returns, where adding more descriptive information initially improves performance but eventually introduces noise or redundancy. Since COCO captions focus on key elements in the image, truncating beyond a certain point likely removes critical content, leading to a steep decline in accuracy after 60%.

Table 2. Performance of different language-only inputs on the VQA-CP v2 test set. Length represents the mean number of tokens in the image descriptions.

Image Description	Length	Accuracy
None (Question-Only)	-	21.39
One Caption	10.5	35.31
Two Captions	21.0	38.49
Three Captions	31.5	40.09
Four Captions	42.0	41.93
Five Captions	52.5	42.34
Narrative	42.9	36.45
Whole (Narrative + Five Captions)	95.3	43.64

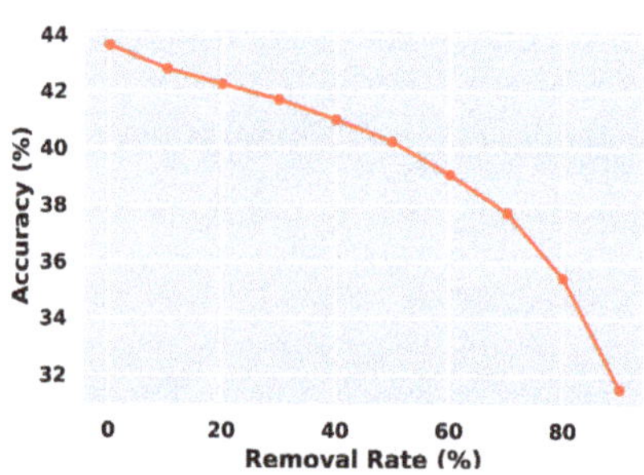

Figure 3. Impact of input sequence truncation on VQA-CP v2 test set accuracy. The graph shows how progressively removing words from the input sequence affected model performance.

4.2. Use of Synthetic Samples

This experiment aimed to evaluate the effectiveness of different data augmentation techniques in improving VQA accuracy. By analyzing how synthetic samples generated through various methods affected the model's performance, we sought to determine which techniques enhanced the model's ability to generalize and handle diverse question types. We specifically tested the impact of these augmentations on the VQA-CP v2 training set, using the full description with the narrative and five captions as input.

The results for each of the proposed data augmentation techniques are shown in Table 3. While most techniques improved accuracy, back translation applied to questions yielded the largest improvement, particularly for Yes/No questions, with a 17.30 point gain. This boost of 17.30 points was calculated as the difference between the baseline Yes/No accuracy of 45.13% and the Yes/No accuracy of 62.43% achieved when the back translation was applied to the questions. This suggests that paraphrasing through back translation introduced a diversity of linguistic structures while preserving the semantic meaning, helping the model generalize better to question variations. In contrast, methods like hypernym/hyponym replacement or color inversion generated smaller improvements, likely because they involved limited word-level changes that did not sufficiently alter the structure of the descriptions or questions to increase generalization significantly. Contextual word replacement for descriptions even led to a performance drop, likely due to the insertion of words that were semantically less relevant, confusing the model during training.

A notable observation is that applying data augmentation to questions consistently produced better results than applying it to descriptions. Among the DAV techniques, hyponym replacement stood out as the most effective, with a significant accuracy boost of 1.62. Interestingly, combining hyponym and hypernym replacements did not improve performance beyond hyponym replacement alone. This indicates that, in some instances, combining synthetic samples from different augmentation techniques can be counterproductive, possibly confusing the model.

Table 3. Results of data augmentation techniques on the VQA-CP v2 test set, showing the impact of different data augmentation methods on model accuracy for Yes/No, Number, and Other question types. D indicates techniques applied to image descriptions, while Q indicates application to questions. The Gap column highlights the improvement in accuracy compared to the baseline, where no synthetic data were used.

	Input Data	Num. Synthetic	Num. Total	Yes/No	Number	Other	Overall	Gap
	Narrative + Five Captions	-	438,183	45.13	20.06	49.33	43.64	-
DAV	w/ Hyponym Replacement	132,570	570,753	45.65	25.36	50.52	45.26	+1.62
	w/ Hypernym Replacement	23,869	462,052	47.28	17.69	49.10	43.70	+0.06
	w/ Hyponym and Hypernym Replacement	183,944	622,177	45.80	21.46	51.15	45.06	+1.42
	w/ Color Inversion	19,308	457,491	45.61	19.93	50.60	44.47	+1.06
	w/ Adversarial Word Replacement	169,929	608,112	44.71	19.84	50.03	43.93	+0.29
	w/ Counterfactual Samples	438,183	876,366	44.20	19.84	52.07	44.86	+1.22
DAL	w/ EDA (D)	438,183	876,366	44.68	20.64	50.08	44.02	+0.38
	w/ EDA (Q)	438,183	876,366	46.86	23.50	50.62	45.39	+1.75
	w/ Contextual Word Replacement (D)	438,183	876,366	44.69	19.40	48.91	43.18	−0.46
	w/ Contextual Word Replacement (Q)	438,183	876,366	46.09	22.49	49.10	44.16	+0.52
	w/ Contextual Word Insertion (D)	438,183	876,366	45.15	19.31	48.86	43.27	−0.37
	w/ Contextual Word Insertion (Q)	438,183	876,366	45.86	21.44	51.10	45.05	+1.41
	w/ Back Translation (D)	438,183	876,366	45.28	21.01	50.89	44.70	+1.06
	w/ Back Translation (Q)	293,811	731,994	62.43	27.15	51.84	51.16	+7.52

4.3. Comparison Against Deep Visual Features

This experiment evaluated the effectiveness of text-based representations in comparison to models using deep visual features. The key question was whether language-only representations can encapsulate the necessary visual information as effectively as traditional visual features. The objective was to assess the potential of text-based approaches as a viable alternative or complement to deep visual features in tasks like VQA, where the understanding of both visual and textual elements is crucial.

We compared our language-only representations (question, narrative, and five captions) with top VQA models that use deep visual features on the VQA-CP v2 and VQA 2.0 datasets. To ensure fairness, we excluded models designed to address language bias [32–34], as these techniques can be applied to any model, including ours. Additionally, we did not use data augmentation for this comparison. Despite the detailed visual information captured by models like VisualBERT, which is trained on image–text pairs, the results in Table 4 demonstrate that language-based models perform competitively. Our approach surpassed many deep visual feature baselines, indicating that well-annotated textual descriptions can effectively capture essential visual details.

One possible explanation for the strong performance of our model is that human-generated image descriptions tend to focus on the most relevant aspects, filtering out unnecessary details that deep visual features might capture. Moreover, text-based representations provide a level of interpretability that may help align the question and description more accurately. However, NSM [65] achieves slightly better results on VQA-CP v2, likely due to its ability to capture more intricate visual details, which can be challenging to express purely through text. Overall, this comparison highlights the advantages of textual representations in tasks where high-level semantic understanding is crucial. However, deep visual features may still hold an edge in tasks requiring precise spatial reasoning or detailed object localization, areas where textual descriptions may fall short.

Table 4. Comparison of language-only models with deep visual feature-based models, showing the performance of various models on the VQA-CP v2 test and VQA 2.0 validation sets. Results marked with * are our re-implementations.

	VQA-CP v2 Test				VQA 2.0 Val			
Model	**Yes/No**	**Number**	**Other**	**Overall**	**Yes/No**	**Number**	**Other**	**Overall**
HAN [66]	52.25	13.79	20.33	28.65	-	-	-	-
MuRel [32]	42.85	13.17	45.04	39.54	-	-	-	65.14
UpDn [29]	42.27	11.93	46.05	39.74	81.18	42.14	55.66	63.48
ReGAT [67]	-	-	-	40.42	-	-	-	67.18
BAN * [30]	43.14	13.63	46.92	40.74	83.19	48.13	57.52	65.93
VisualBERT * [20]	43.30	15.07	47.83	41.51	84.55	48.19	57.29	66.33
NSM [65]	-	-	-	45.80	-	-	-	-
Ours (Narrative + Five Captions)	45.13	20.06	49.33	43.64	87.91	56.47	59.43	69.74

4.4. Back Translation for Other Models

The results in Section 4.2 demonstrate that back translation significantly boosted accuracy in our language-only setting. To assess whether this technique can generalize to other models, we applied back translation to standard VQA models, such as BAN [30] and VisualBERT [20], by adding synthetic back-translated samples to the training set. This experiment aimed to test the generalizability of back translation as a data augmentation technique. We investigated whether the improvements seen in our language-only model also benefited models that incorporate deep visual features, helping to establish back translation as an effective tool across diverse VQA architectures.

We present the results in Table 5. Training BAN and VisualBERT with synthesized back-translated samples significantly boosted performance, with improvements of 2.83 and 5.06 points, respectively. This technique benefited all question types, particularly Yes/No questions, where the improvement was around 12.65 points. These findings align with our model's results, demonstrating that adding synthetically varied questions with the same meaning is highly effective for enhancing model performance.

Table 5. Results of applying back translation to different VQA models in the VQA-CP v2 test set. Gap denotes the improvement achieved by training with synthetic back-translated samples.

Model	Yes/No	Number	Other	Overall	Gap
BAN [30]	43.14	13.63	46.92	40.74	-
w/BT	47.87	16.27	48.76	43.57	+2.83
VisualBERT [20]	43.30	15.07	47.83	41.51	-
w/BT	55.95	17.11	49.74	46.57	+5.06

4.5. Comparison of Language Transformers

In this experiment, we compared the performance of various language-only Transformer models, including BERT [10], XLNet [60], and RoBERTa [9], in both their base and large versions. All models were evaluated using the same input—question, narrative, and five captions. The goal of this experiment was to determine which Transformer architecture is most effective for handling textual representations in VQA. By analyzing the performance of different models, we aimed to gain insights into how various language models manage the complexity of this task.

The results are presented in Table 6. All models exhibited similar performance patterns, with XLNET large achieving the highest accuracy, outperforming RoBERTa large by 0.59%. However, the computational time for XLNET large was approximately 2.7 times longer than for RoBERTa large. Given the minimal accuracy difference, RoBERTa large was a more efficient choice, offering comparable results while significantly reducing training time.

Table 6. Performance comparison of language-only Transformer models on the VQA-CP v2 test set. **Bold** values indicate the highest performance.

Model	Yes/No	Number	Other	Overall
BERT base	42.78	17.53	46.99	41.27
BERT large	42.72	17.43	48.47	42.06
XLNET base	43.49	17.61	48.45	42.30
XLNET large	44.58	**20.67**	**50.52**	**44.23**
RoBERTa base	44.39	17.46	48.74	42.70
RoBERTa large	**45.13**	20.06	49.33	43.64

Summary: Our experiments demonstrate that language-only models, when paired with rich textual descriptions and effective data augmentation, can compete with deep visual feature-based models in VQA tasks. Detailed captions enhance performance, while back translation significantly improves accuracy, especially for Yes/No questions. We also found that models like RoBERTa large provide a strong balance between computational efficiency and accuracy, making them ideal for language-only VQA tasks. Overall, these findings highlight the potential of textual representations as a robust alternative to deep visual features, with wide applicability across different VQA models.

5. In-Depth Analysis of Textual and Visual Representations in VQA

In this section, we provide an in-depth analysis of the strengths and characteristics of textual representations for images, compared to deep visual features. Specifically, we focus on two key analyses: (Section 5.1) examining the overlap in predictions between our language-only model and models using deep visual features, and (Section 5.2) conducting a qualitative analysis of visual examples. For both analyses, our model's input is a combination of the narrative and five captions.

5.1. Error Analysis

We compared our text-only model with models that incorporate deep visual features, examining whether they make similar or different mistakes. We use BAN [30] and VisualBERT [20] as representative models for deep visual features. BAN is a strong pre-Transformer model, while VisualBERT uses multimodal Transformers and integrates both image and caption inputs, making it an intermediate between BAN and our text-only approach.

Figure 4 shows the consistency of correct and incorrect answers across the models. We used a binary accuracy metric for this comparison, where a prediction is considered correct if it matches any ground-truth answer, as opposed to the original non-binary metric used in the main paper [51]. Our model demonstrated high consistency, with similar rates of correct/incorrect predictions for both BAN and VisualBERT. For 80% of the questions, all models gave consistent results (blue part). For 12% of the questions, only our model answered correctly (orange), while this dropped to 8% where only the baseline models answered correctly (red). This supports the idea that textual image representations can compete with deep visual features.

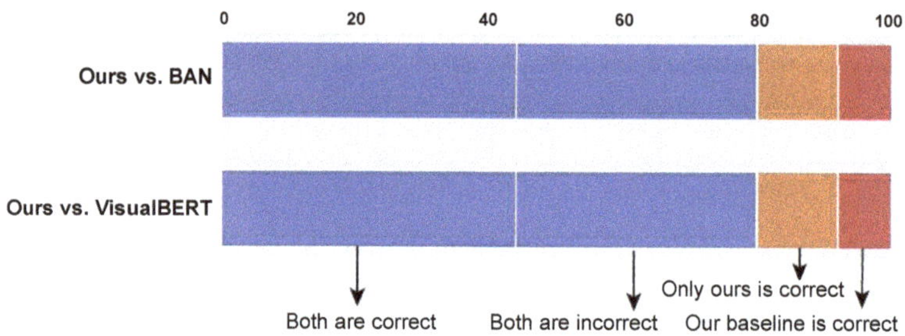

Figure 4. Answer overlap: comparison of prediction agreement between our language-only model, BAN, and VisualBERT. Bar graphs show proportions of identical or differing answers.

5.2. Qualitative Analysis

We analyzed qualitative examples (Figure 5) comparing the predictions of our text-only model, BAN [30], and VisualBERT [20], to identify cases where our method underperformed and suggest potential improvements.

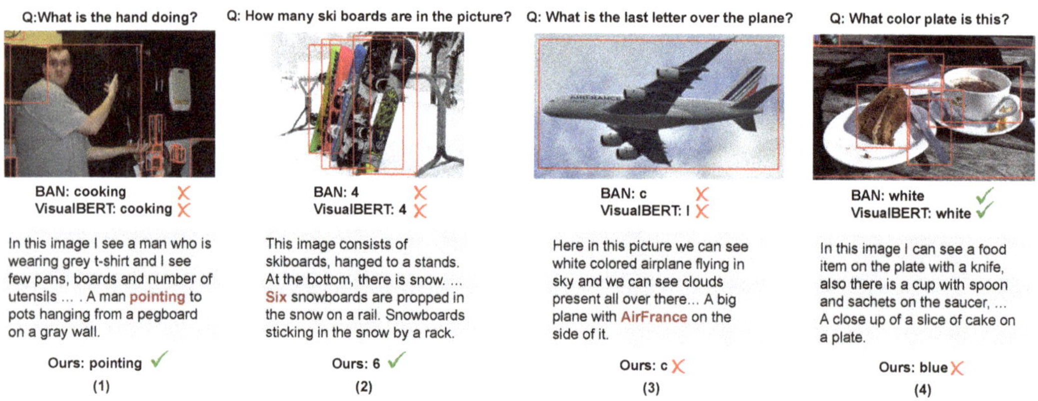

Figure 5. Qualitative comparison: red boxes indicate object detection results by Faster R-CNN with confidence scores over 0.5. Highlighted words in the descriptions correspond to key details relevant to the answers.

In Example (1), our text-only model correctly predicted the man's action based on the description *"A man pointing to pots..."*, while both BAN and VisualBERT incorrectly answered *"cooking"*, likely due to the presence of cooking tools in the scene. This demonstrates how textual representations can more accurately capture actions by relying on explicit information, while deep visual models may misinterpret object presence, underscoring our model's advantage in avoiding irrelevant visual cues.

Example (2) highlights another strength of our method: object counting. The detailed description *"Six snowboards"* enabled our model to correctly predict the answer, whereas the object detectors used in BAN and VisualBERT missed detecting all the relevant objects. This underscores the robustness of our approach in handling precise textual descriptions, which can outperform deep visual features when object detection is incomplete.

However, Example (3) reveals a limitation: despite the description containing the word *"AirFrance"*, our model failed to predict the correct answer. This indicates that our model struggles with precise visual-text alignment, where deep visual features might provide stronger spatial or contextual cues. Improvements could focus on better integrating context from the image to reinforce textual grounding.

Lastly, Example (4) exposes another limitation of our model—handling incomplete or insufficient text input. The lack of essential details in the description led to incorrect predictions. This limitation suggests that future work should aim to enhance the model's ability to infer or handle ambiguity when text descriptions lack critical information.

Overall, this analysis highlights the advantages of our text-based model in capturing detailed, action-related, and count-specific information, often missed by deep visual models. However, it also reveals areas for improvement, particularly in integrating contextual cues from images and addressing gaps in text descriptions for more robust performance.

Summary: In this section, we analyzed the performance of textual representations for VQA compared to models that use deep visual features. Through error analysis, we found that our text-only model can make competitive predictions, often outperforming models that rely on visual features. Qualitative analysis further revealed that textual input excels in capturing actions and counting objects, but struggles with precise visual-text alignment and when descriptions are incomplete. This highlights both the strengths and limitations of text-based models and points to areas for potential improvement.

6. Discussion

Summary of Results and Time Complexity. Our experiments demonstrate that language-only models, particularly when combined with data augmentation techniques like back translation, can achieve competitive performance compared to deep visual models. For instance, back translation improved Yes/No question accuracy by 17.30 points, outperforming most augmentation methods. While deep visual models like NSM slightly outperform our model in some areas, the interpretability and semantic richness of text-based models present a distinct advantage, especially in scenarios requiring human-like reasoning. Additionally, visual feature-based models like BAN and VisualBERT require more time to train than our language-only model. This is due to the additional feature merging module needed to combine image and textual features in these models. For instance, our language-only model trains approximately 3.2 times faster than BAN, making it a more efficient choice in terms of computational time while achieving competitive accuracy.

Comparison between text representation and deep visual features. Directly comparing our language-only model with deep visual feature-based models is challenging due to different inputs—our model uses human-annotated descriptions, while visual models rely on extracted visual features. Human descriptions often align better with the questions, offering a distinct advantage. Despite these differences, our results highlight the parallels and distinctions between text-based and visual features. A key strength of our approach is its interpretability, as human-readable descriptions help explain the model's decisions, making it a valuable baseline for VQA and showing the potential of textual representations as a complement or alternative to visual features, especially when interpretability is key.

Future Research Directions. This study opens up new research avenues for VQA and image understanding. One promising direction is to automatically generate image descriptions as representations, either to supplement or replace deep visual features. This could bridge the gap between textual and visual models, combining the interpretability of text with the precision of deep visual features. Additionally, exploring how textual and visual features can be harmonized to improve models' ability to handle complex reasoning tasks, such as spatial relationships or fine-grained object recognition, is a logical next step. Another direction could involve developing models that dynamically decide when to rely on text versus visual input, optimizing performance based on the complexity of the task at hand.

Additional baselines. While we acknowledge that including a wider range of baseline models would provide a more comprehensive benchmark, the scope of this study focused on representative models that are well-established in the VQA domain. Future work will aim to incorporate a broader selection of models to further evaluate the generalizability of our approach. Given the model-agnostic nature of our method, we anticipate that the benefits observed in this study will extend to other VQA models as well, providing additional insights into the effectiveness of language-based representations.

7. Conclusions

This paper investigated the use of textual representations of images as an alternative to deep visual features for VQA. We also applied data augmentation techniques to both descriptions and questions to expand the training data and improve diversity. Our experiments showed that the language-only model performs competitively with models using deep visual features. Notably, back translation for questions significantly boosted performance. Our findings suggest that machines do not need overly detailed descriptions to understand images—concise, relevant text is sufficient.

Author Contributions: Conceptualization, Y.H., N.G., M.O., C.C. and Y.N.; methodology, Y.H. and N.G.; software, Y.H.; validation, Y.H. and N.G.; formal analysis, Y.H.; investigation, Y.H.; resources, Y.N.; data curation, Y.H.; writing—original draft preparation, Y.H.; writing—review and editing, N.G., M.O., C.C. and Y.N.; visualization, Y.H.; supervision, Y.N.; project administration, Y.N.; funding acquisition, Y.N. All authors have read and agreed to the published version of the manuscript.

Funding: This research was funded by SPS KAKENHI Number JP18H03264 and JP20K19822, and JST CREST Grant Number JPMJCR20D3, Japan.

Data Availability Statement: The data used in this study are publicly available from the following sources: [4,27,51,52].

Conflicts of Interest: Author Mayu Otani is employed by CyberAgent, Inc. The remaining authors declare that the research was conducted in the absence of any commercial or financial relationships that could be construed as a potential conflict of interest. The funding sponsors had no role in the design of the study; in the collection, analyses, or interpretation of data; in the writing of the manuscript, and in the decision to publish the results.

References

1. Ren, S.; He, K.; Girshick, R.B.; Sun, J. Faster R-CNN: Towards Real-Time Object Detection with Region Proposal Networks In Proceedings of the 2015 Advances in Neural Information Processing Systems (NeurIPS), 2015, Ontreal, BC, Canada, 7–12 December 2015; pp. 91–99.
2. You, Q.; Jin, H.; Wang, Z.; Fang, C.; Luo, J. Image Captioning with Semantic Attention. In Proceedings of the 2016 IEEE Conference on Computer Vision and Pattern Recognition (CVPR), Las Vegas, NV, USA, 27–30 June 2016.
3. Yao, T.; Pan, Y.; Li, Y.; Qiu, Z.; Mei, T. Boosting Image Captioning with Attributes. In Proceedings of the 2017 IEEE International Conference on Computer Vision (ICCV), Venice, Italy, 22–29 October 2017.
4. Agrawal, A.; Batra, D.; Parikh, D.; Kembhavi, A. Don't Just Assume; Look and Answer: Overcoming Priors for Visual Question Answering. In Proceedings of the 2018 IEEE Conference on Computer Vision and Pattern Recognition (CVPR), Salt Lake City, UT USA, 18–22 June 2018.
5. Agrawal, A.; Batra, D.; Parikh, D. Analyzing the Behavior of Visual Question Answering Models. In Proceedings of the EMNLP, Austin, TX, USA, 1–5 November 2016.
6. Goyal, Y.; Khot, T.; Summers-Stay, D.; Batra, D.; Parikh, D. Making the V in VQA Matter: Elevating the Role of Image Understanding in Visual Question Answering. In Proceedings of the 2017 IEEE Conference on Computer Vision and Pattern Recognition (CVPR), Honolulu, HI, USA, 21–26 July 2017.
7. Lage, I.; Doshi-Velez, F. Human-in-the-loop learning of interpretable and intuitive representations. In Proceedings of the ICML Workshop on Human Interpretability in Machine Learning, Vienna, Austria, 17 July 2020; Volume 17.

8. Vaswani, A.; Shazeer, N.; Parmar, N.; Uszkoreit, J.; Jones, L.; Gomez, A.N.; Kaiser, L.; Polosukhin, I. Attention is All you Need. In Proceedings of the 2017 Advances in Neural Information Processing Systems (NeurIPS), Long Beach, CA, USA, 4–9 December 2017.
9. Liu, Y.; Ott, M.; Goyal, N.; Du, J.; Joshi, M.; Chen, D.; Levy, O.; Lewis, M.; Zettlemoyer, L.; Stoyanov, V. RoBERTa: A Robustly Optimized BERT Pretraining Approach. *arXiv* **2019**, arXiv:1907.11692.
10. Devlin, J.; Chang, M.; Lee, K.; Toutanova, K. BERT: Pre-training of Deep Bidirectional Transformers for Language Understanding. *NAACL-HLT* **2019**, *1*, 2.
11. Taori, R.; Gulrajani, I.; Zhang, T.; Dubois, Y.; Li, X.; Guestrin, C.; Liang, P.; Hashimoto, T.B. Stanford Alpaca: An Instruction-Following LLaMA Model. 2023. Available online: https://github.com/tatsu-lab/stanford_alpaca (accessed on 28 October 2024).
12. Touvron, H.; Lavril, T.; Izacard, G.; Martinet, X.; Lachaux, M.A.; Lacroix, T.; Rozière, B.; Goyal, N.; Hambro, E.; Azhar, F.; et al. Llama: Open and efficient foundation language models. *arXiv* **2023**, arXiv:2302.13971.
13. Li, J.; Li, D.; Xiong, C.; Hoi, S. Blip: Bootstrapping language-image pre-training for unified vision-language understanding and generation. In Proceedings of the ICML, PMLR, Baltimore, MD, USA, 17–23 July 2022.
14. Chen, X.; Wang, X.; Changpinyo, S.; Piergiovanni, A.; Padlewski, P.; Salz, D.; Goodman, S.; Grycner, A.; Mustafa, B.; Beyer, L.; et al. Pali: A jointly-scaled multilingual language-image model. In Proceedings of the ICLR, Kigali, Rwanda, 1–5 May 2023.
15. Wang, W.; Bao, H.; Dong, L.; Bjorck, J.; Peng, Z.; Liu, Q.; Aggarwal, K.; Mohammed, O.K.; Singhal, S.; Som, S.; et al. Image as a foreign language: BEiT pretraining for vision and vision-language tasks. In Proceedings of the 2023 IEEE Conference on Computer Vision and Pattern Recognition (CVPR), Vancouver, BC, Canada, 18–24 June 2023.
16. Lu, J.; Batra, D.; Parikh, D.; Lee, S. ViLBERT: Pretraining Task-Agnostic Visiolinguistic Representations for Vision-and-Language Tasks. In Proceedings of the 2019 Advances in Neural Information Processing Systems (NeurIPS), Vancouver, BC, Canada, 8–14 December 2019.
17. Tan, H.; Bansal, M. LXMERT: Learning Cross-Modality Encoder Representations from Transformers. In Proceedings of the EMNLP/IJCNLP, Hong Kong, China, 3–7 November 2019.
18. Chen, Y.; Li, L.; Yu, L.; Kholy, A.E.; Ahmed, F.; Gan, Z.; Cheng, Y.; Liu, J. UNITER: UNIversal Image-TExt Representation Learning. In Proceedings of the ECCV, Glasgow, UK, 23–28 August 2020.
19. Su, W.; Zhu, X.; Cao, Y.; Li, B.; Lu, L.; Wei, F.; Dai, J. VL-BERT: Pre-training of Generic Visual-Linguistic Representations. In Proceedings of the ICLR, Addis Ababa, Ethiopia, 30 April 2020.
20. Li, L.H.; Yatskar, M.; Yin, D.; Hsieh, C.J.; Chang, K.W. VisualBERT: A Simple and Performant Baseline for Vision and Language. *arXiv* **2019**, arXiv:1908.03557.
21. Dosovitskiy, A.; Beyer, L.; Kolesnikov, A.; Weissenborn, D.; Zhai, X.; Unterthiner, T.; Dehghani, M.; Minderer, M.; Heigold, G.; Gelly, S.; et al. An image is worth 16x16 words: Transformers for image recognition at scale. In Proceedings of the ICLR, Vienna, Austria, 4 May 2021.
22. Gokhale, T.; Banerjee, P.; Baral, C.; Yang, Y. MUTANT: A Training Paradigm for Out-of-Distribution Generalization in Visual Question Answering. In Proceedings of the EMNLP, Online, 16–20 November 2020.
23. Chen, L.; Yan, X.; Xiao, J.; Zhang, H.; Pu, S.; Zhuang, Y. Counterfactual Samples Synthesizing for Robust Visual Question Answering. In Proceedings of the CVPR, Seattle, WA, USA, 14–19 June 2020.
24. Wei, J.W.; Zou, K. EDA: Easy Data Augmentation Techniques for Boosting Performance on Text Classification Tasks. In Proceedings of the EMNLP/IJCNLP, Hong Kong, China, 3–7 November 2019.
25. Sennrich, R.; Haddow, B.; Birch, A. Improving Neural Machine Translation Models with Monolingual Data. In Proceedings of the ACL, Berlin, Germany, 7–12 August 2016.
26. Yu, A.W.; Dohan, D.; Luong, M.; Zhao, R.; Chen, K.; Norouzi, M.; Le, Q.V. QANet: Combining Local Convolution with Global Self-Attention for Reading Comprehension. In Proceedings of the ICLR, Vancouver, BC, Canada, 30 April–3 May 2018.
27. Chen, X.; Fang, H.; Lin, T.; Vedantam, R.; Gupta, S.; Dollár, P.; Zitnick, C.L. Microsoft COCO Captions: Data Collection and Evaluation Server. *arXiv* **2015**, arXiv:1504.00325.
28. Pont-Tuset, J.; Uijlings, J.R.R.; Changpinyo, S.; Soricut, R.; Ferrari, V. Connecting Vision and Language with Localized Narratives. In Proceedings of the ECCV, Glasgow, UK, 23–28 August 2020.
29. Anderson, P.; He, X.; Buehler, C.; Teney, D.; Johnson, M.; Gould, S.; Zhang, L. Bottom-Up and Top-Down Attention for Image Captioning and Visual Question Answering. In Proceedings of the CVPR, Salt Lake City, UT, USA, 18–22 June 2018.
30. Kim, J.; Jun, J.; Zhang, B. Bilinear Attention Networks. In Proceedings of the 2018 Advances in Neural Information Processing Systems (NeurIPS), Montreal, QC, USA, 3–8 December 2018.
31. Jiang, Y.; Natarajan, V.; Chen, X.; Rohrbach, M.; Batra, D.; Parikh, D. Pythia v0.1: The Winning Entry to the VQA Challenge 2018. *arXiv* **2018**, arXiv:1807.09956.
32. Cadène, R.; Ben-younes, H.; Cord, M.; Thome, N. MUREL: Multimodal Relational Reasoning for Visual Question Answering. In Proceedings of the CVPR, Long Beach, CA, USA, 15–19 June 2019.
33. Cadène, R.; Dancette, C.; Ben-younes, H.; Cord, M.; Parikh, D. RUBi: Reducing Unimodal Biases for Visual Question Answering. In Proceedings of the NeurIPS, Vancouver, BC, Canada, 8–14 December 2019.
34. Clark, C.; Yatskar, M.; Zettlemoyer, L. Don't Take the Easy Way Out: Ensemble Based Methods for Avoiding Known Dataset Biases. In Proceedings of the EMNLP/IJCNLP, Hong Kong, China, 3–7 November 2019.

35. Huang, Z.; Zeng, Z.; Huang, Y.; Liu, B.; Fu, D.; Fu, J. Seeing Out of the Box: End-to-End Pre-Training for Vision-Language Representation Learning. In Proceedings of the CVPR, Nashville, TN, USA, 20–25 June 2021.
36. Rotstein, N.; Bensaïd, D.; Brody, S.; Ganz, R.; Kimmel, R. Fusecap: Leveraging large language models for enriched fused image captions. In Proceedings of the WACV, Waikoloa, HI, USA, 3–8 January 2024.
37. Wang, Z.; Chen, C.; Li, P.; Liu, Y. Filling the image information gap for vqa: Prompting large language models to proactively ask questions. In Proceedings of the EMNLP, Singapore, 6–10 December 2023.
38. Wu, J.; Hu, Z.; Mooney, R.J. Generating question relevant captions to aid visual question answering. In Proceedings of the ACL, Austin, TX, USA, 4–13 October 2019.
39. Banerjee, P.; Gokhale, T.; Yang, Y.; Baral, C. WeaQA: Weak supervision via captions for visual question answering. In Proceedings of the ACL/IJCNLP (Findings), Online, 1–6 August 2020.
40. Zhu, D.; Chen, J.; Haydarov, K.; Shen, X.; Zhang, W.; Elhoseiny, M. Chatgpt asks, blip-2 answers: Automatic questioning towards enriched visual descriptions. *arXiv* **2023**, arXiv:2303.06594.
41. Liu, H.; Li, C.; Wu, Q.; Lee, Y.J. Visual instruction tuning. In Proceedings of the NeurIPS, Vancouver, BC, Canada,9–15 December 2024.
42. Yang, S.; Xiao, L.; Wu, X.; Xu, J.; Wang, L.; He, L. Simple contrastive learning in a self-supervised manner for robust visual question answering. *Comput. Vis. Image Underst.* **2024**, *241*, 103976. [CrossRef]
43. Xiao, L.; Wu, X.; Xu, J.; Li, W.; Jin, C.; He, L. Atlantis: Aesthetic-oriented multiple granularities fusion network for joint multimodal aspect-based sentiment analysis. *Inf. Fusion* **2024**, *106*, 102304. [CrossRef]
44. Shi, X.; Lee, S. Benchmarking out-of-distribution detection in visual question answering. In Proceedings of the WACV, Waikoloa, HI, USA, 3–8 January 2024.
45. Ott, M.; Edunov, S.; Baevski, A.; Fan, A.; Gross, S.; Ng, N.; Grangier, D.; Auli, M. fairseq: A Fast, Extensible Toolkit for Sequence Modeling. In Proceedings of the NAACL-HLT (Demonstrations), Minneapolis, Minnesota, 2–7 June 2019.
46. Socher, R.; Bauer, J.; Manning, C.D.; Ng, A.Y. Parsing with Compositional Vector Grammars. In Proceedings of the ACL, Sofia, Bulgaria, 4–9 August 2013.
47. Hu, M.; Liu, B. Mining and summarizing customer reviews. In Proceedings of the KDD, Seattle, WA, USA, 22–25 August 2004.
48. Pang, B.; Lee, L. A Sentimental Education: Sentiment Analysis Using Subjectivity Summarization Based on Minimum Cuts. In Proceedings of the ACL, Barcelona, Spain, 21–26 July 2004.
49. Li, X.; Roth, D. Learning Question Classifiers. In Proceedings of the COLING, Taipei, Taiwan, 26–30 August 2002.
50. Ganapathibhotla, M.; Liu, B. Mining Opinions in Comparative Sentences. In Proceedings of the COLING, Manchester, UK, 18–22 August 2008.
51. Antol, S.; Agrawal, A.; Lu, J.; Mitchell, M.; Batra, D.; Zitnick, C.L.; Parikh, D. VQA: Visual Question Answering. In Proceedings of the ICCV, Santiago, Chile, 7–13 December 2015.
52. Lin, T.; Maire, M.; Belongie, S.J.; Hays, J.; Perona, P.; Ramanan, D.; Dollár, P.; Zitnick, C.L. Microsoft COCO: Common Objects in Context. In Proceedings of the ECCV, Zurich, Switzerland, 6–12 September 2014.
53. Teney, D.; Abbasnejad, E.; van den Hengel, A. Learning What Makes a Difference from Counterfactual Examples and Gradient Supervision. In Proceedings of the ECCV, Glasgow, UK, 23–28 August 2020.
54. Agarwal, V.; Shetty, R.; Fritz, M. Towards Causal VQA: Revealing and Reducing Spurious Correlations by Invariant and Covariant Semantic Editing. In Proceedings of the CVPR, Seattle, WA, USA, 13–19 June 2020.
55. Goodfellow, I.J.; Pouget-Abadie, J.; Mirza, M.; Xu, B.; Warde-Farley, D.; Ozair, S.; Courville, A.C.; Bengio, Y. Generative Adversarial Nets. In Proceedings of the NIPS, Montreal, QC, Canada, 8–11 December 2014.
56. Miller, G.A. WordNet: A Lexical Database for English. *Commun. ACM* **1995**, *38*, 39–41. [CrossRef]
57. Pennington, J.; Socher, R.; Manning, C.D. Glove: Global Vectors for Word Representation. In Proceedings of the EMNLP, ACL Doha, Qatar, 25–29 October 2014.
58. Selvaraju, R.R.; Cogswell, M.; Das, A.; Vedantam, R.; Parikh, D.; Batra, D. Grad-CAM: Visual Explanations from Deep Networks via Gradient-Based Localization. In Proceedings of the ICCV, Venice, Italy, 22–29 October 2017.
59. Ma, E. NLP Augmentation. 2019. Available online: https://github.com/makcedward/nlpaug (accessed on 28 October 2024).
60. Yang, Z.; Dai, Z.; Yang, Y.; Carbonell, J.G.; Salakhutdinov, R.; Le, Q.V. XLNet: Generalized Autoregressive Pretraining for Language Understanding. In Proceedings of the NeurIPS, Vancouver, BC, Canada, 8–14 December 2019.
61. Huggingface. Huggingface: RoBERTa. 2024. Available online: https://huggingface.co/docs/transformers/model_doc/roberta (accessed on 28 October 2024).
62. Ramachandran, P.; Zoph, B.; Le, Q.V. Swish: A self-gated activation function. *arXiv* **2017**, arXiv:1710.05941.
63. Gordon, J.; Durme, B.V. Reporting bias and knowledge acquisition. In Proceedings of the AKBC@CIKM, San Francisco, CA, USA 27–28 October 2013.
64. Misra, I.; Zitnick, C.L.; Mitchell, M.; Girshick, R.B. Seeing through the Human Reporting Bias: Visual Classifiers from Noisy Human-Centric Labels. In Proceedings of the CVPR, Las Vegas, NV, USA, 26 June–1 July 2016.
65. Hudson, D.A.; Manning, C.D. Learning by Abstraction: The Neural State Machine. In Proceedings of the NeurIPS, Vancouver BC, Canada, 8–14 December 2019.

66. Malinowski, M.; Doersch, C.; Santoro, A.; Battaglia, P.W. Learning Visual Question Answering by Bootstrapping Hard Attention. In Proceedings of the ECCV, Munich, Germany, 8–14 September 2018.
67. Li, L.; Gan, Z.; Cheng, Y.; Liu, J. Relation-Aware Graph Attention Network for Visual Question Answering. In Proceedings of the ICCV, Seoul, Republic of Korea, 27 October–2 November 2019.

electronics

MDPI

Article

SentimentFormer: A Transformer-Based Multimodal Fusion Framework for Enhanced Sentiment Analysis of Memes in Under-Resourced Bangla Language

Fatema Tuj Johora Faria [1], Laith H. Baniata [2,*], Mohammad H. Baniata [3], Mohannad A. Khair [4], Ahmed Ibrahim Bani Ata [5], Chayut Bunterngchit [6] and Sangwoo Kang [2,*]

1 Department of Computer Science and Engineering, Ahsanullah University of Science and Technology, Dhaka 1208, Bangladesh; fatema.faria142@gmail.com
2 School of Computing, Gachon University, Seongnam 13120, Republic of Korea
3 Computer Science Department, Faculty of Information Technology, The World Islamic Sciences and Education University, Amman 11947, Jordan; mohammad.baniata@wise.edu.jo
4 Qatrana Cement Company, Amman 11831, Jordan; mkhair@qatranacement.com
5 Department of Arabic Language, Faculty of Arts and Educational Sciences, Middle East University, Amman 11831, Jordan; a.baniata@meu.edu.jo
6 State Key Laboratory of Multimodal Artificial Intelligence Systems, Institute of Automation, Chinese Academy of Sciences, Beijing 100190, China; chayutb@ia.ac.cn
* Correspondence: laith@gachon.ac.kr (L.H.B.); swkang@gachon.ac.kr (S.K.)

Abstract: Social media has increasingly relied on memes as a tool for expressing opinions, making meme sentiment analysis an emerging area of interest for researchers. While much of the research has focused on English-language memes, under-resourced languages, such as Bengali, have received limited attention. Given the surge in social media use, the need for sentiment analysis of memes in these languages has become critical. One of the primary challenges in this field is the lack of benchmark datasets, particularly in languages with fewer resources. To address this, we used the MemoSen dataset, designed for Bengali, which consists of 4368 memes annotated with three sentiment labels: positive, negative, and neutral. MemoSen is divided into training (70%), test (20%), and validation (10%) sets, with an imbalanced class distribution: 1349 memes in the positive class, 2728 in the negative class, and 291 in the neutral class. Our approach leverages advanced deep learning techniques for multimodal sentiment analysis in Bengali, introducing three hybrid approaches. SentimentTextFormer is a text-based, fine-tuned model that utilizes state-of-the-art transformer architectures to accurately extract sentiment-related insights from Bengali text, capturing nuanced linguistic features. SentimentImageFormer is an image-based model that employs cutting-edge transformer-based techniques for precise sentiment classification through visual data. Lastly, SentimentFormer is a hybrid model that seamlessly integrates both text and image modalities using fusion strategies. Early fusion combines textual and visual features at the input level, enabling the model to jointly learn from both modalities. Late fusion merges the outputs of separate text and image models, preserving their individual strengths for the final prediction. Intermediate fusion integrates textual and visual features at intermediate layers, refining their interactions during processing. These fusion strategies combine the strengths of both textual and visual data, enhancing sentiment analysis by exploiting complementary information from multiple sources. The performance of our models was evaluated using various accuracy metrics, with SentimentTextFormer achieving 73.31% accuracy and SentimentImageFormer attaining 64.72%. The hybrid model, SentimentFormer (SwiftFormer with mBERT), employing intermediate fusion, shows a notable improvement in accuracy, achieving 79.04%, outperforming SentimentTextFormer by 5.73% and SentimentImageFormer by 14.32%. Among the fusion strategies, SentimentFormer (SwiftFormer with mBERT) achieved the highest accuracy of 79.04%, highlighting the effectiveness of our fusion technique and the reliability of our multimodal framework in improving sentiment analysis accuracy across diverse modalities.

Keywords: early fusion; late fusion; intermediate fusion; Bengali language; multimodal sentiment analysis; under-resourced languages; social media; sentiment classification; machine learning

1. Introduction

The rapid growth of internet usage and the development of various Web 2.0 applications have led to a significant increase in the use of social media platforms such as Facebook, X (formerly known as Twitter), and Instagram. These platforms have transformed into spaces where users share their opinions on a wide range of topics, including business, politics, entertainment, and current events. Consequently, automated sentiment analysis of these conversations has attracted significant attention from Natural Language Processing (NLP) researchers, as it helps identify individuals' opinions or sentiments regarding specific events or issues. Most existing research in this field focuses on classifying textual sentiments into three primary categories: positive, negative, and neutral [1,2].

However, the content shared on social media platforms is changing rapidly. More and more content is multimodal, combining images, text, and videos, which has added a new layer to sentiment analysis research [3]. Memes, for example, are becoming a popular way to share information. To understand the sentiment behind memes, it is important to consider multiple types of media at once. Since memes are often created in people's native languages, and social media usage is growing quickly in Bangladesh, there has been a rise in Bengali memes. Bengali, spoken by about 230 million people in Bangladesh and India, is one of the most spoken languages in the world [4].

This increase in Bengali memes has sparked more interest in sentiment analysis for different purposes. One key area is political sentiment analysis [5], which helps understand how people feel about policies and leaders. Other applications include social media emotion classification [6], which helps track user engagement and mental health, and detecting hate speech on online platforms to reduce harmful behaviors. Hate speech in Bengali is a serious concern as it covers a range of issues, from personal complaints to religious, political, and geopolitical conflicts [7,8]. Additionally, research on the level of toxicity against distinct groups in Bangla social media comments has highlighted the severity of harmful content [9]. Sentiment analysis is also being used in areas like news media, where it helps identify biases or frames in news articles and headlines [10]. These developments show how important and complex sentiment analysis is, especially when dealing with diverse types of content and languages.

The literature on sentiment analysis highlights key approaches for understanding emotional responses but also reveals significant gaps, particularly in the integration of multimodal data. Abiola et al. [11] conducted a study on emotional responses to the COVID-19 pandemic using sentiment analysis tools like TextBlob and VADER applied to tweets, uncovering the pandemic's impact on Nigeria's society, environment, and economy. However, while the study used topic modeling and visualized data, it lacked a multimodal approach, failing to incorporate visual data. Similarly, Sudirjo et al. [12] explored

ChatGPT's potential in business customer sentiment analysis, emphasizing its ability to detect customer emotions. Yet, the study relied solely on text, missing the opportunity for multimodal sentiment analysis that could include images or videos. Faria et al. [5] examined political sentiment in the Bangladeshi elections, demonstrating the effectiveness of Pre-trained Language Models (PLMs) like BanglaBERT and Large Language Models (LLMs) like Gemini 1.5 Pro for sentiment detection. Despite the study's focus on Few-Shot learning, it did not utilize multimodal data to enhance sentiment analysis. Rifa et al. [13] proposed a sentiment analysis system for YouTube comments related to Bangla movies and dramas, introducing a dataset of 14,000 preprocessed comments for relevance detection and sentiment analysis. While the study made strides in analyzing sentiment using transformer models, it also lacked multimodal elements, relying solely on text. These studies, despite their contributions, share the limitation of not integrating visual data, which could have provided a more comprehensive understanding of sentiment by combining text with visual or sensory inputs. The absence of multimodal analysis in these works restricts their potential to capture the full range of human emotions and insights, underscoring the need for image–text pairing to deepen sentiment analysis capabilities.

To address the limitations of existing approaches in sentiment analysis for Bangla, this study introduces novel methodologies aimed at improving sentiment classification in this low-resource language. We propose an integrated approach that combines unimodal text and image data with multimodal text–image pair analysis. By fine-tuning state-of-the-art pre-trained models for both text and image data, we enhance the performance of sentiment detection. Furthermore, we explore various fusion strategies to effectively combine textual and visual information, improving accuracy and robustness in sentiment analysis. Through systematic hyperparameter tuning and rigorous evaluation using standard metrics, we ensure the models' optimal performance. Additionally, a comprehensive error analysis helps identify common misclassifications, providing valuable insights for future improvements in sentiment analysis for Bangla and other low-resource languages.

In this paper, we propose several hybrid methodologies aimed at improving sentiment classification for Bangla, a under-resourced language. The contributions of this study are summarized as follows:

- We proposed a three-fold approach for sentiment analysis in Bangla, incorporating unimodal text, unimodal image, and multimodal text–image pair data.
- We developed a systematic framework involving preprocessing, model development, and hyperparameter tuning for each modality, ensuring effective sentiment detection in Bangla.
- We fine-tuned state-of-the-art pre-trained language models (mBERT, XLM-RoBERTa, DistilBERT) for Bangla sentiment classification, introducing a specialized framework tailored for text-based sentiment analysis in the Bangla language.
- We leveraged advanced image classification models (ViT, Swin Transformer, Swift Transformer) for sentiment analysis in images, and introduced a fine-tuned framework for enhancing visual sentiment detection.
- We introduced a hybrid framework combining both textual and visual modalities to improve sentiment classification accuracy, specifically addressing the challenges of sentiment analysis in Bangla.
- We explored three fusion strategies (early fusion, late fusion, intermediate fusion) to effectively combine text and image features, boosting performance in multimodal sentiment analysis for Bangla.

- We conducted systematic hyperparameter tuning for both text and image models, optimizing critical parameters to achieve the best possible performance while maintaining the models' ability to generalize.
- We provided a comprehensive evaluation using metrics such as accuracy, precision, recall, and weighted F1 score, offering valuable benchmarks for future research in sentiment analysis for the Bangla language.
- We performed a comprehensive error analysis for the multimodal approach to identify and address potential weaknesses in sentiment classification. This analysis examined both text and image modalities, pinpointing common misclassifications and their root causes, leading to insights for improving model performance and robustness.

The structure of this paper is as follows: Section 2 provides a comprehensive review of the related literature, establishing the foundation for our research. Section 3 explores the relevant background studies. Section 4 describes the datasets utilized in this study. Section 5 outlines the proposed methodology in detail. Section 6 presents the experiments conducted and analyzes the results. Section 7 discusses the limitations of the study, Section 8 outlines potential directions for future research, and Section 9 summarizes the key findings and conclusions.

2. Literature Reviews

Sentiment analysis has seen substantial progress through both unimodal and multimodal approaches, with notable contributions leveraging diverse datasets and advanced machine learning techniques. Tables 1 and 2 summarize the key findings and methodologies from relevant studies in text-based and image–text pair-based sentiment analysis, respectively.

Table 1. Summary of studies on unimodal (text-based) sentiment analysis.

Authors	Year	Models Employed	Performance Metrics	Key Findings
Abiola et al. [11]	(2023)	Sentiment analysis on 1M Nigerian tweets using TextBlob and VADER; LDA for topic modeling	VADER classified 39.8% positive, TextBlob identified 46.0% neutral, TextBlob was more accurate for neutral	Limited to text data; lacks transformer-based attention mechanisms for deeper sentiment interpretation
Manias et al. [14]	(2023)	Multilingual sentiment analysis using BERT-based models (mBERT, XLM-R, DistilmBERT)	XLM-R achieved F1 score of 0.7642, fine-tuned models performed better than zero-shot models	Limited to text-based classification; no multimodal analysis or domain-specific fine-tuning
Hu et al. [2]	(2024)	Sentiment analysis using ensemble methods, transfer learning, and deep learning (RNNs, transformers)	Naive Bayes (NB) achieved an F1 Score of 0.84	Focused on binary sentiment classification; no multimodal analysis
He et al. [15]	(2024)	Hybrid BERT-CNN-BiLSTM-Att model for sentiment analysis of short movie reviews	Improved accuracy by 5.54% compared to Word2Vec-BiLSTM and BERT-CNN	Restricted to binary sentiment classification; lacked diversity in dataset and multimodal elements
Gu et al. [16]	(2024)	FinBERT-LSTM model integrating stock prices and financial news for sentiment analysis	FinBERT embedding LSTM architecture achieved the highest accuracy of 0.955 at 77 epochs, outperforming other models	Relied solely on financial news and historical stock prices; overlooked multimodal data sources

Table 2. Summary of studies on multimodal (image–text pair-based) sentiment analysis.

Authors	Year	Models Employed	Performance Metrics	Key Findings
Elahi et al. [3]	(2023)	ResNet50, BanglishBERT	weighted F1 score: 0.71	Achieved higher performance than unimodal methods, utilized Explainable AI (XAI) to interpret model behavior. Limited by reliance on CNN architectures and absence of Vision Transformer (ViT).
Hossain et al. [1]	(2022)	ResNet50, BanglaBERT	weighted F1 score: 0.643	Achieved 1.2% improvement in multimodal sentiment classification over unimodal models using early and late fusion techniques. Did not incorporate Vision Transformers or intermediate fusion methods.
Alluri et al. [17]	(2021)	Vision Transformers (ViTs), RoBERTa, SBERT	Macro F1 scores: 0.633 (humor), 0.575 (overall sentiment)	Utilized ViT for image processing and transformer-based models for text analysis. Limited to English-language memes and did not explore variations in Vision Transformer architectures.
Thakkar et al. [18]	(2024)	multilingual BERT, XLM-RoBERTa, CLIP, DINOv2	F1 score: 76.8	Explored multimodal sentiment analysis for multilingual contexts, achieved strong results with sentiment-tuned large language models. Did not explore fusion techniques (early, late, intermediate).

2.1. Unimodal (Text-Based) Approaches in Sentiment Analysis

Abiola et al. [11] analyzed emotional responses to COVID-19 by conducting sentiment analysis on over one million tweets from Nigeria, using TextBlob and VADER for sentiment classification and LDA for topic modeling. Their findings revealed that VADER classified 39.8% of the tweets as positive, 31.3% as neutral, and 28.9% as negative, while TextBlob identified 46.0% as neutral, 36.7% as positive, and 17.3% as negative. Despite the valuable insights provided by this study, it was limited by its unimodal approach, relying solely on text data. The incorporation of multimodal sentiment analysis, which could include images or videos, might have offered richer insights. Furthermore, the absence of transformer-based attention mechanisms in their methodology restricted the depth of sentiment interpretation, especially given that modern models like BERT were capable of offering more nuanced and context-aware sentiment analysis. Similarly, Manias et al. [14] explored multilingual approaches to sentiment and text classification in social media posts, focusing on BERT-based models and a zero-shot classification approach. Their study used four multilingual BERT models (mBERT cased, mBERT uncased, XLM-R, and DistilmBERT) to analyze multilingual datasets, finding that BERT-based classifiers excelled when fine-tuned on multilingual data, achieving high accuracy. While the zero-shot model was efficient and scalable, it provided relatively good results across multiple languages but lagged behind the fine-tuned models in terms of accuracy. The results demonstrated that XLM-R achieved an F1 score of 0.7642, showcasing its robust performance. However, similar to Abiola's study, it was limited by its exclusive focus on text-based classification, without exploring multimodal approaches. Integrating multimodal data, such as images or videos, could have provided a more comprehensive understanding of social media content. Additionally, the reliance on pre-trained models without exploring domain-specific fine-tuning may have reduced the model's effectiveness for certain languages or tasks that were underrepresented in the training data. In contrast, Hu et al. [2] focused on sentiment analysis through advanced NLP techniques, such as ensemble methods, transfer learning, and deep learning architectures. By enhancing the robustness and precision of sentiment predictions, their approach investigated the impact of various models like recurrent neural networks and transformer-based architectures. They also introduced a novel ensemble method that combined multiple classifiers to improve predictive accuracy. However, like the previous studies, this research was limited to a text-based approach, focusing only on binary sentiment classification. Although the robustness of the models employed was notable, the absence of multimodal analysis in their study indicated an opportunity for more comprehensive sentiment analysis that integrated additional data types, such as images, videos, or audio. By incorporating multimodal data, future research could have provided a more nuanced understanding of sentiment in diverse social media contexts. In the same vein, He et al. [15] proposed a BERT-CNN-BiLSTM-Att hybrid model for sentiment analysis of short movie reviews, aiming to address challenges like polysemy and feature extraction in text sentiment analysis. The model employed BERT for dynamic word vectors, CNN for local feature extraction, and BiLSTM for global feature extraction, with an attention mechanism to highlight key information. Experimental results showed that the model outperformed alternatives like Word2Vec-BiLSTM and BERT-CNN, improving accuracy by up to 5.54%. However, like previous studies, this research was restricted to binary sentiment classification. Future research could have explored multiclass classification and expanded the dataset to include diverse elements, such as emoticons, which would have added to the richness of the analysis. Lastly, Gu et al. [16] predicted stock prices by integrating historical stock prices and financial news using the FinBERT-LSTM model. The methodology leveraged the pre-trained FinBERT for sentiment analysis of financial news and combined it with stock market data in an LSTM architecture to forecast stock prices. The results showed that the FinBERT-LSTM model outperformed both standalone LSTM and DNN models in prediction accuracy, as evidenced by metrics like Mean Absolute Error, Mean Absolute Percentage Error, and overall accuracy. The dataset used consisted of over 843,000 articles and stock price data spanning from 2009 to 2020. However, this study was limited by its reliance on only news sentiment and historical prices, potentially overlooking other influential factors that might have impacted stock price predictions. In conclusion, while each of these studies contributed valuable insights into sentiment analysis, they all shared common limitations, such as their exclusive focus on text-based data and the absence of multimodal approaches. Incorporating multimodal data and exploring domain-specific fine-tuning could have enhanced the accuracy and depth of sentiment analysis across various domains.

2.2. Multimodal (Image–Text Pair-Based) Approaches in Sentiment Analysis

Elahi et al. [3] investigated the sentiment analysis of Bengali memes using the newly introduced MemoSen dataset, which fills a critical gap in low-resource language research. Specifically, their study combined ResNet50 for image processing and BanglishBERT for text analysis within a multimodal framework. Notably, this approach achieved a weighted F1 score of 0.71, surpassing unimodal methods. Moreover, Explainable AI (XAI) was employed to interpret model behavior effectively. However, challenges such as an imbalanced dataset and relatively low accuracy were evident. Furthermore, a key limitation was the exclusive reliance on CNN-based architectures like ResNet50 and DenseNet161, without exploring Vision Transformer (ViT) models, which could have offered performance improvements. Similarly, Hossain et al. [1] introduced MemoSen, a novel Bengali multimodal dataset containing 4368 memes annotated with sentiment labels (positive, negative, neutral). They also leveraged ResNet50 for visual analysis and BanglaBERT for textual analysis. By utilizing early and late fusion techniques, their study achieved a weighted F1 score of 0.643 and demonstrated a 1.2% improvement in multimodal sentiment classification over unimodal models. Nevertheless, like Elahi's work, it did not incorporate Vision Transformers or modern variations for visual feature extraction, nor did it investigate intermediate fusion methods. These limitations highlight opportunities for further enhancements in model design and performance evaluation. On the other hand, Alluri et al. [17] focused on meme sentiment analysis using the Memotion dataset, which categorizes memes based on irony, humor, motivation, and overall sentiment. They exclusively employed Vision Transformers (ViTs) for visual representation alongside advanced transformer-based models such as RoBERTa and SBERT for textual and multimodal representations. Their multimodal approaches, including the IMGTXT, IMGSEN, and CAPSEN models, utilized fusion techniques to effectively integrate embeddings and achieved macro F1 scores of 0.633 for humor and 0.575 for overall sentiment. However, despite the robust use of transformer architectures and innovative fusion methods, their study was limited to English-language memes. Furthermore, they did not explore variations in Vision Transformer architectures, which could have provided diverse perspectives and potentially enhanced performance. In contrast, Thakkar et al. [18] addressed the gap in multimodal sentiment analysis by transforming a textual Twitter sentiment dataset into a multimodal format, emphasizing multilingual contexts. Their work utilized pre-trained models such as multilingual BERT, XLM-RoBERTa, CLIP, and DINOv2 for baseline experiments comparing unimodal and multimodal configurations. Through their pipeline, which integrated visual and textual features via concatenation followed by linear projection, they achieved strong results, particularly with sentiment-tuned large language models for text encoding. However, the study did not explore early, late, or intermediate fusion techniques, which could have provided deeper insights into feature integration and potentially improved classification accuracy. Taken together, these studies illustrate significant advancements in multimodal sentiment analysis, particularly for low-resource and multilingual contexts. However, common limitations, such as the lack of exploration into Vision Transformer architectures and intermediate fusion techniques, underscore the need for further investigation to enhance model performance and applicability across diverse datasets.

3. Background Study

3.1. Models for Sentiment Analysis in Bangla Text

The rapid advancements in natural language processing (NLP) have revolutionized sentiment analysis, enabling robust and efficient classification of textual data. For Bangla, a low-resource and linguistically complex language, the development of state-of-the-art (SOTA) models has been particularly impactful. SOTA models such as multilingual BERT (mBERT), XLM-RoBERTa, and DistilBERT have set new benchmarks in Bangla sentiment analysis. These models excel in capturing nuanced linguistic structures and sentiment expressions, making them indispensable tools for this task. By leveraging extensive pre-training on multilingual corpora and applying fine-tuning techniques to Bangla-specific datasets, these models achieve remarkable performance, even in resource-constrained scenarios.

3.1.1. mBERT (multilingual BERT)

mBERT [19], or multilingual BERT, is an extension of Google's original BERT model, designed for multilingual NLP tasks. It employs multiple transformer encoder layers with self-attention mechanisms to understand complex relationships between words in different languages. Pre-trained on a diverse multilingual dataset using masked language modeling (MLM) and next sentence prediction (NSP) tasks, mBERT is highly versatile in cross-lingual tasks. For Bangla sentiment analysis, mBERT provides robust contextual understanding, effectively identifying nuanced sentiment expressions, even in the absence of large-scale annotated datasets.

3.1.2. XLM-RoBERTa

XLM-RoBERTa [20] is a multilingual variant of RoBERTa, optimized for cross-lingual tasks. Unlike mBERT, it focuses exclusively on MLM during pre-training, using massive multilingual corpora such as CommonCrawl to predict masked words. This focused training enhances its cross-lingual generalization and makes it particularly adept for low-resource languages like Bangla. XLM-RoBERTa has proven effective in sentiment analysis by capturing context-rich representations, identifying intricate sentiment cues in Bangla text, and simplifying multilingual workflows with automatic language detection.

3.1.3. DistilBERT

DistilBERT [21] is a lightweight and faster alternative to BERT, trained using knowledge distillation. It retains 97% of BERT's language understanding capabilities while being 40% smaller and 60% faster, making it an efficient option for sentiment analysis tasks. DistilBERT uses masked language modeling (MLM) as its primary pre-training objective. For Bangla sentiment analysis, DistilBERT is highly effective when computational resources are limited. Fine-tuning DistilBERT on Bangla sentiment datasets can yield competitive results, enabling the model to discern subtle sentiment patterns while maintaining high efficiency.

3.2. *Models for Sentiment Analysis in Images*

The rapid advancements in computer vision and multimodal learning have significantly transformed sentiment analysis in images, particularly in the domain of memes, where emotions, humor, and context are often conveyed visually. Effective sentiment analysis for memes requires not only the identification of visual elements but also an understanding of how these elements interact with text to express emotions. The ability to capture emotional cues from image features—such as facial expressions, body language, and scene composition—has become essential for accurately analyzing sentiment in memes. Recent models have leveraged sophisticated techniques, such as vision transformers and multimodal architectures, to enhance the analysis of emotions and sentiments from both the image and text components. Below, we explore several state-of-the-art models that have been developed to address these challenges.

3.2.1. Vision Transformer (ViT)

Vision Transformers (ViTs) [22] provide a novel approach to image processing by using a transformer-based architecture rather than traditional Convolutional Neural Networks (CNNs). In the context of meme sentiment analysis, a ViT divides images into fixed-size patches, which are then transformed into vector representations. These patches capture local image features, such as facial expressions or body language, which are crucial for detecting emotions. By incorporating positional encoding, the ViT preserves the spatial relationships between image components, ensuring that important features are properly contextualized. The model processes the sequence of patch embeddings through transformer encoder blocks, using self-attention mechanisms to understand how various parts of the image relate to one another. This enables the ViT to capture global context in images, such as the interaction between the text and visual elements. The resulting image representations are classified for sentiment, making the ViT highly effective for meme sentiment analysis.

3.2.2. Swin Transformer

Swin Transformer [23] builds upon Vision Transformer architecture by introducing a hierarchical approach to image processing. For meme sentiment analysis, this is particularly advantageous as it allows the model to capture both fine-grained local features (e.g., facial expressions) and the broader global context (e.g., overall image composition). The image is divided into progressively smaller patches, which are processed at different hierarchical levels. This enables Swin Transformer to extract features across scales, enhancing its ability to capture complex emotional cues from both the image and its surrounding context. The shifted window-based self-attention mechanism ensures that the model focuses on important regions, such as the areas around faces or text while maintaining a global context. This hierarchical structure and the attention mechanism make Swin Transformer well-suited for understanding the intricate relationships between visual and textual components in memes, allowing it to accurately predict sentiment.

3.2.3. SwiftFormer

SwiftFormer [24] introduces an efficient additive attention mechanism, which has been shown to reduce the computational complexity of traditional self-attention mechanisms. In the context of meme sentiment analysis, SwiftFormer can capture contextual information from images faster and with fewer resources. This is especially useful for real-time meme sentiment analysis on mobile devices or other resource-constrained environments. By using additive attention rather than matrix multiplication, SwiftFormer retains the ability to focus on important features within the image, such as emotional expressions or key text–image interactions while significantly improving processing speed. This makes SwiftFormer an ideal choice for applications requiring fast and accurate meme sentiment analysis, even in environments with limited computational power.

3.3. *Evaluation Metrics for Sentiment Analysis*

In evaluating the performance of multimodal sentiment analysis tasks, several key metrics play crucial roles in assessing the effectiveness of the models:

3.3.1. Accuracy

Accuracy [25] serves as a fundamental metric for assessing the effectiveness of sentiment analysis models. It quantifies the proportion of correctly classified sentiment instances across both text and image modalities within the dataset. A higher accuracy score indicates that the model has successfully identified sentiment-related information from the multimodal data (e.g., text and image), demonstrating its ability to make correct predictions. Accuracy is a simple but essential metric in determining the model's overall performance in sentiment classification tasks.

$$\text{Accuracy} = \frac{\text{Number of correctly classified sentiment instances}}{\text{Total number of sentiment instances}} \tag{1}$$

3.3.2. Precision

Precision [26] in sentiment analysis refers to the proportion of instances that were correctly predicted as a specific sentiment (e.g., positive) out of all instances predicted as that sentiment. In the context of multimodal sentiment analysis in memes, precision measures how accurately the model identifies positive, negative, or neutral sentiments across all predicted instances of that sentiment.

For a specific sentiment class $c \in \{\text{positive, negative, neutral}\}$, precision is given by:

$$\text{Precision}_c = \frac{\text{TP}_c}{\text{TP}_c + \text{FP}_c} \tag{2}$$

where:

- TP_c (True Positives for class c): The number of instances where sentiment c was correctly predicted as sentiment c.
- FP_c (False Positives for class c): The number of instances where sentiment c was incorrectly predicted, but the true sentiment was not c.

For the overall precision across all sentiment classes, we use the weighted average:

$$\text{Precision}_{\text{macro}} = \frac{1}{C}\sum_{c=1}^{C} \text{Precision}_c \tag{3}$$

where C is the number of sentiment classes (in this case, three: positive, negative, neutral).

3.3.3. Recall

Recall [26] is the proportion of true instances of a specific sentiment class that were correctly identified by the model. In the context of sentiment analysis of memes, recall measures how well the model captures all instances of a specific sentiment, even if it results in false positives. Recall is critical when we aim to ensure that the model identifies every instance of a sentiment, such as detecting all positive or negative memes.

For a specific sentiment class $c \in \{\text{positive, negative, neutral}\}$, recall is given by:

$$\text{Recall}_c = \frac{\text{TP}_c}{\text{TP}_c + \text{FN}_c} \tag{4}$$

where:

- TP_c (True Positives for class c): The number of instances where sentiment c was correctly predicted as sentiment c.
- FN_c (False Negatives for class c): The number of instances where sentiment c was incorrectly predicted as not c (i.e., the model missed an actual instance of sentiment c).

For the overall recall across all sentiment classes, we use the weighted average:

$$\text{Recall}_{\text{macro}} = \frac{1}{C}\sum_{c=1}^{C} \text{Recall}_c \tag{5}$$

where C is the number of sentiment classes (three in this case: positive, negative, neutral).

3.3.4. Weighted F1 score

The weighted F1 score [27] is an extension of the standard weighted F1 score that accounts for the class imbalances in a dataset by assigning different weights to different classes based on their frequency or importance. This metric provides a more accurate reflection of model performance when dealing with datasets where some sentiment classes (e.g., positive, negative, neutral) are underrepresented compared to others. In multimodal sentiment analysis, where the model is expected to analyze data from multiple modalities such as text and images, the weighted F1 score ensures that the evaluation is not disproportionately influenced by dominant classes. The weighted F1 score is calculated by averaging the weighted F1 scores for each class, with each weighted F1 score weighted by the support (the number of true instances) of that class. This allows for a more nuanced understanding of model performance, particularly in situations where some sentiment categories may be less frequent but still critical to the overall analysis.

$$F1_{\text{weighted}} = \sum_{i=1}^{N} w_i \cdot F1_{\text{Sentiment}_i} \tag{6}$$

where:

- w_i is the weight for sentiment class i, calculated as:

$$w_i = \frac{\text{Number of true instances of sentiment class } i}{\text{Total number of instances}}$$

- $F1_{\text{Sentiment}_i}$ is the weighted F1 score for sentiment class i, calculated as:

$$F1_{\text{Sentiment}_i} = \frac{2 \cdot P_{\text{Sentiment}_i} \cdot R_{\text{Sentiment}_i}}{P_{\text{Sentiment}_i} + R_{\text{Sentiment}_i}}$$

- $P_{\text{Sentiment}_i}$ is the precision for sentiment class i, calculated as:

$$P_{\text{Sentiment}_i} = \frac{\text{Correctly classified sentiment instances of class } i}{\text{Total predicted as sentiment instances of class } i}$$

- $R_{\text{Sentiment}_i}$ is the recall for sentiment class i, calculated as:

$$R_{\text{Sentiment}_i} = \frac{\text{Correctly classified sentiment instances of class } i}{\text{Total actual sentiment instances of class } i}$$

4. Dataset Description

In this study, we leverage the MemoSen [1] dataset, a multimodal dataset specifically curated for sentiment analysis in the Bengali language, to conduct our experiments. MemoSen was meticulously developed to address the lack of resources for multimodal sentiment analysis in Bengali. The dataset comprises 4368 memes collected from popular social media platforms such as Facebook, Twitter, and Instagram over a period spanning February 2021 to September 2021. The memes were gathered using targeted keywords such as "Bengali Memes", "Bengali Funny Memes", and "Bengali Troll Memes", ensuring diverse representation across various themes. The dataset includes memes with captions written in Bengali, code-mixed (Bengali and English), or Banglish (code-switched). Memes failing to meet specific criteria, such as those lacking visual or textual components, containing unreadable text, or duplicates, were excluded during curation. The final dataset is annotated into three sentiment categories: positive, negative, and neutral, following rigorous guidelines to ensure consistency and reduce annotation bias. The annotation process was carried out by four graduate students with a background in computer engineering. Initially, the annotators were tasked with determining whether a meme expressed a positive or negative sentiment. If the annotators classified the meme as positive or negative, they were asked to provide the reasoning behind their decision. This reasoning was crucial for resolving any disagreements between annotators. If no clear sentiment was determined, the meme was labeled as neutral. The annotators were trained with examples to ensure they could distinguish between the sentiment classes and provide sound reasoning for their choices. The annotation process was manual, with the final labels being verified by an expert. The expert reviewed any disagreements between the annotators and, after discussing the reasoning behind their choices, set the final label. For each meme, two labels were provided by the initial annotators, and if they agreed, the final label was determined. In cases of disagreement, the expert's judgment was used to finalize the label. To ensure the quality of the annotations, the authors calculated the inter-annotator agreement using the Cohen's Kappa coefficient. The resulting mean Kappa score of 0.674 indicated a moderate level of agreement between the annotators, confirming the consistency of the annotation process. For training and evaluation purposes, the dataset is divided into train (70%), test (20%), and validation (10%) subsets. A detailed class-wise distribution is provided, along with representative examples of memes, including their captions and corresponding sentiment labels. The MemoSen dataset serves as a crucial benchmark for advancing research in multimodal sentiment analysis, especially for low-resource languages such as Bengali. Additionally, Figure 1 presents the distribution of samples across the training, test, and validation sets within the MemoSen dataset. Figure 2 showcases examples from the dataset, including the memes, their captions, and corresponding sentiment labels.

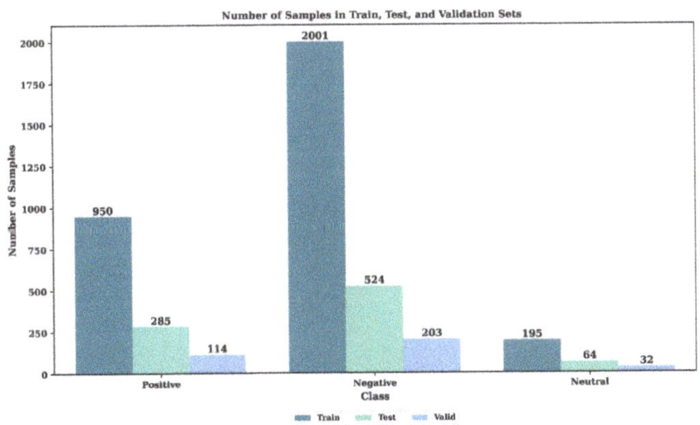

Figure 1. Distribution of samples Across train, test, and validation sets in the MemoSen dataset.

Figure 2. Representative examples from the MemoSen dataset, illustrating memes labeled with positive, neutral, and negative sentiments.

5. Proposed Methodology

We propose three hybrid approaches to multimodal sentiment analysis tailored for Bangla. **"SentimentTextFormer"** is a text-based method focused on accurately identifying sentiment-related information from Bangla texts. **"SentimentImageFormer"** introduces an image-based technique aimed at sentiment analysis, utilizing advanced transformer-based models for precise sentiment classification from visual data. Finally, **"SentimentFormer"** integrates text and image data through hybrid fusion techniques (early fusion, late fusion, and intermediate fusion), enhancing sentiment analysis capabilities across multiple modalities in diverse contexts. Figures 3 and 4 highlight the architectures of SentimentTextFormer and SentimentImageFormer, respectively, while Figure 5 provides an illustrative overview of the SentimentFormer framework.All the code and implementation details for the methodologies discussed in this paper have been made publicly available to ensure transparency and facilitate reproducibility. You can access the complete source code, including the fusion approaches, dimension alignment steps, and hyperparameter schedules, in our GitHub repository: GitHub repository. This repository contains all the necessary scripts and instructions to replicate the experiments and integrate the proposed techniques in your own research.

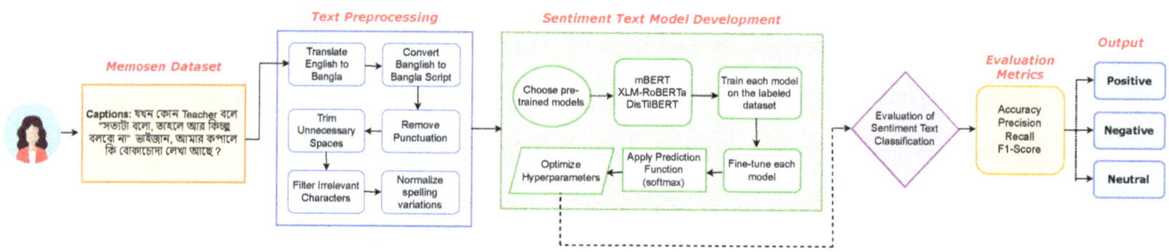

Figure 3. Unimodal sentiment classification framework for Bangla meme captions.

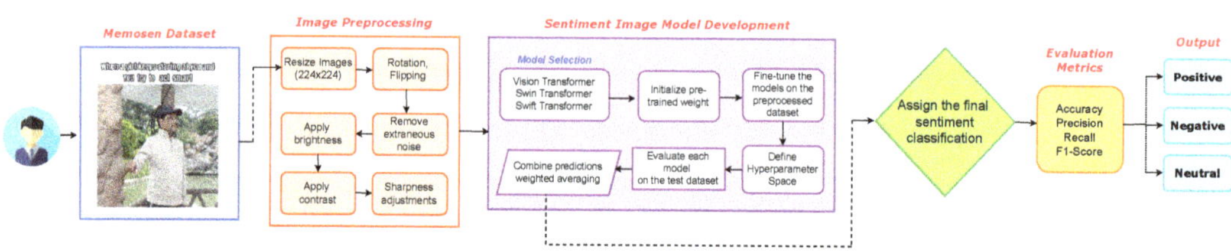

Figure 4. Unimodal sentiment classification framework for meme images.

5.1. Approach 1 for Unimodal Sentiment Analysis Framework for Bangla Captions

(Step 1) Text Preprocessing: Processing Bangla sentiment data presents unique challenges due to the language's rich morphology, flexible syntax, and contextual dependencies. To ensure consistency and relevance for analysis, we employ a systematic approach to preprocessing. First, we address the issue of mixed-language text by translating any English words or phrases into Bangla using Google Translator. While this ensures that the dataset remains monolingual and reduces inconsistencies from cross-lingual sentiment shifts, it may also result in potential information loss. The translation process may not fully capture the nuances of sentiment, as some emotional or contextual subtleties might be lost when converting between languages with different syntactical and cultural structures. This is particularly problematic when dealing with expressions or idioms that do not have direct equivalents in Bangla. Additionally, translation tools like Google Translator might introduce biases or inaccuracies in sentiment representation, further complicating sentiment analysis. We also handle Banglish (Bangla written in Roman script) by converting it into standard Bangla script using tools like Google Translator or Gamista. Since Bangla sentiment often depends on subtle linguistic cues, maintaining script uniformity enhances model performance. Given that punctuation usage in Bangla is inconsistent and sometimes optional—similar to Chinese—we remove punctuation marks such as periods, commas, and exclamation points unless they carry strong sentiment-indicating patterns. Additionally, unnecessary spaces between words are eliminated to maintain text compactness, preventing artificial length distortions. Another significant challenge in Bangla NLP is the presence of spelling variations influenced by dialects, English transliteration, or phonetic inconsistencies. We normalize such variations to ensure that words with the same meaning are consistently represented in the dataset. This step is crucial because state-of-the-art Bangla NLP models, such as mBERT, XLM-RoBERTa, and DisTilBERT, still struggle with non-standard spelling forms due to limited training data and domain diversity. Finally, we filter out irrelevant characters, including special symbols and control characters, that do not contribute to the semantic meaning of the sentiment. These preprocessing steps collectively enhance data quality, ensuring that the sentiment analysis model operates on a clean and standardized dataset despite the inherent complexities of Bangla NLP.

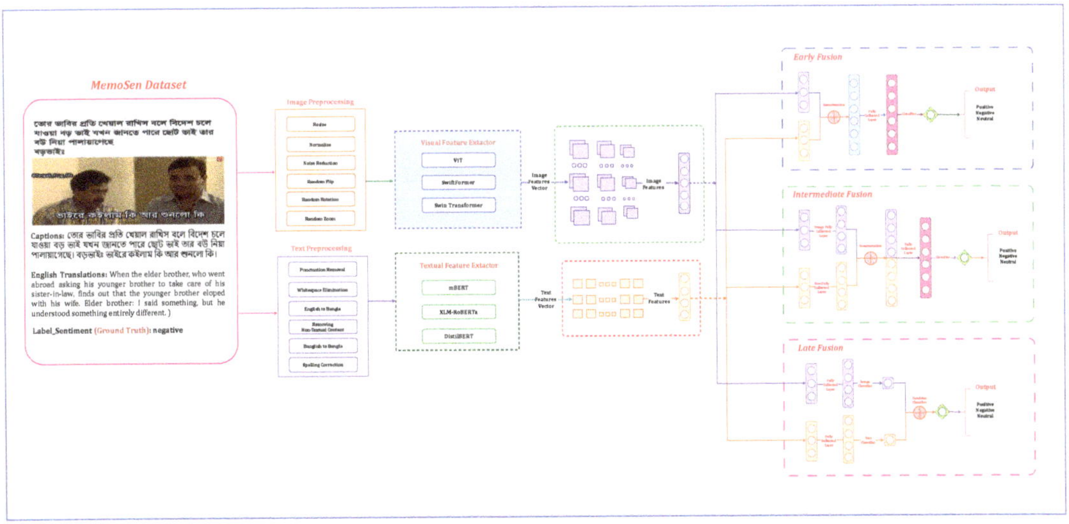

Figure 5. Fusion framework for enhanced multimodal sentiment analysis of Bangla memes.

(Step 2) Sentiment Text Model Development: After text preprocessing, we move forward with developing the model for sentiment analysis. We utilize state-of-the-art pre-trained language models, including mBERT, XLM-RoBERTa, and DisTilBERT, all of which have proven effective in handling a variety of textual data. Each of these models was fine-tuned using the collected Bangla sentiment datasets to tailor them for the specific task of sentiment classification. Fine-tuning involves adjusting the model's parameters using sentiment-labeled data to enhance its performance in categorizing Bangla text into different sentiment classes. This process helps the models better understand and classify the nuanced sentiments expressed in the Bangla language. To address the class imbalance, especially in the neutral sentiment category, we apply the Synthetic Minority Oversampling Technique (SMOTE) to generate synthetic samples for the underrepresented classes. First, we identify the minority class in our sentiment dataset, which is the neutral sentiment category. Using SMOTE, synthetic data points are created by selecting two or more similar instances from the minority class and generating new samples by interpolating their features. These synthetic samples are then integrated into the original dataset, increasing the representation of the minority class while preserving the data's overall distribution. The model is subsequently trained on this oversampled dataset, which aims to provide a more balanced class distribution and improve the model's ability to classify underrepresented sentiment categories, like neutral sentiment.

(Step 3) Hyperparameter Tuning: For Bangla sentiment text identification, hyperparameter tuning plays a crucial role in optimizing model performance. This process involves fine-tuning key hyperparameters such as learning rate, batch size, dropout rate, and the number of training epochs, all of which significantly impact the model's efficiency and performance. We systematically explore different configurations by adjusting these hyperparameters to find the optimal combination. Techniques such as grid search and random search are employed to automate this process, ensuring that the best-performing settings are identified. The model is trained multiple times with varying hyperparameter configurations, and the goal is to strike a balance between model complexity and generalization, allowing the model to accurately classify Bangla sentiment text while avoiding overfitting. Hyperparameter tuning helps in determining the best learning rate for the optimization process, the ideal batch size for training stability, and the appropriate dropout rate to prevent overfitting. Section 6.2 summarizes the results of hyperparameter tuning, showcasing the performance of each model under different settings.

(Step 4) Evaluation of Sentiment Text Classification: After training and fine-tuning the models, we assess their performance in identifying sentiments from Bangla text. Each model is evaluated individually to determine its effectiveness in sentiment classification. The evaluation focuses on key performance metrics such as accuracy, precision, recall, and weighted F1 score. Accuracy measures the overall correctness of the model in identifying sentiments, while precision reflects the model's ability to correctly identify positive sentiment instances. Recall, on the other hand, indicates how well the model identifies all the positive sentiment cases. The weighted F1 score accounts for class imbalances by combining precision and recall, providing a single, balanced measure of the model's performance across all sentiment categories. These metrics offer a comprehensive view of how well the models perform in classifying Bangla text into sentiment categories. Section 6.3 provides a detailed breakdown of the results, showing each model's performance across these key metrics.

Algorithmic Framework for Text-Based Bangla Sentiment Analysis

Text Preprocessing:

Given a Bangla text corpus $D = \{d_1, d_2, \ldots, d_n\}$, the preprocessing begins by translating any English token $e \in d_i$ to Bangla b using:

$$T(e) = b, \quad \forall e \in d_i$$

where T is the translation function.

Next, punctuation and extraneous spaces are removed:

$$\hat{d_i} = \text{RemovePunct}(d_i), \quad \hat{d_i} = \text{TrimSpaces}(\hat{d_i})$$

Irrelevant characters are then filtered out:

$$\tilde{d_i} = \text{FilterChars}(\hat{d_i})$$

The cleaned dataset is represented as:

$$D' = \{\tilde{d_1}, \tilde{d_2}, \ldots, \tilde{d_n}\}$$

Sentiment Text Model Development:

Let the fine-tuning function F operate on pre-trained models M and a labeled Bangla sentiment dataset L:

$$M^* = F(M, L)$$

For models $M \in \{\text{mBERT}, \text{XLM-RoBERTa}, \text{DistilBERT}\}$:

$$M_j^* = F(M_j, L), \quad j = 1, 2, \ldots, k$$

where k is the total number of models.

The output prediction function for sentiment classification is defined as:

$$P(d_i) = \text{softmax}(M^*(\tilde{d_i}))$$

Hyperparameter Tuning:

Let the hyperparameter space be H:

$$H = \{\eta, B, \lambda, E\}$$

where:

- η: Learning rate
- B: Batch size
- λ: Dropout rate
- E: Number of epochs

Define the performance function $\mathcal{P}$ for a hyperparameter configuration $h \in H$:

$$\mathcal{P}(h) = \text{Evaluate}(M^*, h, L)$$

Optimization involves finding:

$$h^* = \arg\max_{h \in H} \mathcal{P}(h)$$

Search techniques can be applied as:

$$h^* = \begin{cases} \text{GridSearch}(H) & \text{if exhaustive search is feasible} \\ \text{RandomSearch}(H) & \text{otherwise} \end{cases}$$

Evaluation of Sentiment Text Classification:

Let the evaluation metrics include:

- **Accuracy (A):**

$$A = \frac{\text{TP} + \text{TN}}{\text{TP} + \text{TN} + \text{FP} + \text{FN}}$$

- **Precision** (P):

$$P = \frac{\mathrm{TP}}{\mathrm{TP} + \mathrm{FP}}$$

- **Recall** (R):

$$R = \frac{\mathrm{TP}}{\mathrm{TP} + \mathrm{FN}}$$

- **Weighted F1 score** ($F1$):

$$F1 = 2 \cdot \frac{P \cdot R}{P + R}$$

For each model M_j^*, calculate:

$$\text{Metrics}_j = \{A_j, P_j, R_j, F1_j\}$$

5.2. Approach 2 for Unimodal Sentiment Analysis Framework for Meme Images

(Step 1) Image Preprocessing: To ensure uniformity in the input size and optimize computational efficiency, we began by resizing the images to a consistent format of 224 × 224 pixels. This resizing step guarantees that the images are suitable for deep learning models while retaining important visual details. In addition, we utilized data augmentation techniques such as rotation, flipping, and other transformations to enrich the dataset and enhance the model's ability to generalize across various scenarios. These modifications introduce variations in the image orientations, which improves the model's robustness when handling new, unseen data. Furthermore, we performed image cleaning to eliminate any extraneous noise or artifacts that could interfere with the model's ability to detect sentiment-specific features. To optimize image quality, we applied image enhancement techniques, including adjustments to brightness, contrast, and sharpness, ensuring that the visual clarity of the images is maximized.

(Step 2) Sentiment Identification Image Model Development: After preprocessing the images, we developed sentiment analysis models using three cutting-edge image classification models: ViT (Vision Transformer), Swin Transformer, and Swift Transformer. ViT leverages a transformer-based approach, dividing images into patches and processing them sequentially to capture global relationships and contextual information. Swin Transformer improves upon ViT by introducing a hierarchical structure and shifting window attention mechanism, enabling it to capture both local and global features more efficiently across varying image scales. Swift Transformer focuses on enhancing computational efficiency by simplifying the attention mechanism, ensuring faster processing without compromising accuracy in detecting sentiment features. By harnessing the unique strengths of these models, we aimed to accurately classify images based on their emotional or sentiment content.

(Step 3) Hyperparameter Tuning: Hyperparameter tuning plays a crucial role in optimizing the performance of sentiment analysis models. This process involves adjusting several key parameters, such as the learning rate, batch size, and regularization strength, to find the optimal configuration that enhances model accuracy. The learning rate determines how quickly the model adjusts its weights during training, with higher rates speeding up learning but potentially causing instability, while lower rates offer slower, more stable convergence. Batch size influences how many images are processed before updating the model weights, with larger batches generally improving model stability but requiring more computational resources. Regularization strength helps prevent overfitting by penalizing complex models that may not generalize well to new data. During tuning, we evaluated model performance using metrics such as accuracy, precision, recall, and weighted F1 score, which collectively provide a comprehensive assessment of how well the model classifies sentiment in images. By systematically experimenting with different hyperparameter combinations, we identified the most effective settings for the models. Section 6.2 showcases the results of the hyperparameter tuning process, detailing the performance of each model under various configurations.

(Step 4) Evaluation of Sentiment Image Analysis: After training and fine-tuning the models, we evaluated their ability to detect sentiment from images. Each model was assessed individually to determine its effectiveness in classifying sentiment. The evaluation process focused on essential performance metrics such as accuracy, precision, recall, and weighted F1 score. Accuracy measures the overall percentage of correct sentiment classifications, precision quantifies the model's ability to correctly identify positive sentiment instances, recall evaluates how well the model identifies all actual positive sentiment cases, and the weighted F1 score provides a balance between precision and recall. Section 6.3 offers a comprehensive analysis of the evaluation outcomes, highlighting the performance of each model based on these critical metrics.

Algorithmic Framework for Image-Based Bangla Sentiment Analysis

Image-Based Bangla Sentiment Analysis:

Given a dataset $\mathcal{D} = \{I_1, I_2, \ldots, I_n\}$ containing n images, the preprocessing steps begin by resizing each image I_i to a uniform dimension of $a \times a$ pixels:

$$\hat{I}_i = \text{Resize}(I_i, a \times a), \quad \forall i \in \{1, \ldots, n\}$$

Next, data augmentation techniques such as random rotation, flipping, and cropping are applied:

$$\tilde{I}_i = \text{Augment}(\hat{I}_i), \quad \forall i \in \{1, \ldots, n\}$$

Noise removal and image enhancement (e.g., adjusting brightness, contrast, and sharpness) are then performed:

$$I'_i = \text{Enhance}(\tilde{I}_i), \quad \forall i \in \{1, \ldots, n\}$$

Model Initialization:

Let the set of models be $\mathcal{M} = \{M_1, M_2, M_3\}$, where each model $M_j \in \mathcal{M}$ is initialized with pre-trained weights.

For each model $M_j \in \mathcal{M}$:

$$M'_j = \text{FineTune}(M_j, \mathcal{D})$$

Hyperparameter Tuning:

Let the hyperparameter space be $H = \{\eta, B, D\}$, where:

- η: Learning rate
- B: Batch size
- D: Dropout rate

For each combination of η, B, and D, train and validate the model M_j:

$$M^*_j = \text{TrainValidate}(M'_j, H)$$

Record performance metrics such as accuracy, precision, recall, and weighted F1 score for each configuration:

$$\mathcal{P}_j = \{A_j, P_j, R_j, F1_j\}, \quad \forall j \in \{1, 2, 3\}$$

Model Evaluation:

For each model M_j, evaluate it on the test dataset $\mathcal{D}_{\text{test}}$:

$$M_j^{\text{eval}} = \text{Evaluate}(M_j, \mathcal{D}_{\text{test}})$$

Compute evaluation metrics for each model:

$$\mathcal{P}_j = \{A_j, P_j, R_j, F1_j\}, \quad \forall j \in \{1, 2, 3\}$$

Prediction Aggregation:

Combine predictions from all models using majority voting or weighted averaging:

$$S_i = \arg\max_k \sum_j w_{M_j} \cdot P_{M_j}(S_i = k), \quad \forall i \in \{1, \ldots, n\}$$

where w_{M_j} represents the model weights, and $P_{M_j}(S_i = k)$ is the probability of sentiment class k.

Final Sentiment Classification:

The final sentiment classification for each image is denoted as:

$$\mathcal{S} = \{S_1, S_2, \ldots, S_n\}$$

where each S_i is the predicted sentiment for image I_i.

Return: Final sentiment classification $\mathcal{S}$.

5.3. Approach 3 for Exploring Different Fusion Techniques in Multimodal Sentiment Analysis

In our approach to multimodal Bangla sentiment analysis, we explored three different fusion techniques: early fusion, late fusion, and intermediate fusion.

(Step 1) Feature Extraction: For text features, we leveraged advanced pre-trained language models, including mBERT, XLM-RoBERTa, and DistilBERT. These models are well-suited for extracting semantic and syntactic information from textual data, allowing us to effectively capture the nuances of sentiment-related expressions in Bangla. mBERT and XLM-RoBERTa excel at handling multilingual text, while DistilBERT provides a lighter and faster alternative while maintaining strong performance. From the text, we extract features such as word embeddings, contextual representations, and sentiment-specific tokens, which help in understanding the sentiment conveyed through the language. In parallel, we extracted image features using state-of-the-art models tailored for sentiment analysis tasks. These models include ViT, Swin Transformer, and Swift Transformer. Each model has been specifically trained to extract visual features from images, such as facial expressions, body language, color patterns, and contextual visual elements, all of which are indicative of sentiment. ViT and Swin Transformer capture global image patterns, while Swift Transformer focuses on more localized, fine-grained image details. The extracted image features provide a rich representation of visual sentiment cues, complementing the text features for a more holistic analysis. By combining these distinct types of features—textual and visual—we ensure that both modalities contribute meaningfully to the sentiment analysis, enhancing the model's ability to accurately understand sentiment in a multimodal context.

(Step 2) Fusion Techniques: We utilized three distinct fusion techniques to effectively combine textual and visual information in our multimodal Bangla sentiment analysis pipeline. Prior to applying these techniques, we focused on extracting rich features from both text and images, ensuring that crucial information from each modality was thoroughly captured. These fusion strategies allow our model to take advantage of the complementary nature of text and image data, improving its ability to accurately analyze sentiment in a multimodal setting. By integrating both textual and visual insights, the model becomes more proficient at identifying and interpreting sentiment, considering both the language and the visual context.

(a) **Early Fusion for Multimodal Sentiment Analysis:** For early fusion [28], we combine representations obtained from both text and image modalities at an early stage, prior to the sentiment classification process. This integration of features from multiple modalities facilitates the creation of joint representations, enabling a more nuanced understanding of sentiment by capturing both linguistic and visual cues. Let $\mathbf{X}$ represent the input features from the text modality and $\mathbf{Y}$ represent those from the image modality. The early fusion process can be mathematically described as:

$$\mathbf{z}_{\text{early}} = f_{\text{fusion}}([\phi_{\text{text}}(f_{\text{text}}(\mathbf{X})); \phi_{\text{image}}(f_{\text{image}}(\mathbf{Y}))])$$

In this equation:

- $\mathbf{X}$ and $\mathbf{Y}$ are the input features from the text and image modalities, respectively.
- $f_{\text{text}}(\cdot)$ and $f_{\text{image}}(\cdot)$ are the feature extraction functions for text and images, respectively.
- $\phi_{\text{text}}(\cdot)$ and $\phi_{\text{image}}(\cdot)$ are non-linear activation functions applied to the extracted features.
- $[\cdot;\cdot]$ denotes the concatenation operation, combining the features from both modalities.
- $f_{\text{fusion}}(\cdot)$ is the function that processes the concatenated features to produce the joint representation.
- $\mathbf{z}_{\text{early}}$ represents the fused features obtained from the early fusion process, which are then fed into a classifier to predict sentiment.

(b) **Late Fusion for Multimodal Sentiment Analysis:** For late fusion [28], we aggregate predictions generated by text and image classification models at a later stage, after individual predictions are made. This technique integrates predictions from individual models to perform comprehensive sentiment analysis, potentially improving the accuracy and robustness of the final predictions. Let $\mathbf{P}_{\text{text}}$ represent the prediction probabilities from the text sentiment classification model and $\mathbf{P}_{\text{image}}$ represent the prediction probabilities from the image sentiment classification model. The late fusion process can be represented as:

$$\mathbf{P}_{\text{fusion}} = \alpha \cdot \mathbf{P}_{\text{text}}(f_{\text{text}}(\mathbf{X})) + (1-\alpha) \cdot \mathbf{P}_{\text{image}}(f_{\text{image}}(\mathbf{Y}))$$

In this equation:

- $\mathbf{X}$ and $\mathbf{Y}$ are the input features from the text and image modalities, respectively.
- $f_{\text{text}}(\cdot)$ and $f_{\text{image}}(\cdot)$ are the feature extraction functions for text and images, respectively.
- $\mathbf{P}_{\text{text}}(f_{\text{text}}(\mathbf{X}))$ represents the prediction probabilities from the text sentiment classification model applied to the text features.
- $\mathbf{P}_{\text{image}}(f_{\text{image}}(\mathbf{Y}))$ represents the prediction probabilities from the image sentiment classification model applied to the image features.
- α is a weighting factor that balances the contributions of text and image predictions, which can be fine-tuned for optimal performance.

- $\mathbf{P}_{\text{fusion}}$ represents the final prediction probabilities obtained from the late fusion process, reflecting the overall sentiment classification result.

(c) **Intermediate Fusion for Multimodal Sentiment Analysis:** For intermediate fusion [28], we merged features extracted from different modalities at an intermediate level of representation. By combining intermediate representations obtained from text and image processing pipelines, this technique captures the nuanced relationships between modalities, thereby facilitating more accurate sentiment analysis. Let $\mathbf{Z}_{\text{text}}$ represent the intermediate features from the text modality, and $\mathbf{Z}_{\text{image}}$ represent the intermediate features from the image modality. The intermediate fusion process can be represented as:

$$\mathbf{Z}_{\text{fusion}} = f_{\text{fusion}}(\phi_{\text{text}}(f_{\text{text}}(\mathbf{X})), \phi_{\text{image}}(f_{\text{image}}(\mathbf{Y})))$$

In this equation:

- $\mathbf{X}$ and $\mathbf{Y}$ are the input features from the text and image modalities, respectively.
- $f_{\text{text}}(\cdot)$ and $f_{\text{image}}(\cdot)$ are the feature extraction functions for text and images, respectively.
- $\phi_{\text{text}}(\cdot)$ and $\phi_{\text{image}}(\cdot)$ are non-linear activation functions applied to the extracted features.
- $\mathbf{Z}_{\text{text}} = \phi_{\text{text}}(f_{\text{text}}(\mathbf{X}))$ represents the intermediate features from the text modality.
- $\mathbf{Z}_{\text{image}} = \phi_{\text{image}}(f_{\text{image}}(\mathbf{Y}))$ represents the intermediate features from the image modality.
- $f_{\text{fusion}}(\cdot,\cdot)$ is the fusion function that combines the intermediate features from both modalities.
- $\mathbf{Z}_{\text{fusion}}$ represents the fused features obtained from the intermediate fusion process.

(Step 3) Hyperparameter Tuning: Hyperparameter tuning was performed to enhance the performance of the multimodal Bangla sentiment analysis models. This process involves adjusting several key parameters, including batch size, learning rate, fusion weight, and regularization strength, to determine the optimal configuration that maximizes performance metrics such as accuracy, precision, recall, and weighted F1 score. Specifically, when applying fusion techniques to combine textual and visual information, hyperparameters play a crucial role in how these two modalities interact and contribute to the final sentiment prediction. In the context of fusion, parameters such as fusion weight determine how much influence the text features and image features will have in the final decision. For example, a higher fusion weight for text features may indicate that textual information is given more importance, while adjusting the weight for image features can help balance the contribution of visual cues. Other hyperparameters, such as the learning rate and batch size, help fine-tune how quickly the model learns from the data and how much data it processes at once, directly impacting the efficiency and effectiveness of the fusion process. Furthermore, regularization parameters help prevent overfitting by controlling the complexity of the model, ensuring that the model generalizes well across unseen data. These tuning processes are essential for achieving the best performance from the multimodal model, as they allow the fusion techniques to adapt optimally to the specific characteristics of the Bangla sentiment analysis task. Section 6.2 display the results of hyperparameter tuning, showcasing how different configurations affect the model's performance across various fusion strategies. These tables provide a detailed comparison of how tuning different parameters influences the model's ability to analyze sentiment in both text and images.

(Step 4) Evaluation of Multimodal Sentiment Analysis: The multimodal sentiment analysis models are evaluated to assess their performance in accurately identifying and classifying sentiment from both textual and visual data sources. Section 6.3 provides a detailed analysis of the performance metrics, such as accuracy, precision, recall, and weighted F1 score, which are computed to measure the effectiveness of the models. These metrics help assess how well the model integrates and interprets both textual and visual features for sentiment classification. Through rigorous evaluation, we ensure that the multimodal approach is robust and effective in real-world sentiment analysis tasks.

Algorithmic Framework for Multimodal-Based Bangla Sentiment Analysis

Feature Extraction: For text and image features, we use the following equations to express the extraction process.

For text feature extraction using pre-trained language models:

$$\mathbf{X} = f_{\text{text}}(\mathbf{T}), \quad \phi_{\text{text}}(\mathbf{X}) = \text{activation}(f_{\text{text}}(\mathbf{T}))$$

where:

- $\mathbf{T}$ represents the raw text input.
- $f_{\text{text}}(\cdot)$ is the feature extraction function for text.
- $\phi_{\text{text}}(\cdot)$ is the activation function applied to the extracted features.

For image feature extraction using pre-trained models:

$$\mathbf{Y} = f_{\text{image}}(\mathbf{I}), \quad \phi_{\text{image}}(\mathbf{Y}) = \text{activation}(f_{\text{image}}(\mathbf{I}))$$

where:

- $\mathbf{I}$ represents the raw image input.
- $f_{\text{image}}(\cdot)$ is the feature extraction function for images.
- $\phi_{\text{image}}(\cdot)$ is the activation function applied to the extracted features.

Fusion Techniques: We apply the following fusion strategies:

(a) **Early Fusion:** The features from both text and image modalities are concatenated before classification. The fusion process is expressed as:

$$\mathbf{z}_{\text{early}} = f_{\text{fusion}}([\phi_{\text{text}}(f_{\text{text}}(\mathbf{X})); \phi_{\text{image}}(f_{\text{image}}(\mathbf{Y}))])$$

where:

- $\mathbf{X}, \mathbf{Y}$ are text and image features.
- $f_{\text{text}}(\cdot), f_{\text{image}}(\cdot)$ are feature extraction functions.
- $\phi_{\text{text}}(\cdot), \phi_{\text{image}}(\cdot)$ are activation functions.
- $f_{\text{fusion}}(\cdot)$ is the fusion function.

(b) **Late Fusion:** The predictions from text and image classifiers are combined using a weighted sum:

$$\mathbf{P}_{\text{fusion}} = \alpha \cdot \mathbf{P}_{\text{text}} + (1 - \alpha) \cdot \mathbf{P}_{\text{image}}$$

where:

- $\mathbf{P}_{\text{text}}, \mathbf{P}_{\text{image}}$ are text and image classifier outputs.
- α is the fusion weight.

(c) **Intermediate Fusion:** The features from both modalities are fused at an intermediate stage:

$$\mathbf{Z}_{\text{fusion}} = f_{\text{fusion}}(\phi_{\text{text}}(f_{\text{text}}(\mathbf{X})), \phi_{\text{image}}(f_{\text{image}}(\mathbf{Y})))$$

where:

- $\mathbf{X}, \mathbf{Y}$ are text and image features.
- $f_{\text{text}}(\cdot), f_{\text{image}}(\cdot)$ are feature extraction functions.
- $\phi_{\text{text}}(\cdot), \phi_{\text{image}}(\cdot)$ are activation functions.
- $f_{\text{fusion}}(\cdot, \cdot)$ is the fusion function.

Hyperparameter Tuning: Hyperparameters are tuned using the following expressions:

For the learning rate (η), batch size (B), and fusion weight (α):

$$\mathcal{L}_{\text{tune}} = \sum_{i=1}^{N} \mathcal{L}_{\text{loss}}(\mathbf{y}_i, \hat{\mathbf{y}}_i; \eta, B, \alpha)$$

where:

- $\mathcal{L}_{\text{loss}}(\cdot)$ is the loss function.
- $\mathbf{y}_i, \hat{\mathbf{y}}_i$ are the true and predicted labels.
- η is the learning rate.
- B is the batch size.
- α is the fusion weight.

The optimization process minimizes the loss $\mathcal{L}_{\text{tune}}$ to find the best hyperparameter settings.

6. Experiments and Result Analysis

6.1. Experimental Setup

The experiments were conducted across multiple environments, including Jupyter Notebook 6.5.5, Kaggle 1.6.17, and Google Colaboratory 0.0.1a2. All experiments were run using Python and PyTorch, with variations in versions across platforms. Specifically, the Jupyter Notebook environments utilized Python 3.8.18 with PyTorch 2.0.1, while the Kaggle setup ran Python 3.10.13 with PyTorch 2.1.2. The Google Colaboratory environment used Python 3.10.12 with PyTorch 2.3.1.

6.2. Hyperparameter Settings

Table 3 provides the hyperparameter settings for both text-based and image-based models used in multimodal sentiment analysis of Bangla memes. For the image-based models, Vision Transformer (ViT), Swin Transformer (SentimentImageFormer), and Swift Transformer are fine-tuned with a batch size of 8 and a learning rate of 0.0001, using the AdamW optimizer. The number of epochs varies slightly: ViT and Swift Transformer are fine-tuned for 45 epochs, while Swin Transformer (SentimentImageFormer) is fine-tuned for 40 epochs. For the text-based models, mBERT (SentimentTextFormer), XLM-RoBERTa, and DistilBERT are fine-tuned with a batch size of 8, a learning rate of 0.0001, and the AdamW optimizer. These models are fine-tuned for either 45 or 50 epochs, with mBERT (SentimentTextFormer) being fine-tuned for 50 epochs and the others for 45 epochs.

Table 3. Hyperparameter settings for text-based and image-based models in multimodal sentiment analysis of Bangla memes.

Approach	Model	Batch Size	Epoch	Learning Rate	Optimizer
Image Based	ViT	8	45	0.0001	AdamW
	Swin Transformer (SentimentImageFormer)	8	40	0.0001	AdamW
	Swift Transformer	8	45	0.0001	AdamW
Text Based	mBERT (SentimentTextFormer)	8	50	0.0001	AdamW
	XLM-RoBERTa	8	45	0.0001	AdamW
	DistilBERT	8	45	0.0001	AdamW

Table 4 provides the hyperparameter settings for early fusion models in the multimodal sentiment analysis of Bangla memes. For the early fusion models, Vision Transformer (ViT) + mBERT, Swin Transformer + mBERT, and Swift Transformer + mBERT are all fine-tuned with a batch size of 8, a learning rate of 0.0001, and the AdamW optimizer. The number of epochs varies: ViT + mBERT is fine-tuned for 40 epochs, Swin Transformer + mBERT for 35 epochs, and Swift Transformer + mBERT for 30 epochs. For the ViT + XLM-RoBERTa, Swin Transformer + XLM-RoBERTa, and Swift Transformer + XLM-RoBERTa models, they are fine-tuned with a learning rate of 0.001, a batch size of 8, and the AdamW optimizer, with epochs ranging from 35 to 40. Similarly, the ViT + DistilBERT, Swin Transformer + DistilBERT, and Swift Transformer + DistilBERT models are fine-tuned with a learning rate of 0.0001 and the AdamW optimizer, and the number of epochs is either 35 or 40 depending on the model.

Table 4. Hyperparameter settings for early fusion in multimodal sentiment analysis of Bangla memes.

Approach	Model	Batch Size	Epoch	Learning Rate	Optimizer
Early fusion	ViT + mBERT	8	40	0.0001	AdamW
	Swin Transformer + mBERT	8	35	0.0001	AdamW
	Swift Transformer + mBERT	8	30	0.0001	AdamW
	ViT + XLM-RoBERTa	8	35	0.001	AdamW
	Swin Transformer + XLM-RoBERTa	8	40	0.001	AdamW
	Swift Transformer + XLM-RoBERTa	8	35	0.001	AdamW
	ViT + DistilBERT	8	35	0.0001	AdamW
	Swin Transformer + DistilBERT	8	35	0.0001	AdamW
	Swift Transformer + DistilBERT	8	40	0.0001	AdamW

Table 5 provides the hyperparameter settings for late fusion models in the multimodal sentiment analysis of Bangla memes. For the late fusion models, Vision Transformer (ViT) + mBERT, Swin Transformer + mBERT, and Swift Transformer + mBERT are all fine-tuned with a batch size of 8 and a learning rate of 0.0001, using the AdamW optimizer. The number of epochs varies: ViT + mBERT is fine-tuned for 40 epochs, Swin Transformer + mBERT for 35 epochs, and Swift Transformer + mBERT for 30 epochs. The models ViT + XLM-RoBERTa, Swin Transformer + XLM-RoBERTa, and Swift Transformer + XLM-RoBERTa are fine-tuned with a learning rate of 0.001, a batch size of 8, and the AdamW optimizer, with epochs ranging from 35 to 40. Similarly, the ViT + DistilBERT, Swin Transformer + DistilBERT, and Swift Transformer + DistilBERT models are fine-tuned with a learning rate of 0.0001 and the AdamW optimizer, and the number of epochs is either 35 or 40 depending on the model.

Table 5. Hyperparameter settings for late fusion in multimodal sentiment analysis of Bangla memes.

Approach	Model	Batch Size	Epoch	Learning Rate	Optimizer
Late fusion	ViT + mBERT	8	40	0.0001	AdamW
	Swin Transformer + mBERT	8	35	0.0001	AdamW
	Swift Transformer + mBERT	8	30	0.0001	AdamW
	ViT + XLM-RoBERTa	8	35	0.001	AdamW
	Swin Transformer + XLM-RoBERTa	8	40	0.001	AdamW
	Swift Transformer + XLM-RoBERTa	8	35	0.001	AdamW
	ViT + DistilBERT	8	35	0.0001	AdamW
	Swin Transformer + DistilBERT	8	35	0.0001	AdamW
	Swift Transformer + DistilBERT	8	40	0.0001	AdamW

Table 6 outlines the hyperparameter settings for intermediate fusion models used in the multimodal sentiment analysis of Bangla memes. For the intermediate fusion models, Vision Transformer (ViT) + mBERT, Swin Transformer + mBERT, and Swift Transformer + mBERT (SentimentFormer) are fine-tuned with a batch size of 8 and a learning rate of 0.0001 using the AdamW optimizer. The number of epochs varies slightly: ViT + mBERT is trained for 40 epochs, Swin Transformer + mBERT for 35 epochs, and Swift Transformer + mBERT for 30 epochs. The ViT + XLM-RoBERTa, Swin Transformer + XLM-RoBERTa, and Swift Transformer + XLM-RoBERTa models are fine-tuned with a learning rate of 0.001, a batch size of 8, and the AdamW optimizer. These models are trained for 35 to 40 epochs. Similarly, the ViT + DistilBERT, Swin Transformer + DistilBERT, and Swift Transformer + DistilBERT models are fine-tuned with a learning rate of 0.0001 and the AdamW optimizer, with the number of epochs ranging from 35 to 40.

Table 6. Hyperparameter settings for intermediate fusion in multimodal sentiment analysis of Bangla memes.

Approach	Model	Batch Size	Epoch	Learning Rate	Optimizer
Intermediate Fusion	ViT + mBERT	8	40	0.0001	AdamW
	Swin Transformer + mBERT	8	35	0.0001	AdamW
	Swift Transformer + mBERT (SentimentFormer)	8	30	0.0001	AdamW
	ViT + XLM-RoBERTa	8	35	0.001	AdamW
	Swin Transformer + XLM-RoBERTa	8	40	0.001	AdamW
	Swift Transformer + XLM-RoBERTa	8	35	0.001	AdamW
	ViT + DistilBERT	8	35	0.0001	AdamW
	Swin Transformer + DistilBERT	8	35	0.0001	AdamW
	Swift Transformer + DistilBERT	8	40	0.0001	AdamW

6.3. Result Analysis

Table 7 presents the performance metrics for multimodal sentiment analysis of memes in Bangla, evaluated across accuracy, precision, recall, and weighted F1 score. Among text-based models, mBERT (SentimentTextFormer) leads with the highest accuracy (73.31%) and a weighted F1 score of 64.34, followed by XLM-RoBERTa (72.85%, weighted F1 score 64.03) and DistilBERT (71.48%, weighted F1 score 62.29). For image-based models, ViT achieves the best accuracy (62.77%) but has lower precision and recall, resulting in a weighted F1 score of 54.14. The Swin and Swift Transformers show similar performance, with accuracies of 64.72% and 63.57%, respectively.

Table 7. Performance metrics of text-based and image-based models for multimodal sentiment analysis of Bangla memes.

Approach	Model	Accuracy	Precision	Recall	Weighted F1 Score
Text Based	mBERT (SentimentTextFormer)	73.31	62.77	68.60	64.34
	XLM-RoBERTa	72.85	62.38	68.35	64.03
	DistilBERT	71.48	60.9	66.14	62.29
Image Based	ViT	62.77	53.26	59.70	54.14
	Swin Transformer (SentimentImageFormer)	64.72	53.39	57.39	54.24
	Swift Transformer	63.57	53.90	59.84	54.79

Table 8 presents the performance metrics for multimodal-based models with early fusion in the context of sentiment analysis of Bangla memes. Among the model combinations, Swin Transformer + XLM-RoBERTa achieves the highest accuracy (75.83%) along with solid precision (64.04%) and recall (67.68%), resulting in a weighted F1 score of 63.88%. Swift Transformer + mBERT closely follows with an accuracy of 74.46%, precision of 63.24%, and recall of 68.82%, leading to a weighted F1 score of 63.69%. Another strong performer is Swin Transformer + mBERT, which achieves an accuracy of 74.68%, with precision (62.97%), recall (67.04%), and a weighted F1 score of 63.03%. Other combinations, such as ViT + mBERT, ViT + XLM-RoBERTa, and ViT + DistilBERT, show lower performances, with accuracies ranging from 69.07% to 72.39%, and weighted F1 scores varying between 55.16% and 59.13%. These results demonstrate that early fusion of image-based models with text-based models, particularly Swin Transformer paired with XLM-RoBERTa, provides the best overall performance for Bangla meme sentiment analysis.

Table 8. Performance metrics for multimodal-based models with early fusion for multimodal sentiment analysis of Bangla memes.

Approach	Model	Accuracy	Precision	Recall	Weighted F1 Score
Early Fusion	ViT + mBERT	72.39	59.67	61.20	59.13
	Swin Transformer + mBERT	74.68	62.97	67.04	63.03
	Swift Transformer + mBERT	74.46	63.24	68.82	63.69
	ViT + XLM-RoBERTa	69.07	56.56	56.19	55.16
	Swin Transformer + XLM-RoBERTa	75.83	64.04	67.68	63.88
	Swift Transformer + XLM-RoBERTa	71.36	58.44	58.00	57.01
	ViT + DistilBERT	70.45	58.03	58.4	56.88
	Swin Transformer + DistilBERT	74.68	62.96	67.58	63.23
	Swift Transformer + DistilBERT	71.82	59.50	60.61	58.56

Table 9 presents the performance metrics for multimodal-based models with late fusion in the context of sentiment analysis of Bangla memes. Among the late fusion models, Swin Transformer + XLM-RoBERTa achieves the highest accuracy (74.8%) with a precision of 60.38%, recall of 60.97%, and a weighted F1 score of 59.82%. The ViT + DistilBERT combination follows with an accuracy of 69.87%, precision of 55.69%, recall of 56.33%, and a weighted F1 score of 55.28%. Swift Transformer + DistilBERT also performs reasonably well, with an accuracy of 68.73% and a weighted F1 score of 54.68%. Other combinations such as ViT + mBERT, ViT + XLM-RoBERTa, and Swift Transformer + XLM-RoBERTa show lower performance, with accuracies ranging from 61.28% to 67.35%, and weighted F1 scores between 47.63% and 52.81%. These results demonstrate that late fusion models, particularly Swin Transformer combined with XLM-RoBERTa, outperform other model combinations in terms of accuracy, precision, recall, and weighted F1 score for Bangla meme sentiment analysis.

Table 9. Performance metrics for multimodal-based models with late fusion for multimodal sentiment analysis of Bangla memes.

Approach	Model	Accuracy	Precision	Recall	Weighted F1 Score
	ViT + mBERT	61.28	48.78	48.05	47.63
	Swin Transformer + mBERT	71.02	56.6	56.97	56.09
	Swift Transformer + mBERT	67.35	53.93	54.78	52.81
	ViT + XLM-RoBERTa	62.43	49.66	48.84	48.49
Late Fusion	Swin Transformer + XLM-RoBERTa	74.8	60.38	60.97	59.82
	Swift Transformer + XLM-RoBERTa	62.77	49.61	50.1	49.02
	ViT + DistilBERT	69.87	55.69	56.33	55.28
	Swin Transformer + DistilBERT	65.29	52.94	53.25	51.98
	Swift Transformer + DistilBERT	68.73	55.04	56.23	54.68

Table 10 presents the performance metrics for multimodal-based models with intermediate fusion in the context of sentiment analysis of Bangla memes. Among the models with intermediate fusion, Swift Transformer combined with mBERT (SentimentFormer) achieves the highest performance, with an accuracy of 79.04%, precision of 71.29%, recall of 77.42%, and a weighted F1 score of 73.28%. Other notable models include Swift Transformer + XLM-RoBERTa, which achieves an accuracy of 74.46%, precision of 65.12%, recall of 71.79%, and a weighted F1 score of 64.84%. Swin Transformer + XLM-RoBERTa follows closely with an accuracy of 72.16%, precision of 62.85%, recall of 70.52%, and a weighted f1 score of 63.17%. In comparison, models such as ViT + mBERT and ViT + XLM-RoBERTa show lower performance, with accuracies ranging from 66.44% to 68.73%, and weighted F1 scores between 56.53% and 58.4%. These results indicate that intermediate fusion, particularly with Swift Transformer and mBERT, leads to the best overall performance for Bangla meme sentiment analysis, outperforming other fusion strategies in terms of accuracy, precision, recall, and weighted F1 score. Figure 6 presents the confusion matrices of SentimentTextFormer, SentimentImageFormer, and SentimentFormer on the MemoSen dataset.

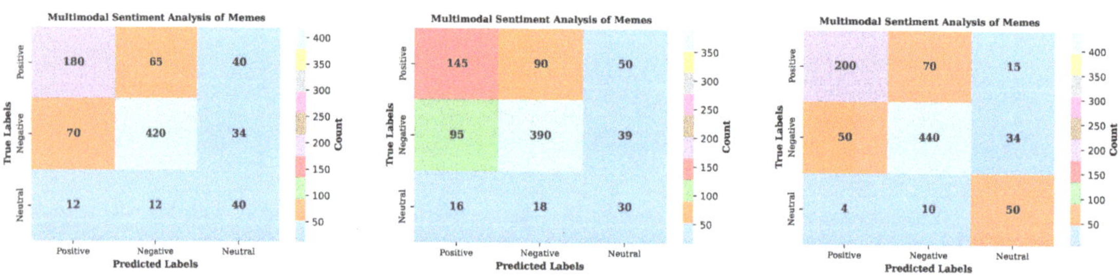

(**a**) SentimentTextFormer (**b**) SentimentImageFormer (**c**) SentimentFormer

Figure 6. Confusion matrices of SentimentTextFormer, SentimentImageFormer, and SentimentFormer showcasing their sentiment classification performance on the MemoSen dataset.

Table 10. Performance metrics for multimodal-based models with intermediate fusion for multimodal sentiment analysis of Bangla memes.

Approach	Model	Accuracy	Precision	Recall	Weighted F1 Score
Intermediate Fusion	ViT + mBERT	68.16	57.83	63.45	58.4
	Swin Transformer + mBERT	68.73	59.8	68.08	60.43
	Swift Transformer + mBERT (SentimentFormer)	79.04	71.29	77.42	73.28
	ViT + XLM-RoBERTa	66.44	56.69	62.23	56.94
	Swin Transformer + XLM-RoBERTa	72.16	62.85	70.52	63.17
	Swift Transformer + XLM-RoBERTa	74.46	65.12	71.79	64.84
	ViT + DistilBERT	66.44	56.35	61.7	56.53
	Swin Transformer + DistilBERT	71.02	61.84	69.35	62.06
	Swift Transformer + DistilBERT	73.31	62.37	68.18	62.86

6.4. Error Analysis

In this section, we examine the limitations and misclassifications encountered during the multimodal sentiment analysis process in memes. By analyzing specific instances in which the model failed to accurately classify the sentiment (positive, negative, or neutral) in meme images and texts, we gain insights into the underlying challenges and areas for improvement. This analysis is crucial for understanding the model's weaknesses, such as difficulties in interpreting sarcasm, context, or visual cues, and for guiding the refinement of multimodal sentiment analysis capabilities. Figure 7 presents a visualization of error analysis for multimodal sentiment analysis in memes.

Figure 7. Error analysis of multimodal sentiment classification in Bengali memes.

6.4.1. Misclassification of Humorous Memes Due to Lack of Contextual Understanding and Cultural Sensitivity in Sentiment Analysis

Image 1 is a meme featuring Tom and Jerry, with Tom sitting on a couch, reading a newspaper, and the text "I am not getting married now, I need my personal space for now" above him. Jerry, standing behind Tom, has the text "You will get married, even your father will get married" above him. Below the image, the text reads "desperate mother for marriage". The intended sentiment is likely positive, with humor derived from the contrast between Tom's desire for personal space and his mother's eagerness for him to marry, creating a relatable and exaggerated situation many young adults can understand.

The humor lies in the exaggerated portrayal of the mother's determination. A model might misclassify it as negative due to several factors. First, text-based sentiment analysis might interpret phrases like "I am not getting married now" and "desperate mother" as negative indicators. Second, the model might lack contextual understanding, failing to grasp the humor in the situation. The contrast between Tom's desire for personal space and his mother's insistence on marriage is key to the humor, which might be missed. Additionally, cultural nuances could play a role, as a model might not fully understand the context of marriage in Bengali society, which the meme is referencing. Lastly, sarcasm and irony often found in memes can be challenging for models to detect, further contributing to the misclassification.

6.4.2. Misclassification of Social Awkwardness as Neutral Sentiment Due to Limited Contextual Understanding in Humorous Memes

Image 2 is a meme featuring a dialogue between two characters. The first character, a customer, is talking to the shopkeeper. The text above the customer reads: "Bought a condom, when I went to my girlfriend's house, I saw him there again". The text above the shopkeeper reads: "Uncle, you?" The intended sentiment of the meme is likely negative, as the humor arises from the awkward and embarrassing situation where the customer encounters the shopkeeper at his girlfriend's house. This unexpected encounter creates a humorous and relatable scenario, but the underlying situation is likely to cause embarrassment and discomfort for the customer. Several factors could lead a model to misclassify the sentiment as neutral: lack of contextual understanding, where the model might not grasp the social awkwardness and embarrassment implied in the situation; a focus on the literal meaning of the text, which does not explicitly convey negative emotions; limited training data, which might not cover similar scenarios involving social awkwardness and embarrassment; and challenges in detecting sarcasm or irony, which are often used in humor and can be difficult for models to interpret correctly.

6.4.3. Misclassification of Humor in Unexpected Interactions Due to Lack of Situational and Cultural Awareness in Sentiment Analysis

Image 3 is a meme featuring a dialogue between two characters. The text above the first character reads, "You won the big lottery, became a millionaire, didn't you?" and the text above the second character reads, "I am Jashim, are you?" The intended sentiment of the meme is likely neutral, with the humor stemming from the unexpected and seemingly random question posed by the second character. It creates a humorous disconnect between the first character's assumed wealth and the second character's seemingly irrelevant question. Several factors could lead a model to misclassify the sentiment as negative. First, the model might not grasp the humor in the situation, interpreting the unexpectedness of the question and the lack of a clear connection to the first character's wealth as dismissive or rude, which could lead to a negative sentiment classification. Additionally, the model might focus on the literal meaning of the text, which does not explicitly convey positive emotions, and fail to recognize the underlying humor and intended lightheartedness of the interaction. If the model was trained on a dataset lacking similar scenarios involving unexpected or random questions, it might struggle to classify the sentiment correctly. Cultural nuances could also play a role, as the humor might be lost on a model that lacks understanding of the Bengali language and the context of such interactions in Bengali society.

6.5. Comparison of Results with Existing Approaches

Table 11 presents a comparison of the performance metrics—precision, recall, and weighted F1 score—of three models for multimodal sentiment analysis of Bangla memes: the proposed SentimentFormer (Swift Transformer + mBERT), Hossain et al. [1] (ResNet50 + CNN), and Elahi et al. [3] (Banglish BERT + ResNet50). The SentimentFormer model outperforms both existing models in all metrics, achieving a precision of 71.29, recall of 77.42, and weighted f1 score of 73.28. In comparison, the model by Hossain et al. [1] scores 66.3 for precision, 62.8 for recall, and 64.3 for weighted F1 score, while the model by Elahi et al. [3] scores 69.0, 74.0, and 71.0, respectively. The SentimentFormer model shows significant improvements, particularly in recall (up by 14.62 over Hossain et al. [1] and 3.42 over Elahi et al. [3]) and weighted F1 score (up by 8.98 over Hossain et al. [1] and 2.28 over Elahi et al. [3]), highlighting the effectiveness of combining Swift Transformer with mBERT and advanced multimodal fusion techniques. This demonstrates that the proposed method is more accurate and better at identifying true positive sentiment, making it a more balanced and robust approach for sentiment analysis in Bangla memes.

Table 11. Performance comparison of proposed method with existing approaches for multimodal sentiment analysis of Bangla memes.

Model	Precision	Recall	Weighted F1 Score
SentimentFormer (proposed method)	71.29	77.42	73.28
Hossain et al. [1] (ResNet50 + CNN)	66.3	62.8	64.3
Elahi et al. [3] (Banglish BERT + ResNet50)	69.0	74.0	71.0

7. Limitations

The MemoSen dataset includes diverse multimodal data for Bangla sentiment analysis, sourced from publicly available platforms such as social media and news articles. While the dataset offers valuable insights for sentiment analysis research in the Bangla language, several inherent limitations must be considered when evaluating its comprehensiveness and generalizability. One key limitation is the representation of regional dialects within the Bengali language. Bengali is spoken in various regions, each with its own dialectal variations, yet the dataset primarily focuses on Bengali memes that may not adequately capture the full diversity of these regional dialects. As a result, the model may struggle to generalize across all Bengali-speaking communities, particularly those whose dialects are underrepresented or absent from the dataset. Another limitation is the restricted scope of sentiment categories. The dataset only includes three broad sentiment labels—positive, negative, and neutral—which may fail to capture the full spectrum of emotions conveyed in memes. Memes often express nuanced sentiments such as sarcasm, humor, irony, or complex emotional gradients, which are difficult to encapsulate within these limited categories. Moreover, the temporal scope of the dataset, covering a specific time period from February to September 2021, introduces potential temporal biases. Meme culture and internet trends evolve quickly, and the sentiments expressed through memes may change over time. As such, the dataset may not fully represent current meme culture or the latest forms of sentiment expression in Bengali-language social media, limiting its applicability to more recent contexts. Additionally, the nature of memes often relies on humor, cultural references, and social commentary that may be rooted in stereotypes or specific societal contexts. As a result, the dataset may inadvertently reinforce or perpetuate negative stereotypes or biases, especially if certain types of memes are more likely to evoke specific sentiments based on cultural or social contexts. This could lead to a skewed understanding of sentiment within the dataset and affect the model's performance in real-world applications where such biases are present.

8. Future Works

In future work, we plan to improve our approach to multimodal sentiment analysis for Bengali memes by exploring several exciting areas. One of the main improvements we want to make is using Explainable AI (XAI) techniques, such as GradCAM++, LayerCAM, and ScoreCAM. These techniques will help us better understand how the model makes its predictions. They will show us which parts of the image and text are most important in deciding the sentiment. This transparency is important because it helps us understand the model's behavior, build trust in it, and make it work better. We also plan to use advanced Vision-Language Models (VLMs) like Claude 3.5 Sonnet and GPT-4, which excel at understanding and generating content that involves both images and text. By using these models, we aim to improve sentiment analysis in memes by generating responses based on different prompting techniques. These techniques could include providing specific instructions about the image or caption, asking the model to focus on certain emotions or elements, or even prompting it to consider various contextual cues. This approach will help the model capture subtle emotional clues, tones, and meanings in memes that simpler models might overlook. By refining the prompts, we can guide the model to generate more accurate and contextually aware responses, leading to a deeper understanding of sentiment in multimodal content. Additionally, we want to create a more inclusive and diverse dataset that includes different regional dialects of Bengali. This will involve collecting memes from areas like Chittagong, Sylhet, and Noakhali, which have unique dialects that are not often included in other datasets. Including these dialects will help our model work better for different Bengali-speaking communities and improve its performance in real-world situations. This will also ensure that the model understands the full richness of the Bengali language, including different cultural and regional expressions. By working on these areas, we hope to create more reliable, accurate, and understandable multimodal sentiment analysis models for Bengali. Our focus will be on capturing the different ways people express sentiments in regional languages and cultures.

9. Conclusions

In this study, we explored the emerging field of multimodal sentiment analysis for Bengali memes using the MemoSen dataset. This dataset consists of 4368 Bengali memes annotated with sentiment labels (positive, negative, and neutral), offering a valuable resource for sentiment analysis in low-resource languages. By proposing and developing innovative hybrid models, SentimentTextFormer, SentimentImageFormer, and SentimentFormer, we demonstrated the potential of combining textual and visual information to improve sentiment classification accuracy. The use of advanced deep learning techniques, such as transformer-based models for both text and image modalities, along with fusion strategies like early, late, and intermediate fusion, significantly enhanced performance. Our models achieved notable results, with SentimentFormer (SwiftFormer with mBERT) reaching an accuracy of 79.04%, showing an improvement of 5.73% over the unimodal text model (SentimentTextFormer) and 14.32% over the unimodal image model (SentimentImageFormer). This demonstrates the effectiveness of our multimodal approach in outperforming both text-only and image-only models. However, there are some limitations in our work, such as the imbalanced class distribution in the MemoSen dataset, which could impact model performance, especially for the minority neutral class. Additionally, despite the improvements achieved, there is potential for further enhancement in handling more complex and diverse meme types. Future work will focus on addressing these limitations, including better handling of class imbalance, exploring more advanced fusion techniques, and expanding the dataset for greater generalization across different meme categories and sentiment nuances.

Author Contributions: F.T.J.F., L.H.B., M.H.B., M.A.K., A.I.B.A., C.B. and S.K. conceptualized and developed the methodology and experiments. F.T.J.F. conducted the experiments, while L.H.B. and S.K. analyzed the data. F.T.J.F. evaluated the results. F.T.J.F. wrote the manuscript, and L.H.B., M.A.K., A.I.B.A. and S.K. reviewed it. All authors have read and approved the final version of the manuscript.

Funding: This work was supported by the Basic Science Research Program through the National Research Foundation of Korea (NRF), funded by the Ministry of Science and ICT under Grant NRF-2022R1A2C1005316.

Data Availability Statement: This study analyzes existing datasets, which have been appropriately cited in the manuscript. No new datasets were created. The analyzed data are publicly available or accessible through the referenced sources.

Conflicts of Interest: Authors Mohannad A. Khair was employed by the company Qatrana Cement Company. The remaining authors declare that the research was conducted in the absence of any commercial or financial relationships that could be construed as a potential conflict of interest.

References

1. Hossain, E.; Sharif, O.; Hoque, M.M. MemoSen: A Multimodal Dataset for Sentiment Analysis of Memes. In Proceedings of the Thirteenth Language Resources and Evaluation Conference, Marseille, France, 20–25 June 2022; pp. 1542–1554.
2. Hu, Z.; Dychka, I.; Potapova, K.; Meliukh, V. Augmenting Sentiment Analysis Prediction in Binary Text Classification through Advanced Natural Language Processing Models and Classifiers. *Int. J. Inf. Technol. Comput. Sci.* **2024**, *16*, 16–31. [CrossRef]
3. Elahi, K.T.; Rahman, T.B.; Shahriar, S.; Sarker, S.; Joy, S.K.S.; Shah, F.M. Explainable Multimodal Sentiment Analysis on Bengali Memes. In Proceedings of the 2023 26th International Conference on Computer and Information Technology (ICCIT), Cox's Bazar, Bangladesh, 13–15 December 2023; pp. 1–6.
4. Faria, F.T.J.; Moin, M.B.; Wase, A.A.; Ahmmed, M.; Sani, M.R.; Muhammad, T. Vashantor: A large-scale multilingual benchmark dataset for automated translation of bangla regional dialects to bangla language. *arXiv* **2023**, arXiv:2311.11142.
5. Faria, F.T.J.; Moin, M.B.; Mumu, R.I.; Abir, M.M.A.; Alfy, A.N.; Alam, M.S. Motamot: A Dataset for Revealing the Supremacy of Large Language Models over Transformer Models in Bengali Political Sentiment Analysis. In Proceedings of the 2024 IEEE Region 10 Symposium (TENSYMP), New Delhi, India, 27–29 September 2024; pp. 1–8.
6. Sharker, A.; Farhab, M.A.R.; Tamanna, T.A.; Rumman, U.; Shawon, M.T.R.; Mandal, N.C. A Cross-Corpus Deep Learning Approach to Social Media Emotion Classification. In Proceedings of the 2022 4th International Conference on Sustainable Technologies for Industry 4.0 (STI), Dhaka, Bangladesh, 17–18 December 2022; pp. 1–6. [CrossRef]
7. Faria, F.T.J.; Baniata, L.H.; Kang, S. Investigating the Predominance of Large Language Models in Low-Resource Bangla Language over Transformer Models for Hate Speech Detection: A Comparative Analysis. *Mathematics* **2024**, *12*, 3687. [CrossRef]
8. Karim, M.R.; Dey, S.K.; Islam, T.; Shajalal, M.; Chakravarthi, B.R. Multimodal hate speech detection from bengali memes and texts. In Proceedings of the International Conference on Speech and Language Technologies for Low-resource Languages, Kalavakkam, India, 23–25 November 2022; pp. 293–308.
9. Moin, M.B.; Debnath, P.; Rifa, U.A.; Anis, R.B. Assessing the Level of Toxicity Against Distinct Groups in Bangla Social Media Comments: A Comprehensive Investigation. *arXiv* **2024**, arXiv:2409.17130.
10. Venugopal, J.P.; Subramanian, A.A.V.; Sundaram, G.; Rivera, M.; Wheeler, P. A Comprehensive Approach to Bias Mitigation for Sentiment Analysis of Social Media Data. *Appl. Sci.* **2024**, *14*, 11471. [CrossRef]
11. Abiola, O.; Abayomi-Alli, A.; Tale, O.A.; Misra, S.; Abayomi-Alli, O. Sentiment analysis of COVID-19 tweets from selected hashtags in Nigeria using VADER and Text Blob analyser. *J. Electr. Syst. Inf. Technol.* **2023**, *10*, 5. [CrossRef]
12. Sudirjo, F.; Diantoro, K.; Al-Gasawneh, J.A.; Azzaakiyyah, H.K.; Ausat, A.M.A. Application of ChatGPT in Improving Customer Sentiment Analysis for Businesses. *J. Teknol. Dan Sist. Inf. Bisnis* **2023**, *5*, 283–288. [CrossRef]
13. Rifa, U.A.; Debnath, P.; Rafa, B.K.; Hridi, S.S.; Rahman, M.A. CineXDrama: Relevance Detection and Sentiment Analysis of Bangla YouTube Comments on Movie-Drama using Transformers: Insights from Interpretability Tool. *arXiv* **2024**, arXiv:2411.06548.

14. Manias, G.; Mavrogiorgou, A.; Kiourtis, A.; Symvoulidis, C.; Kyriazis, D. Multilingual text categorization and sentiment analysis: A comparative analysis of the utilization of multilingual approaches for classifying twitter data. *Neural Comput. Appl.* **2023**, *35*, 21415–21431. [CrossRef] [PubMed]
15. He, A.; Abisado, M. Text Sentiment Analysis of Douban Film Short Comments Based on BERT-CNN-BiLSTM-Att Model. *IEEE Access* **2024**, *12*, 45229–45237. [CrossRef]
16. Gu, W.J.; Zhong, Y.H.; Li, S.Z.; Wei, C.S.; Dong, L.T.; Wang, Z.Y.; Yan, C. Predicting Stock Prices with FinBERT-LSTM: Integrating News Sentiment Analysis. In Proceedings of the 2024 8th International Conference on Cloud and Big Data Computing (ICCBDC '24), Oxford, UK, 15–17 August 2024; Association for Computing Machinery: New York, NY, USA, 2024; pp. 67–72. [CrossRef]
17. Alluri, N.V.; Krishna, N.D. Multi Modal Analysis of memes for Sentiment extraction. In Proceedings of the 2021 Sixth International Conference on Image Information Processing (ICIIP), Shimla, India, 26–28 November 2021; pp. 213–217. [CrossRef]
18. Thakkar, G.; Hakimov, S.; Tadić, M. M2SA: Multimodal and Multilingual Model for Sentiment Analysis of Tweets. *arXiv* **2024**, arXiv:2404.01753.
19. Devlin, J.; Chang, M.W.; Lee, K.; Toutanova, K. Bert: Pre-training of deep bidirectional transformers for language understanding *arXiv* **2018**, arXiv:1810.04805.
20. Conneau, A.; Khandelwal, K.; Goyal, N.; Chaudhary, V.; Wenzek, G.; Guzmán, F.; Grave, E.; Ott, M.; Zettlemoyer, L.; Stoyanov, V. Unsupervised cross-lingual representation learning at scale. *arXiv* **2019**, arXiv:1911.02116.
21. Sanh, V. DistilBERT, a distilled version of BERT: Smaller, faster, cheaper and lighter. *arXiv* **2019**, arXiv:1910.01108.
22. Dosovitskiy, A.D.; Beyer, L.; Kolesnikov, A.; Weissenborn, D.; Zhai, X.; Unterthiner, T.; Dehghani, M.; Minderer, M.; Heigold, G.; Gelly, S.; et al. An image is worth 16x16 words: Transformers for image recognition at scale. *arXiv* **2020**, arXiv:2010.11929.
23. Liu, Z.; Lin, Y.; Cao, Y.; Hu, H.; Wei, Y.; Zhang, Z.; Lin, S.; Guo, B. Swin transformer: Hierarchical vision transformer using shifted windows. In Proceedings of the IEEE/CVF International Conference on Computer Vision, Nashville, TN, USA, 11–15 June 2025; pp. 10012–10022.
24. Shaker, A.; Maaz, M.; Rasheed, H.; Khan, S.; Yang, M.H.; Khan, F.S. Swiftformer: Efficient additive attention for transformer-based real-time mobile vision applications. In Proceedings of the IEEE/CVF International Conference on Computer Vision, Paris, France, 2–3 October 2023; pp. 17425–17436.
25. Liu, B.; Udell, M. Impact of accuracy on model interpretations. *arXiv* **2020**, arXiv:2011.09903.
26. Goutte, C.; Gaussier, E. A Probabilistic Interpretation of Precision, Recall and F-Score, with Implication for Evaluation. In *Advances in Information Retrieval. ECIR 2005. Lecture Notes in Computer Science*; Losada, D.E., Fernández-Luna, J.M., Eds.; Springer Berlin/Heidelberg, Germany, 2005; Volume 3408._25 [CrossRef]
27. Sokolova, M.; Japkowicz, N.; Szpakowicz, S. Beyond Accuracy, F-Score and ROC: A Family of Discriminant Measures for Performance Evaluation. In *AI 2006: Advances in Artificial Intelligence, Lecture Notes in Computer Science*; Springer: Berlin/Heidelberg Germany, 2006; Volume 4304, pp. 1015–1021._114. [CrossRef]
28. Faria, F.T.J.; Moin, M.B.; Rahman, M.M.; Shanto, M.M.A.; Fahim, A.I.; Hoque, M.M. Uddessho: An Extensive Benchmark Dataset for Multimodal Author Intent Classification in Low-Resource Bangla Language. *arXiv* **2024**, arXiv:2409.09504.

electronics

MDPI

Article

Comparative Investigation of GPT and FinBERT's Sentiment Analysis Performance in News Across Different Sectors

Ji-Won Kang and Sun-Yong Choi *

Department of Finance and Big Data, Gachon University, Seongnam 13120, Republic of Korea; kangjiwon5961@gachon.ac.kr

* Correspondence: sunyongchoi@gachon.ac.kr; Tel.: +82-31-750-5387

Abstract: GPT (Generative Pre-trained Transformer) is a groundbreaking generative model that has facilitated substantial progress in natural language processing (NLP). As the GPT-n series has continued to evolve, its applications have garnered considerable attention across various industries, particularly in finance. In contrast, traditional financial research has primarily focused on analyzing structured data such as stock prices. However, recent trends highlight the growing importance of natural language techniques that address unstructured factors like investor sentiment and the impact of news. Positive or negative information about specific companies, industries, or the overall economy found in news or social media can influence investor behavior and market volatility, highlighting the critical need for robust sentiment analysis. In this context, we utilize the state-of-the-art language model GPT and the finance-specific sentiment analysis model FinBERT to perform sentiment and time-series analyses on financial news data, comparing the performance of the two models to demonstrate the potential of GPT. Furthermore, by examining the relationship between sentiment shifts in financial markets and news events, we aim to provide actionable insights for investment decision-making, emphasizing both the performance and interpretability of the models. To enhance the performance of GPT-4o, we employed a systematic approach to prompt design and optimization. This process involved iterative refinement, guided by insights derived from a labeled dataset. This approach emphasized the pivotal importance of prompt design in improving model accuracy, resulting in GPT-4o achieving higher performance than FinBERT. During the experiment phase, sentiment scores were generated from New York Times news data and visualized through time-series graphs for both models. Although both models exhibited similar trends, significant differences arose depending on news content characteristics across categories. According to the results, the performance of GPT-4o, optimized through prompt engineering, outperformed that of FinBERT by up to 10% depending on the sector. These findings emphasize the importance of prompt engineering and demonstrate GPT-4o's potential to improve sentiment analysis. Furthermore, the categorized news data approach suggests potential applications in predicting the outlook of categorized financial products.

Keywords: sentiment analysis; GPT; FinBERT; prompt design; The New York Times

1. Introduction

Large language models (LLMs) are massive deep learning models based on transformer architecture, and they are pre-trained on vast amounts of text data. These models possess the ability to learn from extensive language data, demonstrating remarkable capabilities in natural language processing (NLP) tasks such as language translation, text generation and summarization, sentiment analysis (SA), and question-answering systems. Among these, the Generative Pre-trained Transformer (GPT), first introduced by OpenAI in 2018, has significantly contributed to advancements in NLP. Although its early versions had limitations in solving real-world problems, GPT's emergence brought renewed momentum to AI research, particularly in NLP.

ChatGPT, based on the GPT-3.5 architecture, was introduced by OpenAI as an enhanced version of GPT-3 released in 2022 (https://chatgpt.com/, accessed on 1 January 2025). Unlike its predecessors, which were primarily API-based, ChatGPT's chatbot interface allowed direct user interaction, driving its widespread adoption. Within a week of its launch, ChatGPT surpassed one million users, demonstrating its explosive popularity. The release of GPT-4, incorporating 100 trillion parameters, further accelerated AI advancements, expanding LLMs into multimodal models and intensifying competition in the field. Accordingly, ChatGPT is widely adopted across industries. It assists students in education [1], shows potential in healthcare [2], and enhances finance and business through content creation, customer engagement, and research [3–5].

The rise of ChatGPT has driven innovation in various industries, particularly in business and economics. Researchers have explored its applications in these fields, including prompt engineering techniques to optimize performance [6]. In Section 2.1, we present a concise review of previous studies exploring ChatGPT's performance across various fields.

ChatGPT's growing influence in finance is evident as institutions use LLMs to automate tasks and analyze market behavior. This integration enables advanced applications like sentiment analysis (SA), risk assessment, and investment. SA quantifies subjective elements—emotions, thoughts, and opinions—at document, sentence, and aspect levels to classify sentiment as positive or negative.

In particular, SA traces its roots to early 20th-century public opinion research and computational linguistics studies from the 1990s. Its study expanded in 2004 with internet growth and data proliferation [7]. Recently, machine learning-based approaches have significantly enhanced SA performance [8]. With its growing importance, SA is now widely used by researchers, businesses, governments, and organizations. Ongoing advancements in methods, data, and models continue to enhance its effectiveness [9,10]. We provide a concise review of prior research focused on SA in Section 2.2.

Our study focuses on evaluating the SA performance of GPT-4o, particularly in the context of analyzing news articles across various sectors. To achieve this, we compare and assess the performance of GPT-4o against the FinBERT (Financial Bidirectional Encoder Representations from Transformers) model, which is specifically designed for financial sentiment analysis. Additionally, we employ a sophisticated prompt design process to enhance the accuracy and effectiveness of GPT-4o's sentiment analysis.

The goal of this study is to understand the differences between domain-specific models and general-purpose models, while proposing new possibilities for financial text analysis. This approach aims to provide insights into the capabilities and limitations of GPT-4o in comparison to specialized models like FinBERT.

In conclusion, this study highlights the potential of the general-purpose NLP model, GPT, in sentiment analysis, and seeks to propose new possibilities and directions for research in sentiment analysis.

To do this, we collect news articles from several sectors. Subsequently, we conduct SA on the collected news articles using both GPT-4o and the benchmark model FinBERT. The performance of GPT-4o is influenced by the design of the prompt [11–13]. Accordingly, we employ a refined prompt design process to enhance SA performance. Finally, we compare the SA results from both GPT-4o and FinBERT. In particular, we perform SA using news data through FinBERT, a model specialized in finance. FinBERT, a specialized language model built upon BERT, is tailored for financial language processing. Trained on financial texts, such as news, earnings reports, regulations, and analyst summaries, FinBERT gains prominence for its efficacy in various studies [14–18]. The detailed workflows are provided in Section 3.2.

GPT's use in financial sentiment analysis is still emerging. Although versatile, its lack of financial specialization limits its effectiveness in this domain. Studies have focused on models like FinBERT, which excels in classifying financial sentiment and analyzing market trends [14,15,18,19]. Research comparing GPT to FinBERT and exploring their complementary potential remains limited, restricting insights into GPT's role in financial text analysis. In Section 2.3, we also review previous studies that have utilized FinBERT in various applications.

Consequently, our study makes several significant contributions to the literature. First, we evaluate the performance of GPT-4o in sentiment analysis and compare it with FinBERT, analyzing the relative strengths and weaknesses of each model. Second, we propose a prompt design framework for GPT-4o that can be widely applied across various industry sectors, enhancing both its generalizability and accuracy in sentiment analysis. Third, we generate time-series data for sentiment scores obtained from GPT-4o and FinBERT and conduct an event analysis, introducing a new analytical paradigm that extends beyond traditional technical and fundamental analyses. Ultimately, our findings contribute to the literature by demonstrating the effectiveness of GPT-4o in sentiment analysis and providing a time-series perspective on its performance.

The remainder of this paper is structured as follows: The next section provides a brief review of the existing literature relevant to our study. Section 3 presents the news data and outlines the research design. In Section 4, we report the SA results obtained using GPT-4o and FinBERT, followed by a comparative analysis of their performances. Finally, Section 5 offers a discussion of the findings and concluding remarks.

2. Literature Review

In this section, we review previous studies relevant to our research, focusing on GPT performance, sentiment analysis, and the application of FinBERT.

2.1. The Performance of GPT

Ref. [20] attempted zero-shot and few-shot inference using the Chain-of-Thoughts (COT) methodology with NASDAQ-100 stocks on GPT-4 and supervised fine-tuning with LLaMA. The experimental results demonstrate that these approaches outperform traditional statistical models and machine learning techniques in terms of performance. Ref. [21] utilized GPT-4 to analyze news headlines, Google's sustainability reports, Midwest Energy Emissions Corp's performance records, and Fed FOMC meeting minutes to address four questions arising when applying ML models in accounting. The results demonstrate that GPT-4 is highly accurate and efficient in generating quantitative and logical analyses of textual content. Ref. [22] evaluated whether GPT can assist in stock evaluation using 21 financial knowledge tests. In this test, GPT-3.5 scored 65%, whereas ChatGPT, based on GPT-4, scored an almost perfect 99%, demonstrating that GPT-4 possesses the capability to act as a robo-advisor in current financial matters. Ref. [23] utilized GPT to simplify the process of evaluating publicly listed companies' annual reports and then used the results for machine learning. This shows promising outperformance against the S&P 500 returns, indicating that insights derived from LLMs can be useful features for constructing machine learning models. Ref. [24] investigated the AI quality management (AIQM) of the ChatGPT system in SA by setting prompts and controlling outputs for four types of variations. The evaluation involved Amazon.com review data and the Stanford Sentiment Treebank, demonstrating robustness for all variations but showing weakness in synonymic variations. Ref. [25] prompted ChatGPT-4 to predict earnings announcements and evaluate the relative attractiveness of each S&P 500 company to determine whether ChatGPT-4 can accurately predict stock performance and assist in investment decisions. Using a real-time experiment, the study found a positive correlation between ChatGPT-4 attractiveness ratings and future earnings' announcements as well as stock returns. Ref. [4] evaluated ChatGPT's effectiveness in portfolio management, finding that its asset selections exhibited higher diversity and outperformed random selections. The results suggest ChatGPT's potential as a valuable investment assistant. Ref. [26] analyzed ChatGPT's portfolio recommendations, showing alignment with academic benchmarks across investor profiles. The study highlights ChatGPT's ability to enhance information presentation and support investment decisions. Ref. [27] assessed LLM-based chatbots, including ChatGPT, in cybersecurity, revealing weaknesses in named entity recognition for extracting security-related data. The findings emphasize the need for further refinement in cyber threat detection. Ref. [28] proposed the multimodal fusion Bitcoin (MFB) framework, integrating BiLSTM and BiGRU for market prediction. The study highlights a strong correlation between Bitcoin sentiment and price, reinforcing sentiment analysis in financial forecasting.

GPT models have demonstrated strong potential in data analysis and decision-making support within the financial domain. Various studies indicate that GPT outperforms traditional methodologies in processing complex financial data, asset selection and portfolio construction, market forecasting, and other financial activities. Notably, GPT optimizes investment processes by leveraging high reliability and efficiency, while enhancing the presentation and summarization of information to help users easily understand and utilize key insights. Furthermore, GPT has shown the ability to adapt to specific financial contexts, offering tailored recommendations based on investor profiles and outperforming traditional robo-advisors in certain cases. This suggests that GPT can transcend its role as a mere analytical tool to become a crucial assistant in financial advisory and research. Its sophisticated language processing and reasoning capabilities provide the potential to enhance efficiency in financial research and practice, strengthen decision-making support, and open new possibilities for delivering financial services.

2.2. Sentiment Analysis

Ref. [29] proposed Instruct-FinGPT, trained by fine-tuning LaMA with Twitter financial news and the FiQA dataset. It demonstrates superiority over widely used LLMs in scenarios where understanding of numbers and context is crucial. Ref. [30] bootstrapped a smaller student model, Charformer (CF), by tuning it with COT-integrated data from social media platforms such as Reddit and FiQA. Despite its smaller size, it achieved comparable or superior performance to existing state-of-the-art models in terms of financial outlook for companies. Ref. [31] utilized instruction tuning and retrieval augmentation modules with Llama-7B, initialized to train on Twitter financial news and the FiQA dataset. Consequently, it exhibited significantly superior performance in financial SA compared to ChatGPT and LLaMA. Ref. [32] performed tasks such as SA, HC and NER by instructing and tuning various open LLMs. Utilizing datasets such as FPR, FiQA-SA, Headline Dataset, NER Dataset, and FinRED, it demonstrated remarkable generalization ability in zero-shot tasks. Ref. [33] conducted financial SA on corporate financial reports using four LLMs, including OpenAI's ChatGPT (GPT-3.5), through prompt engineering. The results indicate that the performance and output quality of the LLMs vary depending on the prompt design, content of the reports, and complexity of the task, highlighting the importance of prompt design in achieving optimal results. Ref. [34] analyzed sentiment analysis methods using GPT, showing that prompt engineering, fine-tuning, and embedding classification outperform state-of-the-art models. The study highlights GPT's strength in handling context, sarcasm, and linguistic challenges in sentiment analysis. Ref. [35] introduced MarketSenseAI, leveraging GPT-4's reasoning for stock selection. Integrating Chain of Thought and In-Context Learning, the framework enhances AI-driven investment decision-making by improving signal accuracy and reliability. Ref. [36] integrated emotion lexicons with ChatGPT to enhance empathetic responses in psychotherapy. Using therapy transcripts, they improved GPT's empathy, coherence, and fluency, emphasizing the role of emotional embeddings in LLM performance.

Recent studies in financial sentiment analysis have focused on utilizing GPT to analyze the complex relationships between financial data and market sentiment. These studies reveal that GPT outperforms traditional models, significantly enhancing the accuracy and efficiency of sentiment analysis through advanced capabilities such as context understanding, addressing complex linguistic challenges, zero-shot learning, and retrieval augmentation. Furthermore, prompt engineering and systematic data calibration have been identified as critical factors influencing model performance. Emphasis has also been placed on adopting approaches that consider the unique context and complexity of financial data. These advancements enable the effective detection of sentiment patterns across diverse data sources such as news, social media, and financial reports, linking them to practical applications such as market prediction, investment decision support, and financial risk management. Collectively, these studies highlight the potential of GPT-based sentiment analysis as a powerful tool for understanding and interpreting market sentiment, thereby expanding its performance and applicability.

2.3. The Application of FinBERT

Ref. [18] evaluated FinBERT for sentiment classification in financial texts, showing it outperforms benchmark models, including dictionaries and machine learning algorithms, by leveraging contextual information effectively. Ref. [14] fine-tuned BERT to create FinBERT and demonstrated its superior sentiment classification accuracy over general BERT using financial datasets, confirming its applicability in finance. Ref. [37] analyzed unstructured financial text from Bursa Malaysia reports, comparing MiniLM and FinBERT. The results highlight FinBERT's effectiveness in categorizing Key Audit Matters, emphasizing the value of domain-specific models. Ref. [38] explored financial sentiment analysis in the forex market, showing that ChatGPT 3.5's zero-shot prompt approach outperforms FinBERT in predicting market returns from news headlines. Ref. [39] demonstrated the vulnerability of keyword-based sentiment models, using adversarial attacks on GPT-3 and contrasting its susceptibility with FinBERT in financial text analysis.

In the financial sector, FinBERT outperforms other machine learning algorithms, including BERT, in sentiment analysis and classification tasks, demonstrating significant potential for financial text analysis. It has proven to be highly effective in extracting insights from diverse financial data, contributing to the literature on financial text analysis. Additionally, FinBERT can match or even surpass GPT's performance in certain cases, making it a suitable benchmark model for comparisons in financial applications.

Building on the existing literature discussed above, it is evident that GPT's performance is advancing rapidly across various fields. Sentiment analyses based on text data are becoming increasingly significant and widely utilized. Notably, there has been a growing number of studies employing FinBERT, a model specialized in the financial domain, for sentiment analysis.

In this study, we apply GPT, which has demonstrated exceptional performance, to sentiment analysis and compare its results with those of FinBERT. Furthermore, we conduct performance comparisons across financial and non-financial domains using sector-specific news text data. This approach allows us to comprehensively evaluate GPT's sentiment analysis performance, offering new insights beyond the scope of previous studies.

3. Data Description and Research Design

3.1. Datasets

In this section, we present the datasets used in our study. Initially, we collected labeled data to perform the prompt design. We utilized the News SA Dataset provided by Kaggle (https://www.kaggle.com/datasets/clovisdalmolinvieira/news-sentiment-analysis, accessed on 1 January 2025) and converted the CSV file into a DataFrame format. From the available columns, we focused on the "Headline", "Description", "Sector", and "Sentiment" fields. These data were categorized by news sectors, specifically "Business", "Health", and "Technology", by aligning it with the corresponding categories.

To ensure the quality of our dataset and minimize potential biases that could impact model performance, we performed several preprocessing steps.

First, we applied preprocessing to the headline and description columns, which involved removing content within parentheses and brackets, as well as eliminating HTML entities and special characters. Specifically, we used regular expressions to delete any text enclosed in parentheses () and brackets [], removing unnecessary information from the headlines. For example, the headline "NMCB 18 and 647th Civil Engineer Squadron Learn New Technology from ERDC [Image 9 of 11]" was cleaned to "NMCB 18 and 647th Civil Engineer Squadron Learn New Technology from ERDC". Additionally, since news article data often contain HTML-encoded characters such as &#;number, , and –, we replaced them to ensure a more natural text format. Furthermore, we removed URLs from the description column, as they can introduce irrelevant information in news article analysis. By identifying and eliminating these URLs, we reduced noise that could affect model training and data analysis.

Finally, we removed duplicate rows to ensure data consistency. The deleted records were exact duplicates, and among the 500 records in each category, 136 records were removed from the Business category, 130 from Technology, and 179 from Health. Additionally, we removed unnecessary symbols and extraneous text to further refine the dataset and improve overall data quality.

Table 1 presents the number of data points for each category, along with the distribution of sentiment labels: positive, negative, and neutral. For the "Business" category, there are a total of 364 data points, with 254 being labeled as "positive", 48 as "negative", and 62 as "neutral". The "Health" category comprises a total of 321 data points, with 170 labeled as "positive", 75 as "negative", and 76 as "neutral". Finally, the "Technology" category contains a total of 370 data points, with 239 labeled as "positive", 56 as "negative", and 75 as "neutral".

Table 1. Label distribution across different categories. Num. = number.

Sector	Total Num.	Positive Num.	Negative Num.	Neutral Num.
Business	364	254	48	62
Health	321	170	75	76
Technology	370	239	56	75

The classification of sentiment into "positive", "neutral", or "negative" may introduce subjective biases. However, many previous studies on sentiment analysis have commonly adopted this three-category approach [40–47]. Following this standard, our study also applies sentiment analysis to news articles using these three classes.

To enhance the performance of FinBERT, we conducted fine-tuning using a financial news text dataset labeled with sentiment. This dataset, provided by Kaggle (www.kaggle.com/datasets/antobenedetti/finance-news-sentiments, accessed on 1 January 2025), consists of 32,583 financial news articles. The dataset was originally in CSV format, which was converted into a DataFrame format. It contains two primary columns: text and sentiment. The text column provides summaries of news articles, while the sentiment column contains sentiment labels for each article.

The sentiment labels categorize each article as either positive, neutral, or negative. During the fine-tuning process, these labels were mapped to integers in accordance with FinBERT's classification system: neutral was mapped to 0, positive to 1, and negative to 2. This label conversion ensured compatibility with the model's input format, facilitating the sentiment classification task.

In the data preprocessing phase, rows containing null and duplicated values were removed to maintain the quality of the dataset. After this cleaning process, a total of 32,417 valid entries remained, which were subsequently used for fine-tuning.

Table 2 presents the number of data points for each sentiment label in the dataset used for FinBERT fine-tuning. It consists of 10,841 positive samples, 10,752 neutral samples, and 10,824 negative samples.

Table 2. Label distribution for FinBERT fine-tuning.

Sentiment	Number
Positive	10,841
Neutral	10,752
Negative	10,824

For the experiment data, we collected news articles from The New York Times. Using the Selenium library for dynamic crawling, we aligned the data with news sector classifications based on categories provided by The New York Times. For the business category, we collected articles from April 2024 to June 2024, from May 2023 to July 2024 for health, and from September 2023 to July 2024 for technology. We extracted the headline, description, and date of each article using relevant HTML tags and merged this information into a DataFrame. A total of 1010 data points were used in the analysis. Figure 1 shows a sample collection of New York Times articles.

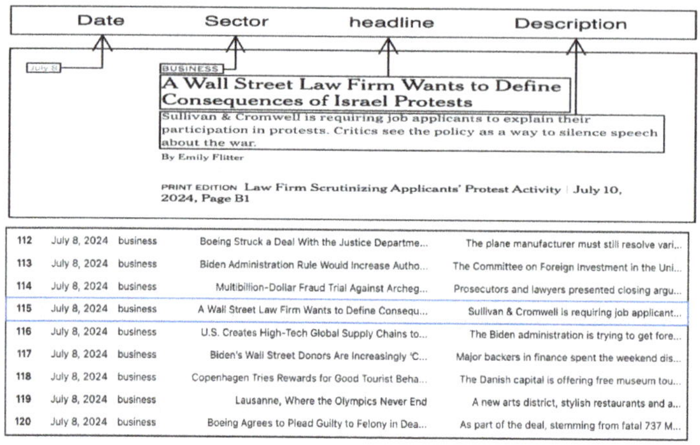

Figure 1. The New York Times data collection example.

3.2. Research Design

In this section, we provide a detailed explanation of how the experiments were designed.

Figure 2 illustrates the overall process of our study. Our research process can be broadly divided into three stages: data collection, GPT-4o prompt engineering&FinBERT fine-tuning, and SA. Each stage is executed from top to bottom, with arrows indicating the flow of the process. Rectangles represent research activities, whereas diamonds indicate the corresponding outcomes. A detailed, step-by-step description is provided below.

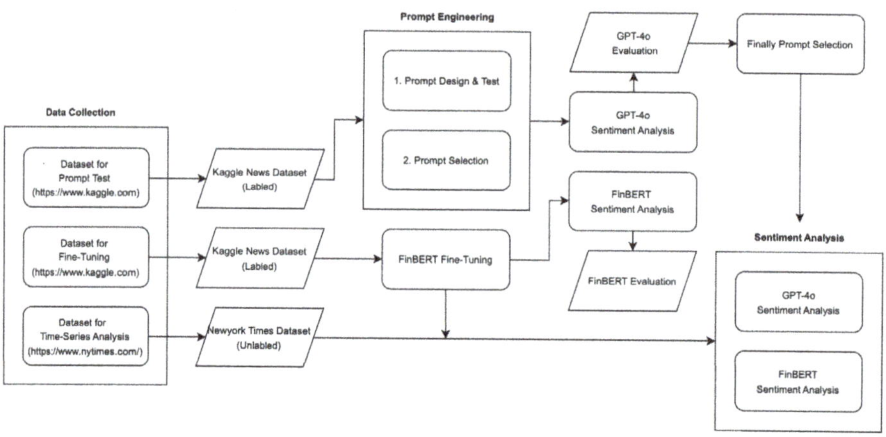

Figure 2. Flow chart.

- **Step 1**: In the first stage, news articles from three sectors (business, health, and technology) were collected. Each article included information on the headline, description, date, and sector. Kaggle's SA dataset was used for the prompt design, while the experiment data were dynamically crawled from The New York Times, collecting news from each sector. Additionally, we collected a sentiment analysis (SA) dataset from Kaggle, which consists of news summary text and sentiment labels, to fine-tune FinBERT.
  The entire dataset collected for sector-specific SA was categorized into three sectors: business, health, and technology. For SA, text data containing sector, news headline, and news description variables were utilized. FinBERT used merged text comprising

sector, headline, and description, while GPT-4o incorporated these variables into prompts using Python 3's f-string method.

- **Step 2**: In the second stage of our study, SA was conducted on the collected news articles using both GPT-4o and the benchmark model FinBERT for prompt design and performance comparison. FinBERT, being pre-trained on financial text data, offers superior SA performance compared to general language models, making it a valuable reference for assessing GPT-4o's capabilities.
  To enhance FinBERT's performance on financial news sentiment analysis, we performed a fine-tuning process specifically tailored for this domain. The fine-tuning was conducted using a financial news dataset provided by Kaggle, where each news article was labeled as positive, neutral, or negative based on its sentiment.
  The dataset was split into a training set (80%) and a validation set (20%) using stratified sampling to preserve the class distribution across both subsets. This prepared dataset was then utilized for model training and performance evaluation.
  During training, we conducted a random search to determine the optimal hyperparameters, including the learning rate, number of epochs, and batch size. The AdamW optimizer was used for parameter optimization, and cross-entropy loss was applied as the loss function, as it is well suited for multi-class classification tasks.
  At the end of each epoch, the model's generalization performance was assessed using the validation dataset. A linear learning rate scheduler was also implemented to gradually reduce the learning rate as training progressed, ensuring smoother convergence.
  Subsequently, we conducted SA on labeled Kaggle news datasets using the fine-tuned FinBERT model. For GPT-4o, a refined prompt design process was implemented to improve SA performance. This involved analyzing cases where FinBERT misclassified sector-specific news sentiment (5 samples per sector, totaling 15 samples). Eight prompts, referenced from benchmark papers, were utilized for these samples. Based on performance, the two most effective prompts were selected. Two additional prompts similar to each were created, resulting in a total of six final prompts applied to the dataset.
  The following describes the process of SA using the GPT-4o model based on prompt design. The prompt design is developed with reference to benchmark papers [13,20,38,48], and its return format outputs the sentiment of the text data (positive, neutral, negative) along with the corresponding probability values on both models, enabling a precise assessment of sentiment intensity.
- **Step 3**: In the third stage, during the experiment phase, the best-performing prompt from the prompt design phase was selected for SA on The New York Times data. FinBERT was also used in this stage to evaluate and compare SA performance. Ultimately, the time-varying results for the experiment data were derived using the best-performing prompt along with both the GPT-4o and FinBERT models, enabling a comparative analysis.

Each piece of news data, modified according to sector, headline, and description, was analyzed through the GPT-4o API, which was pre-built as a Python module. This module was designed based on GPT-4o and was implemented to receive three parameters—system, assistant, and user—and it ultimately returns the SA results. Table A2 provides the roles of the three parameters. In this study, the "system" parameter was excluded, and only the "assistant" and "user" parameters were utilized for prompt engineering. To ensure consistency in the output, the "assistant" parameter was fixed while the user input was adjusted to optimize the prompts. The "assistant" prompt used in this study is provided in Table A3.

4. Empirical Results

We first present the results of SA conducted using GPT-4o and FinBERT on the Kaggle dataset. Specifically, we leverage this labeled dataset to design prompts optimized for GPT-4o to perform SA. In Section 4.1, we illustrate our prompt design process with accompanying diagrams. Subsequently, we present the results of emotional analysis using GPT-4o and FinBERT on The New York Times dataset.

4.1. Prompt Design Results

First, we present a detailed account of the prompt design process for GPT-4o. We generated the initial eight candidate prompts from previous studies [11–13]. The eight initial candidate prompts are listed in Table A1.

To evaluate the sentiment analysis performance of the model on labeled data, i.e., the Kaggle dataset, we used four classification performance metrics (accuracy, precision, recall, and F1-score). Before explaining the performance metrics, the actual class in a classification problem can be defined as **true** or **false**. **True** indicates that the model's prediction is correct, while **false** indicates that the model's prediction is incorrect. The predicted class returned by the model can be defined as **positive** or **Negative**. **Positive** indicates that the model predicted the sentiment as positive, and **negative** indicates that the model predicted the sentiment as negative.

Therefore, the following outcomes can occur in classification performance: First, when the model makes correct predictions, true positive (TP) and true negative (TN) can occur. True positive (TP) indicates that the model predicted positive, and the actual sentiment is also positive. True negative (TN) indicates that the model predicted negative, and the actual sentiment is also negative. When the model makes incorrect predictions, false positive (FP) and false negative (FN) can occur. False positive (FP) indicates that the model predicted positive, but the actual sentiment is negative. False negative (FN) indicates that the model predicted negative, but the actual sentiment is positive.

Accuracy measures the proportion of correct predictions out of the total number of predictions. It represents the frequency at which the classifier makes correct predictions.

$$\text{Accuracy} = \frac{TP + TN}{TP + TN + FP + FN}$$

Precision (positive predictive value) measures the proportion of TP results among all positive predictions made by the model.

$$\text{Precision} = \frac{TP}{TP + FP}$$

Recall (sensitivity or true-positive rate) measures the proportion of TP results out of all actual positive cases.

$$\text{Recall} = \frac{TP}{TP + FN}$$

F1-score is the harmonic mean of precision and recall. This metric balances the two, particularly when there is an imbalance in class distribution.

$$\text{F1-Score} = 2 \times \frac{\text{Precision} \times \text{Recall}}{\text{Precision} + \text{Recall}}$$

Additionally, our study considers the macro average (Macro avg.) as it involves a multi-class classification problem. This approach calculates the arithmetic mean of individual metrics (precision, recall, and F1-score) across all classes, ensuring equal weight for each class. As a result, it provides an unbiased evaluation even in imbalanced datasets where certain classes have significantly more samples than others. In particular, we use the **Macro F1-score** to assess the overall balance of the model's performance.

$$\text{Macro F1-score} = \frac{1}{N}\sum_{i=1}^{N}\text{F1-score}_i$$

where N represents the number of classes, and the Macro F1-score is obtained by averaging the F1-scores of all classes.

Using the performance indicators above, we compared the accuracy values of FinBERT and GPT-4o to assess their performance.

Our initial test with eight candidate prompts revealed that their structure had a significant impact on GPT-4o's performance. Specifically, Prompt 5 and Prompt 6 demonstrated the best performance for the business sector, while Prompt 5 was most effective for the health sector and Prompt 6 for the tech sector.

Based on these results, we selected Prompt 5 and Prompt 6 as the top-performing prompts. To further refine our approach, we created six additional prompts by modifying these two—generating two variations for each prompt (prompt5-1, prompt5-2, prompt6-1, and prompt6-2). These processes are illustrated in Figure 3. These variations involved rearranging sentence structures or replacing words with similar meanings while maintaining the original intent. The final set of six refined prompts is presented in Table 3. We then applied these prompts to the labeled dataset to evaluate their effectiveness.

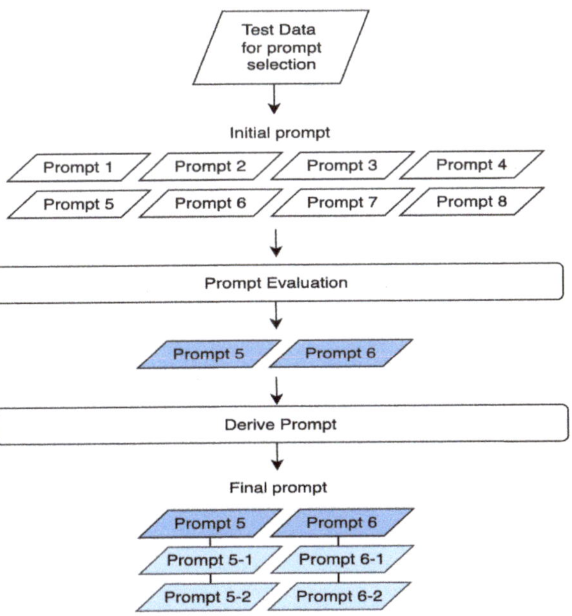

Figure 3. Prompt design process.

Table 3. Prompt design for user.

Role	Prompt
user5	Given the news related to the {sector} industry, classify the sentiment as positive, negative, or neutral, based on the headline {headline}, description {description} and provide the probability value for your response.
user5-1	Classify the sentiment of the given news headline {headline} and description {description}, which are closely related to the {sector} industry, as positive, negative, or neutral, and provide the probability values for your classification.
user5-2	Using the headline {headline} and description {description} of news related to the {sector} industry, classify the sentiment as positive, negative, or neutral, and provide the probability values for your response.
user6	Given the news related to the {sector} industry, classify the sentiment as positive for buy, negative for sell, or neutral for hold position, based on the headline {headline}, description {description} and provide the probability value for your response.
user6-1	Classify the sentiment of the given news headline {headline} and description {description}, which are closely related to the {sector} industry, as positive for buy, negative for sell, or neutral for hold position, and provide the probability values for your classification.
user6-2	Using the headline {headline} and description {description} of news related to the {sector} industry, classify the sentiment as positive for buy, negative for sell, or neutral for hold position, and provide the probability values for your response.

The performance of SA using the six different prompts (Table 3) across sectors was evaluated as follows. We provide the SA results for FinBERT and GPT-4o in Tables 4–7. For the business sector, the average accuracy was 0.43; for the health sector, it was 0.42; and for the technology sector, it was 0.53. On the other hand, the accuracy of FinBERT in the business, health, and technology sectors was 0.38, 0.39, and 0.44, respectively, with GPT-4o outperforming FinBERT by an average of approximately 0.06. Based on the performance by prompt, p5 (user2-1 + assistant) achieved the highest accuracy of 0.45 in the business sector. In the health sector, p3 (user1-2 + assistant) and p5 (user2-1 + assistant) both achieved the highest accuracy of 0.43. In the technology sector, p3 (user1-2 + assistant) and p5 (user2-1 + assistant) also recorded the highest accuracy of 0.55. Therefore, we adopted p5, which exhibited the highest performance, and we applied it to the model for the experiment data.

Table 4. Performance table of FinBERT.

Sector	Business			Health			Technology		
Label	Precision	Recall	F1-Score	Precision	Recall	F1-Score	Precision	Recall	F1-Score
Positive	0.84	0.33	0.47	0.69	0.24	0.36	0.77	0.44	0.56
Negative	0.23	0.24	0.23	0.33	0.41	0.37	0.20	0.14	0.16
Neutral	0.20	0.81	0.32	0.31	0.71	0.43	0.26	0.67	0.37
Macro avg			0.34			0.39			0.37
Accuracy			**0.38**			**0.39**			**0.44**

Table 5. Performance table of GPT-4o: business. Notes. The maximum achieved accuracy is 0.45.

Sector	**Business**								
Prompt	p1 (user5 + assistant)			p2 (user5-1 + assistant)			p3 (user5-2 + assistant)		
Label	Precision	Recall	F1-score	Precision	Recall	F1-score	Precision	Recall	F1-score
Negative	0.26	0.44	0.33	0.27	0.42	0.33	0.23	0.34	0.27
Neutral	0.15	0.31	0.20	0.12	0.29	0.17	0.13	0.29	0.18
Positive	0.75	0.46	0.57	0.73	0.43	0.54	0.73	0.47	0.57
Macro avg			0.27			0.34			0.34
Accuracy			**0.44**			**0.41**			**0.42**
Prompt	p4 (user6 + assistant)			p5 (user6-1 + assistant)			p6 (user6-2 + assistant)		
Label	Precision	Recall	F1-score	Precision	Recall	F1-score	Precision	Recall	F1-score
Negative	0.26	0.42	0.32	0.25	0.42	0.32	0.24	0.40	0.30
Neutral	0.13	0.27	0.17	0.15	0.29	0.20	0.13	0.23	0.16
Positive	0.74	0.47	0.57	0.73	0.48	0.58	0.73	0.49	0.59
Macro avg			0.36			0.37			0.35
Accuracy			**0.43**			**0.45**			**0.44**

To gain a comprehensive understanding of the differences in sentiment analysis mechanisms and performance between GPT-4o and FinBERT, an in-depth investigation was conducted into cases where the two models produced different predictions. The analysis focused on two key scenarios: instances where GPT-4o correctly classified sentiment and FinBERT misclassified it, and instances where FinBERT correctly classified sentiment and GPT-4o misclassified it. The objective of this study was to identify patterns in misclassification and explore the underlying factors contributing to these discrepancies.

Table 6. Performance table of GPT-4o: health. Notes. The maximum achieved accuracy is 0.43.

Sector	**Health**								
Prompt	p1 (user5 + assistant)			p2 (user5-1 + assistant)			p3 (user5-2 + assistant)		
Label	Precision	Recall	F1-score	Precision	Recall	F1-score	Precision	Recall	F1-score
Negative	0.33	0.55	0.41	0.32	0.50	0.39	0.34	0.54	0.41
Neutral	0.32	0.36	0.34	0.33	0.43	0.37	0.29	0.32	0.33
Positive	0.62	0.39	0.48	0.61	0.38	0.47	0.62	0.42	0.50
Macro avg			0.41			0.41			0.41
Accuracy			**0.42**			**0.42**			**0.43**
Prompt	p4 (user6 + assistant)			p5 (user6-1 + assistant)			p6 (user6-2 + assistant)		
Label	Precision	Recall	F1-score	Precision	Recall	F1-score	Precision	Recall	F1-score
Negative	0.31	0.51	0.38	0.32	0.55	0.41	0.32	0.53	0.40
Neutral	0.27	0.33	0.30	0.32	0.31	0.31	0.29	0.31	0.30
Positive	0.62	0.36	0.46	0.61	0.43	0.51	0.60	0.42	0.49
Macro avg			0.38			0.41			0.40
Accuracy			**0.39**			**0.43**			**0.42**

Table 7. Performance table of GPT-4o: technology. Notes. The maximum achieved accuracy is 0.55.

Sector	Technology								
Prompt	p1 (user5 + assistant)			p2 (user5-1 + assistant)			p3 (user5-2 + assistant)		
Label	Precision	Recall	F1-score	Precision	Recall	F1-score	Precision	Recall	F1-score
Negative	0.15	0.12	0.14	0.12	0.12	0.15	0.16	0.11	0.13
Neutral	0.36	0.43	0.39	0.27	0.48	0.34	0.34	0.43	0.38
Positive	0.69	0.67	0.68	0.66	0.55	0.66	0.69	0.69	0.69
Macro avg			0.40			0.37			0.40
Accuracy			**0.54**			**0.47**			**0.55**
Prompt	p4 (user6 + assistant)			p5 (user6-1 + assistant)			p6 (user6-2 + assistant)		
Label	Precision	Recall	F1-score	Precision	Recall	F1-score	Precision	Recall	F1-score
Negative	0.12	0.12	0.12	0.14	0.12	0.13	0.13	0.12	0.13
Neutral	0.28	0.29	0.29	0.38	0.37	0.38	0.31	0.27	0.29
Positive	0.68	0.66	0.67	0.69	0.67	0.69	0.68	0.72	0.70
Macro avg			0.36			0.40			0.37
Accuracy			**0.51**			**0.55**			**0.54**

First, in cases where GPT correctly classified sentiment and FinBERT misclassified it, the findings indicate that FinBERT consistently exhibits a tendency to misclassify positive or negative sentiments as neutral across all three sectors: business, health, and technology. In the business sector, 85% of misclassified cases were labeled as neutral by FinBERT, while in the health and technology sectors, 78% and 86% of cases, respectively, were also categorized as neutral. A closer examination suggests that FinBERT systematically underestimates sentiment, particularly for news articles conveying implicit positivity. This pattern was especially evident in the business sector, where articles highlighting urban development and business growth were misclassified as neutral. This misclassification appears to stem from FinBERT's reliance on explicit financial terminology to determine sentiment, making it less effective in interpreting sentiment in a broader news context where financial implications are more subtle.

A similar trend was observed in the health and technology sectors. FinBERT frequently misclassified articles discussing medical advancements, healthcare service expansions, and infrastructure improvements as neutral, whereas GPT-4o successfully identified the positive sentiment in these reports. Likewise, in the technology sector, FinBERT often failed to recognize the optimistic tone in articles about technological breakthroughs, misclassifying them as neutral, while GPT-4o consistently detected their positive sentiment.

On the other hand, in cases where FinBERT correctly classified sentiment while GPT-4o misclassified it, GPT-4o displayed a tendency to overestimate sentiment by incorrectly labeling neutral articles as either positive or negative. Specifically, in the business sector, 48% of neutral cases were misclassified by GPT-4o, while in the health and technology sectors, the misclassification rates reached 54% and 65%, respectively. A notable example includes an article about women leaders in business, which was primarily an informational piece but was misclassified as positive by GPT-4o. Similarly, factual reports about health risks were often misclassified as negative by GPT-4o due to its tendency to over-rely on emotionally charged keywords, leading to sentiment overestimation in neutral contexts.

These findings highlight fundamental differences in how GPT-4o and FinBERT approach sentiment classification. FinBERT's misclassification tendencies can be attributed to its training data, which are heavily focused on financial news, making it highly sensitive to explicit financial sentiment but less effective at recognizing sentiment in broader contexts. Additionally, its reliance on keyword- and phrase-based sentiment cues limits its ability to capture subtle contextual nuances in sentiment analysis.

In contrast, GPT-4o demonstrates superior contextual awareness, allowing it to capture sentiment more effectively across diverse news topics. This capability enables GPT-4o to correctly classify implicitly positive news articles that FinBERT misclassifies as neutral. However, GPT-4o's tendency to misclassify neutral articles as either positive or negative highlights its sensitivity to emotionally charged language, sometimes leading to sentiment overestimation.

Overall, this analysis suggests that GPT-4o is better suited for general-purpose sentiment analyses due to its context-aware approach, while FinBERT's keyword-based method is more effective for domain-specific financial sentiment analyses. A hybrid sentiment analysis strategy that leverages the strengths of both models could enhance classification accuracy. Future research should explore refining FinBERT's training data with more diverse news sources and integrating context-aware methodologies similar to those employed by GPT-4o to develop more robust sentiment analysis models.

4.2. Experiment Results

In this section, we present the results of an SA conducted using GPT-4o and FinBERT on a dataset consisting of The New York Times news articles. Specifically, we investigated GPT-4o's sentiment responses based on prompts crafted through the detailed design process outlined in the previous section.

We performed SA on a news dataset, categorizing sentiments into three classes—positive, neutral, and negative—along with their corresponding probability values. As multiple news articles can exist for a given date, we, respectively, defined S_k^t and P_k^t as the sentiment label and corresponding probability for the k-th news article on day t, where t represents the date and k is the index of news articles for that date ($k = 1, 2, \ldots, n$).

To quantify the sentiment labels, we mapped positive to +1, neutral to 0, and negative to -1, and multiplied each by the respective probability P_k. Thus, $S_k \times P_k$ gives the quantified sentiment score for each news article, which we define as N_k^t. Finally, to compute the overall sentiment value for a given date, we calculated the average of the quantified sentiment scores for all news articles on that day. The sentiment score for day t, N^t, is given by

$$C_t = \frac{\sum_k N_k^t}{n}, \tag{1}$$

where n refers to all news articles for the day t. This represents the final daily sentiment score for the given date.

The sentiment scores were calculated using both GPT-4o and FinBERT across the three sectors. A five-day moving average was then applied to ensure a more stable analysis.

Table 8 presents the descriptive statistics for each sector after applying a five-day moving average to the computed sentiment scores C_t in (1). The table includes the mean, maximum, minimum, standard deviation (Std. Dev.), and skewness for the business, health, and technology sectors, with all values rounded to three decimal places. These statistics provide valuable insights into the distribution of sentiment probabilities across sectors.

Table 8. Summary statistics for the sentiment scores C_t.

			GPT-4o		
Sector	Mean	Max.	Min.	Std.Dev.	Skewness
Business	−0.144	0.055	−0.421	0.098	−0.475
Health	−0.170	0.590	−0.759	0.251	0.368
Technology	−0.143	0.272	−0.653	0.180	−0.219
			FinBERT		
Sector	Mean	Max.	Min.	Std.Dev.	Skewness
Business	−0.159	0.005	−0.332	0.063	−0.119
Health	−0.194	0.150	−0.558	0.125	−0.010
Technology	−0.177	0.155	−0.606	0.149	−0.188

According to the mean values, both GPT-4o and FinBERT exhibit negative averages across all sectors, indicating that negative sentiment was predominant in the news overall. Moreover, FinBERT consistently reports lower mean sentiment scores than GPT-4o across all sectors, suggesting that it captures negative sentiment more strongly.

Regarding the maximum values, a score approaching 1 signifies periods of highly dominant positive sentiment. GPT-4o's results indicate that the health sector reaches the highest maximum value of 0.590, while the business sector records a considerably lower maximum of 0.055. Similarly, FinBERT shows relatively higher maximum values of 0.150 and 0.155 for the health and technology sectors, respectively, while the business sector records an exceptionally low maximum of 0.005. This suggests that positive sentiment was significantly less prevalent in the business sector across all models.

A minimum value approaching −1 signifies periods of intense negative sentiment. In GPT-4o's results, the health sector exhibits the lowest minimum value of −0.759, while the technology sector also shows substantial negativity with a minimum of −0.653. FinBERT follows a similar trend, reporting minimum values of −0.558 and −0.606 in the health and technology sectors, respectively. These results indicate that negative sentiment was particularly dominant in these sectors during specific periods.

In terms of standard deviation, GPT-4o consistently exhibits higher variability across all sectors compared to FinBERT. Notably, in the health sector, GPT-4o has a standard deviation of 0.251, which is approximately twice as large as FinBERT's 0.125. This suggests that GPT-4o produces sentiment scores with greater variability, whereas FinBERT offers more stable and moderate assessments.

Regarding skewness, FinBERT maintains values close to zero across all sectors, suggesting that its sentiment score distributions are relatively symmetric. In contrast, GPT-4o demonstrates sector-dependent skewness, with sentiment distributions exhibiting either positive or negative skewness depending on the sector.

In summary, the two models demonstrate distinct tendencies in sentiment interpretation. FinBERT consistently captures negative sentiment more strongly than GPT-4o and provides a more conservative evaluation with a narrower range of sentiment scores. On the other hand, GPT-4o tends to assign more extreme sentiment values and is more sensitive to positive sentiment than FinBERT. These findings underscore the potential benefits of integrating the complementary strengths of both models to enhance the balance and comprehensiveness of sentiment analysis.

We display the results of these calculations in Figures 4–6, which correspond to the business, health, and technology sectors, respectively.

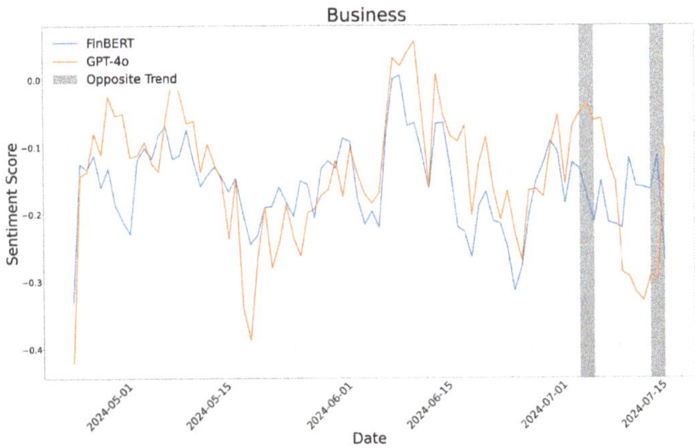

Figure 4. Sentiment score moving average: business.

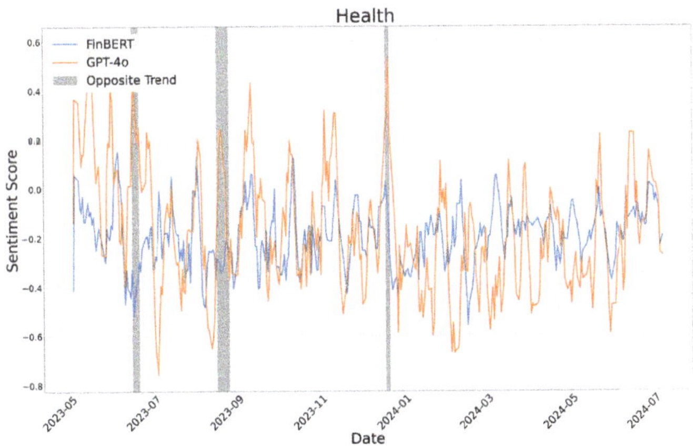

Figure 5. Sentiment score moving average: health.

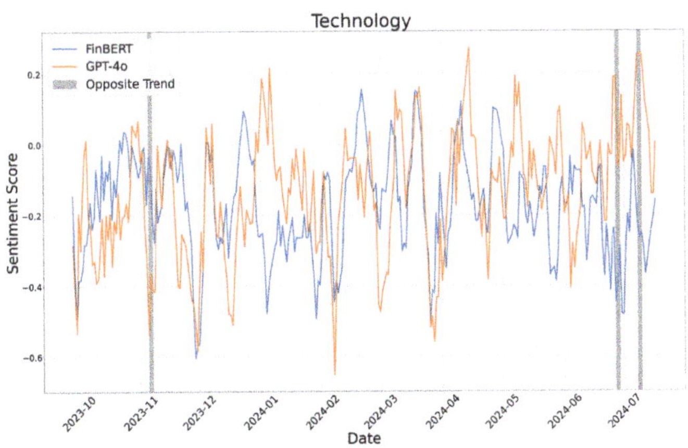

Figure 6. Sentiment score moving average: technology.

Figures 4–6 illustrate the sentiment trends across different sectors over time. The x-axis represents the publication date of the news articles, while the y-axis shows sentiment scores calculated using a five-day moving average. The sentiment scores generated by FinBERT and GPT-4o are represented by blue and orange lines, respectively. Although both models exhibit similar overall trends, there are specific periods where their sentiment classifications diverge significantly. These discrepancies, highlighted with gray boxes in the figures, provide insights into the underlying differences in how each model interprets sentiment.

In the business sector, FinBERT generally exhibited a more conservative stance, often classifying financial and legal discussions as neutral or negative, whereas GPT-4o tended to provide a more optimistic interpretation. For instance, in "Paramount Agrees to Merge With Skydance", GPT-4o recognized the positive outlook on the corporate merger and assigned a high sentiment score, while FinBERT classified it as neutral. Conversely, in "New Plan to Target Russia's Oil Revenue Brings Debate in the White House", FinBERT identified concerns about gasoline price fluctuations and assigned a negative sentiment score, while GPT-4o maintained a neutral stance. Additionally, when news content was framed as a question or contained ambiguous interpretations, FinBERT predominantly assigned neutral sentiment scores, whereas GPT-4o was more likely to classify such content as either strongly positive or negative. For example, in "Is It Silicon Valley's Job to Make Guaranteed Income a Reality?", FinBERT categorized the sentiment as neutral, while GPT-4o interpreted it optimistically and assigned a positive sentiment score.

A similar pattern was observed in the health sector, where GPT-4o emphasized the positive aspects of scientific research and technological advancements, while FinBERT remained neutral or negative. For instance, in "Scientists Debut Lab Models of Human Embryos", which described a breakthrough in stem cell research, GPT-4o assigned a positive sentiment score, whereas FinBERT classified it as negative. However, in cases involving disease outbreaks and medical risks, GPT-4o assigned stronger negative sentiment scores compared to FinBERT. This was evident in "Women May Face Higher Risk of Stroke Following Infertility Treatment", where GPT-4o classified the sentiment as negative, while FinBERT remained neutral.

In the technology sector, the differences in sentiment classification were largely driven by the models' respective approaches to sentiment detection. FinBERT relied primarily on individual keywords, often resulting in neutral classifications when sentiment cues were implicit. In contrast, GPT-4o analyzed the broader context of the news article. For instance, in "U.S. Creates High-Tech Global Supply Chains to Blunt Risks Tied to China", FinBERT focused on the word "risks" and classified the sentiment as negative, whereas GPT-4o considered the broader economic context and assigned a positive sentiment score. Similarly, in "OpenAI Lets Mom-and-Pop Shops Customize ChatGPT", GPT-4o identified the opportunities for small businesses and assigned a positive sentiment, while FinBERT, relying on individual keywords, classified the article as neutral.

In summary, FinBERT and GPT-4o adopt different sentiment analysis approaches. FinBERT's keyword-driven method detects explicit sentiment but often classifies implied sentiment as neutral. In contrast, GPT-4o's context-aware approach captures subtle sentiment shifts but may sometimes overestimate their intensity. FinBERT's precision suits financial reports and legal documents, while GPT-4o's holistic interpretation is better for market trends, innovations, and socio-economic analysis. Given these strengths and limitations, a hybrid sentiment analysis approach—combining FinBERT's keyword-based detection with GPT-4o's contextual comprehension—could improve classification accuracy while enhancing robustness and reliability across finance, healthcare, and technology.

4.3. The Relationship Between the Stock Market and Sentiment

Finally, to evaluate the applicability of the sentiment analysis results derived from this study, we conducted a comparative analysis between sector-specific stock prices and sentiment scores over time. The sentiment score was obtained using GPT-4o, the primary model of this study, and the comparison process with stock market data was as follows:

First, sector-specific closing price data were collected from the S&P 500 index. Subsequently, only stock price data corresponding to the dates of the sentiment-analyzed news data were selected for comparison. This step ensured that the sentiment variations in news data and stock price fluctuations were analyzed over the same time period.

However, since sentiment scores and stock prices have different scales, several preprocessing steps were implemented to facilitate a consistent comparison. First, to better capture stock price volatility, closing price data were transformed into log returns. Next, a five-day moving average was applied to smooth out short-term fluctuations, following the same procedure used for sentiment scores. Finally, both sentiment scores and stock prices were normalized using MinMaxScaler to scale the values within the range of -1 to 1, allowing for more intuitive comparisons.

The following graph visualizes the time-series trends of GPT-4o's sentiment scores and sector-specific stock prices, where the green line represents stock price trends, and the red line represents sentiment score trends.

The analysis of the graph indicates that, except for the business sector with a relatively short period of time, most sectors exhibit similar patterns in sentiment scores and stock price movements. In particular, there are multiple instances where an increase in sentiment scores corresponds to an increase in stock prices, and a decrease in sentiment scores coincides with a decline in stock prices. These findings suggest that sentiment analysis results may be correlated with stock market movements to some extent.

These results imply that news sentiment analysis could serve as a complementary indicator for stock market prediction, particularly in sectors where sentiment variations are closely associated with stock price fluctuations. Future studies should aim to further quantify this relationship by integrating sentiment analysis into predictive stock market models and evaluating their forecasting performance.

Meanwhile, sector-specific stock prices can be considered an external factor. According to Figures 7–9, sentiment scores appear to reflect market conditions to some extent based on sector-specific stock prices. Consequently, the sentiment analysis results can be interpreted as incorporating some contextual information related to external factors, specifically the stock market.

Figure 7. Time-series of GPT-4o's sentiment scores and adjusted business sector prices.

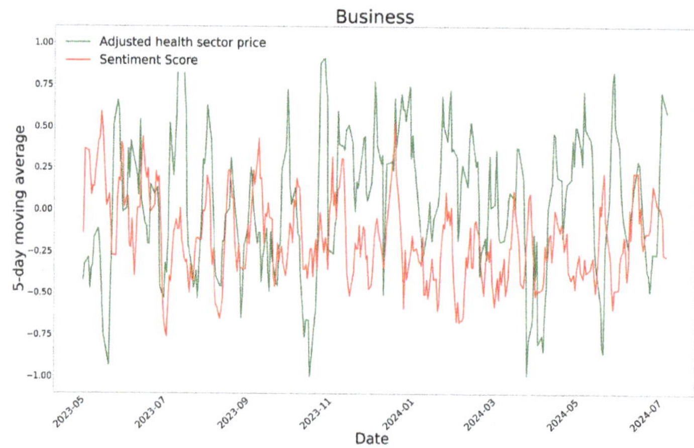

Figure 8. Time-series of GPT-4o's sentiment scores and adjusted health sector prices.

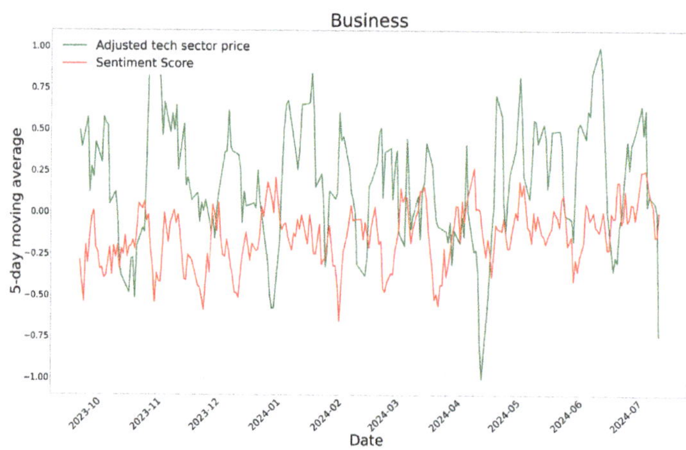

Figure 9. Time-series of GPT-4o's sentiment scores and adjusted tech sector prices.

5. Discussion and Concluding Remarks

In this study, sentiment analysis (SA) was conducted on categorized news data using GPT-4o and FinBERT. To establish the fine-tuning process, prompt design, and experimental datasets, news data were obtained from Kaggle and supplemented with additional data collected through dynamic crawling from The New York Times. Subsequently, SA was performed using GPT-4o and FinBERT by leveraging headlines, descriptions, and sectors from the labeled news data in Kaggle. To further enhance the performance of FinBERT and GPT-4o in SA, fine-tuning and prompt engineering techniques were applied, respectively. We sampled five data points for each sector, selected the two best-performing prompts, and then generated four additional derivative prompts, resulting in a total of six prompts from the prompts' design step. We utilized a confusion matrix as the performance evaluation metric and found that, across all sectors, the performance of GPT-4o with the optimized prompt design outperformed the fine-tuned FinBERT model.

Next, we conducted a time-series analysis of sentiment scores from both models on unlabeled data to examine their sentiment trends over time. Although both models generally exhibited similar trends, they showed contrasting sentiment shifts in certain periods, highlighting fundamental differences in their sentiment evaluation mechanisms. Additionally, we compared the sentiment trends of GPT-4o with sector-specific stock return data. Although variations were observed across sectors, the overall sentiment trends closely aligned with stock return movements.

According to the SA results, the key findings are as follows: First, when comparing the sentiment score graphs across the three analyzed categories, the overall trends of the two models were generally similar. However, some opposing trends were observed in this process. It was found that FinBERT relies on a keyword-based approach, effectively detecting explicit sentiment but often classifying implicit sentiment as neutral. In contrast, GPT-4o adopts a context-aware strategy, assessing sentiment based on the overall narrative and thematic implications. As a result, while GPT-4o captures subtle emotional shifts, it may occasionally overlook the importance of explicitly emotional terms.

Second, sector-specific analyses reveal that in the business sector, FinBERT tends to interpret financial and legal news in a more conservative and negative manner, whereas GPT-4o provides a more optimistic perspective. In the health sector, GPT-4o frequently assigns a more positive sentiment to scientific research and technological advancements, while FinBERT often remains neutral. Additionally, for news related to disease outbreaks and medical risks, GPT-4o tends to classify such news as more negative, while FinBERT maintains a neutral stance. In the technology sector, FinBERT's keyword-based classification makes it more sensitive to certain negative keywords, whereas GPT-4o, by considering the broader context, often interprets news more positively.

Finally, an analysis of these contrasting periods across the three sectors revealed a common factor contributing to the significant differences in sentiment interpretation between the two models: ambiguous topics where sentiment varied depending on subjective perspectives. These articles often addressed complex ethical dilemmas without clear resolutions, leading to substantial variations in how the two models interpreted and classified sentiment.

This study presents several distinguishing features compared with previous studies. First, we categorized the nature of the news into specific categories and utilized the news category, headline, and description for modeling. Second, we iteratively refined and evaluated the performance of the prompts using a labeled text dataset, progressively working toward an optimal design. A notable aspect of this approach was the clear delineation of roles—system, user, and assistant—within the GPT-4o prompt design process, executed via the API during both the prompt design and experiment phases. This separation allowed for a more focused evaluation of each parameter's contribution to the model performance. We then conducted a comparative analysis of GPT-4o and FinBERT across different sectors and prompt designs. Finally, using The New York Times dataset, we generated daily sentiment scores to explore time-varying characteristics and investigated the anomalies identified through this process.

Furthermore, our findings present several significant implications. First, FinBERT, renowned for its effectiveness in financial text analysis and sentiment classification, excels in domain-specific tasks due to its pretraining on financial data. However, news datasets often encompass diverse topics beyond finance, limiting FinBERT's adaptability as a specialized model. In contrast, GPT-4, trained on a broad dataset with billions of parameters, exhibits strong general-purpose performance across various tasks, including finance. This flexibility suggests that GPT-4 may outperform FinBERT in tasks involving diverse content, such as news datasets. In addition, GPT-4o utilized prompts optimized through the prompt engineering process. The results, depicted in time series graphs, demonstrated similar overall trends but emphasized differences during instances of specific terms, abbreviations, or ambiguous expressions related to judgments or ethical dilemmas. These ambiguous expressions posed challenges for accurate interpretation due to their inherent subjectivity. GPT-4, with its capability to generate multi-contextual interpretations, outperformed FinBERT, which primarily focuses on single-context analysis. This made GPT-4 more effective at handling subtle and complex textual content.

Second, prompt engineering plays a critical role in maximizing GPT's performance, particularly for interpreting ambiguous sentences. By refining context or incorporating additional details into prompts, GPT can provide more accurate or multifaceted interpretations. This synergy between GPT and prompt engineering enables flexible and creative processing of ambiguous text. Choosing the appropriate model—BERT or GPT—and optimizing prompt design based on the data and analysis goals is essential for effective results.

In addition, the main findings of this study provide several practical applications. First, by providing a sentiment score for each sector, the results can be utilized for price prediction, including forecasting the stock index, sector index or ETFs [49–52]. Second, through the time-varying analysis of both models, we identified which news characteristics and content cause differences between the two models, specifically leading to ambiguity in SA. This could be explored as a research topic regarding the factors causing ambiguity in news sentiment and their handling, which could be useful for SA of news in the future.

Nevertheless, we discuss several limitations of this study. First, the dataset used for prompt design was relatively small, consisting of approximately 300 samples per sector. In contrast, the experiment dataset was considerably larger, with around 1000 samples. The limited size of the prompt design dataset can be attributed to the stringent requirement that news articles be specifically labeled by sector, which significantly restricted the available data. Second, the prompt design dataset exhibited an unbalanced distribution of sentiment labels. Of the approximately 300 samples per sector, around 200 were labeled as positive, while the remaining samples were evenly split between negative and neutral labels. This imbalance arose from the challenge of collecting sufficient labeled news data for each sector. Thirdly, our sentiment analysis was conducted in a single experimental setting and did not account for various market conditions, which may limit its generalizability across all market environments. However, through performance analysis across different sectors (business, technology, health, etc.), we observed the potential superiority of GPT-4o over FinBERT. In future research, we plan to incorporate sentiment analysis that considers market volatility and major financial events, allowing us to further examine how various economic factors influence sentiment analysis results.

Finally, we analyzed the time-varying trends of GPT-4o and FinBERT on the experiment dataset and examined the prominent features in the graphs and their underlying causes. However, because the crawled The New York Times dataset lacks labeled sentiment values, it was challenging to evaluate the performance with specific metrics. This study primarily focused on analyzing the sentiment scores generated by GPT-4o and FinBERT in relation to changes over time. Future research could explore obtaining labeled sentiment data for The New York Times articles or utilizing an alternative news dataset with pre-existing sentiment labels. Additionally, extending the data collection period to cover a longer time period could provide more comprehensive insights into sentiment trends over an extended period. Although this would be a time-consuming process, it would enable a more rigorous comparison of the sentiment scores produced by GPT-4o and FinBERT.

Based on the framework and results of this study, we propose several directions for future research. First, to mitigate the limitations associated with small dataset sizes, future research could explore expanding sector-specific datasets with sentiment labels or applying sentiment analysis to larger datasets using GPT. Similarly, we suggest conducting sentiment analysis on a wider range of new and diverse datasets as a potential direction for future studies. This approach is expected to enhance the robustness of the findings presented in this study. Second, this study exclusively utilized the GPT-4o model as the LLM for sentiment analysis. Moreover, recent developments have introduced various LLM models, such as Gemini and Llama. Future research could explore sentiment analysis using these models or compare their results to those of GPT-4. Third, in this study, sentiment analysis was limited to three categories: positive, negative, and neutral. However, exploring finer sentiment labels could unlock significant potential across various fields. Therefore, future research could investigate sentiment analysis beyond these three categories, focusing on a broader range of emotional labels. Our study has a limitation in that it does not provide explanatory power for model decisions. However, this is not a constraint unique to our research but rather a broader limitation inherent to LLMs. Consequently, enhancing the interpretability of pre-trained transformer models, such as GPT-4o and FinBERT, represents a significant avenue for future research.

Author Contributions: Conceptualization, S.-Y.C.; data curation, J.-W.K.; formal analysis, J.-W.K. and S.-Y.C.; funding acquisition, S.-Y.C.; investigation, J.-W.K. and S.-Y.C.; methodology, J.-W.K.; software, J.-W.K.; writing—original draft preparation, J.-W.K. and S.-Y.C.; writing—review and editing, J.-W.K. and S.-Y.C. All authors have read and agreed to the published version of the manuscript.

Funding: The work of S.-Y. Choi was supported by the National Research Foundation of Korea (NRF) grant funded by the Korea Government (MSIT) (No. RS-2024-00454493) and the Gachon University research fund of 2024 (GCU-202404060001).

Data Availability Statement: The data presented in this study are available upon request from the corresponding author.

Conflicts of Interest: The authors declare no conflicts of interest.

Appendix A. GPT-4o Prompts and API

Table A1. The initial Prompts.

Role	Prompt
user1	You are an excellent financial {sector} expert who trades by accurately analyzing the sentiment related to given news. When news headlines {headline} and descriptions {description} are provided, you can respond as follows: sentiment of news: positive, sentiment of news: negative, sentiment of news: neutral
user2	You are an excellent {sector} Sentiment analysis model trained on financial news headlines and descriptions. When news is provided as (headline: {headline}, description: {description}), you return the following: sentiment: {{sentiment}}, probability: {{probability}}.
user3	You are an excellent {sector} sentiment analysis service of a financial news. When news headlines {headline} and descriptions {description} are provided, you can respond like this: sentiment of news: positive, positive probability: {{probability}}; sentiment of news: negative, negative probability: {{probability}}; sentiment of news: neutral, neutral probability: {{probability}}; you must choose one.
user4	The given the news related to the {sector} industry, how do you feel about the headline {headline} and description {description}? Answer in one token: positive, negative, or neutral.
user5	The given the news related to the {sector} industry, how do you feel about the headline {headline} and description {description}? Answer in one token: positive for buy, negative for sell, or neutral for hold position.
user6	The given the news related to the {sector} industry, classify the sentiment as positive, negative, or neutral, based on the headline {headline}, description {description} and provide the probability value for your response.
user7	The given the news related to the {sector} industry, classify the sentiment as positive for buy, negative for sell, or neutral for hold position, based on the headline {headline}, description {description} and provide the probability value for your response.
user8	This text presents the news headline {headline} and description {description} for the {sector} industry. Based on this information, would you sell, buy, or hold an ETF in the {sector} industry? The sentiment of the news can be positive for buying, negative for selling, or neutral for holding. Answer in one token with the sentiment.

Table A2 presents the main parameters that can be input based on the usage of the GPT-4o API. The following three parameters each serve a specific role. "System" refers to the content requested by the user, and while optional, it assigns a role that aligns with the purpose of using GPT-4o. "User" is mandatory and provides the request or opinion that GPT-4o should respond to. "Assistant" is optional, and although it has the function of storing previous assistant responses, it can also be written by the user to provide an example of the desired behavior.

Table A2. API parameter definitions.

Role	Description
system	This message sets the behavior of the AI. It defines the tone or rules of the conversation, guiding how the AI should respond. It helps shape the overall interaction between the user and the AI.
assistant	This message represents the AI's response. Based on the {system} and {user} messages, the AI generates an appropriate reply. It keeps the conversation going.
user	This message contains the user's question or request to the AI. It provides the topic for the conversation and prompts the AI to respond. It reflects the user's actual input.

Table A3 contains information about the "assistant" among the GPT-4o API parameters. It serves as an example to output the sentiment and probability of the news in a consistent format when the content of the news is provided through the "user".

Table A3. Prompt design for assistant.

Role	Prompt
assistant	When news is provided, you can respond with sentiment of news: positive, positive probability: {probability}, or sentiment of news: negative, negative probability: {probability}, or sentiment of news: neutral, neutral probability: {probability}. Answer with just one sentence.

References

1. Javaid, M.; Haleem, A.; Singh, R.P.; Khan, S.; Khan, I.H. Unlocking the opportunities through ChatGPT Tool towards ameliorating the education system. *BenchCouncil Trans. Benchmarks Stand. Eval.* **2023**, *3*, 100115. [CrossRef]
2. Kung, T.H.; Cheatham, M.; Medenilla, A.; Sillos, C.; De Leon, L.; Elepaño, C.; Madriaga, M.; Aggabao, R.; Diaz-Candido, G.; Maningo, J.; et al. Performance of ChatGPT on USMLE: Potential for AI-assisted medical education using large language models. *PLoS Digit. Health* **2023**, *2*, e0000198. [CrossRef] [PubMed]
3. Raj, R.; Singh, A.; Kumar, V.; Verma, P. Analyzing the potential benefits and use cases of ChatGPT as a tool for improving the efficiency and effectiveness of business operations. *BenchCouncil Trans. Benchmarks, Stand. Eval.* **2023**, *3*, 100140. [CrossRef]
4. Ko, H.; Lee, J. Can ChatGPT improve investment decisions? From a portfolio management perspective. *Financ. Res. Lett.* **2024**, *64*, 105433. [CrossRef]
5. Dowling, M.; Lucey, B. ChatGPT for (finance) research: The Bananarama conjecture. *Financ. Res. Lett.* **2023**, *53*, 103662. [CrossRef]
6. Han, Y.; Hou, J.; Sun, Y. Research and Application of GPT-Based Large Language Models in Business and Economics: A Systematic Literature Review in Progress. In Proceedings of the 2023 IEEE International Conference on Computing (ICOCO), Langkawi Island, Malaysia, 9–12 October 2023; pp. 118–123.
7. Mäntylä, M.V.; Graziotin, D.; Kuutila, M. The evolution of sentiment analysis—A review of research topics, venues, and top cited papers. *Comput. Sci. Rev.* **2018**, *27*, 16–32. [CrossRef]
8. Collobert, R.; Weston, J.; Bottou, L.; Karlen, M.; Kavukcuoglu, K.; Kuksa, P. Natural language processing (almost) from scratch. *J. Mach. Learn. Res.* **2011**, *12*, 2493–2537.
9. Birjali, M.; Kasri, M.; Beni-Hssane, A. A comprehensive survey on sentiment analysis: Approaches, challenges and trends. *Knowl.-Based Syst.* **2021**, *226*, 107134. [CrossRef]
10. Yu, L.C.; Wu, J.L.; Chang, P.C.; Chu, H.S. Using a contextual entropy model to expand emotion words and their intensity for the sentiment classification of stock market news. *Knowl.-Based Syst.* **2013**, *41*, 89–97. [CrossRef]
11. Zhu, X.; Kuang, Z.; Zhang, L. A prompt model with combined semantic refinement for aspect sentiment analysis. *Inf. Process. Manag.* **2023**, *60*, 103462. [CrossRef]
12. Xue, H.; Salim, F.D. Promptcast: A new prompt-based learning paradigm for time series forecasting. *IEEE Trans. Knowl. Data Eng.* **2023**, *36*, 6851–6864. [CrossRef]
13. Sun, S.; Pan, X.; Yang, T.; Gao, J. STID-Prompt: Prompt learning for sentiment-topic-importance detection in financial news. *Knowl.-Based Syst.* **2024**, *284*, 111347. [CrossRef]
14. Yang, Y.; Uy, M.C.S.; Huang, A. Finbert: A pretrained language model for financial communications. *arXiv* **2020**, arXiv:2006.08097.
15. Sidogi, T.; Mbuvha, R.; Marwala, T. Stock price prediction using sentiment analysis. In Proceedings of the 2021 IEEE International Conference on Systems, Man, and Cybernetics (SMC), Melbourne, Australia, 17–20 October 2021; pp. 46–51.

16. Liu, Z.; Huang, D.; Huang, K.; Li, Z.; Zhao, J. Finbert: A pre-trained financial language representation model for financial text mining. In Proceedings of the Twenty-Ninth International Conference on International Joint Conferences on Artificial Intelligence, Online, 7–15 January 2021; pp. 4513–4519.
17. Fazlija, B.; Harder, P. Using financial news sentiment for stock price direction prediction. *Mathematics* **2022**, *10*, 2156. [CrossRef]
18. Huang, A.H.; Wang, H.; Yang, Y. FinBERT: A large language model for extracting information from financial text. *Contemp Account. Res.* **2023**, *40*, 806–841. [CrossRef]
19. Girsang, A.S.; Stanley. Cryptocurrency Price Prediction Based Social Network Sentiment Analysis Using LSTM-GRU and FinBERT. *IEEE Access* **2023**, *11*, 120530–120540. [CrossRef]
20. Yu, X.; Chen, Z.; Ling, Y.; Dong, S.; Liu, Z.; Lu, Y. Temporal Data Meets LLM–Explainable Financial Time Series Forecasting *arXiv* **2023**, arXiv:2306.11025.
21. Cao, Y.; Zhai, J. Bridging the gap–the impact of ChatGPT on financial research. *J. Chin. Econ. Bus. Stud.* **2023**, *21*, 177–191 [CrossRef]
22. Niszczota, P.; Abbas, S. GPT has become financially literate: Insights from financial literacy tests of GPT and a preliminary test of how people use it as a source of advice. *Financ. Res. Lett.* **2023**, *58*, 104333. [CrossRef]
23. Gupta, U. GPT-InvestAR: Enhancing stock investment strategies through annual report analysis with large language models *arXiv* **2023**, arXiv:2309.03079. [CrossRef]
24. Ouyang, T.; MaungMaung, A.; Konishi, K.; Seo, Y.; Echizen, I. Stability Analysis of ChatGPT-based Sentiment Analysis in AI Quality Assurance. *Electronics* **2024**, *13*, 5043. [CrossRef]
25. Pelster, M.; Val, J. Can ChatGPT assist in picking stocks? *Financ. Res. Lett.* **2024**, *59*, 104786. [CrossRef]
26. Oehler, A.; Horn, M. Does ChatGPT provide better advice than robo-advisors? *Financ. Res. Lett.* **2024**, *60*, 104898. [CrossRef]
27. Shafee, S.; Bessani, A.; Ferreira, P.M. Evaluation of LLM-based chatbots for OSINT-based Cyber Threat Awareness. *Expert Syst Appl.* **2024**, *261*, 125509. [CrossRef]
28. Han, P.; Chen, H.; Rasool, A.; Jiang, Q.; Yang, M. MFB: A generalized multimodal fusion approach for bitcoin price prediction using time-lagged sentiment and indicator features. *Expert Syst. Appl.* **2025**, *261*, 125515. [CrossRef]
29. Zhang, B.; Yang, H.; Liu, X.Y. Instruct-fingpt: Financial sentiment analysis by instruction tuning of general-purpose large language models. *arXiv* **2023**, arXiv:2306.12659. [CrossRef]
30. Deng, X.; Bashlovkina, V.; Han, F.; Baumgartner, S.; Bendersky, M. What do llms know about financial markets? a case study on reddit market sentiment analysis. In Proceedings of the Companion Proceedings of the ACM Web Conference 2023, Austin, TX USA, 30 April–4 May 2023; pp. 107–110.
31. Zhang, B.; Yang, H.; Zhou, T.; Ali Babar, M.; Liu, X.Y. Enhancing financial sentiment analysis via retrieval augmented large language models. In Proceedings of the Fourth ACM International Conference on AI in Finance, Brooklyn, NY, USA, 27–29 November 2023; pp. 349–356.
32. Wang, N.; Yang, H.; Wang, C.D. Fingpt: Instruction tuning benchmark for open-source large language models in financial datasets. *arXiv* **2023**, arXiv:2310.04793.
33. Ahmed, R.; Rauf, S.A.; Latif, S. Leveraging Large Language Models and Prompt Settings for Context-Aware Financial Sentiment Analysis. In Proceedings of the 2024 5th International Conference on Advancements in Computational Sciences (ICACS), Lahore Pakistan, 19–20 February 2024; pp. 1–9.
34. Kheiri, K.; Karimi, H. Sentimentgpt: Exploiting gpt for advanced sentiment analysis and its departure from current machine learning. *arXiv* **2023**, arXiv:2307.10234.
35. Fatouros, G.; Metaxas, K.; Soldatos, J.; Kyriazis, D. Can large language models beat wall street? unveiling the potential of ai in stock selection. *arXiv* **2024**, arXiv:2401.03737. [CrossRef]
36. Rasool, A.; Shahzad, M.I.; Aslam, H.; Chan, V. Emotion-Aware Response Generation Using Affect-Enriched Embeddings with LLMs. *arXiv* **2024**, arXiv:2410.01306.
37. Alias, M.S.; Fuad, M.H.; Hoong, X.L.F.; Hin, E.G.Y. Financial Text Categorisation with FinBERT on Key Audit Matters. In Proceedings of the 2023 IEEE Symposium on Computers & Informatics (ISCI), Shah Alam, Malaysia, 14–15 October 2023 pp. 63–69.
38. Fatouros, G.; Soldatos, J.; Kouroumali, K.; Makridis, G.; Kyriazis, D. Transforming sentiment analysis in the financial domain with ChatGPT. *Mach. Learn. Appl.* **2023**, *14*, 100508. [CrossRef]
39. Leippold, M. Sentiment spin: Attacking financial sentiment with GPT-3. *Financ. Res. Lett.* **2023**, *55*, 103957. [CrossRef]
40. Mandloi, L.; Patel, R. Twitter sentiments analysis using machine learninig methods. In Proceedings of the 2020 International Conference for Emerging Technology (INCET), Belgaum, India, 5–7 June 2020; pp. 1–5.
41. Wang, T.; Lu, K.; Chow, K.P.; Zhu, Q. COVID-19 sensing: Negative sentiment analysis on social media in China via BERT model *IEEE Access* **2020**, *8*, 138162–138169. [CrossRef] [PubMed]

42. Ray, B.; Garain, A.; Sarkar, R. An ensemble-based hotel recommender system using sentiment analysis and aspect categorization of hotel reviews. *Appl. Soft Comput.* **2021**, *98*, 106935. [CrossRef]
43. Halder, S. Finbert-lstm: Deep learning based stock price prediction using news sentiment analysis. *arXiv* **2022**, arXiv:2211.07392.
44. Chiranjeevi, P.; Rajaram, A. A lightweight deep learning model based recommender system by sentiment analysis. *J. Intell. Fuzzy Syst.* **2023**, *44*, 10537–10550. [CrossRef]
45. Gössi, S.; Chen, Z.; Kim, W.; Bermeitinger, B.; Handschuh, S. FinBERT-FOMC: Fine-Tuned FinBERT Model with sentiment focus method for enhancing sentiment analysis of FOMC minutes. In Proceedings of the Fourth ACM International Conference on AI in Finance, Brooklyn, NY, USA, 27–29 November 2023; pp. 357–364.
46. Okey, O.D.; Udo, E.U.; Rosa, R.L.; Rodríguez, D.Z.; Kleinschmidt, J.H. Investigating ChatGPT and cybersecurity: A perspective on topic modeling and sentiment analysis. *Comput. Secur.* **2023**, *135*, 103476. [CrossRef]
47. Branco, A.; Parada, D.; Silva, M.; Mendonça, F.; Mostafa, S.S.; Morgado-Dias, F. Sentiment Analysis in Portuguese Restaurant Reviews: Application of Transformer Models in Edge Computing. *Electronics* **2024**, *13*, 589. [CrossRef]
48. Li, X.; Chan, S.; Zhu, X.; Pei, Y.; Ma, Z.; Liu, X.; Shah, S. Are ChatGPT and GPT-4 general-purpose solvers for financial text analytics? A study on several typical tasks. *arXiv* **2023**, arXiv:2305.05862.
49. Jing, N.; Wu, Z.; Wang, H. A hybrid model integrating deep learning with investor sentiment analysis for stock price prediction. *Expert Syst. Appl.* **2021**, *178*, 115019. [CrossRef]
50. Ho, T.T.; Huang, Y. Stock price movement prediction using sentiment analysis and CandleStick chart representation. *Sensors* **2021**, *21*, 7957. [CrossRef]
51. Kim, J.; Kim, H.S.; Choi, S.Y. Forecasting the S&P 500 index using mathematical-based sentiment analysis and deep learning models: A FinBERT transformer model and LSTM. *Axioms* **2023**, *12*, 835. [CrossRef]
52. Shobayo, O.; Adeyemi-Longe, S.; Popoola, O.; Ogunleye, B. Innovative Sentiment Analysis and Prediction of Stock Price Using FinBERT, GPT-4 and Logistic Regression: A Data-Driven Approach. *Big Data Cogn. Comput.* **2024**, *8*, 143. [CrossRef]

electronics

MDPI

Article

DeepSeek-V3, GPT-4, Phi-4, and LLaMA-3.3 Generate Correct Code for LoRaWAN-Related Engineering Tasks

Daniel Fernandes [1,*], João P. Matos-Carvalho [2,3], Carlos M. Fernandes [1,3] and Nuno Fachada [1,3]

[1] Copelabs, Lusófona University, 1749-024 Lisbon, Portugal; p7582@ulusofona.pt (C.M.F.); nuno.fachada@ulusofona.pt (N.F.)
[2] LASIGE, Departamento de Informática, Faculdade de Ciências, Universidade de Lisboa, 1749-016 Lisbon, Portugal; jpecarvalho@ciencias.ulisboa.pt
[3] Center of Technology and Systems (UNINOVA-CTS) and Associated Lab of Intelligent Systems (LASI), 2829-516 Caparica, Portugal
* Correspondence: daniel.fernandes@ulusofona.pt

Abstract: This paper investigates the performance of 16 Large Language Models (LLMs) in automating LoRaWAN-related engineering tasks involving optimal placement of drones and received power calculation under progressively complex zero-shot, natural language prompts. The primary research question is whether lightweight, locally executed LLMs can generate correct Python code for these tasks. To assess this, we compared locally run models against state-of-the-art alternatives, such as GPT-4 and DeepSeek-V3, which served as reference points. By extracting and executing the Python functions generated by each model, we evaluated their outputs on a zero-to-five scale. Results show that while DeepSeek-V3 and GPT-4 consistently provided accurate solutions, certain smaller models—particularly Phi-4 and LLaMA-3.3—also demonstrated strong performance, underscoring the viability of lightweight alternatives. Other models exhibited errors stemming from incomplete understanding or syntactic issues. These findings illustrate the potential of LLM-based approaches for specialized engineering applications while highlighting the need for careful model selection, rigorous prompt design, and targeted domain fine-tuning to achieve reliable outcomes.

Keywords: LoRaWAN; large language models; UAV placement; code generation; IoT

1. Introduction

The rapid expansion of Internet of Things (IoT) applications has led to increased attention to Low-Power Wide-Area Network (LPWAN) technologies, such as LoRa Wide Area Network (LoRaWAN), which provide long-range communication with low power consumption [1]. LoRaWAN networks are particularly appealing for rural areas, where infrastructure constraints can pose significant challenges to traditional wireless communication systems [2]. In this context, the integration of Unmanned Aerial Vehicles (UAVs) as mobile relays has emerged as a promising solution, enabling flexible deployments and extended coverage [3]. Determining the UAV position that minimizes signal propagation loss and assessing the corresponding received power are critical for ensuring reliable connectivity and resource-efficient operations in these rural scenarios [4].

Parallel to these developments in wireless communications, Large Language Models (LLMs) have shown rapid progress. Modern LLMs—including GPT-4 [5], recent open-source offerings locally installable with Ollama [6], and novel models such as

DeepSeek [7]—have shown substantial capabilities in understanding complex tasks and generating functional code for engineering problems [5]. Furthermore, these models demonstrate a broad applicability beyond code generation, including text clustering [8], text summarization [9], machine translation [10], and text classification/question answering [11]. However, despite these advancements, the effectiveness of lightweight, locally executed models in generating correct and efficient solutions for domain-specific engineering tasks remains an open question [12].

This study investigates whether lightweight and locally executed LLMs can generate correct Python code for UAV planning tasks in LoRaWAN environments. Specifically, we assess 16 different LLMs by evaluating their ability to generate Python functions that determine the optimal UAV position from a discrete set of candidate locations, minimizing propagation loss, and computing the corresponding received power (in dBm). Our primary goal is to compare the performance of locally run models, such as LLaMA-3.3 [13] and Phi-4 [14], against state-of-the-art large models such as GPT-4 [5] and DeepSeek-V3 [7], accessed via their online application programming interfaces (APIs). The inclusion of these larger models serves as a reference point to establish that such tasks can indeed be solved using advanced LLMs, allowing for a meaningful comparison with the performance of smaller, locally executed alternatives. The evaluation uses a zero-shot natural language prompt configuration, and correctness is measured through a scoring system based on function extraction and execution results.

Despite significant progress in AI assisted UAV deployment, previous research has largely overlooked the unique communication and operational constraints inherent to LoRaWAN environments. LoRaWAN deployments pose distinct challenges such as stringent power limitations, specialized propagation characteristics at lower frequencies, and long-range communication requirements that differ fundamentally from scenarios commonly studied in existing UAV-AI literature. Existing approaches primarily focus on UAV trajectory planning, mission coordination, or visual scene understanding tasks, without explicitly addressing scenarios involving the low-power, wide-area network constraints and signal propagation peculiarities of LoRaWAN systems. This gap motivates our study, which specifically examines whether LLMs—particularly lightweight, locally executable variants—can effectively generate Python code to solve UAV placement and received power calculation tasks uniquely relevant to LoRaWAN environments.

The findings of this study are significant for two main reasons. First, they illustrate the extent to which lightweight, locally run LLMs can perform domain-specific engineering tasks, providing insight into their potential as cost-effective alternatives to proprietary, large-scale models [15]. Second, these findings may offer practical guidance not only for practitioners integrating LLM-generated code into IoT and UAV communication workflows but also for those in a wide range of other fields, as they highlight critical considerations such as reliability, correctness, and maintainability. The subsequent sections of this paper are organized as follows. Section 2 provides background information on the use of LLMs for human–UAV interaction and code generation, also discussing relevant aspects of prompt design. Section 3 describes the materials and methods employed, including the engineering problem context, prompt structure, model selection, and evaluation metrics. Results are presented in Section 4, followed by a detailed discussion in Section 5. Section 6 outlines the study's limitations and opportunities for future research. Finally, Section 7 concludes the paper with final remarks and recommendations.

2. Background

In this section, we start by addressing the general goal of integrating LLMs with UAVs to improve the behavior, organization, and communication of autonomous systems, as well as the specific implementation of UAVs as mobile relays and antennas in LoRoWAN environments. In Section 2.2, we focus on the specific task of generating code for autonomous devices and on how LLMs are being used to incorporate code generation at different levels of workflow. Finally, in Section 2.3, we briefly discuss prompt engineering and its principles, the benefits and drawbacks of conversational and structured prompting, and how prompt design impacts code generation or task planning.

2.1. LLMs for Human–UAV Interaction

The nature of UAVs, namely their collective organization and communication requirements, strongly encourages integration with Artificial Intelligence (AI) algorithms. The recent emergence of LLM technologies in particular is inspiring new frameworks and prototypes for communication and design of several autonomous systems, and UAVs are no exception. As LLMs learning and adaptation capabilities in uncertain and dynamic environments grow and approach human-level proficiency, the scientific literature on the subject steadily increases [16,17]. Currently, there is a significant amount of knowledge on LLMs for human–UAV interaction. For a review on the state-of-the art literature on LLMs and UAVs, please refer to [16]. For a discussion of key areas where LLMs can impact UAVs, we urge the reader to refer to the paper by Phadke et al. [17]. In the following paragraphs, we discuss some recent developments on the usage of natural language models for controlling UAVs.

In [18], Aikins et al. present LEVIOSA, a framework for the generation of UAV trajectory based on text and speech. The authors use several LLMs to convert natural language prompts into sets of coordinates to guide the UAVs and low-level controllers to control each device in its path, aiming for accuracy, synchronization, and collision avoidance. LEVIOSA was tested on various scenarios with promising results.

Cui et al. [19] propose a Task Planning for Multi-UAV System (TPML) that uses LLMs as interfaces to translate UAV's operator instructions into executable codes. After validating the system in simulation environments and real-wold scenarios, the authors argue that TPML is able to control multiple UAVs in both synchronous and asynchronous missions with a single natural language input.

While most of the studies on natural language processing for UAVs focus on processing the user messages to program or optimize UAV behavior, others try to provide UVAs with scene descriptions skills in natural language, taking advantage of their capacity to acquire visual cues of the environment. In [20], the authors use LLMs and Visual Language Models (VLMs) to provide UAVs with the ability of scene description using natural language. The generated tests were subject to a readability test, some achieving a high school senior reading level (level 12 in the Gunning fog index).

In [21], the authors discuss a framework that integrates a novel factorization method—QTRAN—in a multi-agent reinforcement learning algorithm (MARL) [22] with an LLM to optimize UAV trajectories, overcoming limitations of value decomposition algorithms for trajectory planning, as they have difficulties in associating local observations with the global state of UAV swarms. Although QTRAN overcomes some of the limitations of standard MARLs, its performance can still be improved, namely by enhancing the representation network. For that purpose, the authors incorporate LLMs in the framework, boosting its overall performance in trajectory optimization and outperforming other reinforcement learning methods.

LPWAN-based systems are one of the emerging technologies in which UAVs are being tested and deployed. LPWANS, and LoROWANs in particular, rely on a set of fixed sensor stations, which measure and transmit a number of environmental data to a central unit. Traditionally, these stations are static, cover only very small areas and can be impaired by natural disasters. Due to their mobility, UAVs can act as moving communication nodes, which solves some of the limitations of static LoROWANs.

Several methods have been proposed to integrate UAVs in LoROWANs. In [23], UAVs are used to transfer information from ground-based LORAWAN nodes to the base station. The architecture of the systems thus consists of two layers, the first being the ground nodes that transmit data using LoRaWAN and the second the swarm of drones communicating over a WiFi ad hoc network. To enhance the performance of the systems, a distributed topology algorithm periodically adapts the UAV topology to the position of the ground nodes. In [24], the authors describe an air quality monitor system based on a LORAWAN and UAVs. In [25], a UAV emergency monitoring system using a LORAWAN is proposed to overcome the limitations of ground stations in disaster scenarios. Finally, Arroyo et al. [26] propose a UAV and LOROWAN system that enables data transfer from sensors to a central system and then use machine learning to classify the data. To the extent of our knowledge, there are no studies on the integration of LLMs and UAVs in a LoRaWAN environment.

2.2. Code Generation with LLMs

The landscape of AI-assisted programming has evolved significantly, with extensive research focusing on natural language generation and understanding of large codebases [27]. Shortly after their inception, some LLMs demonstrated capabilities in code assistance and code generation, even from natural language specifications. In the first models, those skills were somewhat limited and the output often required post-processing steps to improve the quality of the suggested code [28]. But LLMs quickly evolved, and their ability to provide executable code in due time improved significantly [29]. Furthermore, derivations of popular LLMs, like Open AI Codex [30], a descendant of ChatGPT-3, and Code Llama [13], Meta's programming tool, emerged as specialized models for coding. Nowadays, AI-assisted programming is a common practice in industry.

In the context of code generation for autonomous devices, Vemprala et al. [31] explore ChatGPT's ability on several robot-oriented tasks, including code synthesis. The authors present a framework for robot control that requires designing and implementing a library of APIs receptive to prompt engineering for ChatGPT. The proposed framework allows the generated code to be tested, verified, and validated by a user through simulation and manual inspection.

In [32], the authors adapt LLMs trained on code completion for writing robot policy code according to natural language prompts. The generated robot policies exhibit spatial-geometric reasoning and are able to prescribe precise values to ambiguous descriptions. By relying on a hierarchical prompting strategy, their approach is able to write more complex code and solve 39.8% of the problems on the HumanEval [30] benchmark.

Luo et al. [33] use LLMs to generate robot control programs, testing and optimizing the output in a simulation environment. After a number of optimization rounds, the robot control codes are deployed on a real robot for construction assembly tasks. The experiments show that their approach can improve the quality of the generated code, thus simplifying the robot control process and facilitating the automation of construction tasks.

2.3. Prompt Design

The piece of text or set of instructions that the user provides to an LLM to generate a specific response is called a prompt. Designing effective prompts is essential to take advantage of the potential of LLMs, and in a few years the craft established as a field of research and development of its own [34].

Prompting strategies can be broadly classified into structured and unstructured approaches. Structured prompting employs precise instructions with explicitly defined inputs, outputs, and constraints, often leading to more reliable and accurate code generation. However, structured prompts typically require a deeper understanding of both the problem domain and the underlying model, potentially limiting flexibility and accessibility. Conversely, unstructured prompting uses intuitive, conversational language, making it accessible to a broader audience, reflecting realistic scenarios where users may not possess specialized knowledge of prompt crafting. However, this can result in less consistent outputs due to inherent ambiguity.

Prompts may also be categorized based on the number of illustrative examples provided: zero-shot prompts provide no examples, one-shot prompts include a single example, and few-shot prompts incorporate multiple examples. Empirical research supports the trade-offs associated with different prompt styles; for instance, Liang et al. [32] demonstrate that structured, code-based prompts generally yield superior results for robot-related reasoning tasks compared to natural language prompts. However, advances in LLM technology continue to improve the viability of unstructured, natural language prompting in complex domains such as robotics [31]. Further improvements in output coherence have also been observed through structured reasoning techniques such as chain-of-thought (CoT) prompting [33,35].

In this study, we follow a natural language zero-shot prompt strategy, in which the request is performed in a relatively unstructured fashion without any examples. Nonetheless, established best practices for engineering-focused code generation were followed by explicitly specifying function inputs, expected return types, and required libraries, thus improving the clarity and reproducibility of the generated code [36].

3. Materials and Methods

This section starts with an overview of the theoretical context that informs our prompt design in Section 3.1. Next, Section 3.2 presents the proposed prompts and their respective scenarios. Section 3.3 describes and justifies the models analyzed in this study. Section 3.4 then outlines the prompting and response processing pipeline. The section concludes with a description of the experimental setup in Section 3.5, including all tested inputs for both the LLMs and the generated Python functions, the expected function results, and the evaluation metrics used.

3.1. Theoretical Context

The IoT paradigm refers to the interconnection of physical devices that collect, exchange, and process data over the Internet or other communication networks. According to Sanguesa et al. [37], it is estimated that by 2030, there will be approximately 125 billion IoT devices, ranging from simple temperature and humidity sensors to more complex sensors used in sectors such as agriculture and industry. The main goal of these sensors is to simplify and optimize daily activities. One of the challenges associated with this paradigm is the large volume of data generated and how it is processed. A potential solution for data collection is the use of UAVs, which can fly over (or carry) multiple sensors along a predefined path planning. These UAVs may or may not be capable of transmitting data in real time to a base station (BS). However, to use UAVs efficiently, it is often necessary to calculate their location and send control commands to adjust their position or even modify their flight path. Therefore, reliable communication between the UAV and a base station is crucial. One possible communication protocol for this purpose is LoRaWAN, which is based on LoRa (long-range) communication and enables effective long-distance data transmission [38,39]. Essentially, LoRa communication establishes a link between two points: the transmitter—in this case, the BS—and the receiver, i.e., the UAV. This communication is based on classical propagation models, such as those found in reference [40].

Regarding the modulation of a communication channel, the received power at the antenna (p_r) depends on factors such as the transmit power (p_t), the gain of the antennas (g_r and g_t), the distance between the antennas (r), and the losses during transmission (free-space attenuation). Equation (1) represents the propagation loss l_F between the two points:

$$l_F = \frac{p_t \cdot g_r \cdot g_t}{p_r} = \left(\frac{4\pi r}{\lambda}\right)^2 = \left(\frac{4\pi r f}{c}\right)^2 \tag{1}$$

where λ represents the wavelength. In particular, $\lambda = \frac{c}{f}$, with c representing the speed of light and f the frequency, which in Europe is 868 MHz.

A lower propagation loss results in a stronger received signal. Propagation losses are typically expressed in dB units, and for a distance in meters and a frequency in Hz, Equation (1) can be rewritten as Equation (2), which represents the Free Space Path Loss formula. This formula is valid under free-space conditions, assuming a direct, unobstructed line of sight. In terms of notation, lowercase variables denote linear values, whereas uppercase variables denote logarithmic values.

$$L_F(dB) = 20\log(r_m) + 20\log(f_{Hz}) - 147.55 \tag{2}$$

To estimate the received power, it is necessary to consider the transmitted power, the gain of the transmitting and receiving antennas, and the path losses that occur during transmission. Thus, Equation (3), derived from Equation (1), can be written as

$$P_{r(dBm)} = P_t + G_t + G_r - L_F \tag{3}$$

3.2. Scenarios and Prompts

To evaluate the LLM models, three zero-shot prompts with increasing levels of difficulty were designed—see Table 1. In this context, 'zero-shot' refers to prompts that do not provide any examples to the model being tested. Furthermore, these prompts use natural language, meaning that they are relatively unstructured and have undergone minimal refinement, apart from ensuring technical precision and clarity. This approach was chosen as it more closely follows real-world scenarios where domain experts may rely on direct, straightforward queries to achieve their goals.

The specific request posed by these prompts is for the LLM to identify, from a set of points, the point where the value of L_F is the lowest or to determine the received power at that point (i.e., the point with the lowest L_F). In all scenarios, a frequency of 868 MHz is considered, as well as a rural area where LoRa communication is possible up to 10 km. Both antennas are assumed to have a gain of 2.5 dBi each.

To simplify post-processing of responses, all prompts specify the available libraries, the expected indentation type, and that the return function should be self-contained—i.e., all required code including constants and auxiliary functions should be defined within the requested function.

Table 1. Prompts designed for this study, requiring the tested LLMs to generate Python functions that solve increasingly complex tasks related to LoRaWAN and UAVs.

Prompt 1

```
Consider that the LoRaWAN communication protocol is being used in a rural scenario where a base station communicates with a UAV
at a communication frequency of 868 MHz. Assume a system with two axes (the x-axis and the y-axis) and that the base station is
in position (0,0). Also, assume that all positions are in kilometers (km).

Create a Python function called `index_position()` which accepts a list of tuples, with each (x, y) tuple representing a possible
position in which the UAV can be placed with respect to the base station. This function should return the list index of the tuple
(i.e., UAV position) which minimizes the propagation loss. Assume that the math and numpy libraries are imported as follows, and
no more libraries can be used:

import math
import numpy as np

Beyond importing these libraries, the `index_position()` function must be self-contained. In other words, all variables,
constants, or helper functions must be defined within the `index_position()` function. Provide Python code with 4-space
indentation following PEP 8.
```

Prompt 2

```
Consider that the LoRaWAN communication protocol is being used in a rural scenario where a base station communicates with a UAV
at a communication frequency of 868 MHz. Assume a system with two axes (the latitude axis and the longitude axis) where each
value is given in decimal degrees.

Create a Python function called `index_position()` which accepts a list of (latitude, longitude) tuples. The first tuple in this
list represents the position of the base station, while the remaining tuples represent possible positions in which the UAV can be
placed. This function should return the list index of the tuple which minimizes the propagation loss. Assume that the math and
numpy libraries are imported as follows, and no more libraries can be used:

import math
import numpy as np

Beyond importing these libraries, the `index_position()` function must be self-contained. In other words, all variables,
constants, or helper functions must be defined within the `index_position()` function. Provide Python code with 4-space
indentation following PEP 8.
```

Prompt 3

```
Consider that the LoRaWAN communication protocol is being used in a rural scenario where a base station communicates with a UAV at
a communication frequency of 868 MHz, with a transmission power of 27 dBm. Both the transmitter and UAV antennas have a gain of
2.5 dBi. Assume a system with two axes (the latitude axis and the longitude axis) where each value is given in decimal degrees.

Create a Python function called `power_received()` which accepts a list of (latitude, longitude) tuples. The first tuple in this
list represents the position of the base station, while the remaining tuples represent possible positions in which the UAV can be
placed. This function should return the power received (in dBm) by the UAV at the position that minimizes the propagation loss.
Assume that the math and numpy libraries are imported as follows, and no more libraries can be used:

import math
import numpy as np

Beyond importing these libraries, the `power_received()` function must be self-contained. In other words, all variables,
constants, or helper functions must be defined within the `power_received()` function. Provide Python code with 4-space
indentation following PEP 8.
```

The first prompt is presented in the first row of Table 1. In this simpler scenario, the BS and the UAV's possible positions, measured in kilometers (km), are defined within a coordinate system with two axes: the x-axis and the y-axis. The BS is fixed at position $(0,0)$, while the UAV's possible positions are provided as an input array to the function generated by the LLMs. To solve this problem, LLMs must generate a Python function that calculates the distance (e.g., Euclidean) between the BS and each possible UAV position, applies Equation (2) to compute power losses, and returns the index of the position with the lowest loss. The LLM must ensure that power losses maintain a one-to-one correspondence with the UAV positions to return the correct index.

Prompt 2, shown in the second row of Table 1, increases the complexity by considering geographical coordinates—latitude and longitude—instead of a simple (x, y) axis. LLMs must use a different method to calculate the distances between the UAV's position and the BS, such as Haversine's formula. This prompt further increases the difficulty by requiring that the UAV's position be given as the first element of the input array. Consequently, the generated functions must extract this information and return an index greater than zero, as index zero contains the UAV's position.

Prompt 3, presented in the last row of Table 1, closely resembles Prompt 2. However, instead of returning the index with the lowest loss, the generated function must return the value of that loss by applying Equation (3).

3.3. LLMs Considered

The LLMs models used in this paper were chosen based on their impact in AI research, innovative approaches, and performance across different domains such as programming, advanced reasoning, and computational efficiency. Table 2 lists and characterizes the LLMs selected for this study. For the remainder of this paper, the number of parameters associated with each model is expressed in billions or trillions with an uppercase B and T, respectively.

Table 2. Characteristics and main purpose of the LLMs tested in this study. 'Size' indicates the number of parameters in billions (B) or trillions (T). 'Tag' corresponds to the specific model version invoked in the respective API calls.

Family	Version	Size	Tag	Main Purpose
DeepSeek [7,41]	R1	7B	`deepseek-r1:7b`	Computationally efficient distilled reasoning model.
	R1	70B	`deepseek-r1:70b`	Distilled reasoning model balancing performance and computational efficiency.
	V3	671B	`deepseek-v3`	Mixture-of-Experts general-purpose model.
Gemma [42,43]	1.1	2B	`gemma:2b`	Lightweight model for dialogue, instruction-following, and coding.
	2.0	2B	`gemma2:2b`	Compact general-purpose model trained with knowledge distillation.
GPT [5]	4	1.76T *	`gpt-4-0613`	Multimodal model optimized by OpenAI for text, audio, and image processing.
LLaMA [13]	3.2	3B	`llama3.2:3b`	Lightweight text-only model for multilingual dialogue and text summarization.
	3.3	70B	`llama3.3:70b`	Text-only model for deeper comprehension multilingual conversation.
	code	7B	`codellama:7b`	Code generation model.
Mistral [44]	0.3	7B	`mistral:7b`	Efficient model for text and code generation, supports function calling.
Phi [14]	4.0	14B	`phi4:14b`	Reasoning model trained using high-quality synthetic data.
Qwen [45,46]	2.5-coder	0.5B	`qwen2.5-coder:0.5b`	Code generation model.
	2.5-coder	1.5B	`qwen2.5-coder:1.5b`	Code generation model.
	2.5-coder	3B	`qwen2.5-coder:3b`	Code generation model.
	2.5	0.5B	`qwen2.5:0.5b`	General-purpose language model.
	qwq	32B	`qwq:32b`	Advanced reasoning model for complex problem-solving tasks.

* Unofficial estimate.

The DeepSeek family of models includes a range of architectures designed to balance performance and computational efficiency. DeepSeek-R1 (7B) and DeepSeek-R1 (70B) are distilled versions derived from the larger DeepSeek-R1 model (671B)—based on the Qwen and LLaMA architectures—to retain significant reasoning capabilities while reducing hardware demands [41]. In contrast, DeepSeek-V3 (671B) is a Mixture-of-Experts model designed to perform well in diverse tasks [7]. Considering these models is crucial due to their varied architectures and training methodologies, which offer insights into the trade-offs between model size, training techniques, and task-specific performance. The V3 671B model was selected over its more developed R1 counterpart, as initial trials demonstrated it was sufficiently accurate for the prompts presented in Section 3.2, providing a balance between performance and cost.

The Gemma model family [42,43], developed by Google DeepMind, comprises open models derived from the research and technology behind the Gemini models. While influenced by Gemini, Gemma is fully open-source and designed for efficient language understanding and reasoning. The lightweight Gemma v1.1 (2B) and Gemma2 (2B) implementations are optimized for resource-limited environments. Gemma2 (2B) incorporates knowledge distillation, improving efficiency and performance relative to its size. These models were included to assess the trade-offs in model scaling, particularly for the real-time and cost-sensitive applications associated with the tested prompts.

OpenAI's Generative Pre-trained Transformer (GPT) models are proprietary LLMs designed to understand and generate human-like text, facilitating tasks such as drafting documents, coding, and responding to queries [5]. Their popularity and advanced capabilities make them essential subjects in LLM comparison studies. In this context, GPT-4-0613 was selected over newer models such as GPT-4o and o1, as preliminary tests indicated its performance was sufficient for the presented prompts, therefore reducing costs.

The LLaMA series by Meta AI includes models optimized for various applications [13]. LLaMA-3.2 (3B) is a lightweight, multilingual model suited for mobile and edge devices, appropriate for text summarization and classification. LLaMA-3.3 (70B) is a larger, instruction-tuned model with superior performance in natural conversation and multilingual tasks. Code Llama (7B) specializes in code generation and understanding. Testing these three models is important for evaluating how model size, specialization, and efficiency in the LLaMA family impacts performance across the three implemented prompts.

The Mistral family of language models [44], developed by the French company Mistral AI, stands out for its efficient architecture and strong performance. Mistral models achieve high accuracy with fewer parameters, making them more accessible and computationally efficient compared to many large-scale models. The Mistral v0.3 (7B) model exemplifies this approach, demonstrating capabilities in text and code generation, conversation, and function calling, while effectively handling longer sequences. Its open-source nature offers a valuable option for research and application development, providing a European alternative to models predominantly from U.S.- and China-based companies.

The Phi model family [14], developed by Microsoft Research, is focused on the role of high-quality synthetic data for improving reasoning in compact language models. Phi-4, a 14-billion parameter model, prioritizes synthetic data to improve problem-solving in mathematics and coding, outperforming its teacher model, GPT-4, on several benchmarks. Unlike models that primarily scale with size, Phi-4 follows a distinct training approach, making it important to compare against other LLMs. Its relatively small size also makes it relevant for low-resource environments, where optimizing data efficiency can be a crucial factor in model deployment.

The Qwen model family, developed by Alibaba Cloud, includes general-purpose [45] and code-specialized [46] LLMs over a wide range of sizes. Their scalability, architectural optimizations, and strong reasoning capabilities make them valuable for benchmarking efficiency and specialization. Here, the most recent 2.5 versions are tested—namely the specialized coder implementations (0.5B, 1.5B, and 3B) and the general-purpose 0.5B model—as well as QwQ (Qwen with Questions) 32B model with advanced reasoning capabilities.

3.4. Implementation

The pipeline for submitting a prompt to an LLM, obtaining a response, extracting a Python function, and executing it is illustrated in Figure 1. The process begins by iterating through a predefined set of LLMs, seeds, temperatures, and prompts. Each prompt is submitted to the corresponding LLM, and its response is stored in a text file. Next, the function from each stored response is extracted by searching for the function definition (e.g., '`def requested_function():`') and capturing all internal code up to the last properly indented '`return`' statement. This ensures that functions defined within the external function do not prematurely terminate the extraction. The extracted function is then recorded in a Python file for execution. If the function is not successfully extracted—such as when the defined function name does not match the expected one—this information is logged in the results file, and a score of zero is assigned for that LLM, seed, temperature, and prompt combination.

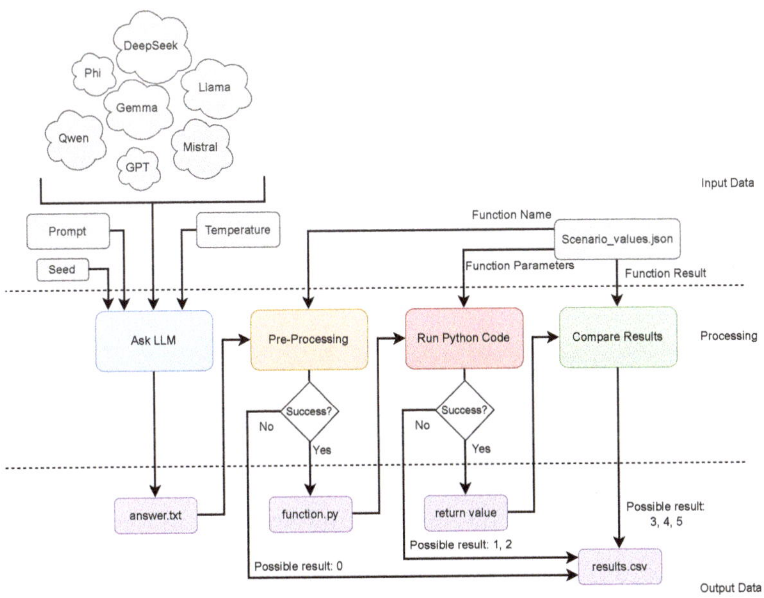

Figure 1. Validation pipeline for the results of LLMs under study.

If the Python function is correctly generated and extracted, it is tested under Python 3.9.6 using the data provided for each scenario (presented in Section 3.5). One of three possible outcomes may occur:

- The code contains a syntax error and does not compile, in which case a score of 1 is recorded in the results file;

- The code executes but encounters a runtime error, resulting in an exception, in which case a score of 2 is stored in the results file;
- The code executes successfully and returns a result, in which case the score ranges from 3 to 5, as detailed below.

If the code executes successfully, the function's output is evaluated as follows: if the returned value is of a different type than expected (e.g., a `float` instead of an `int`), a score of 3 is recorded in the results file. This type check is performed broadly; for example, if an integer is expected, types such as `int`, `np.int32`, or `np.int64` are considered valid (where `np` refers to the NumPy library). If the type is correct, the next step is to verify whether the returned value matches the expected value. For floating-point comparisons, a tolerance of 1% is allowed. If the result is incorrect, a score of 4 is assigned. Finally, if the returned value is correct, a score of 5 is recorded, indicating 100% functionally correct code. At the end of this process, a file containing all recorded scores is available for analysis.

In summary, scores between 0 and 5 are characterized as follows:

0. No Python file was generated—This indicates that the LLM did not generate a Python function or that the generated function does not have the name specified in the prompt.
1. Syntax error—The code does not compile.
2. Runtime error—The code is valid Python but has logic incongruencies and/or does not conform to the prompt requirements.
3. Code runs but returns an incorrect data type—For Prompts 1 and 2, it should return an integer (the index value), while in Prompt 3, it should return a float.
4. Code runs but returns an incorrect result.
5. Code runs and returns the correct result.

3.5. Experimental Setup

To thoroughly test the capabilities of the models listed in Section 3.3, the prompts presented in Section 3.2 were individually submitted to LLMs using six different pseudo-random number generator seeds across six temperature values, in a total of 36 submissions per prompt for each LLM. Temperatures were increased in 0.2 increments from 0.0 to 1.0 for locally executed LLMs via Ollama. Although Ollama accepts temperatures in the range of 0.0–1.0, both DeepSeek-V3 and GPT-4, executed through their online APIs, accept temperatures in the 0.0–2.0 range. Therefore, temperatures were doubled for these models. For example, and for the purpose of this study, a temperature of 0.6 in local models is doubled to 1.2 when submitting a prompt to online LLMs.

The LLM-generated Python functions were tested with the following input data, and return values for each prompt were expected:

Prompt 1 The input data are an array of four positions, namely $[(2,5),(7,7),(1,8),(1,0.5)]$. The expected return value is 3, corresponding to coordinate $(1,0.5)$, which is the closest one to the BS, which is fixed at $(0,0)$.

Prompt 2 The input data are an array containing the following coordinates:

$$\begin{array}{lcl} \text{BS / UAV} & \rightarrow & (38.759297963817374, -9.154483012234662) \\ \text{Position 1} & \rightarrow & (38.749330295687805, -9.15304293547367) \\ \text{Position 2} & \rightarrow & (38.75727072916799, -9.157797377555926) \\ \text{Position 3} & \rightarrow & (38.737648166512336, -9.138660615310467) \\ \text{Position 4} & \rightarrow & (38.76841010033327, -9.160013961052972) \end{array}$$

The expected return value is 2, corresponding to the index of Position 2, which minimizes the power loss.

Prompt 3 The input data are the same as in Prompt 2, but the expected value is −50.33 dBm, which is the minimal loss, obtained at Position 2.

As described in Section 3.4, the capabilities of the different LLMs in correctly answering Prompts 1–3 are assessed using a score between 0 and 5. For six submissions (one per seed) for each prompt–model–temperature combination, four summary statistics are calculated and presented: the mean score, a non-parametric 95% confidence interval around the mean, the percentage of perfect scores (score equal to 5), and a histogram of score distribution. These metrics allow for a detailed performance investigation of the capabilities of the 16 tested models to generate Python code to solve the three progressively complex LoRaWAN-related prompts.

In addition to these summary statistics, a formal statistical comparison between models is conducted using stratified permutation tests [47]. To account for varying prompt difficulty, model performance is stratified by prompt, allowing all three prompts to be included in a unified testing procedure. For each pairwise comparison between two models at a given temperature, scores are pooled by prompt (six scores per model per prompt, 12 in total), and a one-sided permutation test is applied. The test statistic is the sum of mean rank differences across prompts. All $\binom{12}{6} = 924$ possible permutations of model labels are precomputed per prompt, and 1000 stratified permutations are generated by randomly selecting one permutation per prompt and combining them. The resulting null distribution is used to estimate the probability of obtaining a test statistic as large or larger than the observed one under the null hypothesis of no difference. The tests are one-sided, since the goal is to determine whether one model significantly outperforms another—not whether it is worse. Finally, multiple testing correction is applied using the Benjamini–Hochberg procedure to control the false discovery rate (FDR) across all comparisons [48].

4. Results

Results for the simpler Prompt 1 are shown in Figure 2 and Table 3. While all models generated accurate code for certain seed/temperature combinations, DeepSeek-V3 and Phi-4 stood out, consistently providing correct answers across all seeds and temperatures. The three LLaMA models, the three Qwen coder models, and GPT-4 also demonstrated strong performance, reliably generating correct code for at least a subset of temperature values—typically at lower settings. Interestingly, GPT-4 exhibited a significant drop in answer quality at temperatures of 1.6 and higher (i.e., 2×0.8), with responses becoming essentially random at the highest temperature. In contrast, the DeepSeek-R1 models (7B and 70B), the Gemma models (2B), the Mistral model (7B), and the non-coder Qwen models (2.5–0.5B and QwQ-32B) failed to consistently produce correct answers.

Results for the slightly more complex Prompt 2, for which the UAV position is given as a function argument (i.e., it is not predefined within the function) and actual geographical coordinates are used, are shown in Figure 3 and Table 4. Only four models consistently generated accurate code: the larger online DeepSeek-V3 and GPT-4 models, as well as the smaller, locally tested LLaMA-3.3 and Phi-4. However, the drop in performance for GPT-4 at higher temperatures is even more pronounced for this prompt. Conversely, Gemma (2B), Mistral (7B), and both 0.5B Qwen models failed to produce a single correct answer.

Prompt 3, while similar to Prompt 2 in many respects, requires the requested function to return a concrete power loss value rather than merely the index of the position with the lowest loss. This distinction arguably makes it the most complex task for the models evaluated in this study. The results for this prompt are presented in Figure 4 and Table 5. The same four models continued to generate accurate code consistently, though within a more limited range of temperature settings. DeepSeek-V3 demonstrated the highest overall consistency, reliably producing correct code at temperatures of 0.8 (2×0.4) and 1.2 (2×0.6), while maintaining a high percentage of accurate responses across the remaining temperatures. GPT-4 and Phi-4 achieved 100% accuracy when the temperature was set to zero. However, while Phi-4 remained highly consistent at higher temperatures, GPT-4 exhibited a significant decline in performance. LLaMA-3.3 also demonstrated strong consistency, achieving 100% accuracy in all runs at temperatures of 0.2 and 0.4. None of the remaining models were able to successfully complete this task. The only exception was Qwen's QwQ (32B), which generated a single correct response at a temperature of 0.6. However, beyond this isolated instance, it predominantly produced code containing invalid syntax or runtime errors.

Figure 5 presents a pairwise significance heatmap based on p-values from a stratified permutation test, after FDR multiple testing correction, indicating which models (in rows) statistically outperformed others (in columns) across temperatures. Table 6 summarizes these results, showing the number of models each system significantly outperformed at each temperature, as well as the overall total across all temperatures. These results reinforce what was observed in the descriptive statistics—namely that DeepSeek-V3, GPT-4, Phi-4, and LLaMA-3.3 are the most consistent and competitive models in these engineering tasks. At nearly all temperature levels, these models significantly outperformed the majority of alternatives, with corrected p-values below the 0.05 threshold in a substantial number of pairwise comparisons. In particular, DeepSeek-V3, Phi-4, and LLaMA-3.3 achieved the highest number of significant wins at every temperature, while GPT-4 showed similarly strong performance at lower temperatures but exhibited a sharp decline in statistical superiority as temperature increased.

In contrast, the two DeepSeek-R1 models, as well as QwQ, registered very few significant wins at any temperature. Crucially, their only advantages were against GPT-4 at higher temperatures, where its output becomes increasingly random and unsuitable for these types of coding tasks. This further confirms their limited effectiveness, as already observed in previous results. An additional insight—less apparent in the descriptive statistics but clearly highlighted in Table 6—is the lack of correlation between model size and performance within the Qwen coder family. Specifically, the 1.5B Qwen coder model achieved the fourth highest total number of pairwise wins (47), surpassing even GPT-4 (45), while the larger 3B variant achieved roughly half as many.

Finally, Figure 6 presents the mean scores for the tested models across all three prompts, aggregating results from all seeds and temperature settings. While the initial assumption was that Prompts 1 to 3 increase in complexity, and the results thus far appear to support this hypothesis, Figure 6 provides a more comprehensive perspective. For most models, the mean score declines progressively with increasing prompt complexity, reinforcing this assumption. However, exceptions include both Gemma models and the non-coder Qwen-2.5 model, where the score reduction is not strictly monotonic. Another observation from this figure is that the highest performing models—DeepSeek-V3, GPT-4, LLaMA-3.3, and Phi-4—maintain consistent performance across prompts, with only a slight decline in mean score as complexity increases.

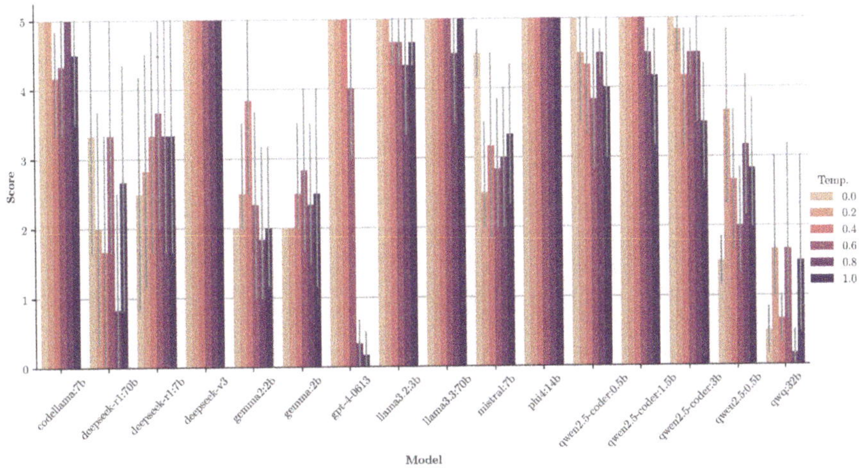

Figure 2. Prompt 1 mean answer score for the tested models over several temperatures. Each combination of model and temperature was tested with 6 different seeds. Error bars denote a 95% confidence interval. Temperatures for online models, `deepseek-v3` and `gpt-4-0613`, are twice the displayed values.

Table 3. Prompt 1 answer statistics, namely the percentage of correct answers (score equal to 5) and histogram of scores (0–5) for the tested models over several temperatures. Each combination of model and temperature was tested with 6 different seeds. Temperatures for online models, `deepseek-v3` and `gpt-4-0613`, are twice the displayed values.

Model	Temperature						
	0.0	0.2	0.4	0.6	0.8	1.0	Overall
`codellama:7b`	100.0%	100.0%	50.0%	66.7%	100.0%	83.3%	83.3%
`deepseek-r1:70b`	66.7%	33.3%	33.3%	66.7%	16.7%	50.0%	44.4%
`deepseek-r1:7b`	50.0%	50.0%	50.0%	66.7%	66.7%	66.7%	58.3%
`deepseek-v3`	100.0%	100.0%	100.0%	100.0%	100.0%	100.0%	100.0%
`gemma2:2b`	0.0%	16.7%	66.7%	33.3%	16.7%	16.7%	25.0%
`gemma:2b`	0.0%	0.0%	16.7%	33.3%	16.7%	33.3%	16.7%
`gpt-4-0613`	100.0%	100.0%	100.0%	66.7%	0.0%	0.0%	61.1%
`llama3.2:3b`	100.0%	100.0%	66.7%	66.7%	66.7%	66.7%	77.8%
`llama3.3:70b`	100.0%	100.0%	100.0%	100.0%	83.3%	100.0%	97.2%
`mistral:7b`	50.0%	16.7%	50.0%	16.7%	33.3%	33.3%	33.3%
`phi4:14b`	100.0%	100.0%	100.0%	100.0%	100.0%	100.0%	100.0%
`qwen2.5-coder:0.5b`	100.0%	83.3%	66.7%	50.0%	50.0%	66.7%	69.4%
`qwen2.5-coder:1.5b`	100.0%	100.0%	100.0%	100.0%	50.0%	50.0%	83.3%
`qwen2.5-coder:3b`	100.0%	83.3%	50.0%	50.0%	83.3%	16.7%	63.9%
`qwen2.5:0.5b`	0.0%	50.0%	16.7%	0.0%	16.7%	16.7%	16.7%
`qwq:32b`	0.0%	16.7%	0.0%	16.7%	0.0%	16.7%	8.3%

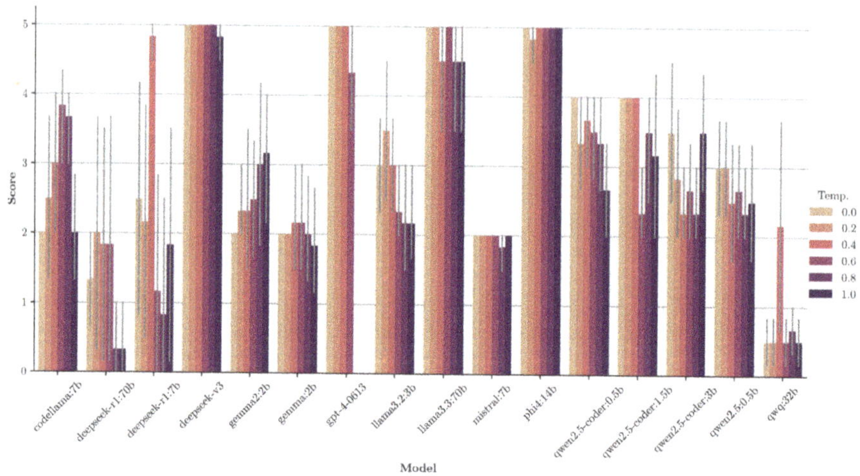

Figure 3. Prompt 2 mean answer score for the tested models over several temperatures. Each combination of model and temperature was tested with 6 different seeds. Error bars denote a 95% confidence interval. Temperatures for online models, `deepseek-v3` and `gpt-4-0613`, are twice the displayed values.

Table 4. Prompt 2 answer statistics, namely the percentage of correct answers (score equal to 5) and histogram of scores (0–5) for the tested models over several temperatures. Each combination of model and temperature was tested with 6 different seeds. Temperatures for online models, `deepseek-v3` and `gpt-4-0613`, are twice the displayed values.

Model	Temperature						
	0.0	0.2	0.4	0.6	0.8	1.0	Overall
`codellama:7b`	0.0%	16.7%	16.7%	16.7%	0.0%	0.0%	8.3%
`deepseek-r1:70b`	0.0%	33.3%	33.3%	33.3%	0.0%	0.0%	16.7%
`deepseek-r1:7b`	50.0%	33.3%	83.3%	16.7%	16.7%	33.3%	38.9%
`deepseek-v3`	100.0%	100.0%	100.0%	100.0%	100.0%	83.3%	97.2%
`gemma2:2b`	0.0%	0.0%	16.7%	0.0%	16.7%	0.0%	5.6%
`gemma:2b`	0.0%	0.0%	0.0%	0.0%	0.0%	0.0%	0.0%
`gpt-4-0613`	100.0%	100.0%	100.0%	66.7%	0.0%	0.0%	61.1%
`llama3.2:3b`	0.0%	50.0%	0.0%	0.0%	0.0%	0.0%	8.3%
`llama3.3:70b`	100.0%	100.0%	83.3%	100.0%	83.3%	83.3%	91.7%
`mistral:7b`	0.0%	0.0%	0.0%	0.0%	0.0%	0.0%	0.0%
`phi4:14b`	100.0%	83.3%	100.0%	100.0%	100.0%	100.0%	97.2%
`qwen2.5-coder:0.5b`	0.0%	0.0%	0.0%	0.0%	0.0%	0.0%	0.0%
`qwen2.5-coder:1.5b`	0.0%	0.0%	0.0%	0.0%	0.0%	33.3%	5.6%
`qwen2.5-coder:3b`	50.0%	16.7%	0.0%	0.0%	0.0%	16.7%	13.9%
`qwen2.5:0.5b`	0.0%	0.0%	0.0%	0.0%	0.0%	0.0%	0.0%
`qwq:32b`	0.0%	0.0%	33.3%	0.0%	0.0%	0.0%	5.6%

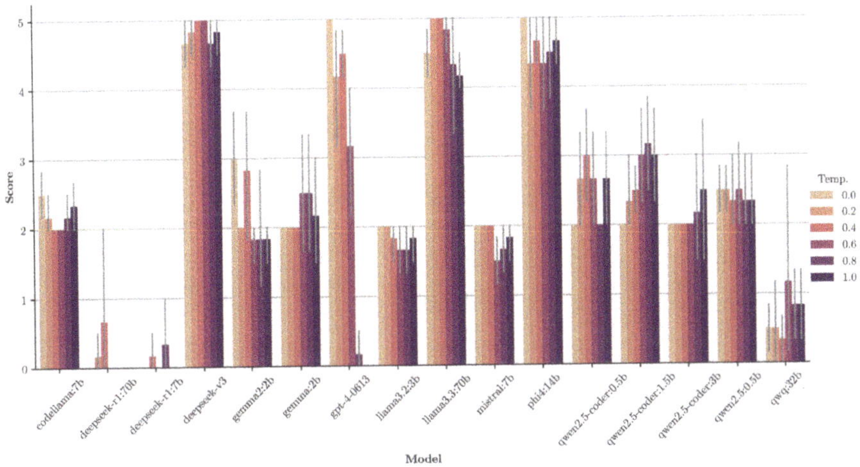

Figure 4. Prompt 3 mean answer score for the tested models over several temperatures. Each combination of model and temperature was tested with 6 different seeds. Error bars denote a 95% confidence interval. Temperatures for online models, `deepseek-v3` and `gpt-4-0613`, are twice the displayed values.

Table 5. Prompt 3 answer statistics, namely the percentage of correct answers (score equal to 5) and histogram of scores (0–5) for the tested models over several temperatures. Each combination of model and temperature was tested with 6 different seeds. Temperatures for online models, `deepseek-v3` and `gpt-4-0613`, are twice the displayed values.

Model	**Temperature**						
	0.0	**0.2**	**0.4**	**0.6**	**0.8**	**1.0**	**Overall**
`codellama:7b`	0.0%	0.0%	0.0%	0.0%	0.0%	0.0%	0.0%
`deepseek-r1:70b`	0.0%	0.0%	0.0%	0.0%	0.0%	0.0%	0.0%
`deepseek-r1:7b`	0.0%	0.0%	0.0%	0.0%	0.0%	0.0%	0.0%
`deepseek-v3`	66.7%	83.3%	100.0%	100.0%	66.7%	83.3%	83.3%
`gemma2:2b`	0.0%	0.0%	0.0%	0.0%	0.0%	0.0%	0.0%
`gemma:2b`	0.0%	0.0%	0.0%	0.0%	0.0%	0.0%	0.0%
`gpt-4-0613`	100.0%	50.0%	50.0%	0.0%	0.0%	0.0%	33.3%
`llama3.2:3b`	0.0%	0.0%	0.0%	0.0%	0.0%	0.0%	0.0%
`llama3.3:70b`	50.0%	100.0%	100.0%	83.3%	66.7%	16.7%	69.4%
`mistral:7b`	0.0%	0.0%	0.0%	0.0%	0.0%	0.0%	0.0%
`phi4:14b`	100.0%	66.7%	66.7%	66.7%	66.7%	66.7%	72.2%
`qwen2.5-coder:0.5b`	0.0%	0.0%	0.0%	0.0%	0.0%	0.0%	0.0%
`qwen2.5-coder:1.5b`	0.0%	0.0%	0.0%	0.0%	0.0%	0.0%	0.0%
`qwen2.5-coder:3b`	0.0%	0.0%	0.0%	0.0%	0.0%	0.0%	0.0%
`qwen2.5:0.5b`	0.0%	0.0%	0.0%	0.0%	0.0%	0.0%	0.0%
`qwq:32b`	0.0%	0.0%	0.0%	16.7%	0.0%	0.0%	2.8%

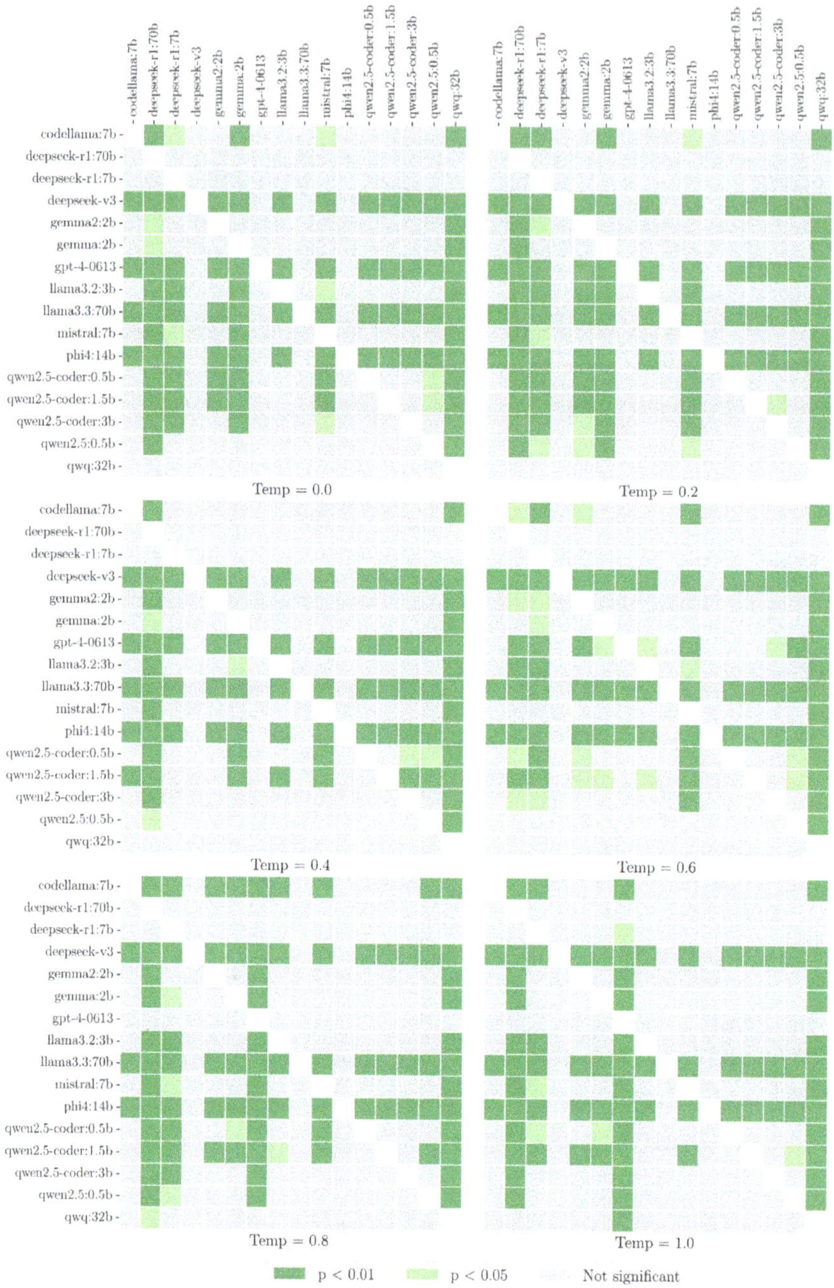

Figure 5. Pairwise significance heatmap of model performance comparisons for the three prompts across temperatures. Each colored block represents the p-value of a one-sided, rank-based stratified permutation test between two models (model in row vs. model in column) for a given temperature. Cells are colored based on statistical significance after Benjamini–Hochberg FDR multiple testing correction: dark green indicates a significant advantage of the model in the row against the model in the column ($p < 0.01$), light green indicates moderate significant advantage ($p < 0.05$), and light gray denotes no significant difference. Temperatures for online models, `deepseek-v3` and `gpt-4-0613`, are twice the displayed values.

Table 6. Number of statistically significant pairwise wins (corrected $p < 0.05$) per model across temperature settings. Bold values indicate the highest number of wins for each temperature column (including ties). Each cell represents how many times a given model significantly outperformed others at the corresponding temperature. Temperatures for online models, `deepseek-v3` and `gpt-4-0613`, are twice the displayed values.

Model	Temperature						
	0.0	0.2	0.4	0.6	0.8	1.0	Overall
`codellama:7b`	5	5	2	5	9	4	30
`deepseek-r1:70b`	0	0	0	0	0	0	0
`deepseek-r1:7b`	0	0	0	0	0	1	1
`deepseek-v3`	**12**	**12**	**12**	**13**	**13**	**13**	**75**
`gemma2:2b`	2	3	2	3	3	3	16
`gemma:2b`	2	2	2	2	4	3	15
`gpt-4-0613`	**12**	**12**	**12**	9	0	0	45
`llama3.2:3b`	5	6	3	4	4	4	26
`llama3.3:70b`	**12**	**12**	**12**	**13**	**13**	**13**	**75**
`mistral:7b`	4	3	2	1	4	4	18
`phi4:14b`	**12**	**12**	**12**	**13**	**13**	**13**	**75**
`qwen2.5-coder:0.5b`	7	6	6	6	6	5	36
`qwen2.5-coder:1.5b`	7	7	8	8	9	8	47
`qwen2.5-coder:3b`	5	6	2	4	4	3	24
`qwen2.5:0.5b`	2	6	2	1	4	3	18
`qwq:32b`	0	0	0	0	1	1	2

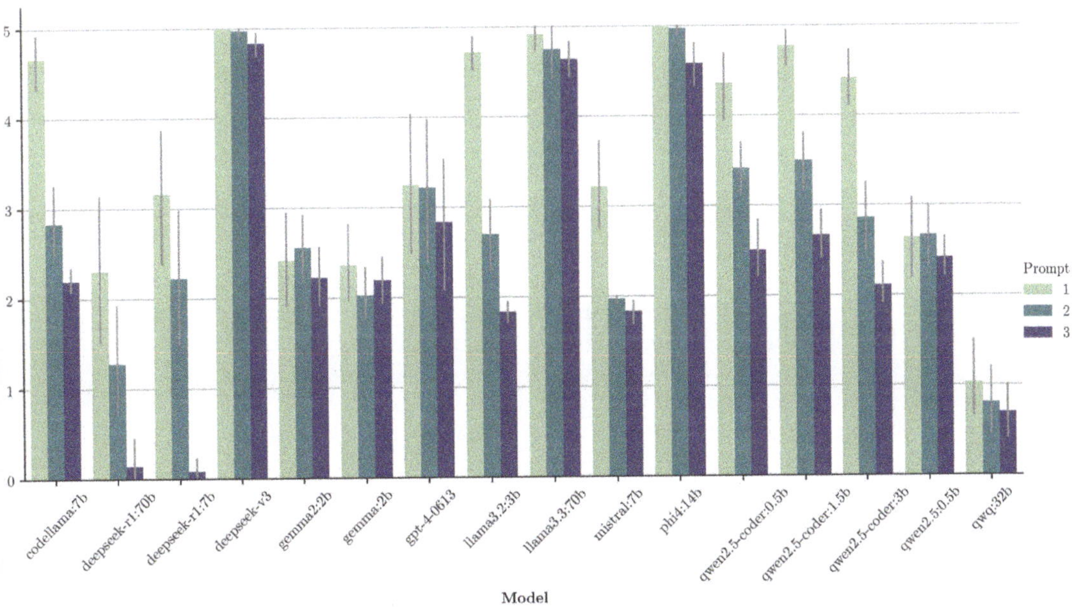

Figure 6. Mean answer score for the tested models and the three prompts. Each combination of model and prompt was tested 36 times (6 seeds $\times$ 6 temperatures). Error bars denote a 95% confidence interval.

5. Discussion

Within the DeepSeek model family, there was a surprising discrepancy between the well-performing DeepSeek-V3 and the underperforming DeepSeek-R1 models. The DeepSeek-R1 versions (7B and 70B), despite their larger parameter counts, rarely generated correct code. Interestingly, the DeepSeek-R1 models, as well as Qwen's QwQ (32B), tended to generate answers over five times longer than those from other models, yet without improved correctness. While these verbose outputs are particularly noticeable, we did not investigate the reasons behind them because this lies beyond the scope of this study. Nonetheless, the generated data—as well as further analyses on this matter—are available on Zenodo (https://doi.org/10.5281/zenodo.14888673) and may be addressed in future studies.

An important observation is that GPT-4 exhibits essentially random outputs when operating at higher temperatures. This behavior aligns with OpenAI's own documentation, which indicates that temperatures above 1.2 or 1.4 may lead to increasingly stochastic completions. In contrast, the other top-performing models in this study—DeepSeek-V3, LLaMA-3.3, and Phi-4—remain relatively robust under higher temperature settings. These considerations indicate that temperature influences each model differently. Differences in temperature scaling ranges (0–1 vs. 0–2) further complicate direct comparisons.

Although one might expect a clear correlation between model size and code generation quality, results support a more involved situation among locally run models. Larger models such as DeepSeek-R1 (70B) and QwQ (32B) do not necessarily outperform smaller alternatives: their answers were typically long yet largely incorrect. Conversely, some mid- to large-scale models, such as Phi-4 (14B) and LLaMA-3.3 (70B), consistently provided accurate solutions to all prompts. Another example, LLaMA-3.2 (3B), showed reasonable performance for simpler tasks but struggled with more complex prompts, highlighting a lower boundary for parameter count beyond which performance degrades. In contrast, Qwen's smaller coder models (0.5B, 1.5B, 3B) did not show any clear advantage with increasing size, confirming that raw parameter counts alone are insufficient to predict success across different tasks.

Within the Gemini-based lineage, Gemma-2 offered marginal improvements over its older v1.1 sibling, though neither model consistently produced correct outputs. On the other hand, LLaMA-3.3 (70B) clearly outperformed the related LLaMA-3.2 (3B), a result likely driven by its substantially larger parameter count. Phi-4 merits special mention for delivering accurate code across all tasks, seeds, and temperatures, while requiring considerably fewer parameters (14B) than the largest competitors. This affords Phi-4 a strong performance/size ratio among the locally executed models.

To support these observations, a stratified permutation test with FDR correction was applied across all model pairs and temperatures. The resulting significance heatmap and win counts showed strong agreement with the descriptive statistics. DeepSeek-V3, Phi-4, and LLaMA-3.3 consistently achieved the highest number of statistically significant wins, while GPT-4 also dominated at lower temperatures. These results reinforce that the observed differences in model performance are statistically meaningful and not artifacts of randomness or scoring variability.

From a broader perspective, these findings support the notion that carefully tuned, locally run models can achieve near-state-of-the-art performance in specialized Python code generation tasks without necessarily relying on proprietary solutions. Specifically, both Phi-4 and LLaMA-3.3 proved capable of reliably generating correct solutions for the type of UAV/LoRaWAN planning prompts tested in this work. Their consistency in providing accurate answers under varying seeds and temperature conditions places them among the top-performing models overall, comparable to GPT-4 and DeepSeek-V3. These results address the central research question: lightweight and locally executed LLMs can, in fact, generate correct Python code for relatively simple LoRaWAN and UAV planning tasks, provided that their parameter counts and training procedures meet a certain threshold of quality and scale. The performance of Phi-4 was particularly impressive, especially considering it is a relatively lightweight model.

6. Limitations

Despite the insights gained from this study, several limitations should be acknowledged. First, the selection of models, while diverse, was not exhaustive. Only a subset of locally run lightweight models was evaluated, and online testing was limited to GPT-4 and DeepSeek-V3. Several potentially relevant models, such as Claude, Mistral (larger online versions), and specialized coding models (e.g., Gemma Coder or DeepSeek Coder), were not included. This restricted scope leaves open the possibility that other models may perform competitively or even outperform those tested in this study.

Second, model outputs were assessed solely based on functional correctness, without a detailed qualitative analysis of the responses. This introduces the risk that some answers classified as correct may not have been genuinely derived but instead relied on unintended memorization, dataset leakage, or other forms of 'cheating'. While this concern is most relevant for Prompts 1 and 2, where only an index is returned, Prompt 3 mitigates this issue by requiring a real-valued output. Nevertheless, a more rigorous analysis of response quality—including potential hallucinations, redundant reasoning, and incorrect assumptions—would strengthen future work.

Third, the study relied on a single test case per function, which limits the robustness of correctness assessments. A more comprehensive evaluation would include multiple test cases per function, ensuring that responses generalize beyond a specific input scenario. This is particularly relevant given the stochastic nature of LLM-generated code, where seemingly minor variations in the prompt or execution conditions can lead to significant changes in output validity.

Fourth, all evaluations were conducted using zero-shot natural language prompts, without fine-tuning or explicit prompt engineering. While this choice aligns with practical use cases where domain experts may rely on straightforward instructions, further experimentation with prompt optimization strategies—such as chain-of-thought prompting or few-shot learning—could provide deeper insights into model capabilities.

Additionally, the study focused on relatively simple UAV/LoRaWAN planning tasks. While these scenarios are relevant to real-world applications, they do not necessarily capture the full complexity of autonomous UAV coordination, network interference, or real-time decision-making in dynamic environments. The strong performance of top models suggests they may be capable of handling more complex scenarios, but this remains an open question for future research.

A final limitation concerns the use of statistical significance testing. While stratified permutation tests confirmed the robustness of performance differences, they do not account for the magnitude or practical implications of those differences. Moreover, the use of discrete, ordinal scores simplifies model outputs and may obscure subtle qualitative distinctions. Although multiple testing correction was applied to reduce false positives, this also reduces sensitivity to borderline effects. Additionally, comparisons at non-zero temperatures should be interpreted with caution, as temperature scaling is handled differently across models, potentially resulting in varying degrees of output randomness for the same nominal value. These tests therefore complement, but do not replace, the broader descriptive analysis presented earlier.

These limitations do not diminish the validity of the study's conclusions but highlight areas for refinement in subsequent investigations. A broader model selection, more rigorous evaluation metrics, and extended task complexity would further improve the understanding of LLMs' capabilities in UAV and LoRaWAN-related computational tasks.

7. Conclusions

This paper analyzed the capabilities of 16 LLMs to generate Python functions for practical LoRaWAN-related engineering tasks involving UAV placement and signal propagation. By progressively increasing the complexity of prompts, we evaluated each model's ability to return valid and correct solutions under a standardized scoring system. The findings indicate that several recent models—particularly DeepSeek-V3, GPT-4, LLaMA-3.3, and Phi-4—consistently generated accurate and executable functions. Particularly, Phi-4 displayed exceptional performance despite its relatively lightweight architecture, demonstrating that well-optimized, smaller-scale models can be highly effective for specialized engineering applications. Models that did not achieve high scores often struggled with prompt interpretation, code syntax, or domain-specific computations, underlining the need for careful prompt engineering and model fine-tuning in similar applications.

The demonstrated viability of lightweight and locally executed LLMs for specialized engineering tasks such as UAV planning in LoRaWAN environments suggests that these models could significantly lower computational barriers and costs, allowing for broader and more flexible integration of AI-driven code generation into practical engineering workflows.

While this study highlighted the strong potential of LLMs in engineering workflows, certain limitations must be acknowledged, including the constrained model selection, the single test case per function, and the absence of qualitative analysis of responses. However, these limitations present opportunities for future research. Expanding test sets, incorporating more complex domain requirements, and evaluating additional models—particularly other lightweight alternatives—could further enrich our understanding of LLM-driven code generation in wireless communications and related fields. Future research could also explore the incorporation of reinforcement learning with human feedback to further improve the code generation capabilities of lightweight LLMs [49].

Author Contributions: Conceptualization, D.F., J.P.M.-C. and N.F.; methodology, D.F., J.P.M.-C. and N.F.; software, D.F., J.P.M.-C. and N.F.; validation, D.F., J.P.M.-C. and C.M.F.; formal analysis, N.F.; investigation, D.F. and C.M.F.; resources, D.F. and J.P.M.-C.; data curation, N.F.; writing—original draft preparation, D.F., J.P.M.-C., C.M.F. and N.F.; writing—review and editing, D.F., J.P.M.-C., C.M.F. and N.F.; visualization, N.F. All authors have read and agreed to the published version of the manuscript.

Funding: This research was partially funded by: Fundação para a Ciência e a Tecnologia (FCT, https://ror.org/00snfqn58, accessed on 26 March 2025) under Grants Copelabs ref. UIDB/04111/2020, Centro de Tecnologias e Sistemas (CTS) ref. UIDB/00066/2020, LASIGE Research Unit ref. UIDB/00408/2025, and COFAC ref. CEECINST/00002/2021/CP2788/CT0001; Instituto Lusófono de Investigação e Desenvolvimento (ILIND, Portugal) under Project COFAC/ILIND/COPELABS-/1/2024; and, Ministerio de Ciencia, Innovación y Universidades (MICIU/AEI/10.13039/501100011033, https://ror.org/05r0vyz12, accessed on 26 March 2025) under Project PID2023-147409NB-C21.

Data Availability Statement: The data generated by this study and respective analysis are available at https://doi.org/10.5281/zenodo.14888673 under the CC-BY license.

Conflicts of Interest: The authors declare no conflicts of interest.

Abbreviations and Symbols

The following abbreviations are used in this manuscript:

AI	Artificial Intelligence
API	Application Programming Interface
BS	Base Station
CoT	Chain of Thought
FDR	False Discovery Rate
GPT	Generative Pre-trained Transformer
IoT	Internet of Things
LLM	Large Language Model
LoRa	Long-range
LoRaWAN	LoRa Wide Area Network
LPWAN	Low-Power Wide-Area Network
MARL	Multi-Agent Reinforcement Learning algorithm
TPML	Task Planning for Multi-UAV System
UAV	Unmaned Aerial Vehicle
VML	Visual Language Models

The following symbols are used in this manuscript:

λ	Wavelength
c	Speed of light
f	Frequency
G_r	Gain of the receiving antenna
G_t	Gain of the transmitting antenna
L_F	Propagation loss
P_r	Received power
P_t	Transmit power
r	Distance between the antennas

?eferences

Petajajarvi, J.; Mikhaylov, K.; Roivainen, A.; Hanninen, T.; Pettissalo, M. On the coverage of LPWANs: Range evaluation and channel attenuation model for LoRa technology. In Proceedings of the 2015 14th International Conference on ITS Telecommunications (ITST), Copenhagen, Denmark, 2–4 December 2015; IEEE: New York, NY, USA, 2015; pp. 55–59. [CrossRef]

Augustin, A.; Yi, J.; Clausen, T.; Townsley, W.M. A study of LoRa: Long range & low power networks for the internet of things. *Sensors* **2016**, *16*, 1466. [CrossRef] [PubMed]

Mozaffari, M.; Saad, W.; Bennis, M.; Debbah, M. Wireless communication using unmanned aerial vehicles (UAVs): Optimal transport theory for hover time optimization. *IEEE Trans. Wirel. Commun.* **2017**, *16*, 8052–8066. [CrossRef]

Sanchez-Iborra, R.; Sanchez-Gomez, J.; Ballesta-Viñas, J.; Cano, M.D.; Skarmeta, A.F. Performance evaluation of LoRa considering scenario conditions. *Sensors* **2018**, *18*, 772. [CrossRef] [PubMed]

Achiam, J.; Adler, S.; Agarwal, S.; Ahmad, L.; Akkaya, I.; Aleman, F.L.; Almeida, D.; Altenschmidt, J.; Altman, S.; Anadkat, S.; et al. GPT-4 Technical Report. *arXiv* **2024**, arXiv:2303.08774. [CrossRef]

Morgan, J.; Chiang, M. Ollama: Get Up and Running with Large Language Models. GitHub. 2023. Available online: https://ollama.com/ (accessed on 10 February 2025).

Liu, A.; Feng, B.; Xue, B.; Wang, B.; Wu, B.; Lu, C.; Zhao, C.; Deng, C.; Zhang, C.; Ruan, C.; et al. DeepSeek-V3 Technical Report. *arXiv* **2024**, arXiv:2412.19437. [CrossRef]

Petukhova, A.; Matos-Carvalho, J.P.; Fachada, N. Text clustering with large language model embeddings. *Int. J. Cogn. Comput. Eng.* **2025**, *6*, 100–108. [CrossRef]

Lewis, M.; Liu, Y.; Goyal, N.; Ghazvininejad, M.; Mohamed, A.; Levy, O.; Stoyanov, V.; Zettlemoyer, L. BART: Denoising Sequence-to-Sequence Pre-training for Natural Language Generation, Translation, and Comprehension. In Proceedings of the 58th Annual Meeting of the Association for Computational Linguistics, Online, 5–10 July 2020; Jurafsky, D., Chai, J., Schluter, N., Tetreault, J., Eds.; Association for Computational Linguistics: Cambridge, MA, USA, 2020; pp. 7871–7880. [CrossRef]

10. Alves, D.M.; Pombal, J.; Guerreiro, N.M.; Martins, P.H.; Alves, J.; Farajian, A.; Peters, B.; Rei, R.; Fernandes, P.; Agrawal, S.; et al. Tower: An Open Multilingual Large Language Model for Translation-Related Tasks. *arXiv* **2024**, arXiv:2402.17733. [CrossRef]
11. Yang, Z.; Dai, Z.; Yang, Y.; Carbonell, J.; Salakhutdinov, R.; Le, Q.V. XLNet: Generalized Autoregressive Pretraining for Language Understanding. In Proceedings of the 33rd International Conference on Neural Information Processing Systems, 2019, NeurIPS Vancouver, BC, Canada, 8–14 December 2019; pp. 5753–5763.
12. Gu, X.; Chen, M.; Lin, Y.; Hu, Y.; Zhang, H.; Wan, C.; Wei, Z.; Xu, Y.; Wang, J. On the effectiveness of large language models in domain-specific code generation. *ACM Trans. Softw. Eng. Methodol.* **2024**, *34*, 1–22. [CrossRef]
13. Grattafiori, A.; Dubey, A.; Jauhri, A.; Pandey, A.; Kadian, A.; Al-Dahle, A.; Letman, A.; Mathur, A.; Schelten, A.; Vaughan, A. et al. The Llama 3 Herd of Models. *arXiv* **2024**, arXiv:2407.21783. [CrossRef]
14. Abdin, M.; Aneja, J.; Behl, H.; Bubeck, S.; Eldan, R.; Gunasekar, S.; Harrison, M.; Hewett, R.J.; Javaheripi, M.; Kauffmann, P.; et al. Phi-4 technical report. *arXiv* **2024**, arXiv:2412.08905. [CrossRef]
15. Ling, C.; Zhao, X.; Lu, J.; Deng, C.; Zheng, C.; Wang, J.; Chowdhury, T.; Li, Y.; Cui, H.; Zhang, X.; et al. Domain specialization as the key to make large language models disruptive: A comprehensive survey. *arXiv* **2024**, arXiv:2305.18703. [CrossRef]
16. Javaid, S.; Fahim, H.; He, B.; Saeed, N. Large Language Models for UAVs: Current State and Pathways to the Future. *IEEE Open J. Veh. Technol.* **2024**, *5*, 1166–1192. [CrossRef]
17. Phadke, A.; Hadimlioglu, A.; Chu, T.; Sekharan, C.N. Integrating large language models for UAV control in simulated environments: A modular interaction approach. *arXiv* **2024**, arXiv:2410.17602. [CrossRef]
18. Aikins, G.; Dao, M.P.; Moukpe, K.J.; Eskridge, T.C.; Nguyen, K.D. LEVIOSA: Natural Language-Based Uncrewed Aerial Vehicle Trajectory Generation. *Electronics* **2024**, *13*, 4508. [CrossRef]
19. Cui, J.; Liu, G.; Wang, H.; Yu, Y.; Yang, J. TPML: Task Planning for Multi-UAV System with Large Language Models. In Proceedings of the 2024 IEEE 18th International Conference on Control & Automation (ICCA), Reykjavik, Iceland, 18–21 June 2024; IEEE: New York, NY, USA, 2024; pp. 886–891. [CrossRef]
20. de Curtò, J.; de Zarzà, I.; Calafate, C.T. Semantic Scene Understanding with Large Language Models on Unmanned Aerial Vehicles. *Drones* **2023**, *7*, 114. [CrossRef]
21. Zhu, F.; Huang, F.; Yu, Y.; Liu, G.; Huang, T. Task Offloading with LLM-Enhanced Multi-Agent Reinforcement Learning in UAV-Assisted Edge Computing. *Sensors* **2024**, *25*, 175. [CrossRef]
22. Son, K.; Kim, D.; Kang, W.J.; Hostallero, D.E.; Yi, Y. QTRAN: Learning to Factorize with Transformation for Cooperative Multi-Agent Reinforcement Learning. In Proceedings of the 36th International Conference on Machine Learning, PMLR, Long Beach, CA, USA, 9–15 June 2019; Volume 97, pp. 5887–5896.
23. Saraereh, O.A.; Alsaraira, A.; Khan, I.; Uthansakul, P. Performance Evaluation of UAV-Enabled LoRa Networks for Disaster Management Applications. *Sensors* **2020**, *20*, 2396. [CrossRef] [PubMed]
24. Chen, L.Y.; Huang, H.S.; Wu, C.J.; Tsai, Y.T.; Chang, Y.S. A LoRa-Based Air Quality Monitor on Unmanned Aerial Vehicle for Smart City. In Proceedings of the 2018 International Conference on System Science and Engineering (ICSSE), New Taipei City, Taiwan, 28–30 June 2018; pp. 1–5. [CrossRef]
25. Pan, M.; Chen, C.; Yin, X.; Huang, Z. UAV-Aided Emergency Environmental Monitoring in Infrastructure-Less Areas: LoRa Mesh Networking Approach. *IEEE Internet Things J.* **2022**, *9*, 2918–2932. [CrossRef]
26. Arroyo, P.; Herrero, J.L.; Lozano, J.; Montero, P. Integrating LoRa-Based Communications into Unmanned Aerial Vehicles for Data Acquisition from Terrestrial Beacons. *Electronics* **2022**, *11*, 1865. [CrossRef]
27. Wong, M.F.; Guo, S.; Hang, C.N.; Ho, S.W.; Tan, C.W. Natural language generation and understanding of big code for AI-assisted programming: A review. *Entropy* **2023**, *25*, 888. [CrossRef]
28. Jain, N.; Vaidyanath, S.; Iyer, A.; Natarajan, N.; Parthasarathy, S.; Rajamani, S.; Sharma, R. Jigsaw: Large language models meet program synthesis. In Proceedings of the 44th International Conference on Software Engineering, Pittsburgh, PA, USA, 21–29 May 2022; ICSE '22, pp. 1219–1231. [CrossRef]
29. Brown, T.; Mann, B.; Ryder, N.; Subbiah, M.; Kaplan, J.D.; Dhariwal, P.; Neelakantan, A.; Shyam, P.; Sastry, G.; Askell, A.; et al. Language models are few-shot learners. In Proceedings of the 34th Conference on Neural Information Processing Systems NeurIPS 2020, Vancouver, BC, Canada, 6–12 December 2020; Volume 33, pp. 1877–1901.
30. Chen, M.; Tworek, J.; Jun, H.; Yuan, Q.; Pinto, H.P.D.O.; Kaplan, J.; Edwards, H.; Burda, Y.; Joseph, N.; Brockman, G.; et al. Evaluating large language models trained on code. *arXiv* **2021**, arXiv:2107.03374. [CrossRef]
31. Vemprala, S.; Bonatti, R.; Bucker, A.; Kapoor, A. ChatGPT for robotics: Design principles and model abilities. *arXiv* **2023**, arXiv:2306.17582. [CrossRef]
32. Liang, J.; Huang, W.; Xia, F.; Xu, P.; Hausman, K.; Ichter, B.; Florence, P.; Zeng, A. Code as Policies: Language Model Programs for Embodied Control. In Proceedings of the 2023 IEEE International Conference on Robotics and Automation (ICRA), London, UK, 29 May–2 June 2023; IEEE: New York, NY, USA, 2023; pp. 9493–9500. [CrossRef]

33. Luo, H.; Wu, J.; Liu, J.; Antwi-Afari, M.F. Large language model-based code generation for the control of construction assembly robots: A hierarchical generation approach. *Dev. Built Environ.* **2024**, *19*, 100488. [CrossRef]
34. Amatriain, X. Prompt design and engineering: Introduction and advanced methods. *arXiv* **2024**, arXiv:2401.14423. [CrossRef]
35. Wei, J.; Wang, X.; Schuurmans, D.; Bosma, M.; Ichter, B.; Xia, F.; Chi, E.H.; Le, Q.V.; Zhou, D. Chain-of-thought prompting elicits reasoning in large language models. In Proceedings of the 36th International Conference on Neural Information Processing Systems, New Orleans, LA, USA, 28 November–9 December 2022; Curran Associates Inc.: Newry, UK, 2022; Volume 35, pp. 24824–24837.
36. Li, Y.; Shi, J.; Zhang, Z. An approach for rapid source code development based on ChatGPT and prompt engineering. *IEEE Access* **2024**, *12*, 53074–53087. [CrossRef]
37. Sanguesa, J.A.; Torres-Sanz, V.; Serna, F.; Martinez, F.J.; Garrido, P.; Calafate, C.T. Improving LoRaWAN Connectivity in Smart Agriculture Contexts Using Aerial IoT. In Proceedings of the 2023 IEEE Globecom Workshops (GC Wkshps), Kuala Lumpur, Malaysia, 4–8 December 2023; IEEE: New York, NY, USA, 2023; pp. 1027–1032. [CrossRef]
38. Raimundo, A.; Fernandes, D.; Gomes, D.; Postolache, O.; Sebastião, P.; Cercas, F. UAV GNSS Position Corrections based on IoT LoRaWAN Communication Protocol. In Proceedings of the 2018 International Symposium in Sensing and Instrumentation in IoT Era (ISSI), Shanghai, China, 6–7 September 2018; IEEE: New York, NY, USA, 2018; pp. 1–5. [CrossRef]
39. Ghazali, M.H.M.; Teoh, K.; Rahiman, W. A Systematic Review of Real-Time Deployments of UAV-Based LoRa Communication Network. *IEEE Access* **2021**, *9*, 124817–124830. [CrossRef]
40. Saunders, S.R.; Aragón-Zavala, A. *Antennas and Propagation for Wireless Communication Systems*, 2nd ed.; J. Wiley & Sons: Hoboken, NJ, USA, 2024.
41. Guo, D.; Yang, D.; Zhang, H.; Song, J.; Zhang, R.; Xu, R.; Zhu, Q.; Ma, S.; Wang, P.; Bi, X.; et al. DeepSeek-R1: Incentivizing reasoning capability in llms via reinforcement learning. *arXiv* **2025**, arXiv:2501.12948. [CrossRef]
42. Mesnard, T.; Hardin, C.; Dadashi, R.; Bhupatiraju, S.; Pathak, S.; Sifre, L.; Rivière, M.; Kale, M.S.; Love, J.; Tafti, P.; et al. Gemma: Open models based on Gemini research and technology. *arXiv* **2024**, arXiv:2403.08295. [CrossRef]
43. Riviere, M.; Pathak, S.; Sessa, P.G.; Hardin, C.; Bhupatiraju, S.; Hussenot, L.; Mesnard, T.; Shahriari, B.; Ramé, A.; Ferret, J.; et al. Gemma 2: Improving open language models at a practical size. *arXiv* **2024**, arXiv:2408.00118. [CrossRef]
44. Jiang, A.Q.; Sablayrolles, A.; Mensch, A.; Bamford, C.; Chaplot, D.S.; Casas, D.d.l.; Bressand, F.; Lengyel, G.; Lample, G.; Saulnier, L.; et al. Mistral 7B. *arXiv* **2023**, arXiv:2310.06825. [CrossRef]
45. Yang, A.; Yang, B.; Zhang, B.; Hui, B.; Zheng, B.; Yu, B.; Li, C.; Liu, D.; Huang, F.; Wei, H.; et al. Qwen2.5 technical report. *arXiv* **2025**, arXiv:2412.15115. [CrossRef]
46. Hui, B.; Yang, J.; Cui, Z.; Yang, J.; Liu, D.; Zhang, L.; Liu, T.; Zhang, J.; Yu, B.; Lu, K.; et al. Qwen2.5-Coder Technical Report. *arXiv* **2025**, arXiv:2409.12186. [CrossRef]
47. Good, P.I. *Permutation, Parametric and Bootstrap Tests of Hypotheses: A Practical Guide to Resampling Methods for Testing Hypotheses*, 3rd ed.; Springer Series in Statistics; Springer: Berlin/Heidelberg, Germany, 2004. [CrossRef]
48. Benjamini, Y.; Hochberg, Y. Controlling the false discovery rate: A practical and powerful approach to multiple testing. *J. R. Stat. Soc. Ser. B (Methodol.)* **1995**, *57*, 289–300. [CrossRef]
49. Wong, M.F.; Tan, C.W. Aligning Crowd-Sourced Human Feedback for Reinforcement Learning on Code Generation by Large Language Models. *IEEE Trans. Big Data* **2024**. [CrossRef]

MDPI AG
Grosspeteranlage 5
4052 Basel
Switzerland
Tel.: +41 61 683 77 34

Electronics Editorial Office
E-mail: electronics@mdpi.com
www.mdpi.com/journal/electronics

www.ingramcontent.com/pod-product-compliance
Lightning Source LLC
Chambersburg PA
CBHW040819250926
51850CB00007BA/1207
* 9 7 8 3 7 2 5 8 5 1 7 7 5 *